ORDINARY
GERMANS IN
EXTRAORDINARY
TIMES

H.E.STERN.   JULI 1909.

Frontis: Bookplate featuring Hildesheim's Roland Fountain,
Rosebush, and the Star of David

ORDINARY GERMANS IN EXTRAORDINARY TIMES

The Nazi Revolution in Hildesheim

Andrew Stuart Bergerson

Indiana University Press

Bloomington and Indianapolis

This book is a publication of

Indiana University Press
601 North Morton Street
Bloomington, IN 47404-3797 USA

http://iupress.indiana.edu

Telephone orders	800-842-6796
Fax orders	812-855-7931
Orders by e-mail	iuporder@indiana.edu

© 2004 by Andrew Stuart Bergerson

The paper used in this publication meets the minimum requirements of
American National Standard for Information Sciences—Permanence
of Paper for Printed Library Materials, ANSI Z39.48-1984.

Manufactured in the United States of America

Library of Congress Cataloging-in-Publication Data

Bergerson, Andrew Stuart.
  Ordinary Germans in extraordinary times : the Nazi revolution in
Hildesheim / Andrew Stuart Bergerson.
      p. cm.
  Includes bibliographical references and index.
  ISBN 0-253-34465-4 (cloth : alk. paper)
  1. National socialism—Germany—Hildesheim. 2. Hildesheim
(Germany)—Social life and customs—20th century.
3. Ethnology—Germany—Hildesheim—History—20th century.
I. Title.
  DD901.H66B47 2004
  943'.595—dc22
                                        2004003780

1 2 3 4 5 09 08 07 06 05 04

To my father,
Steven,
who made it possible

The laws to be promulgated will issue from manners and will mirror them. Frenchmen, you are too intelligent to fail to sense that new government will require new manners.

—Le Marquis de Sade,
"Yet another effort, Frenchmen,
if you would become Republicans," in
La Philosophie dans le boudoir, 1795

Contents

Illustrations

Preface

THIS BOOK CONCERNS the deeds of ordinary people during the Third Reich. It hopes to serve as both a classic history of the Nazi revolution as well as a cultural history of everyday life (*Alltagsgeschichte*). This book is also addressed to very different audiences at the same time: to both popular and academic readers; to German historians and Holocaust scholars interested in questions of Nazi state and society as well as cultural anthropologists, critical theorists, and other scholars interested in the historicity of cultural practices. Coherently synthesizing these contradictions has been the major challenge of researching and writing this history. Since analogous contradictions lie at the core of the everyday life I seek to describe, it is fitting that they remain only partially resolved in my account. Interested readers are invited to turn to the appendix for a more technical discussion of these historiographic, theoretical, and methodological issues. Still, the reader will notice that I sometimes use technical terms in the text to describe the behavior of ordinary people. These are printed in italics when first mentioned (e.g., *conviviality*). Key terms for which I provide a more detailed definition in the appendix appear in boldface when first mentioned (e.g., **eigensinn**). Although the use of theoretical concepts may disturb the steady flow of the story, this is as it should be. A critical analysis of everyday life, particularly during the Third Reich, cannot rely simply on the language of common sense without running the risk of reiterating its myths.

Acknowledgments

THE RESEARCH FOR this study was made possible by a generous grant from the Friedrich-Weinhagen Stiftung in Hildesheim. An exploratory visit to Hildesheim was funded by a Mellon Summer Research Grant. For their friendly and cooperative assistance, I would like to thank the directors and staff of many institutions in Hildesheim: the Stadtarchiv und -bibliothek, the Bistumsarchiv and Dombibliothek, the Pfarrei St. Godehard, the Magdalenenhof Altersheim, and the *Hildesheimer Allgemeine Zeitung*. In the United States, I would like to recognize the support and assistance of the Departments of History at the University of Chicago, Franklin and Marshall College, and the University of Missouri–Kansas City as well as the staff at Indiana University Press.

For their constructive criticism and personal assistance, I would like to thank Alessandro Baldioli, Barbara Bayley, Robert Beachy, James A. Bell, Daphne Berdahl, Jana Beznoskova, John Borneman, Peg Boucher, John Boyer, Matti Bunzl, Alon Confino, Alicia Cozine, Adam Daniel, Marion Deshmukh, Martina Elstner, Peter Fritzsche, Bartira Galati, Hans-Jürgen Hahn, Gesine Hasselhof (as well as her father and friends), the Heep family, Günther Hein, Matthias Heine, Alois and Lydia Hemmerde, Shannon Jackson, Jennifer Jenkins, Jeanette Louise Jones, Jonnie Kaiser, Hans and Monika Kehr, Moses Kimchi-Mehl, Brett Klopp, Sonja Koch, Stefanie Krause, Kathryn Krug, Kate Lacey, Gayle A. Levy, Julie Lindstrom, Alf Lüdtke, Thomas Mache, Gerlind and Magali Mander, Maria Mitchell, Joseph Perry, Guillaume de Sion, Bruce Moran, H. Glenn Penny III, David Pickus, Anne Röhrig, Eve Rosenhaft, Elizabeth Sage, Stefan Sanders, Theresa Sanislo, June Schapiro, Hans-Dieter Schmid, Jörg Schneider, Phyllis Soybel-Butler, Martin Spiller, Andreas Steding, Helga Stein, Hans Steinke, Guy Stern, Gifford Teeple, Barbara Thimm, Rudolf Thomasius, Bernd-Jürgen Warneken, Stephanie Willadsen, Reiner Wahl, Britta Weidtke, Kerstin Witt, Stefan Wolff, Eric Zolov as well as the members of the Association for Integrative Studies, the Central European Studies Workshop at the University of Chicago, the Forschungsinstitut regionale Gesellschaftsentwicklung e. V. at the Universität Hannover, the Midwest Graduate Seminar in German

Studies, the Midwest German History Workshop, the Washington Area German History Seminar, the "Work of Memory in Germany" Workshop, the Institute for European Studies at Cornell University, the German history graduate students at the University of Illinois at Urbana-Champaign and at Georgia State University, as well as the Interdisciplinary Faculty Workshops at the University of Missouri–Kansas City.

A special note of respect and appreciation goes to my mentors: Isabel Hull and Terence Cole; Andrew Apter, Leora Auslander, and John Boyer; and especially Michael Geyer. I would also like to thank the Buerstedde family of Hildesheim for their special efforts on my behalf: they were always ready to help me find my way and feel at home in Hildesheim. This study could never have become a reality without the unwavering support of my family and relatives. Most especially, I would like to thank my interview partners, many of whom are no longer here to read these lines of appreciation. I hope that this book does justice to the Hildesheim of their youth.

Abbreviations

BAH	Bistumsarchiv Hildesheim
BA-P	Bundesarchiv-Potsdam
D/	Slide number
EGb	*Evangelisches Gemeindeblatt für Hildesheim*
G/	Cassette number & side
Gestapo	Secret State Police
HAb	*Hildesheimer Abendblatt*
HAZ	*Hildesheimer Allgemeine Zeitung*
HB	*Hildesheimer Beobachter*
HeZ	*Hildesheimische Zeitung*
HJ	Hitler Youth
HVb	*Hildesheimer Volksblatt*
KPD	Communist Party of Germany
NSDAP	National Socialist German Workers' Party
R/	Approx. cycle number
SA	Storm Troop
SAH	Stadtarchiv Hildesheim
SDR	*Statistik des deutschen Reichs*
Sopade	Social-Democratic Party of Germany in Exile
SPD	Social-Democratic Party of Germany
SS	Protection Squad
VVNH	Verein der Verfolgten des Naziregimes Hildesheim

ORDINARY
GERMANS IN
EXTRAORDINARY
TIMES

Introduction: New Manners

From Zbaszyn to Hildesheim

BERNWARD NEDDERICH (A pseudonym) was a so-called Eastern Jew (*Ost-jude*). He was born in Warsaw in 1914 but grew up in Hildesheim, a socially diverse, mid-sized, provincial town in northwest Germany. On 27–28 October 1938, the Nazi regime expelled some 17,000 Polish Jews to an internment camp in Zbaszyn, Poland.[1] Bernward's sisters had all been born in Hildesheim and possessed German passports, but they too were deported because their parents were Polish citizens. Bernward and his brother escaped this fate only because they had already emigrated to Palestine. As Lotte, his oldest sister, wrote (in a letter to him dated 1 November):

> Everything happened so suddenly that it took us totally by surprise. In the evening, four men came and said that we must leave Germany in two hours. You can imagine our state. We could not take anything with us. Papa took a few suits with him and a little linen. Don't worry about us. . . . We have written to our relatives in Warsaw and have already received an answer. . . . We hope to see you soon.

Without an immigration certificate from the British in Palestine, Bernward could not get his family out of Zbaszyn. On 2 December 1939, Lotte reported that the families Beim, Schwer, Zinn, and Zucker, all former Hildesheimers, were still trapped in Zbaszyn, though she had heard that the camp would soon get overfilled. Bernward lost track of them after they moved back to Warsaw. He never heard from any of them again.

Sarah Meyer had been friends with Gustie Beim in spite of the fact that Sarah's family were German Jews and Gustie's were Polish Jews; relations between these groups had not always been smooth. Sarah never heard from Gustie after Gustie too was deported to Zbaszyn in 1938. When I interviewed Sarah (see note on reference system),[2] Bernward's letters served as sufficient verification of what she had long suspected but never fully accepted about the fate of her playmate: Gustie had been killed in a ghetto, camp, or gas chamber.

Around the same time, Georg Brzezinski was stationed at an army depot near a Polish city that contained a large Jewish ghetto. The depot subcontracted some 140 Jews from the SS. Georg insisted that, in spite of the risk of retribution from the SS, "they" treated "their" Jews well, and he even developed a friendship with one of them. Yet whenever I asked him about the ultimate fate of these Jews, he spoke of their murder in the passive, as if he had been only an ordinary German. Quite beyond his control, the SS came under cover of "night and fog," he explained, and took the Jews away.[3] In keeping with his view of himself as an ordinary person, Georg had described the so-called Final Solution (*Endlösung*) to the Jewish Question using a phrase taken from Nazi propaganda. Yet back in Hildesheim, the Brzezinskis had lived quite close to the Nedderichs and the Meyers. At times over the course of the interwar years, they had even been neighbors.

Studies of the Holocaust and the implementation of Nazi racial policy are typically prefaced by the long history of latent antisemitism in Germany and Europe; Nazi ideology and propaganda; and the Nazi seizure of power, their anti-Jewish legislation, and their violence against the Jews during the 1930s. The story of the Holocaust per se usually begins with the so-called *Kristallnacht* (The Night of Broken Glass) of 9–10 November 1938. In response to the plight of his family (like Bernward's, it had been expelled from Germany), Herschel Grynszpan shot a diplomat in the German embassy in Paris. Using this incident as an excuse, the Nazi regime orchestrated a nationwide pogrom. Concluding with the first wave of deportations of German Jews to concentration camps, Kristallnacht marked a major step towards state-sponsored genocide.[4]

The Nazi regime began to organize a bureaucratic–industrial system of mass murder in 1941. In Hildesheim, the next wave of deportations took place in 1942. On 31 March and 23 July, the Nazi regime relocated most of the two hundred or so remaining Jews to ghettos, concentration camps, and ultimately death camps: Theresienstadt, Belzec, Majdanek, Sorbibor. Only twelve Jews remained during the rest of the war, all of whom were involved in mixed marriages. The deportations to Zbaszyn thus marked a critical turning point for Hildesheim's Jews. After 1938 they increasingly became the victims of organized genocide, even though roughly two-thirds of them had already been forced into exile or suicide.[5]

Due to the horror of Nazi crimes against humanity, studies of the Holocaust tend to focus on these latter stages of deportation, concentration, and murder. We know far less about the earlier process: the role of ordinary Germans in alienating their neighbors and abandoning them to the machinations of the Nazi regime. This book seeks to provide a more precise and rich account of that story. It shifts our attention from Zbaszyn back to Hildesheim. It uses ordinary Hildesheimers as an archetype for the larger problem of the complicity of ordinary people in revolutionary historical transformations and inhumane systems of mass destruction. Yet it revisits a core of persistent questions about the Nazi revolution specific to modern German history: the Nazi seizure of power; the coordination (*Gleichschaltung*) of a civil society to fit the principles of the Nazi racist community (*Volksgemeinschaft*); the modernization of German society as an indirect result of Nazi policy; the alienation, aryanization, exile, and deportation of Nazi victims, particularly the Jews; and the place of the Nazi past in memory (*Vergangenheitsbewältigung*). Less typically, this book applies ethnographic theories and methods to these grand historical questions of revolution and mass murder.

This book tries to reconstruct social relations on an informal level that historians rarely study directly: friendship and neighborliness. At the core of our understanding of Nazi fascism (and totalitarianism more generally) lie presumptions about *conviviality* (*Geselligkeit*). The Third Reich claimed to replace the modern, individualistic society of the Weimar Republic with a *völkisch* (folk) community that recreated bonds of friendship and neighborliness among the German volk united behind the *Führer* (leader). At the same time, it limited membership in this community according to racist principles and discouraged sympathy for "outsiders." In effect, the Reich alienated and murdered some of its people in order to integrate and reward others. Its opponents and victims feared denunciation from friends and neighbors as much as the terror of the Nazi regime itself. Both fascists and antifascists were as sensitive to the daily informal interactions of ordinary people as much as they politicized those relationships. Yet historians of the period have not yet systematically studied how ordinary Germans actually interacted in everyday life. We tend to focus either on formal institutions (associations, bureaucracies, businesses, parties) or on social groups as defined by their formal associations (different classes, confessions, ethnicities, gender, sexualities). Such studies tend to prove what they assume: the coherence of these subcultures, as if institutions shaped history. In this study I investigate how different kinds of ordinary people interacted informally—and helped shape history in the process.

This book also shifts attention away from kinds of people (collaborators, victims, resistance fighters, workers, women, Jews) to kinds of behavior. It describes how Hildesheimers negotiated the public and the private in the semi-permeable terrain of conviviality. I focus on informal social behaviors: how Hildesheimers made friends with a few and kept most just as neighbors, exchanged greetings with acquaintances and offered helpful assistance when they were in need, learned about neighbors and took part in their lives, decorated their homes and bodies, cleaned their common streets and courtyards, expressed political positions yet preserved civility in the local public sphere. In the process of these informal interactions, ordinary Hildesheimers helped shape the character of their local society. This focus on actual deeds will highlight the historical consequences of the "symbolic actions" of ordinary people engaged in interactive "debate" in the public sphere.

To be sure, everyday life in Hildesheim included far more than just these aspects. Conviviality was closely related to family life and club meetings that, along with labor and business, often had an "everyday" quality. Even the makers and executors of public policy often experienced a sense of normalcy. For the most part, however, I am concerned with individual behavior outside and in between these institutional settings. Members of formally constituted social, economic, and political groups interacted informally with others as neighbors and sometimes as friends. Structured by specific customs, convivial interactions not only defined the nature and shape of human interaction on this most immediate level; conviviality also framed subsequent social, economic, and political relations. Particularly in provincial towns like Hildesheim, a proper greeting and a neighborly chat represented a primary foundation for the construction of more complicated relationships of *sociability*, exchange, and politics. Conviviality also represented "the public" to any given individual: one often thought of friends and neighbors when one imagined society at large.

To reconstruct the history of conviviality during the turbulent interwar years, I focused my attention on the case-study community of Hildesheim, illustrated in Figure 1. As I argue in more detail in the appendix, Hildesheim is unique among the many communities of Germany because it almost perfectly reflected the social and economic composition of the Weimar Republic in 1925: e.g., in terms of the distribution of men and women, Catholics and Protestants, Jews and Gentiles, working classes and middle classes, as well as the growth, scale, and diversity of its economy. It is therefore ideally suited to study how the individual members of these divergent groups interacted in everyday life. Hildesheim experienced the full range of historical events and crises that plagued modern Germany. Hildesheimers also consistently voted in almost the same percentages as Germans did more generally. On the one hand, Hildesheimers interpreted these similarities to mean that their community was typical and representative of the German nation. On the other hand, they interpreted these similarities to mean that the residents were politically moderate: i.e., neither violent nor particularly strong supporters of radical political parties. In reality, the rise of the Nazi party in Hildesheim almost precisely reflects national trends. Hildesheimers liked to imagine that they were ordinary; my research sought to discover how they negotiated such extraordinary times.

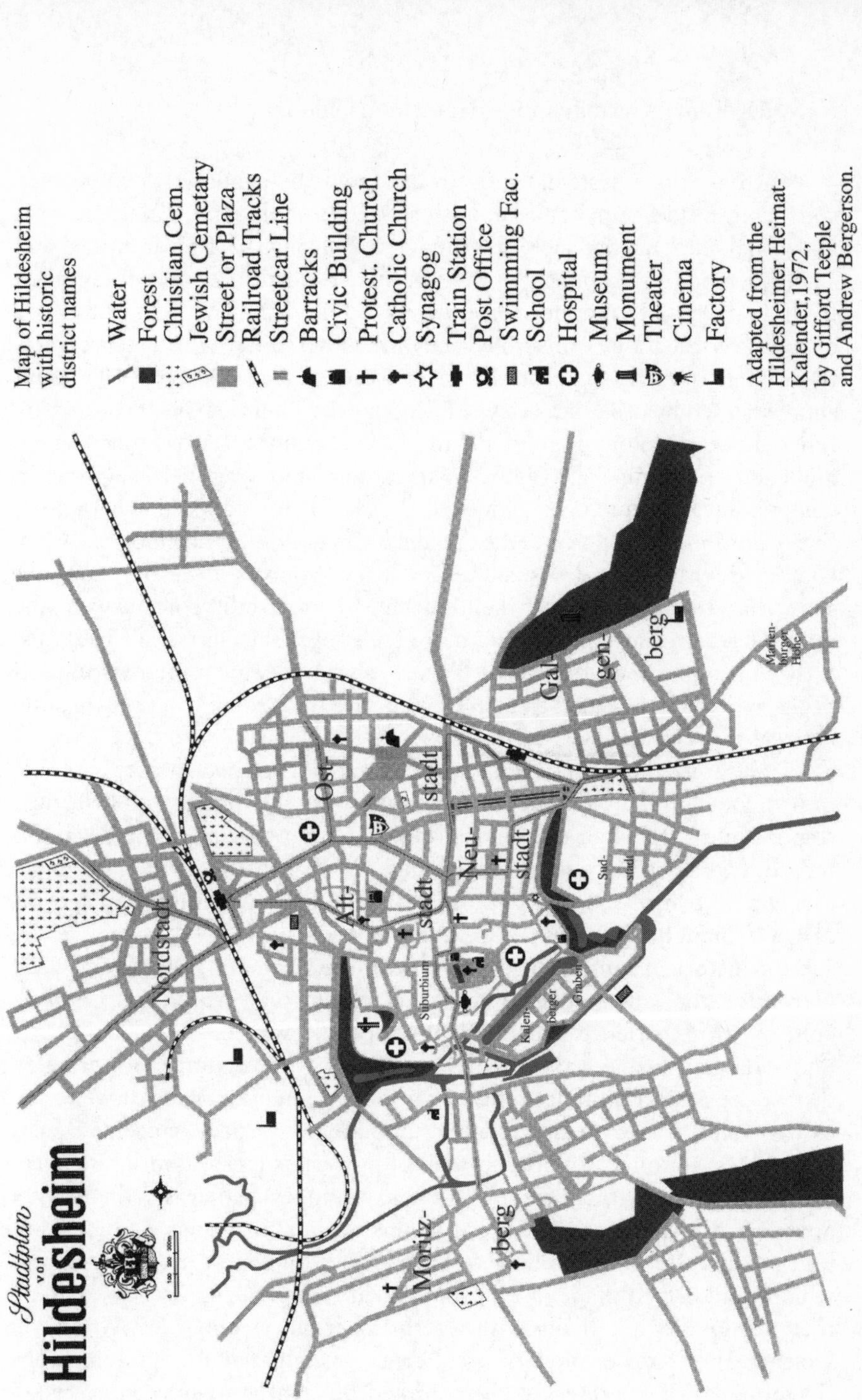

Stadtplan von Hildesheim
Map of Hildesheim with historic district names
Water
Forest
Christian Cem.
Jewish Cemetary
Street or Plaza
Railroad Tracks
Streetcar Line
Barracks
Civic Building
Protest. Church
Catholic Church
Synagog
Train Station
Post Office
Swimming Fac.
School
Hospital
Museum
Monument
Theater
Cinema
Factory
Adapted from the Hildesheimer Heimat-Kalender,1972, by Gifford Teeple and Andrew Bergerson.
Nordstadt
Alt-stadt
Ost-stadt
Neu-stadt
Gal-gen-berg
Moritz-berg
Suburbium
Kalen-berger Graben
Süd-stadt
Marien-burger Höhe

Figure 1. Map of interwar Hildesheim

To that end, I systematically investigated the available documentary sources in Hildesheim concerning this period: public and private, textual and visual, fictional and factual, primary and secondary. They informed and supplemented this account. But the story itself is driven by anecdotes taken from an extensive interview process, including some two hundred hours of tape-recorded and transcribed narrative interviews, with a representative sample of thirty-six Hildesheimers born between 1900 and 1930, and supplemented by other interviews. I describe my interview partners and my research methodology in more detail in the appendix ("A Ringing Tour"); and I address the question of how historians can interpret their memories in Chapter 8 ("Epistemologies") once readers have been exposed to enough of their anecdotes to appreciate the content and style of their memories. When combined with archival, visual, and published sources, these oral histories show that, by subtly altering their customs of conviviality, ordinary people made Germany more fascist and more racist over the course of the 1930s. If they disguised their role in the Nazi revolution behind a pre-existing veil of the everyday, they also created that culture of normalcy in part through their customs of conviviality.

Here, I use the term *ordinary* to describe not so much a particular set of people who remained outside the circles of public power and historical responsibility. To be ordinary was to engage in a specific cultural gambit for survival. A creative response to rapid and disruptive historical change, this way of behaving was a characteristically modern, rather than specifically German, habit of daily life; yet in the end, this study does look at the specific historical consequences when ordinary Germans behaved this way. *Normalcy*, too, refers not to a natural state but to a by-product of human culture: an experience generated by a specific way of being, believing, and behaving. In the wake of the First World War, a culture of normalcy denied the prewar assumption that every individual made small, yet critical, contributions to realizing some utopian future or a reinvented past. In its place, normalcy offered the veil of powerlessness and insignificance. By circumscribing their responsibilities, ordinary people set themselves apart from history writ large. Insofar as all human beings by definition take meaningful action in their own lived environment, ordinary men and women still helped shape history; but the culture of normalcy now enabled them to do so while living with a self-deception of innocence. Given the violence and chaos of modern life, normalcy made day-to-day living considerably easier; it preserved their limited but real autonomy in everyday life.

How ordinary people maintained a culture of normalcy while nonetheless transforming *friends* and *neighbors* into *Jews* and *Aryans*[6] is something that the cultural history of conviviality in interwar Hildesheim can help us better understand. Interwar Hildesheimers laid claim to status and power among friends and neighbors—in fantasy when necessary, in reality when possible. To disguise their aspirations from public criticism, they cultivated this new self behind the veil of the everyday afforded by conviviality. To maintain that self during *hard times,* they found useful, and sometimes sincerely believed, a range of attitudes from generational differences to latent antisemitism.[7] Yet no matter how veiled in conviviality, this everyday competition for status and power soon acquired a dynamism of its own. The Nazi movement proved particularly effective at using informal social relations to conduct politics by other means, just as ardent Nazis became skillful in using conviviality to their personal and political advantage. Self-cultivation was a significant factor in the Nazi revolution as it was in the Holocaust. For the many people not initially committed to Nazi principles, fascism and racism provided both the means to break through traditional social constraints as well as a direction to guide their new aspirations.[8] The Third Reich thus created a revolutionary context in which some ordinary people could try to realize their dreams; only reluctantly did they recognize it as a living nightmare.

Making Hildesheim Fascist

Serious revolutionaries know that a new political, social, or economic order requires new manners. Establishing a dictatorship through a coup d'état is one matter, but there can be no totalitarian revolution without an equally essential change in ways of life. I use the term *totalitarian* not to emphasize similarities between fascism and communism, but to distinguish it from the more general category of dictators. I see a significant difference between a terror state based primarily on formal authority seized from above and one grounded also in informal dynamics for laying claim to power and status from below, such that coordinated processes in state and society affirm and enforce each other.[9] This book tells the story of that everyday, cultural revolution: of ordinary people transforming a civil society into a fascist–racist community imbued with the principles of national socialism.[10]

The first part of the book focuses on tactics of *eigensinn* (pronounced: ey' gən zin). A German word that refers both to child-like obstinacy as well as a sense of oneself, I use it here to refer to the many creative ways that ordinary people manipulated circumstances to challenge power relations and to cultivate an identity that corresponds to their self-image. In individual terms, eigensinn feels good because even a brief symbolic display of mockery empowers and validates one's sense of self. In interpersonal terms, eigensinn helps shape the character of that local society. Yet on all sides, eigensinn is typically dismissed as the prank or parody of an underdog.

An *open secret*, everyone relies at times on the contradictions in eigensinn to navigate everyday life; but few wish to think critically about it, because that cultural regime of knowledge and ignorance preserves their maneuverability in everyday life. Contradictory at their core, tactics of eigensinn generate a culture of normalcy that denies their own significance.

The first chapter explores forms of neighborly civility in these terms. Interwar Hildesheimers used a friendly greeting to negotiate their conflicting needs for mutual respect and social hierarchy, intimacy and distance. The ritual repetition of greeting represented an *eigensinnig* response to the latent civil war in the Weimar Republic that provided stability in hard times. Designed to negotiate similarities and differences across social and political divides, the customs of conviviality were necessarily shared across those cleavages. Yet conviviality did as much to preserve those boundaries as to overcome them. By drawing attention to what they did rather than to what they believed, Hildesheimers kept civil society civil. Nonetheless, Hildesheimers got to know their neighbors selectively: alienating some and integrating others into their corner neighborhoods. They did so in order to lay claim to status and power for themselves, what they called *niveau*, even though that identity was largely a fantasy. The second chapter will therefore demonstrate that a subtle form of self-cultivation stood at the core of neighborly relations. A culture of normalcy protected eigensinn from critical reflection in order to preserve that minimal degree of maneuverability.

These customs may strike the reader as remarkably familiar and ordinary, but in a study of everyday life, this is as it should be. These chapters also illustrate my interpretive technique. They use anecdotes not so much as objective evidence of actual individuals, names, and places, but as a guide to the relatively consistent style with which my interview partners negotiated informal social relations. The facts under scrutiny are the artifacts of habit recovered in *body narratives*: stories of habits creatively enacted. Yet these *habit memories* are precisely what can get us back to politics and history. Ordinary Hildesheimers readily transposed existing tactics for dealing with neighbors onto new situations. Ritualized greetings could negotiate one's relationship with any neighbor, from a flasher or prostitute to an Eastern Jew or an ardent Nazi. The latter could exploit changing habits of headdress—relevant here as the hats Hildesheimers used while greeting each other—for their political purposes, though these innovations were similarly introduced as tactics of eigensinn. Ritual repetition disguised changes in conviviality; Hildesheimers could thus introduce revolution behind the veil of the everyday.

Chapter 3 investigates exchange relations with the same eye towards transposition. Hildesheimers drew a distinction between sharing resources among neighbors or shopping in corner stores as compared to making purchases in the central business district. Young Hildesheimers also took walks through the central business district in the early evening, calling this *The Stroll*. Rebelling against their parents, they experimented cautiously with both economic and sexual desire. They learned to cultivate fantasies of upward social mobility that did not correspond to their reality, and to desire consumer goods that they could not yet really afford. Reinventing customs of conviviality, these younger Hildesheimers contributed to the long-term process of modernization by undermining the hold of local traditions. Ardent Nazis went further: they could easily adjust the strolls' cultural logic to correspond to critical elements of Nazi propaganda, since the central business district was associated with both modernity and Jewishness in contrast to the "authenticity" of their corner neighborhoods. Framed within conviviality, ordinary Hildesheimers could readily adopt remarkably modern, potentially antisemitic ways of life.

The Weimar Republic witnessed a large degree of political mobilization and political violence, bordering on a civil war. With activities ranging from parades by day or night and the display of flags and uniforms, to assassinations, street fights, and attempted coups, participation in the one often led to the other. Yet if my interview partners recounted any stories about street politics, they preferred to relate anecdotes of how they practiced politics by other, indirect means. They politicized conviviality in the sense of both laying claim to individual power and status among friends and neighbors as well as trying to influence the political system through informal social relations. They then purged the neighborhood of all evidence of transgression through communal rituals of purification. Chapter 4 describes how Hildesheimers could understand themselves as normal all the while that they cultivated power in and politicized everyday life. Through convivial customs of ritual ablution, Hildesheimers hid these bids for formal and informal dominance behind the veil of the ordinary—and resurrected their sense of belonging to a *moral community*.

The second part of the book focuses on strategies for *herrschaft* (pronounced: hĕr' schäft). A German term for hegemony or dominance, I use it here to refer to those ways in which ordinary people tried to alter the circumstances of everyday life in the hopes of promoting a social and political order in which they would hold power and status. Because dominion in everyday life functions best when ordinary people accept its essential principles as a natural part of the human condition, the actual process of colonizing everyday life must also remain an open secret. Like tactics of eigensinn, strategies for herrschaft generate a culture of normalcy, and conviviality in interwar Hildesheim was replete with them. Also like tactics of eigensinn, strategies for herrschaft helped drive the Nazi revolution. Here again, I am not so much interested in what Hildesheimers believed as in what they did:

what kinds of principles they made normal by enacting them in the everyday. In her seminal 1987 article, Heide Gerstenberger defined this process as *fascisizing*. Reviving her argument, Chapter 5 will provide rich anecdotal evidence of the public debate over nazification, expressed in terms of how ordinary Hildesheimers decorated their homes and greeted their neighbors. It will show that they coordinated informal social relations to fit the policies and principles of the Third Reich behind the veil of the everyday. It will also remind us that, in spite of the fact that my interview partners often narrated them as if they were two different stories, the modernization of everyday life was part and parcel of its nazification.

The remaining chapters trace the everyday dynamic of the Nazi revolution further by exploring the consequences of this public debate. Focusing on the behavior of those Hildesheimers ideologically committed to and against the Third Reich, Chapter 6 will show that these attempts to colonize everyday life effectively polarized informal social relations into formal categories of resistance and collaboration. The dual politicization and criminalization of conviviality created a communicative crisis, undermining the ability of activists on both sides to measure the commitment of ordinary people to the Nazi cause. It also created a pragmatic crisis in conviviality as such: ordinary Hildesheimers undermined their own informal mechanisms for negotiating social relations. In response, they turned increasingly to the Nazi regime to administer conviviality, and thereby to restore the moral community, on their behalf. The seventh chapter will explore this unforeseen consequence of the Nazi revolution in terms of cultural pollution. Though the Nazi regime based its policies for scatological social groups (like forced laborers and prisoners of war) on customary rituals for dealing with dirt and disease, the formal application of informal principles created a far more brutal system of social engineering; and yet it was ordinary people who turned to the Nazi regime to protect their moral community.

When ordinary people accustomed themselves to Nazi habits, they laid the everyday foundations for Nazi totalitarianism. In anthropological terms, the very success of the Nazi revolution against *societas* (existing social hierarchies and power relations) to create a fascist–racist *communitas* (a temporary, anti-structural, ritual space of liberation, equality, and belonging) encouraged a shift back from politicized conviviality to bureaucratic administration. This model of everyday life thus helps us account for the shift in Nazi policy from informal to formal management that recent scholarship associates with the transition to war (ca. 1937–41).[11] But it will not get us all the way to the Holocaust. The Final Solution was not an inevitable outcome of the cultural process outlined here. Many other factors such as a racist ideology, a polycratic regime, as well as the pressures and brutality of war helped translate local customs into mass murder. Ordinary people had to continue to implement racism and fascism inside and outside of Germany. Nonetheless, these chapters do describe the indigenous process of how interwar Hildesheimers first learned the Nazi habits that later facilitated genocide. Arguably, ordinary people welcomed Nazi programs for social engineering in part because the struggle to colonize everyday life from above and below had so undermined the functionality of conviviality.

None of my interview partners admitted to any crimes against humanity, either because they did not perpetrate any or because they falsified the past. Since this history relies so centrally on the way that my interview partners remembered and represented their past, the final chapter will revisit the classic excuse that ordinary people simply did not know about Nazi crimes against humanity. Yet when viewed in the context of the preceding cultural history, these epistemologies of the Holocaust suggest that we need to invert the standard model of how history and memory relate. Accordingly, I place this chapter on memory at the end of the study to restore the original sequence of events. My interview partners described conviviality in interwar Hildesheim according to the idiosyncratic way that they cultivated status and power in the past. They tried to preserve a coherent sense of self over the years. For both personal and political reasons, they wanted to imagine that they had been essentially consistent in behavior. As a result, their contemporary self-presentation closely reflected their historical self-cultivation, and, in self-reflection, disclosed its discrepancies. Though often mistaken or cagey in terms of more factual forms of memory, these habit memories provide us with a sound basis for insight into everyday life when my interview partners first formed those habits, as they first cultivated those selves.

Alf Lüdtke has argued that memories of German victimization at the end of the Second World War are "associated in consciousness with the concatenation of terror and suffering *caused* by Germans themselves—and highlighted the fact that many Germans at the time also realized this connection." The personal actions and experience of self-styled ordinary Germans can never really be separated "from the *context* of their genesis and impact."[12] Narrative interviews provide an essential source for reconstructing how ordinary people responded to, and helped shape, world history precisely because there is no such thing as normalcy after all. Oral history can help us understand how ordinary people have since dealt with the Nazi past by revealing to us how they first dealt with the Nazi present.

PART I
EIGENSINN

1 | Civility

DURING THE 1920s, salutations served as one foundation for Hildesheim's civil society. Hildesheimers offered a friendly greeting as the overture for the exchange of ideas, goods, currency, and services. A friendly greeting between friends and neighbors generated a sense of integration in a community of equals, though notably, Hildesheimers used the same customs of conviviality to lay claim simultaneously to status and power in a diverse and hierarchical society. They negotiated these contradictory desires with a friendly greeting, keeping neighbors "neither too close nor too far." Thus a proper salutation did more than just initiate the other, "more important" relationships and exchanges that constituted the economy and shaped the polity. Significant for its own sake, a proper greeting preserved that minimal amount of respect necessary to keep neighborly relations civil.

This cultural mechanism is hardly new. In his travel log for the journal *Le Tour du Monde* in 1883 (reprinted 1974: 7), E. del Monte wrote that Hildesheimers responded politely and in kind whenever he said *good evening*. Yet the particular circumstances of interwar Germany exacerbated the need for soothing salutations. The Weimar Republic witnessed acrimonious political debate, a high degree of political mobilization, as well as noteworthy incidents of political violence from street fighting and vandalism to assassination and coups d'état. In this context, seemingly ordinary neighborly interactions often threatened to release barely contained animosities. In response, Hildesheimers issued a proper greeting in order to bind their neighbors into moral relationships of reciprocity. Salutations thus afforded ordinary Hildesheimers a sense of control over circumstances that seemed out of their control. Greetings evoked a sense of community within a modern and modernizing society. They promised a fair and salutary outcome to social relations in an era of uncertainty. Above all, they presumed—and thereby generated—a sense of normalcy in extraordinary times.

Good Day

German salutations were sufficiently diverse that folklorist Karl Prause could publish a 250-page survey of them in 1930, using both dialectical dictionaries and questionnaires. In the colloquial High German of towns, Prause argued, you *offered the time of day: good morning, good day, good evening,* or *good night.* Perhaps you inquired as to your neighbor's condition if you had not seen that neighbor for a long time. Yet this salutation remained formulaic. "In town, one often greeted only to attend to the responsibility to be polite." Just saying *good day* would be taken as unfriendly or insulting in the countryside. Rural salutations, he offered as a contrast, were more evocative of trust, and involved a longer conversation: what my interview partners also called *taking part (Anteil nehmen)* in the lives of neighbors. The so-called rural man could also sometimes greet by asking a question or making a joke. More so than *good day,* such greetings match the etymology of the word *grüssen*: these salutations were a means *to address someone (anreden).* According to Prause, rural greetings preserved native customs both as language and as social life. Unfortunately, a rise in commuter traffic and the Great War helped dissolve the urban–rural distinction so significant to folklorists like Prause (§3). When migrants moved from the countryside to provincial towns like Hildesheim, they abandoned their rural dialects and adopted more "civilized" manners.

Prause's urban–rural dichotomy arose more from cultural pessimism than social-scientific accuracy. His exaggerated, temporal hierarchy of allegedly authentic rural salutations over modern, urban ones reproduced a politicized distinction of community and society that had a long tradition in German academic research (Bendix 1997; Liebersohn 1988; Tönnies 1988). My interview partners strongly disagreed with Prause's argument about the superficiality of urban greetings. Heinrich Weber recalled his stepmother's encounters with neighbors in the 1920s:

> We all knew each other, and it was always a—we could say—almost a friendship with neighbors. At least a good acquaintanceship. I know that not only would they greet but they would also detain each other with: *How's it going? How are things with you? What's up at home?* and vice versa, as it were. This was how the neighborhood got informed about everything—what I was doing in the future, who was getting married among the daughters or sons. (G/145b R/170)

Whenever Günther Seidner ran into people he knew, he greeted them, gave them his hand, and asked how things were going for them (G/81b R/80). As a matter of habit and propriety, Hildesheimers took part in the life and work of their fellows through greeting.

Prause noted that German speakers were changing their forms of salutations. Greetings were becoming shorter, more frequent, and more fleeting, so that the semantic and etymological meanings of the phrases were losing their social significance. For example, *good day* (*Guten Tag*), already an abbreviated version of *may God grant you a good day* (*Gott gebe Dir guten Tag*), got shortened in contemporary practice to *g' day* (*'n Tag*). A long phrase was not necessary since circumstance and style already conveyed the fact that one was greeting (§5). Only the sentiment of greeting remained, not what was said as such but the fact that one greeted one's neighbors. Prause also noted the converse tendency: some changes in greeting highlighted semantics. German speakers had used the French salutation *adieu* since the twelfth century, but the German Language Association succeeded in almost entirely eliminating the word from parlance during the First World War. Hildesheimers corroborated this change. As Friedrich Rother told another interviewer: "In 1914 when the war broke out, suddenly it became taboo or forbidden to say *adieu* from one day to the next. We always used to say *adieu* or *dieu*. It's like saying *bye* [*Tschüss*]. . . . We were no longer allowed to say it . . . because it was French!" (SAH 904–1/43b R/10). *Adieu* was replaced with *auf Wiedersehen*, the German translation of *au revoir*. Prause even discovered more complex shifts in the scope of neighborliness. He noted that, whereas *until we meet again* implied a trusted, friendly relationship before the war, it was also used in the interwar years in more neutral relationships, such as those that involved shopping (§50–51). Clearly, the style of salutations was changing dynamically in the first decades of the twentieth century. Facing pressure from state and society, salutations were becoming more fleeting, formulaic, and pragmatic, more "German" and urban in style, perhaps also serving expanded functions.

My interview partners insisted that they always *offered the time of day* (*die Tageszeit bieten*) to the neighbors they knew. This general expression for salutations disguised within it a large range of different expressions in the Hildesheim region, such as *what's new?* (*Was gibt's Neues?*) or *is the advice any good?* (*Ist der Rat gut?*), both used when greeting more than one person already engaged in a conversation (Prause §1, 2, 6, 7, 11, 12). Most salutations were optative and reflected religious influences: as in wishing that God would grant your neighbor a *good day,* and so on. Other greetings expressed subordination and submission, such as *at your service* (*Ihr Diener;* in Latin, *servus*). Prause insisted that submissive salutations were not Germanic in origin and were used only by businessmen, students, servants, and the military (§4, 25, 27). Karl Rudolph, involved in a fraternal group in Hildesheim, referred to a boy's proper greeting in those terms: *making a servant* (*Diener machen,* described below). Although few Hildesheimers used this expression for greeting, the words still reveal the normative logic of greeting in interwar Hildesheim. While greeting, speakers were supposed to subordinate themselves. The question is to whom—or to what—were they showing respect.

Karl Rudolph's family did not establish any close relationships with their neighbors. He knew them all by name, of course, but he knew them not because they met socially. He knew them because he greeted them. "This was hammered into my head since I was small: with neighbors, you greet." So I asked Karl to describe how he greeted a neighbor. "With a *servant*." Karl bowed his head to imaginary neighbors. Then, imagining that they were walking past him, or he them, he looked to the side, following their relative position. "Head down like this, greet [with a] *good day,* looking in at them at the same time." The head was neither down nor up, but to the side "like this: *good day* no? *good day.*" That is, both neighbors bowed simultaneously while looking into each other's eyes and continuing on their way. You walked past "a little bowed [*gebeugt*]—down." Both were slightly, but equally, humbled (G/180b R/185). Girls *curtsied,* Käthe Stolte explained. When they were on their way somewhere, perhaps back home from church or out on a Sunday stroll, and they met some acquaintances of her parents,

> Then we greeted them. First my parents. We always stood mostly some two steps apart, as was proper. And then it was our turn. Then they would greet, and if they greeted us, then we children, we girls made a curtsy.

Then Käthe asked me: "Do you know how to make a curtsy?" I lied, saying that I did not, because I wanted her to explain it to me in her terms. Käthe said that she had learned to curtsy in dance class. Our interview suddenly became my first *Tanzstunde.* Käthe stood up from her sofa and moved around the coffee table to the only part of her salon where she could move freely. "You can stay seated," she reassured me.

> Let's say, for instance . . . that we have seen each other and you have just greeted my parents, and now it's the children's turn. Then you reach out your hand to me and then we have to make a curtsy—

Which Käthe did.

> One knee under—. But then you have to look the people in the eye, don't look down. My parents always used to say, "If you look down, then you are not honest, then you have something to hide. One has to look the people in the eye!"

Käthe's hand was presented to me neither to be kissed (palm down), nor for her to kiss mine (palm up). Hildesheimers did not kiss hands while greeting. Correct hand position was in a handshake, side to side (G/186a R/345).

Greeting was neither a rarefied discourse of what was said nor just the gestures of hands and bodies; it was the synthetic enactment of both. During their interviews, Käthe and Karl "narrated" greeting as they remembered it, neither as text nor as gesture but as a habit. Physicality was central to greeting. While greeting, neighbors touched each other in what was per-haps the only opportunity for physical contact in polite, public interaction. Clearly, servants and curtsies were not acts of subordination to neighbors as social superiors. Adults greeted each other as equals, and even though children humbly waited for adults to greet them first, the children were nonetheless taught to look adults in the eyes. In bowing to each other at the same time, holding hands side-by-side, and keeping direct eye contact, the Hildesheimers publicly and mutually recognized their equality of status. Eye contact does not naturally create a sense of equality and integration. It other contexts, it could just as readily be considered predatory (E. Anderson 1990: 171, 220–21). In interwar Hildesheim, however, this particular style of greeting enacted principles of liberalism and established the foundations of a civil society.

The objects of respect to which Hildesheimers subordinated themselves were none other than the universalized, self-legislating individual in them-selves and their neighbors. This ideal stands at the core of the Enlightenment concept of ethical behavior, as Immanuel Kant defined it: "The dignity of human beings consists of this ability to morally legislate for all of society, although under the conditions that you subordinate yourself to this same legislation as well" (1786: 439–40). In such a civil society, then, "the actual object of respect" becomes "this ideal will—a potential for all of us." Shared ethical standards made neighbors seem trustworthy. A mutual greeting as-sured Hildesheimers that they all subordinated themselves to these same imperatives. Greeting thus served as more than just the ritual glue binding individualized agents and rationalized institutions into an experience of co-herence in daily life. At every interpersonal encounter in the neighborhood, Hildesheimers symbolically demonstrated their respect for their neighbors (one formulation of Kant's categorical imperative) and literally bowed be-fore the imperative to greet—though they watched carefully to make sure their neighbors did as well. Greeting not only laid the foundations for a civil society in Hildesheim; it also legislated a moral community (see also Simmel 1989, vol. 2: 308–16).

This ideal only partially corresponded to the realities of everyday life. In Hildesheim, there were many social distinctions that the forms of greet-ing seemed to reinforce (see also Althusser 1971). Girls curtsied and boys bowed. Children waited for their parents to greet their neighbors and greet-ed if and only if they were greeted by adults first. Girls curtsied only up to a certain age (G/192a R/325) and boys who went to *Gymnasium* (an elite high school), like Karl Rudolph, raised their school caps when they said *good day* (which Karl did for me too, G/180b R/185). Prause (§3) even argued that the melody and style of the salutation expressed hierarchies of class. For the most part, however, Hildesheimers downplayed such divisive aspects of greeting in their narratives.

Overriding the shock of difference imposed by a neighbor's social background was the act of greeting itself. Ulrike Volkmann did not have a close relationship with her working-class neighbors. She was not permitted to play with them because they were Protestant (and she was Catholic), because they did not attend an upper school (and she did), and because they lived in a building nicknamed *The Flea Barracks*. Her mother avoided long conversations with them but still greeted them when they met on the street (G/59b R/110). Similarly, Käthe Stolte's parents did not have a close relationship with their neighbors, but "there were no differences there. We knew of course who they were and everyone greeted everyone else. Everyone spoke with them. I never noticed any differences!" (G/184b R/400). Mandatory greeting inverted, equalized, and erased social hierarchies, flattening structure in a fleeting moment of anti-structure. By emphasizing the fact of greeting over its many forms, salutations could accomplish this temporary transcendence of societas in communitas.

Once they made greeting mandatory in all neighborly circumstances, Hildesheimers could then hide their eigensinn behind it. With good reason, Heinrich Weber was terrified of Ernst Ehrlicher. Not only was Ehrlicher the mayor of Hildesheim, but he was also Heinrich's boss. But that fear did not extend into the streets of town. For instance, Heinrich told the following story to an interviewer: Ehrlicher drove to work at nine in the morning every day, for he was a very punctual man. Every morning, Stöber, a pewterer, stood at his door as the mayor drove past and took out his watch, as if to check the accuracy of his watch by the mayor or the mayor by the watch. One day when the mayor seemed late, Stöber greeted him with: "Hm, is the time correct or am I late?" The mayor replied: "I already came to work!" (SAH 904-1/56b R/00). The ritual repetition of greeting, here literally *offering the time of day,* made this kind of eigensinn possible. The mayor had to tolerate this challenge to his work ethic because Stöber veiled his criticism behind a mandatory greeting.

This tactic worked only if every Hildesheimer always greeted every neighbor he or she knew. Günther Seidner explained, "Yes, we were raised to greet adults on the street. . . . If you had a cap, you had to take off the cap. . . . If you had nothing on your head, then you made a short"—Günther never finished his sentence, but bowed his head as an example. "You said *good day* whenever you knew someone. . . . You knew each other and greeted each other" (G/79b R/360). Walking down the street, outside of church, in corner stores, Hildesheimers ritually repeated their greetings to all neighbors: *good day, Mr. So-and-So, how are you.* "In that style," Frieda Stolzenberg told me. "You were nice and polite" (G/19b R/70, 390; see also G/130b R/140). Stopping at the barber to call her father for the midday meal, Ulrike Volkmann made a curtsy and said *good day* to the men in the shop. "That went without question" (G/59b R/63).

Parents taught the ritual repetition of greeting to children by example. "When I went out with my father," Georg Brzezinski explained, "then the hat was constantly off, you know. . . . When I walked with my father and he greeted people, then I had to greet also!" Once hats were removed, a long conversation would ensue, "which was naturally so uncomfortable for me at that age" (G/92a R/200). By the time Friedrich Rother was fifteen, he had started to play *Ladies and Gentlemen* with the young girls on his street all on his own. "We sat across from each other. We greeted each other politely." Friedrich put out his hand to illustrate the process for me. "Perhaps [we then tried] a few dance steps, or something like that, no?" (G/54a R/310). Other children needed more discipline. Käthe Stolte was often sent unescorted to St. Bernward's Church for the *Andacht* (the Catholic service at two in the afternoon). Sometimes her parents stayed home in the Nordstadt to sew or read, so she and her siblings would walk south of the railroad tracks to church with a group of neighborhood children. The pastor would teach them about Christian precepts, and then ask them questions that they had to answer. Meanwhile, the adult members of the church would watch her carefully to see if she greeted every one of them properly with a curtsy.

> My parents' generation knew absolutely everyone. So they all paid close attention to see if we greeted. . . . If . . . for instance . . . we had not greeted, looked at them in a friendly manner, or made a curtsy and given them our hand, then they would have complained to my parents and then we would have gotten a fleecing as to why, wherefore, and for what reason we did not. (G/184b R/130, G/186a R/395, G/186b R/00)

Adult Hildesheimers took part in the lives of neighbors, and they made sure that children did so too.

While walking down the street, Hildesheimers were constantly tipping their hats, curtsying, offering the time of day, taking part in their neighbors' lives. To appreciate this preoccupation with neighborhood civility, however, we must locate it in its historical context. Prior to 1914, the Second Empire served as the cornerstone for the Hildesheimers' cosmology: it provided a sense of stability in rapidly changing times and a lodestone by which residents could compass their way through everyday life, even in the negative for those who disagreed with the regime politically. Crisis after crisis then shook

Hildesheim in the decade from 1914 to 1924: war, suffering, protest, defeat, collapse, revolution, demobilization, hyperinflation, stabilization. Once the formal institutions of state and society proved to be unreliable, the streets of Hildesheim became a battleground for strategies for herrschaft among competing factions. The fledgling republic did not help much: it provided only an uncertain democracy, collapsing morals, and inverted social hierarchies. Ordinary Hildesheimers faced the typical contradictions of classic modernity: of uneven development, of a future that promised much and a present that delivered little (*Ungleichzeitigkeiten;* Bloch 1962; Harootunian 2000; Peukert 1987).

Hildesheimers responded with innovations of their own: tactics of eigensinn designed to help them survive the tribulations of modernization. In sharp contrast to the failure of formal institutions, a proper greeting offered Hildesheimers the promise of a reasonable outcome for their agency. Greeting's ritual repetition publicly demonstrated their willingness to abide by and reproduce those common standards. Greeting thus restored their faith in the potentiality of social relations per se (following Simmel 1989, vol. 2: 308–16). Serving the function of politics, though by other means, it represented that reasonable survival tactic through which ordinary Hildesheimers could find a modicum of stability in hard and rapidly changing times.

A Proper Greeting

Hildesheimers turned to greeting in order to circumvent social crisis on a systemic level, in part because they had learned of its functionality on an individual level. Many, if not most, young Hildesheimers learned how to make a proper curtsy or bow during tanzstunde (see Figure 2). "This was a very important time," Lotte Schohl recalled. Almost all of the girls in the lower second class of the Goethe School took dance lessons in the hall of the Civic Theater in 1935.

> First we went to step class. That was for girls only. There we *learned to move,* as the dance instructor was wont to say. We were supposed to learn how to behave: how to walk, how to bow, how to make a formal curtsy, how to behave near young men. That was four hours before the big opening of dancing classes, and in the last hour, as we girls came out, there stood the boys from the upper second class—the *young gentlemen* as they were called back then—all in a row and looking at who came in: us. Then there was the big presentation evening. You got a new dress. You did up your hair especially nicely. You were horribly excited; I was at least.

Lotte did not have any brothers, so she was not accustomed to having social contact with young men.

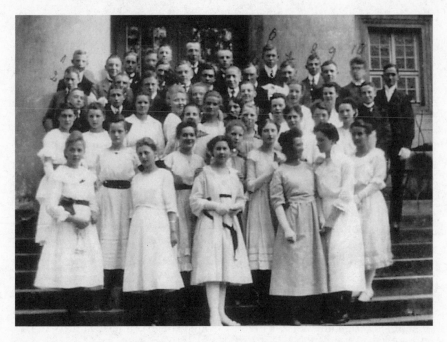

Figure 2. Dance class, in front of the Civic Theater, 1919 (D/584). As a young woman, my interview partner had inscribed numbers near certain gentlemen's heads and their names on the back.

The young men wore dark suits, had white gloves on, and were just as excited as we were. We had to sit in a long row of stools and the gentlemen came in. The dance instructor said to us fifteen-year-olds: "Ladies, may I present to you the gentlemen of dance class!" They were called out alphabetically, the gentlemen. They had to take three steps forward and one step back—

Lotte laughed.

—put the back foot to the right, make their bows, and then they were permitted to sit back down again. After that, the dance teacher said: "Gentlemen, I now present to you the ladies of dance class!" and then we had to take three steps forward, make our curtsies, bow, and then return to our seats. And then light music was played and the dance teacher said, "Gentlemen, I ask you to invite [one of the ladies to dance]."

Lotte's story built to a climax.

And there we sat and were terrified that we could be the last one [to be asked]. It was such that every lady got a gentleman. But it was horribly exciting. Today that is not how it is; that was really a good feeling. (G/6b R/end, G/7a R/00; see also G/9a R/40, G/13b R/170, G/74b R/15, G/182a R/00)

Many families sent their children to tanzstunde regardless of whether they had the requisite means or background. Participation in dance class reflected their claim to future status. Contact between girls and boys in public settings was closely monitored by adults, so for many, dance class also provided the first official contact with the opposite gender. It is hardly surprising then that Lotte Schohl felt so much anxiety there. When she was fourteen years old, she was still playing with dolls. A mere year later, she was confirmed, went to dance class, and suddenly found that she was "grown up." In dance class, her identity and future prospects in the public sphere were at stake (G/6b R/end, G/7a R/00). Dance class was highly ritualized to ease children into these scary, new circumstances. A partner was literally called the *Dance Class Gentleman* or the *Dance Class Lady,* and it was expected that every young man would dance with every young woman at the table at which they were seated during balls (G/4a R/290, G/5a R/210). In dance class, every Lady got her Gentleman, as Lotte explained with relief (and in contrast to the uncertainty of informal social relations in the 1990s). That is, tanzstunde taught Lotte that greetings were the opening gesture towards a specific kind of heterosexual–patriarchal order. Formalized greetings reassured her that everyone would find a place in civil society in the end.

This happy outcome was hardly assured in informal social life. My interview partners recounted various circumstances in which Hildesheimers had to negotiate treacherous social encounters. These moments involved a sense of isolation, improper sexual expression, social deviancy, and outright animosity in the neighborhood. Yet the pragmatic lesson of each story was that such rough waters could be navigated smoothly through the use of a proper greeting. Greeting buried social conflicts under a shroud of normalcy.

In response to systematic questions about their parents' activities, my interview partners sometimes found themselves face-to-face with the fact that their fathers and especially their mothers lived their lives in almost total social isolation. Yet my interview partners found solace by saying that their parents always greeted their neighbors (G/86b R/30, G/73a R/190, G/74a R/150, G/74b R/200). For instance, I asked Otto Koch to whom his mother could talk about her husband's alcohol problem, since she had no support network of relatives and friends. Otto replied that she chatted with one neighbor "from window to window: *Good day! How are things? The sun is shining today! It's good, the weather! What are the prospects?* And so on. Yes, these general, meaningless conversations. . . . Just empty words" (G/44b R/300). A pragmatist, Otto's mother filled the gap in her life created by alienation with a neighborly greeting.

Greeting also negotiated the potentially sexualized interaction between neighbors. In a poem for Ida Rolf on her ninetieth birthday (in the author's possession), a "dear neighborly friend" recognized the elderly woman's accomplishments, wished her health and happiness, and then added:

Yes, what more gifts should I give to you?	Ja, was soll Ich Dir noch bescheren?
I think, Ignaz [Mr. Rolf] would not forbid me,	Ich denk, der Ignaz wird's nicht verwehren
since I should close with a loving greeting,	drum sei's mit liebem Gruss zum Schluss
to give you a heartfelt birthday kiss!	ein herzhafter Geburtstagskuss!
As long as the sun will shine on us both	Solang uns Zwein die Sonn noch scheint
I remain your old, true friend!	bleib ich Ihr alter treuer Freund!

A request for a kiss between neighbors could easily have been mistaken for an amorous advance. To desexualize it, this neighbor framed it within a "loving greeting" from an "old, true friend." Greetings effaced sexual transgressions (see also G/79b R/360).

Greetings also reinforced the sense that neighborhoods worked in spite of social diversity. Ulrich Gerke cited various examples from everyday life to prove to me that confessional difference was not a problem in his neighborhood. He noted that Catholic and Protestant children played together and attended each other's churches out of curiosity. Ulrich then cited the example of the pastor of the Catholic parish of St. Bernward, a "populist" who stopped by to chat with Ulrich's mother about groceries. "Protestants or Catholics it made no difference. When he came into the house, he said *good day* to everyone, and even greeted, no?" (G/86a R/355). In his neighborhood, some people were more private than others, Helmut Rabitz said, but "they greeted each other. The children all learned to greet and did it also. That was a self-evident thing." Helmut never said if the relations between neighbors were good or bad in the context of social diversity (which was my question). Instead, he described the habit of exchanging greetings (G/51a R/95).

Georg Brzezinski started to laugh when he described the neighbors who lived one door down from his childhood home. They had joined two homes together into one larger building, but because the town was constructing a trolley line on their street that required their homes being set further back, they were forced to rebuild entirely. Georg's family maintained a "good neighborly relationship" with this family, but when Georg explained what he meant by this, he got uncomfortable. They greeted each other if they saw each other, he said, but his family did not have any social intercourse with them. "They bore a certain grudge against us back then." Again interrupting his narrative with laughter, Georg said that his neighbors were jealous of his family because his neighbors had to rebuild their home. He began to explain that the issue "really went a little further than that." Georg never clarified why. His father was active in politics, so perhaps they blamed him for creating the problem in the first place; or perhaps they were angry that they, and not the Brzezinskis, had to move their home back. But both possible explanations must remain pure speculation because Georg shifted his narrative yet again away from these underlying tensions to the topic of salutations. "You said *good day* and such, but there again, there was no large amount of social intercourse" (G/90a R/290, G/90b R/00).

Hildesheimers did not greet just because the custom was proper behavior, ingrained since childhood. They also greeted selfishly to produce an experience they desperately desired. The ritual repetition of greeting gave them a sense of equality, homogeneity, and community in the midst of their increasingly modern society. In hard times, it restored their faith in the viability of civil society and a reasonable outcome for their agency. It compensated for an absence of reliable friendship in the face of difficult personal problems. Most importantly, a greeting disguised social difference and even defused personal animosities behind the veil of propriety. It did not transcend the barriers of social difference, but it did make it possible for political opponents to cohabitate as neighbors. Hildesheimers greeted especially in moments of interpersonal tension or social crisis because a salutation reinforced social bonds while the neighborhood was teetering on the brink of dysfunction. That is, greeting was a way "to come to terms with an environment they see as not always welcoming or safe" (E. Anderson 1990: 169). Interwar Hildesheimers greeted to keep their civil society civil.

This preservative function of greeting can be best illustrated by cases of its inverse: not greeting (cf. E. Anderson 1990: 168–72). Not greeting your neighbor implied arrogance, registered the presence of an unresolved or irresolvable conflict, or symbolized both. Prause wrote (§142):

> In the countryside, those who do not greet are considered to be proud, arrogant, and uneducated. Even from temporary strangers, the peasant expects a greeting at least. Those who walk past without greeting often have to hear mocking and uncouth expressions.

In Hildesheim, C. J.'s "Story of Old Jürgen," a serialized narrative in the *Evangelische Gemeindeblatt* (EGb) in the Summer of 1926 (May: 5–6; June: 4–5; July: 4) gave an example of the consequences of not greeting. It was a story of two enemies.

> Once he encountered me on my way. I did not greet him but just walked by him. So he yelled after me: "Are you that proud, Malte? Is that the best way to make a complaint? Are you finished yet? You know of course, *whoever buries the greetings of another—*

A Protestant publication, the EGb exhorted its readership to greet neighbors no matter what their personal differences. Nonetheless, Theresa Stoffregen's grandfather "buried" his greetings in one instance. He went to court with a neighbor on Langer Hagen over the ownership of some carrier pigeons. Theresa doubted that her grandfather greeted this neighbor on the street. "In this, grandfather was stubbornly defiant" (*konsequent;* G/191a R/300).

Not greeting was an extreme measure that dissolved a neighborhood's social relations. Johanna Ernst always greeted with *very fine day.* "I am that kind of a person." She greeted elderly people, who could not see very well, with a *good day, Mr. or Mrs. So-and-so* and a wave of the hand, so they could see the greeting, "and always in a friendly manner." But she had only the strongest words for people who do not greet properly:

> What I cannot tolerate at all is when someone greets . . . and they only do this: mouth open and no noise comes out. I greet [them] once, the second time I wave or look in another direction. There I am totally harsh. I cannot tolerate that. . . . If I think about it, that is just unbelievable. Either I greet properly or not at all. This is a question of your outlook. You either have to be friendly or things can't proceed any further [*geht nichts drüber*]. You don't lose anything by it [*da bricht man sich nichts ab*]. But if greeting hurts you, well, then [I] do it once, twice maybe, then I make a stupid face, look to the other side of the street, see no one. . . . If they only open their mouth, what should you [do] with such people? How should you greet them? It has no purpose. (G/130b R/140)

The absence of proper greeting not only registered conflict but also broke the bonds of reciprocity and trust. Without a proper greeting, further social interaction seemed neither possible nor purposeful. Without a proper greeting, civil society seemed to collapse.

By always greeting their neighbors, Hildesheimers preserved the integrity of community against the constant threat of disintegration. It was only late in the interview process that Theresa Stoffregen mentioned neighbors who lived in *back houses*: those homes set off from the street behind other homes. These neighbors were usually much poorer than the rest of the population. Still, she insisted that she always greeted them. "Oh yes, they were still respected. Of course, of course" (G/193a R/105). Margareta Averdieck lived in her youth above an older, unmarried man and his aunt. The man was probably an epileptic and "one of those angry old men." He complained to her mother whenever Margareta and her sister were loud, such as when they ran or leaped up or down the wood stairs. Once, she and her mother returned from the theater wearing shoes and their neighbor screamed at them, saying that they should take off their shoes (even though, according to Margareta, they rarely wore fancy shoes). As a result of these incidents, the relationship was never a good one between the neighbors. Still, "my mother was not the type to—," Margareta could not give voice to her dark thoughts. She shifted her narrative. "She was always friendly afterwards. Yes, superficially, but never without a greeting. Never that she would walk past them without greeting. It was never like that" (G/75a R/00).

The ritual repetition of a proper greeting should be understood as a tactic of eigensinn: a self-expressive, nonconformist revolt against an unstable world in a vain attempt to recreate stability. Greeting restored a sense of control over one's environment for ordinary Hildesheimers. It also reasserted a sense of communal order against the constant threat of disintegration into an alienated, potentially violent society. Precisely because it had to be shared between neighbors of different social backgrounds and political beliefs, that same act of eigensinn helped constitute a mass culture of conviviality that transgressed, but did not transcend, existing social and political divisions. Responding creatively, ordinary Hildesheimers modernized neighborliness to survive the crises of classic modernity.

Good Day and Goodbye

Hildesheimers greeted all of their neighbors, but they did not greet all their neighbors in the same way. They believed strongly in equality of dignity but did not recognize equality of status nor the notion of being equally intimate with all. Hildesheimers needed a custom that could move individual neighbors back and forth along a range of familiarity from best friend to complete stranger, and correspondingly up or down a hierarchy of status from people-to-emulate to people-who-should-emulate-you. That is, they needed a way to greet their neighbors selectively that would integrate *or alienate* them according to the needs of the greeter.

Prause described how greetings could be used to set degrees of intimacy. "One meets someone, wishes him a *good day* as a salutation. Since one does not want to enter into a conversation with him, one adds immediately the fare-thee-well of *goodbye*" (§64). Examples from the interviews abound in which Hildesheimers used some form of *good day and goodbye* to limit a relationship (G/21b R/55, G/24b R/290, G/26b R/215, G/30a R/30, G/34a R/335, 395, G/42b R/180, G/179b R/385). Before or after church, Helmut Rabitz's family would greet their neighbors with: *How is it going? How are things with you?* or simply *good day*. This greeting did not imply intimacy. When I asked if they used the southern German greeting, *God be with you* (*Grüss Gott*), he replied, "no, *good day and goodbye*." He laughed sardonically and shifted his narrative to details about the Sunday meal just as he had left the church and his neighbors: as quickly as possible (G/51a R/130, 155). Theodora Algermissen lived near, and played in, a Jewish cemetery. Sometimes Jews came to visit the burial grounds, though this occurred infrequently because the gravestones dated from before the First War. Since she did not know these people, she said, *good day* "and there you had it" (G/2a R/180; see also G/1a R/190, G/22b R/260, G/42b R/50).

The emphasis in such anecdotes lay not on the greeting itself but on the absence of something *more* than just greeting (cf. E. Anderson 1990: 170). Jürgen Ludewig's family had good contact with their relations on his mother's side that included visits and play dates with cousins, but he had no contact with relatives on his father's side. "No visits, you could say. *Good day and goodbye,* as it was said" (G/103a R/380). Jürgen claimed that he greeted everyone he knew in the neighborhood. "There were no distinctions there." The children played together, after all. Still, the adults did not have social contact. "They lived more or less for themselves, withdrawn. . . . I'll say it this way, yes: I close my house door and then I will have nothing to do with anyone else." Isolation was not limited to specific camps or between them; it was generally true among all neighbors in interwar Hildesheim:

> Everyone was on their own. If you met someone outside, sometimes [you would say] *good day and goodbye* as it was said, where[by] you did not want to or were not able to or had no time to talk to them. . . . And sometimes . . . if you were a bit more familiar, then you would exchange a few words. . . . Everyone knew each other well on the street. Everyone greeted everyone who walked past. But that was all.

Jürgen's account should not be read as if greetings were formulae applicable for all circumstances, individuals, groups, or regions (G/103b R/240; cf. G/107b R/280). Individuals negotiated their own relationship with each neighbor in their own way (a topic addressed in the next chapter). Bernward Nedderich's family did not have that much contact with his neighbors in the Altstadt. Consequently, he could remember few of them. Even though his family was Jewish, he did not believe that religious differences accounted for this distance (a conclusion with which Jürgen, among others, agreed). "It was just that everyone lived more or less in their own four walls, yes. You met each other, said *good morning* said *good evening* yes. It was always a very good relationship" (G/156b R/100; see also G/140a R/90). Hildesheimers also did not always use the specific phrase *good day and goodbye* to create distance, and *good day* to create intimacy. As a body narrative, this expression attempted to represent an intuitive, pragmatic distinction between slightly different styles of greeting that were hard to describe in words. Yet precisely because it relied on a very subtle shift in style rather than an overt semantic difference (different words with different meanings), Hildesheimers could preserve their propriety and their distance through the "same" greeting.

In everyday use, greeting your neighbors in no way obligated a close relationship. Martha Paul neither knew her landlords nor knew or visited the neighbors who lived in her building. Yet she did not consider her relationships unfriendly. "We said *hello* and *goodbye, good morning* and *good afternoon.* . . . Hildesheimers were that way: *muffelig*" (she said the word for *grumpy* in German, though the rest of our interviews were in English; G/96a R/375, G/100a R/85). Greeting could just as easily create isolation as integration. Stella Storch's father worked as a typesetter at one of the local newspapers, but he had been educated at gymnasium. "God, how should I say this?" Stella interrupted herself. "That was something different." His social life and discussions were limited to his nuclear family. He would talk to his neighbors, of course, "but not extensively: *good day, Mr. So-and-so,* and *how are you?* and nothing [else]" (G/24b R/340; see also G/161b R/75, G/165b R/00, G/172b R/120, G/179b R/155, G/177a R/125). With *good day and goodbye,* Hildesheimers could exclude certain neighbors without offense.

Greeting defined relationships not just by what was said but by what was not said. When Hildesheimers said that they greeted their neighbors, they could have been implying an inclusion, an exclusion, or even both. Friedrich Rother had "hardly any" relationship with his neighbors in the 1930s and early 1940s. "Still [we] greeted, naturally. If we met on the street, we talked to each other. But no visits and such like were made" (G/55b R/00). The way he greeted excluded these neighbors from a closer friendship, while the fact of the greeting effectively included these same individuals in the category of neighbors. *Good day and goodbye* preserved greeting as a local custom without over-obligating the greeter to any particular relationship or identity. Friedrich described the dualities and dynamism of greeting with sarcastic self-awareness. Among his neighbors, he claimed that he maintained

> a very good relationship. No terrific friendships. Both parents used to say, "you have to get along well, but not too close." There is a saying in Hildesheim that goes: *so close, so far* [*so dicke, so dunne*]. It means that if you have a close friendship, and then a conflict arises in it, then it will become a bad fight, no? You have to get along with the neighbors, say *have a nice day,* and when there are festivities, celebrate with them—but not too close.

Friedrich then described a neighbor who lived on the same floor as his mother.

> They were sisters, the two of them. But they never spoke to each other in the informal. . . . As close as the friendship becomes, that is how far apart it will drift afterwards. Enmity arises from all things. (*von alles wirkt die Feindschaft aus* [*sic*]; G/54b R/170)

Friedrich intentionally walked a fine line among friends and neighbors. He maximized his security among his neighbors without risking the dangers of

closer friendships. His definition of *not too close, not too far* was idiosyncratic and contextual, but all interwar Hildesheimers greeted at times with
some version of *good day and goodbye.* Greeting was dynamic in this way:
it expressed a public identity and allowed one to lay claim to status without
insulting one's neighbors. Overtly, it created a sense of community at the
same time that it covertly preserved a sense of social hierarchy.

At the core of greeting therefore stood its normalcy. These customs
of conviviality hid the presence of interpersonal tactics and social conflict behind the veil of communal harmony and custom. They enabled
Hildesheimers to imagine that they lived in a world free of self-promotion
and conflict, all the while that they promoted themselves vis-à-vis their
neighbors. Heinrich Weber, who did not go to gymnasium, described his interactions with the daughters of a wealthy, socially connected bicycle dealer
in Hildesheim who did. His grandmother used to tell him: "When you are
walking by, and these two girls walk past you, then you take off your cap
and say *very fine day indeed,* just like a proper young boy." Heinrich admitted that greeting in this sense reflected a society based on subordination, and
then he laughed (G/144a R/30). He had unwittingly admitted that interwar
Hildesheimers created alienation as well as integration among neighbors.
A *good day* on its own held a dangerous potential for excessive intimacy. It
opened the floodgates of community, equality, and homogeneity (e.g., G/33a
R/330). Hence the necessity of some version of *goodbye.* It kept boys like
Heinrich in their place.

When Theresa Stoffregen was a young girl, one of her neighbors "had
visits from men" for which she received payment. Theresa could not remember actually having encountered this prostitute on the street: she lived
a quiet, retired life. Still, everyone knew her profession. Another neighbor
was "deformed" and did not suffer it well. He liked to chat up young girls
and was known to periodically reveal himself to them (curiously, he was a
tailor by profession). He never confronted Theresa in this way, nor had her
mother informed her as a young girl about the details of his misbehavior.
She simply warned Theresa to avoid him. I asked Theresa if she greeted these
two neighbors. She replied:

> Yes of course, of course, of course. As I said, we were encouraged back
> then to greet people, [and especially] everyone in the neighborhood, com-
> pletely regardless of what was up, no? . . . Propriety demanded that you
> greet when you [met] a neighbor. It was your duty to greet. That was just
> the tenor, no?

The norm of greeting just barely disguised its actual enactment, however.
With most neighbors, Theresa's mother asked how's it going, what's up,
or chatted across a fence with them. However, with these two particular

neighbors, "we did not let ourselves get into a longer conversation. . . . Of course we had to say good day. But otherwise, the least possible." As a child, Theresa could not simply cut off an adult who was speaking to her, and she lacked the sophistication to subtly but politely end a greeting with an adult. So her mother advised her to say that she had to run home quickly because her mother needed her. In retrospect, Theresa laughed at this ploy:

> Mother always said to us: no contact whatsoever with strange men. And this guy was actually not a stranger to us at all. So she probably told [us to say] *good day and goodbye* and that is it! No more! Yeah, she used to teach us such things on the sly. (*auf dem Weg gegeben;* G/190b R/00, G/191a R/165; cf. G/138a R/175, G/6a R/350)

The dynamism of greeting enabled girls like Theresa to avoid contact with potentially dangerous neighbors while continuing to afford them the respect due them as neighbors. In effect however, Theresa just publicly admitted that she had manipulated greeting to create hierarchies of familiarity and status where there should have been none. She clearly had more control over her life, and impact on her neighbors' lives, than she claimed. She laughed uncomfortably, then, because she had just let the cat of eigensinn out of her bag of everyday tactics.

Johanna Ernst liked some neighbors more than others. Sometimes they gossiped a lot, so she did two things: she avoided them by walking on the other side of the street, and she simultaneously greeted them in a friendly manner from a distance. "I won't admit to this, but it is true. You don't want to offend anyone." Appropriately, she located this transgressive tactic within a narrative that reiterated the imperative to greet. She said that she demanded proper greetings from her neighbors and from children. Which neighbors were gossips was also not mentioned, just the fact that she knew them all and greeted them all properly (G/130b R/140). "Let's say it this way," she later explained about her relationship with her neighbors. "You did not have conflict—for me, still to this day—so long as everyone [says] Oh, *hello* Johanna! Oh, *greetings to you*! . . . Conflict or something like that, we did not know it. We just did not have it. If you did not like someone particularly, [you said] *hello, greetings* or something, and off you went. That happens here also." She then got nervous. Caught red-handed treating some neighbors differently from others, Johanna had tarnished her claim to be just an ordinary Hildesheimer. "Do you have the tape recorder on?" she asked (G/131a R/65).

My interview partners remembered these tactics of eigensinn because it was through these cultural mechanisms that they negotiated difficult contradictions in everyday life, and because it was through these mechanisms of creating distinction that they felt most like themselves. By narrating these curious, funny, or awkward stories of self-expression, however, they revealed that they created both integration and alienation in their neighborhood. So greeting in interwar Hildesheim was as self-effacing as it was dynamic. It facilitated eigensinn by hiding it behind the veil of everyday life. More accurately, greeting evoked a sense of normalcy to preserve one's maneuverability in everyday life.

Transpositions

We now have a relatively clear picture of the *habitus* (Bourdieu 1989) of greeting in interwar Hildesheim: the underlying cultural logic that ordinary Hildesheimers enacted in ritual. Regulative, it provided a shared framework through which ordinary Hildesheimers interpreted and responded to certain social situations. Yet it was not proscriptive. Ordinary Hildesheimers determined for themselves how and when to apply it. They did so carefully and creatively, adjusting their greetings to meet the demands of different circumstances. They even transposed this habitus onto new or difficult circumstances. That is, they relied on salutations to negotiate everyday life not simply because greetings were normative but primarily because they were useful. A greeting best filled those awkward moments when Hildesheimers wanted to preserve community integrity, yet desired to keep their distance from certain neighbors. Greeting helped them disguise their role in shaping the boundaries and character of that moral community. Those neighbors whom they kept at a distance could be sexual deviants, social inferiors, gossips, or any other set of individuals deemed dangerous on a communal or interpersonal level. Greeting could enable them to deal with them all with equal finesse by giving informal encounters with them a veneer of normalcy.

Hildesheim was riven by cleavages of class, confession, ethnicity, race, gender, age, and sexuality, and many of these identities translated directly into rival political beliefs. Still, the town constituted an essentially civil society. What made it civil was not the degree of integration in any formal sense of intermarriage, common associations, or umbrella political parties: that is, homogenization or assimilation (for Hildesheim, cf. Schneider 1998: II. 11, IV). Hildesheim was civil because of ritual integration on this informal level (Henry 1984). Hildesheimers greeted all of the neighbors they knew—and disguised their responsibility for ignoring the rest. The question here is not whether this greeting was heartfelt, but to recognize that neighborliness provided a mechanism for Hildesheimers to decide that for themselves on an individual basis—and still treat all of their neighbors with respect. Its civility also had precious little to do with the degree to which anti-Catholic, anti-communist, antisemitic, or other prejudicial sentiments were latent or even overt in interwar Hildesheim. All of these attitudes were evident in Hildesheim in the 1920s. But Hildesheimers nonetheless experienced their town as essentially civil because they treated their neighbors like neighbors regardless of their attitudes or beliefs (cf. Schneider 1998: II. 12). Precisely because there were such radically different opinions at large in the political culture, and because these political differences were sometimes expressed through violence (if not directly in Hildesheim then still in the national news), interwar Hildesheimers made a point of greeting their neighbors, to keep civil society civil.

They could even be Nazis. For instance, Lena Turz had no friends other than her husband. As a Catholic wife of an artisan, she kept her distance from all of her neighbors in order to preserve an image of herself as having a certain superiority. So she greeted alcoholic landlords, local store own-ers, elite employers, socialists, communists, and national socialists with much the same greeting: *good day and goodbye* (G/65b R/215, 275, 445, G/66a R/130, 350, G/67a R/120, 320, G/67b R/50; see also G/168b R/110, G/160b R/165). Even with the family who lived below her, the Müllers, who threatened to denounce her husband to the party, Lena always preserved "otherwise a good relationship as such. We did not get in their way." As she was wont to say, "we did not go visiting from one house to another. We said *day* to their *day, good day and good day* and nothing else, no?" (G/67a R/320).

Theodora Algermissen believed that her relationships with her neigh-bors remained consistent during the interwar years. The one exception was the teacher who lived in the house in front of theirs: *the SA man*. Since he did not really play a role in the neighborhood anyway, this exception did not make much of a difference to her. It was not even a matter of being careful with what you said around him. "In any case, you only said *good day* or further *see you later* to him." Theodora then laughed at her own comment. "Nothing else at all." She laughed again. "He lived in the house, but we had no relationship whatsoever with him. We said *good day and goodbye*" (G/5a R/600). The conclusion to be drawn from these anecdotes is not that my interview partners treated all neighbors the same throughout the interwar period, which their own testimony later disavowed, or that they all avoided Nazi neighbors like good antifascists, since they may just have been trying to distance themselves from these neighbors in memory. Rather, the point is that, in the historic past as in the interview present, ordinary Hildesheimers used greetings flexibly and dynamically to create distance with neighbors with whom they did not wish to be associated—including Nazis. As individuals, they may or may not have lied about their politics, but as Hildesheimers, they negotiated those decisions with the aid of the relatively consistent cultural logic of greeting. This habitus was addictive precisely because it enabled them to cultivate their identities in response to changing circumstances and yet act as if they had done nothing new, different, or selfish.

Above all, a transposed greeting preserved a sense of normalcy. Dietrich Vornfett's family never had a particularly good relationship with their neighbors across the hall, the glass blower named Rath. Or at least it was not as close as their relationships with some of the other neighbors. "It was not bad but it was not particularly good, you know. It was just like neighbors who lived in the same house and did not know each other especially well, no?" Dietrich played with the Rath boy as a child because "he was good in math and I was bad in math." In their youth, the Rath boy was also Dietrich's only serious competition in diving. But they got along well nonetheless. "He was not my friend, but a good acquaintance." They negotiated these boundaries in the usual way. When Dietrich saw the Raths on the street as a child, they did not chat. Dietrich just greeted with *good day, Mr. or Mrs. Rath.* Then Dietrich felt the political winds changing in his neighborhood at the onset of 1933. Suddenly both of the youngest Rath boys joined the SS. The one who used to compete with Dietrich in diving became an arch-Nazi. In later years, Dietrich heard through the grapevine that he was one of the men who set the Hildesheim synagogue on fire and that he died himself in a firebomb in 1945. Still, the Raths never said anything antisemitic directly to the Vornfetts, who were Jewish. In 1933, Dietrich still greeted the Rath family in spite of the change in politics. He did nothing special when he saw Günther Rath walking in his SS uniform. Dietrich just said *good day* to him, and he said *good day* back. When I asked if Günther greeted with *heil hitler!* Dietrich said that Günther probably had but that he was not paying much attention right then. He suggested that he had been distracted by a love affair with a married woman in communist circles (G/151b R/60, G/152b R/140, 200, 245, G/153a R/140), but clearly, the ritual repetition of greeting also preserved a sense of normalcy in extraordinary times.

Hildesheimers transposed their older customs of greeting into the new political circumstances of the Third Reich. The tactics that Theresa had used to deal with flashers, Lena now applied to party members, Theodora to the SA man, and Dietrich to the SS. Of course, the stakes of neighborly relations had changed in the 1930s with the rise of the Nazi party (during the elections of 1930) and its seizure of power (officially in 1933). Still, the revolutionary qualities of the Third Reich were precisely what the Hildesheimers were trying to hide when they continued to greet all of their neighbors, including ardent Nazis. In spite of the Nazi revolution, the ritual repetition of greeting preserved a sense of normalcy.

In 1935, shortly before he was arrested for passing on anti-Nazi propaganda, Otto Koch moved to a new address in the Oststadt. Like many other Hildesheimers, Otto had two Nazis as neighbors. One neighbor was nicknamed Fritz. Otto described him as a good acquaintance, though not a best friend. They were part of a set of families who celebrated holidays together, exchanged potato pancakes, and even spoke to each other in the informal. The children played together in the same courtyard and the adults drank and sang songs in their apartments, even when there was supposed to be a blackout due to air raids. Otto accounts for these close neighborly relations (of all times, during the Third Reich) because they were all good, nice people, because they were also politically "untalented" people, and because he avoided talking about politics with them in any serious fashion. Fritz was not a member of the social-democratic party but voted for them as long as he could still vote. Later, Fritz was pressured to join the Nazis and become a block warden because he was in the police. He conformed. Yet he also warned Otto to be careful when he suspected that something was in the works in Nazi circles. Otto said of him: "I am indebted to him for a lot. Things did not go especially well for me with the Nazis." Otto understated his own biography: he had been arrested for passing resistance literature. Meanwhile Karl, the other neighbor, was Otto's school chum and had joined the Gestapo. Their relationship was not especially good, Otto laughed. "Once I knew that he was with the Gestapo, or worked for the Gestapo, then everything was of course very: . . . *good day,* Karl! . . . *good day, goodbye,* and the end" (G/43b R/180, G/45a R/320, G/45b R/00, G/48a R/40).

Everyday life during the Third Reich cannot be characterized as either normal or abnormal, integrative or alienating. Normalcy and abnormality, community and society, are not objective categories but subjective experiences produced through cultural mechanisms. Otto, Fritz, and Karl and their families all lived in the same neighborhood. They all greeted each other in spite of Otto's resistance to the Nazi regime, Karl's participation in it, and Fritz's conformity and nonconformity. They could continue to behave as neighbors by applying the relatively independent cultural logic of greeting to their new Nazi circumstances. Greeting did not ignore these political differences; by contrast, it took them very seriously. It afforded Otto the opportunity to adjust his relationships with his neighbors according to new circumstances, in this case political, without losing his sense of normalcy. In extraordinary times, a careful greeting helped them all live ordinary lives.

Tipping Your Hat

In an era of latent civil war and rapid social change, the ritual repetition of greeting effaced social differences and created a sense of community. By contrast, Hildesheimers used hats to identify differences and reinforce social hierarchies. Men tipped their hat while greeting their neighbors, but hats restored to the wearer that social identity that had been effaced while greeting. In this sense, the greeting and the hat-greeted-with were caught in a dialectic of eigensinn and herrschaft. By affording all of their neighbors the same proper greeting, Hildesheimers temporarily denied the salience of formal institutions and social divisions; but by greeting with a tip of the hat, they reintroduced the authority of formal hierarchies into informal enactments. Because hats were used to lay claim to distinction during an expression of equality, hats objectified (*reified*) those hierarchical social relations, and even seemed to acquire a degree of power over their wearer (as a *fetish*). Although based on limited data (see also Benjamin 1978: 48–49), an exploration of headdress in interwar Hildesheim will also suggest a central argument of this book: that eigensinn in the 1920s became herrschaft in the 1930s.

A hat spoke wonders about its wearer. First, headdress marked age. Every class in every school in town had its own cap, differentiated by the color of the hat and the color of the ribbons; and every Hildesheimer could decode this visual language. Showing me his school-cap collection from the 1930s, Karl Rudolph explained that the black hats were for the sixth and fifth classes, the red for the upper third and lower second classes, and the blue for the upper second, lower first, and upper first classes. If you still wore the same hat in the following year, Karl added, then the whole neighborhood knew that you had not been promoted to the next grade. Local historians Bernhard Gerlach and Hermann Seeland clarified this social dynamic: *veterans* who wore the same colors for a second year received a supplemental ribbon, "out of respect for one's elders" (1950: 204; see also G/13a R/180). Adult males did not wear school caps at all.

Second, Hildesheim's schools were divided by confession, so Hildesheimers could also tell for the most part who was Catholic and who was Protestant. "It made a colorful picture, you know, when the schools got out at midday and the kids from the various schools, each with their caps," Georg Brzezinski explained. "Well, so, that was just natural, what was proper" (*was sich gehörte;* G/5a R/250, G/13a R/180, G/92a R/200, G/192a R/300). In retrospect, we can see that the traditions of the 1920s were invented in the 1880s. According to Gerlach and Seeland (1950: 203; see also the image in Brinkmann 1993: 63), it was during the *Gründerzeit* (after the unification of Germany in 1871) that these forms and colors became universal in Hildesheim's schools. Still in the 1920s, caps, perhaps more than any other resource in Hildesheim, highlighted the diversity of the town's social life.

Third, hats marked gender: only boys were supposed to wear school caps. To be sure, the standards for gender had changed in the 1920s.

According to an anonymous Hildesheimer in the article "Sun-Umbrella and the Lady," appearing in the *Hildesheimische Zeitung* (HeZ) on 6 June 1925 (130: 3), traditionally women would never have left the house without a hat on their head, a veil before their face, and gloves on their hands. Yet young girls of 1925 would have been shocked by such a "fairy-tale," the author believed. Meanwhile, even their mothers wore a hat only if "it is new and various friends have not yet seen it. But very frequently, Mommy's bobbed hair appears unadorned on the street, for it is healthy, after all, to let your head get sun regularly." The author blamed the disappearance of *the Lady,* and her hat, on the rising popularity of sports and other outdoor leisure-time activities as well as on the emergence of a so-called *New Woman* who could play tennis, ride a motorcycle, and above all, purchase consumer products. To this Hildesheimer, attire in 1925 was no longer based on traditional norms but on personal pleasure and consumption; and with fashion were changing both the markings of gender and the forms of conviviality.

This generational shift away from hats, veils, and gloves corresponded to the general change in women's fashion during the 1920s towards more androgynous attire (Guenther 1997). In Hildesheim, girls like Dora Pröbst and Thekla Mestmacher sometimes wore hats and even gloves to prove that they were grown up. Sunday afternoons in interwar Hildesheim would have been boring for a young woman like Thekla had it not been for the opportunity to go sun-bathing and swimming during the summer. There she and her friends wore a hat as part of elaborate outfits designed to make them look beautiful: an integral aspect of this leisure-time activity. By contrast, older women, according to Dora, would never have gone to religious services without a hat (G/15b R/40, G/16b R/260, G/128b R/180, 250). Hats had been normative for the prewar generation but were becoming one option among many for the interwar generation. As was the case for greetings more generally, consumers in 1925 could choose which consumer goods shaped the identity that they desired to express at that moment in terms of gender, generation, sexuality, and lifestyle.[1]

Akin to the custom of greeting with which it was so closely associated, headdress facilitated the cultivation of particular identities in the local public sphere. Probably a member of the older generation, the anonymous author of the article mentioned above was criticizing precisely that new notion, part and parcel of a consumer society, that propriety could be sacrificed for the sake of eigensinn. The author was distressed by the very historicity of conviviality that eigensinn and consumerism presumed. In stark contrast to articles in the same issue about modern lifestyles and new technology, the author appealed to a romanticized memory of stable gender relations in a bygone era. Taking part in his neighbor's lives, the author reminded fellow Hildesheimers, especially females, of what was considered good manners in town: obedience to local cultural imperatives. In a society on the brink of chaos, he seemed to suggest, civility and normalcy would be preserved only if everyone respected the same rules of style.

Fourth, headdress marked class. Among adult males, Theresa Stoffregen explained, "the workers wore these caps back then, these peaked caps, and those with a stiff hat, they were in an office" (G/192a R/300). In Theresa's neighborhood, for instance, most of the men were artisans, at least those whose children she played with. The sole exception was one man, the father of one of her playmates, who lived on Langer Hagen and worked for the town. "He walked around with a stiff hat. You know, our fathers only had caps and this man went around with a stiff hat." Theresa laughed. "Because he wore his stiff hat to work, people said, 'There goes the Mayor of Langer Hagen!' . . . He was small and proud" (G/191b R/25). A local chronicler recorded the death of *Geheime Sanitätsrat* (Privy Councilor) Dr. Joseph Koh on 30 March 1916 with the same kind of mockery. He had been a "noteworthy sight in the cityscape. He almost always wore a top hat but also carried his umbrella upright in his jacket pocket" (SAH 801: 5/186e). Like titles, hats located their wearers within a rigid hierarchy of social status. Even visually, the working classes were subordinated to their betters, as seen in Figure 3. Their peaked caps were of similar shape and size to a boy's school cap, both shorter and less upright than the top hats of the educated elite.

Taken together, these various elements of headdress made one's formal identity transparent. The German expression *to have something on your hat* meant the public demonstration of a social identity or opinion (G/103b R/300). Hats marked interwar Hildesheimers in terms of age, confession, gender, generation, and class. Caught in this web of reification, the hat could even represent the person. Günther Seidner told me how teachers used to discipline children in public for smoking cigarettes. He then noted "if a teacher today would give someone a slap to the cheeks or something like that, then they could take their hat with them in the morning" (G/82b R/00): their hat, and therefore they, would be asked to leave. While showing me a photo of herself with a student at the local architecture school in 1929 (D/918), Thekla Mestmacher explained to me that he "wore a hat instead of a school cap." She then excused his behavior by explaining that he had come from Argentina and had only been studying in Hildesheim. Though he had relatives in the Nordstadt, his headdress still marked him as a foreigner.

Given this equation of hats with formal social identities, it almost seems to have been the case that to acquire a new identity, one simply needed to switch one's headdress. During the First World War, the town of Hildesheim agreed to cooperate with the German-Turkish Union in organizing exchange programs and financial support for Turkish students to attend Hildesheim schools. One such student, Mehmed Musaffer, came from a Constanti-

Figure 3. Working-class boys' handball team, 1930 (D/974).

nople family high in the Turkish government and was to attend the Arts and Crafts School in the Knochenhaueramtshaus. On 30 November 1916, the school administration informed Mayor Ehrlicher (SAH 102/6316) that Musaffer had found a room at Sedanstrasse 45 in the home of a woman who regularly took in foreign students, but this was not precisely how things were supposed to have work out. Someone from the business office of the school had been sent to meet Musaffer at the train station to take him on a tour of various apartments before he would make his selection. Yet, "the agreed-upon sign—the Turkish head covering—was not seen, since the Turk had . . . exchanged his Turkish head covering with a German one so as not to stand out. Hence the tour guide could not execute his office." The school administration believed that this room would be suitable for Musaffer but were disturbed by the town's evident lack of hospitality to guests. This anecdote reinforces the conclusion that a proper hat was required to properly identify people in the local public sphere. Hildesheimers used greetings to erase social distinctions and establish reciprocity and trust in their community. However, they used hats-greeted-with to locate their neighbors back into formal social hierarchies of age, confession, generation, gender, class, as well as ethnicity. Mehmed had not become German per se when he changed his headdress, but when he adopted local styles of conviviality, it was harder to identify him as a foreigner.

Interwar Hildesheimers used hats to reinforce *societas* in the context of the ritual invocation of *communitas*. As a result, hats came to represent that social identity in commodified form, and even acquired a sense of authority alienated from the wearer. Precisely because of the rigidity of this semiotic system, resentment and resistance against it spread in interwar Hildesheim. For instance, Theodora Algermissen's partner in dance class (ca. 1934) went to gymnasium even though his parents were workers, yet he chose not to don a school cap because of its class implications:

> With his inclinations towards socialism, a school cap was for him a symbol of class and he discarded it. And so, he wore a hat and not a school cap. . . . He was one of the first who threw his [cap] away and only went out with a felt hat, because he was anti-Nazi. He was a socialist. But because that was not so welcomed at our home, we never spoke about it.

Theodora laughed. Since he was an upstanding fellow, she could ignore his politics and enjoy his company. "But I knew that he had another opinion [than I], a fact which was documented just by his felt hat" (G/4b R/170, G/5a R/250). In a culture in which top hats, peaked caps, and school caps marked rigid social hierarchies, the choice to wear a fedora expressed one's *eigensinnig* desire to transcend this system of categories entirely. This association is also evident in the "artistic self-portrait" from 1929, seen in Figure 4. Reminiscent of gangster movies from the same era, the fedora in this image cultivated an identity for a rebellious outsider.

Arguably, the fedora appealed to Hildesheimers in part because it enabled them to transcend, at least in cultural terms, the social cleavages that characterized their society. Some of the children of workers already began to wear them in 1930, as seen in Figures 3 and 4. Similarly, only some of the oldest students attending the Catholic gymnasium Josephinum dared to wear a felt hat at this stage, and even then, only on the way to a pub and never on the main streets of town where they could be seen by their teachers. School caps fell out of fashion after Easter of 1938 among the upper classes; they disappeared entirely by 1941. While caps emphasized particular identities, wearing a fedora expressed uniformity. Contrary to what one might expect, this change in custom was not ordered by the Nazi regime: peers in the HJ made fun of students wearing their school caps (Gerlach and Seeland 1950: 204). That the fedora was nonetheless common among Nazi supporters is clear from the photograph of Hitler's visit to Hildesheim in 1934, shown in Figure 5. The fedora corresponded to the political ideal of a united, homogeneous Aryan race. Meanwhile, social-democratic workers, and even their wives, wore fedoras when they walked around the walls

Figure 4. Artistic self-portrait with felt hat, ca. 1929 (D/967).

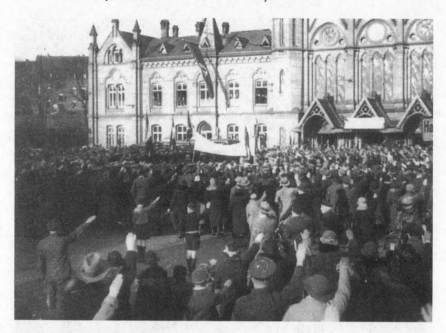

Figure 5. Greeting Adolf Hitler at the train station, October 1934.
Courtesy of: SAH 951/1790/2.

Figure 6. Two working-class families on a long walk, 1943 (D/953).

of town in 1943, as seen in Figure 6. For the first time in residents' recent memory, nationalists and socialists, Catholics and Protestants, and even men and women could wear the "same" headdress.

Meanwhile, Hitler rarely wore a hat, and many Nazi organizations preferred to leave their members bareheaded. Like the New Woman described in the article above, a bare head also offered a symbolic third way between capitalism and socialism. It represented a healthy, natural style that was central to the Nazi's eugenic platform. Arguably more so than even the fedora, a bare head marked a rejection of the rigid social hierarchies that characterized the Wilhelmine Empire and persisted into the Weimar Republic. A bare head also marked an attempt to transcend the social cleavages of class and confession in a mass society of Aryans. With women in braids again, the only distinctions left were those "natural" ones: of gender.

Before the *First War* (as my interview partners often called it), men wore hats and women carried parasols; the socialist working classes wore peaked caps; and the national-liberal middle classes wore top hats. During the interwar years, individual Hildesheimers expressed their rebellion against the rigidity of these options by adopting new fashions: a bob, a fedora, a bare head. These new fashions reduced class and confessional differences as well as gender, to some degree (though gender was still marked even in the case of "androgynous" fashions like the fedora and a bare head). These new cultural forms benefited the Nazi regime politically, but they were not imposed on Hildesheimers simply by a totalitarian state or a fashion industry; both were persistently ambiguous about the new fashions for the new Germany (Guenther 1997). Rather, the modernization of headdress resulted from a dialectic of eigensinn and herrschaft negotiated in the informal context of conviviality. This new, mass culture offered a legitimate medium for both the emergence of a mass consumer society as well as the homogeneity desired by a totalitarian regime. As the interwar period drew to a close, these acts of eigensinn against the rigidity of Wilhelmine society had become acts of conformity to the herrschaft of the Nazi regime.

Franz Meissner remembered how, after 1934, the only place where Jewish artists could appear in public legally for concerts was the synagogue. To make sure that nothing anti-Nazi was being preached during such events, a Gestapo officer or a member of the SA came by, sometimes in normal clothes, other times in uniform. Franz could not remember these details precisely, but he was sure that his grandfather always went up to these Nazis, saying, "Please, enjoy yourself; please put a hat on," and that they did (G/162a R/106). It was a sign of respect to take off one's hat in a building in interwar Hildesheim. Gestapo officers were quick to hit a Jew if he did not remove his hat when entering their office (see Schneider 1998: III. 11, cf. G/172b R/15). In synagogue, however, men wore hats according to

Jewish custom. The idea of a Nazi officer obeying Jewish religious practice is absurd, but this was Hildesheim. Just two years prior, it had still been a civil society in which neighbors respected collective customs. A mandatory greeting and a tip of the hat had symbolically established this foundation of civility. Ordinary Hildesheimers had subscribed to it so vehemently in part because it permitted them to lay claim to superior status and alternate identities without losing their sense of integration in a moral community and, above all, without losing their sense of normalcy. They used these same tactics to circumvent ardent Nazis in the neighborhood, or even, in pure eigensinn, to remind Gestapo officers of the habits of civility that they used to share.

2 | Niveau

GROWING UP IN interwar Hildesheim, Lotte Schohl did not think consciously or critically about her neighborhood. "Neighborhood was something completely normal. You lived on a street where many people lived. You knew each of them, greeted them, chatted with them. As a child, I hardly thought seriously about it at all" (G/8a R/160). Here, Lotte reiterated the central myth of everyday life: neighborhood simply *was*. One accepted its reality as natural. Its boundaries, contents, and character were imposed on innocent Hildesheimers. Neighborliness did not change historically. It certainly did not change history. Above all, Lotte took no responsibility for its nature. Yet once she began to talk about neighborhood in general, she reminded herself of her own experiences in and around her home in Hildesheim. Lotte then slipped from collective into personal memories. She described how neighbors in Hildesheim knew each other, greeted, and even chatted with each other. Lotte's neighborhood now seemed much more proactive, its denizens far less innocent. Her anecdotes implied that her neighbors constituted their own communities through specific customs and therefore their direct agency. My interview partners moved back and forth between these two layers of memory: collective memory as depicted in official histories (both national and local), in which Hildesheimers appear as pawns of circumstance and statesmen; and personal memories, in which neighbors shaped their own neighborhoods to suit their own purposes.

The latter memories were *dangerous* because they challenged official narratives and disrupted the myths of normalcy (Benjamin 1968; Harootunian 2000; Ostovich 2002). This version of *deep history* threatens to subvert the assumption of imposed circumstances and revise that collective wisdom about everyday life (cf. Apter 1992: 21). For instance, Thekla Mestmacher was wont to describe Hildesheim as if it were small enough that one could feel like one knew, or at least recognized, everyone there. Because she always ran into people on the street that she knew, she felt the town was not very big after all, that it stood within the range of perception for an ordinary individual (*noch so überschauen dadurch;* G/13a R/250, G/16b R/280). Over the course of my stay in Hildesheim, I ran into her several times on the street, at which point she would reiterate her assertion: "You see, Mr. Bergerson, Hildesheim is visible at a glance [*doch überschaubar*], as I said." Günther Seidner used the expression *übersichtlich* to make the same point (G/81b R/60). Hans Teich concurred (1979: 64): "in old Hildesheim, a mid-sized town, everyone knew almost everyone else."

In reality, interwar Hildesheim was sufficiently large a town (of fifty to sixty thousand people) that one could not know everyone personally. Hildesheimers had to make selections. And the problem with choice is that it implies some degree of free will, some form of agency. Günther insisted that the children in his neighborhood played together regardless of confession or status in the community. Yet when I asked if he could recall any antisocial types in his childhood neighborhood, he responded: "On this street, actually no. It was up at the corner . . . that is where I first heard about a family. . . . There was a trial with stepfather and daughter somehow—but this lay outside of our area." In this anecdote about sexual misconduct, the scope of Günther's knowledge seemed outside his control. And then Günther slipped into a deeper, more dangerous history:

> Otherwise, all of the people on the whole street, we knew each other there, you greeted each other, and the kids played together, with the small reservation: if you were a convinced Catholic [or] Protestant, then perhaps just with a bit, a certain distance. (G/79b R/325, G/81b R/150)

Günther revealed an open secret about neighborliness: Hildesheimers knew their neighbors selectively, flexibly, contingently. When playing on the street, Günther's family limited the horizon of their experience by knowing, greeting, playing, and taking part in the lives of only certain neighbors. This horizon of ignorance produced a sense of integration within its imaginary bounds and alienation beyond those bounds, but denied its own role in this process. To function as a *moral* community, this kind of neighborhood had to presume its own normalcy.

On the one hand, then, this idiosyncratic community reflected its residents' sense of self. Loyal Protestants, the Seidners kept a certain distance from Catholic neighbors. To lay claim to their own respectability, they had nothing whatsoever to do with sexual miscreants. Necessarily enacted in the local public sphere, these patterns of hidden knowledge and feigned ignorance also broadcasted these claims about themselves to neighbors, revealing their religious politics, their moral fiber. On the other hand, the habits of self-cultivation gave shape to that community as it was actually lived. I refer to this smallest microcosm of the local public sphere as their *corner neighborhood*: that area nearest to their place of residence in which they personally knew their neighbors. In extreme cases, the scope of the corner neighborhood ranged from homes and shops on several nearby streets to only one or two buildings; most of my interview partners (twenty-five out of thirty-eight) included only that one residential building and perhaps a few neighboring homes in the immediate proximity to the building. Far smaller than administrative districts determined by governments or even the historic districts labeled on contemporary maps, in their corner neighborhoods Hildesheimers constituted an identity for themselves and felt that they belonged. Reciprocally, they drew the boundaries of their corner neighborhoods primarily by *not* knowing certain neighbors.

Consider how six women described their corner neighborhoods during the interview process. Some belonged to the proletariat, some to the bourgeoisie; some were Protestants, some Catholics; but they all shared a common style of neighborliness. These customs of conviviality were designed to enable them to negotiate these formal social distinctions with grace and without responsibility. Highly conscious of status, they acquired cultural capital in the corner neighborhood through self-alienation. They highlighted their relevance by making unfamiliar those neighbors whom they considered their social inferiors (cf. Bourdieu 1984; Foucault 1977, 1980; Schutz and Luckmann 1973: 324–25). In typically modern terms, the distinction they imagined for themselves stood in sharp contrast to their actual social position in a rigid social hierarchy. Their corner neighborhoods matched their subjective fantasies and not their objective realities. Consequently, they experienced their corner neighborhoods as spaces of eigensinn: of self-expressive revolt against their position in the social hierarchy (though not against the hierarchy itself). This tactic was pleasurable because it served as an informal means to transcend the constraints of their real circumstances. It is also for this reason that they insisted on the normalcy of conviviality. For their fantasy to remain uncontested by social reality, they had to act as if their social superiority were given.

Dreams

When I asked Lotte to describe her neighborhood, she listed the divisions and residents of her house: a bakery on the ground floor, an unmarried woman with her brother on the first floor, and Lotte's own family on the second floor. Behind the house was a courtyard with a bake house. On one side stood the corner house where the street opened onto a larger plaza; on the other side was a wall beyond which lay a butcher's store and home similarly equipped with a courtyard used for business purposes. Lotte was not forthcoming with the names of her neighbors. She was confused about the profession of their downstairs neighbor, and could not say whether he was the director of a bank or a brewery. Our discussion of neighbors evoked only one anecdote that concerned this man's unmarried sister, the woman was "an unfriendly lady for whom I was always too loud. When I went down the [wood] steps, she would open up her door and say, 'Do be a bit quieter for once!'" (G/6a R/200). Lotte played with other children on the street or in the adjacent plaza, yet she called them her *friends* rather than *neighbors* (G/6a R/270; cf. her sister's account: G/75a R/20).

The absence of relevant neighbors in Lotte's childhood cannot be explained by the limitations of plazas, street corners, or walls, nor the actual absence of other people. Her family made choices based on concerns for local status: "I grew up in a bourgeois family that maintained a certain *niveau,* or wanted to achieve it, who had the *dream* of preparing their children for life, which for girls meant that they should someday marry" (G/7a R/115, my emphasis; see also R/55).

They developed another, more subtle tactic for realizing their dreams. Lotte was the daughter of a purchasing agent at a local department store (G/7a R/180, 290). According to the 1930 address book for Hildesheim (pp. 97–98), the house next door contained a tobacconist, an innkeeper, and a lower bureaucrat at the railroad; other merchants, artisans, workers, and servants lived on their street. None of them fit her family's social aspirations—that certain level of sophistication and distinction expressed with the French term *niveau.* The Schohls used the brick wall just outside their home to keep those neighbors at bay who, they wanted to believe, were their inferiors.

Thekla Mestmacher and Günther Seidner had led me to believe that everyone knew each other in the Hildesheim of their youth and that the town's streets were experienced as neighborly spaces. Lotte's personal memories contradicted that official narrative of universal conviviality: Lotte did not fight with her neighbors, but she also spoke little with them. "There was no close relationship between the neighbors." They continued to behave this way after her family moved to another street in the same part of town in 1932. "Some very nice people lived in our house with us who perhaps shared the same social position. . . . Yet on the whole we had little contact with neighbors. I do not know why" (G/7a R/125, G/7b R/230). In order to imagine their niveau, Lotte and her family distanced themselves from most of their neighbors.

Frieda Stolzenberg started in a social position far preferable to Lotte's. Frieda was the middle child of nine from a family of well-situated merchants. Her family did not own the building in which they lived in the Altstadt (see Figure 1), but they managed a leather goods store in it and did well for themselves. Their success was reflected in the presence of electricity, a telephone, flush toilets, and a bathtub inside their apartment before *the First War.* When Frieda identified her neighbors on a main shopping street of Hildesheim, she named storeowners surrounding her home: that is to say, she recalled merchants of her class. By contrast, she knew the residents who rented the upper stories of these buildings only vaguely (G/18a R/185), though she believed that most were members of the educated middle class. According to address books for 1910 and 1914 however, her street was in fact quite mixed. Skilled and unskilled workers lived right next to merchants, professionals, and white-collar workers. Social stratification often corresponded to altitude: it was the stores on the ground floor and owners who lived on the first floor who remained foremost in Frieda's memory, not the workers renting apartments in the upper stories. Certainly the visual experience of store windows and names on storefronts contributed to the features that she knew or remembered. Yet she also described a social environment that reflected her own sense of identity and status. Knowing neighbors like herself, she could claim that her street was "all merchants," all "well-situated" people (G/18a R/185, 430). The working classes were less predominant in her memory not because of post facto repression but because she had known her neighbors selectively even as a child.

Frieda, whose family was Catholic, mentioned that Hildesheimers took no notice of the confessional affiliation of their merchants. Nonetheless, she remembered which of her neighbors belonged to which religious group (G/18b R/120). Similarly, she mentioned teasing a little girl who lived in the apartment "above" her. This girl was the daughter of the owners of the building who also owned a shop on the street. In reality, the girl lived not above but next door to Frieda (G/18a R/ 200). The renting working classes could remain irrelevant within the network of merchant neighbors and homeowners. By contrast, shopkeepers and landlords could not be ignored because they held an unavoidable presence in the network of neighborly ownership and exchange; landlords stood "above" renters even if they lived next to them. Yet Frieda temporarily inverted the power relations between owners and renters through teasing. Eigensinn gave her a brief respite from her feeling of inferiority.

By 1920, Frieda's family moved to the new, suburban district of the Oststadt, an area populated mostly by the educated, financial, and managerial bourgeoisie. A few workers and artisans did live in the upper stories of these homes, but Frieda did not know of them at all nor where a working-class district might be found (G/18a R/430, G/18b R/80). She remembered only one family of close neighbors: the family von Oppeln. Also merchants, they had lived on the same street as the Stolzenbergs and moved with them into the suburban periphery. To be sure, this family was also noble and had contacts with other aristocrats. Her own parents did not traffic in such circles (i.e., as friends); at most they chatted on the street (as neighbors). "That we were permitted to play with their children at all was something special," she explained. "The nobility was indeed superior to us"

(G/18b R/420, SAH 904-1/37, R/140). Still Frieda got along with her neighbors, she remembered.

Frieda did not so much identify with the Oststadt at large but rather with her house itself, seen in Figure 7 (G/20a R/260). Still, Frieda explained that her *Heimat* (home) was still in the Oststadt, not the Altstadt. In the Altstadt, they had been but one successful merchant family among many and had rented their residence from a merchant-landlord. In the Oststadt, they owned a beautiful home and the only neighbors they knew were Catholic nobles. In this new corner neighborhood more than ever before, they made themselves relevant.

Good Times, Good Friends

Self-alienation creates distinction. Regardless of their precise location on the social scale, Hildesheimer families could aspire to categories to which they did not in fact belong by alienating themselves from their neighbors. They transcended their objective identities by constructing corner neighborhoods to match their subjective fantasies. Consider the extreme examples of Lena Turz and Stella Storch.

Like her mother, Lena ironed clothes in the homes of wealthy Hildesheimers. Her mother had built a clientele for herself through referrals. In fact, all of her mother's clients were members of the same *Kaffeekränzchen,* a friendship circle that met regularly in each person's house for coffee, cake, and light conversation. Members of a kränzchen shared many things: common interests, loves, even maids. "It all passes from one to the next," Lena explained. In interwar Hildesheim, friendships of this kind presumed an essential identity among its members, illustrated even in clothing. For instance, the circle of friends seen in Figure 8 met every week. "We would read together," my interview partner (not Lena) annotated. "We were kind of interested in things. [We did] not just chatter!" Lena had no such kränchen; and her mother's relationship with the wives of bank directors, factory owners, and even the county president was purely professional.

> They did not do anything together, I mean nothing. [Her employer] always came in and looked to see what my mother had ironed, or later what I had ironed . . . and then we would exchange a word, maybe *good day* but otherwise nothing. There was no relationship between them. The wife of the county president or of a factory director, they would never go out fancy with a washing woman!

The fact that Lena grew up with the children of these bourgeois families counted only when they met on the street; then they would "get along fine" (*gut zusammen fertig kommen*). Yet the children never played together

Figure 7. House in the Oststadt, after 1917 (D/587).

Figure 8. Kränzschen posing in sailor uniforms, ca. 1917 (D/727).

or visited each other. "There was a certain distance, from the other side, not at all from us, but—"Lena said with a smile, "those were good times" (G/66a R/115).

Saturday afternoons, when such kränzchen typically met, Lena's mother would be busy cleaning her apartment and its windows.

> Her kränzchen was her children . . . She was always away ironing, she did not have any time at all. She was happy if she ever had some free time for her household. Cleaning—my Mommie did not let anyone take that over. Grandmother did not do it accurately enough. (G/66a R/115)

In fact, Lena's parents had no friends at all. Her family did not even have contact with their neighbors. To be sure, she made short conversation with them in the stairwell about whatever was current news. They would comment, perhaps, on hearing of someone getting drafted during the war, or they perhaps would give a small gift from the whole house when someone died. But she and her family never went visiting. Lena's mother "did not really have the time to go running from one to the other" (*von eins zum andere' zu laufen*: G/66a R/170; see also R/285), a phrase that Lena repeated frequently in the interviews when I asked about relations in her corner neighborhood. Even among colleagues, where the men spoke in the informal (*du* instead of *Sie*), visits were never options. Speaking of her father, she explained that "no, he did not do that. My father came back from the factory . . . sat himself down [in his seat] and did not move from there" (*und da sass fest*, G/65b R/275).

Lena conducted her life in a similar fashion: she had no friends besides her husband. She had little contact with neighbors because they were all people "below" her: communists, divorced women, drinkers. One exception was a neighbor who lived across the hall from her later in life; yet she only really had contact with the family's children, not with the adults. The one friendship she had made in her life, with a fellow domestic servant, was short-lived. Her friend married well and her spouse's mother forced her to cut off all relations with Lena because Lena was no longer an appropriate social contact. This hurt Lena so deeply that she never found a replacement (see also Bergerson 1993).

Like Lena, Stella Storch's family had little contact with their neighbors. Her father was a head typesetter who did little more than greet his neighbors: at most they discussed health problems. They did not borrow food or money from their neighbors. Each family faced fate on their own. They were all master artisans, but Stella's father had been educated at gymnasium, while his neighbors had merely learned a trade. So there was no social contact outside the nuclear family; even from the extended family there were few visits (G/24a R/250, G/24b R/15, 135, 255, 330). After she married a mechanic who worked at the plastic factory in Moritzberg and established her own household, Stella conducted her life in much the same manner. She did not get close to any one particular neighbor. "May I be a little arrogant?" she asked rhetorically. I said that she may. "They were all people with a household, yes," she continued, "but nothing else." Stella "was already attending continuing education back then." By contrast, her neighbors were all "vulgar people": they were "housewives" to be sure, "but they would have never gone further." They never came up with the idea of attending continuing education classes in the evening. "This niveau was not there" (G/24b R/150).

Certainly there were real constraints on working-class families that partially explain their informal alienation. Factors such as time, money, and energy contributed. Working-class families also faced a social hierarchy that seemed impermeable to upward mobility as well as social *cleavages* that seemed impermeable to sympathetic contact (Best 1989; Falter 1992; Jones 1988; Lepsius 1973; Rohe 1992; for Hildesheim see Knott 1980; Riekenberg 1982; Wichard 1975). But too often, academics involved in German studies view these social identities in terms of rigid, binary dyads (bourgeois–proletarian; masculine–feminine; Protestant–Catholic; Aryan–Jewish; straight–gay) as if these groups were locked in a *clinch,* a boxing term that refers to the situation when two opponents hold each other's bodies so closely that they prevent both from striking. This is particularly true of the working classes, the Catholics, and the Protestant middle classes. The German term for these divergent *social milieux* is *Lager;* meaning *camp,* it holds the connotation of mutually armed and besieged encampments. The antithesis between these camps was so striking a reality in modern Germany, especially in terms of their formal political, economic, and social institutions, that these categories seem impermeable to change or transgression (adapting Scott 1988, 1991).

In reality, individual Hildesheimers who formally belonged to different and distinct sociological categories still had to cultivate those identities informally and negotiate them in mixed neighborhoods. Nearly all of Hildesheim was relatively diverse in terms of class and confession. Even in most of the wealthier districts, workers lived in the upper stories of homes or on adjacent streets, as did Jürgen Ludewig, who lived modestly on Braunschweiger Strasse next to the elegant Sedanstrasse. Similarly, the Nordstadt had a reputation for being a working-class district, but middle-class families lived there too, like Thekla Mestmacher (G/12b R/110). Many of my interview partners moved to a variety of neighborhoods in Hildesheim. Particularly in the 1920s, these sociopolitical milieux were also being undermined by new forms of mass culture and social segmentation based on age and gender as well as the experiences of war, revolution, and hyperinflation (Childers 1983; Negt and Kluge 1993; Peukert 1987: 149–74). Faced with uncertainty and diversity in the local public sphere, many felt the need to clarify their identities. They used customs of conviviality to help them accomplish these contradictory goals: to cultivate a subjective sense of self beyond their objective reality, to break out of this clinch.

Stella and Lena could neither overcome nor ignore their subordination to and exclusion from the social circles of the bourgeoisie, but they could and did decide not to have neighborly contact with people they considered to be beneath them. Themselves victims of a status-conscious society, they imposed analogous standards on others in order to reinforce their own imagined status. This way of cultivating niveau for themselves left them remarkably alienated: from above by the wives of bank directors and from below by their own conceit. But neither of them claimed to have missed something in their lives. When I asked them to whom they could bring their problems, they both responded that they did not have any problems that required a friend's advice or help. When her husband could no longer provide for her, Lena did not even take her father's offer to return to his household and leave her husband. Divorce was out of the question for her. She did not bring her problems to others, even to her family. Likewise, Stella felt that there were good relations among the neighbors within her apartment house, though there was no community, no togetherness. She explained that she helped her neighbors when someone died to cope with their grief, but she herself would not bring her own problems to them (G/24b R/135, 150, 290). "One moment!" Stella interrupted. She recounted how she gave birth to her daughter in 1930. Her husband was sound asleep. In spite of her labor pains, she tried to not wake him because he had been "up the whole night playing dance music" and had to report to work in the factory at six the next morning. When she finally did wake him and send him to get the midwife, it was too late: she ended up bringing her daughter into the world on her own. "Friends?" Stella added a few moments later. "No, no. I did not try so hard. I had an especially good friend in my husband and I had my three children" (G/26b R/180).

In terms of their objective relationship to the means of production, the Turz and Storch families fell from artisanal training into proletarian employment. In terms of their friendships, they had little formal access to middle-class circles, except in service roles. In terms of neighborliness, however, they constructed their status informally by exclusion: by not knowing and despising their proletarian neighbors, even if this resulted in their own, almost complete alienation. The same pattern was true of upper-class families like the Schohls and the Stolzenbergs. Families of diverse social backgrounds ranging from unskilled laborers to entrepreneurs transcended the social category to which they objectively belonged by sacrificing neighborly relationships.

Making the Best of What You Have

Women, in particular, seemed to play an especially important role in the process of establishing respectability through self-alienation. This was not so much due to the assumption that women were actually more closely engaged in neighborliness than men (Kaplan 1998) as to the fact that, in a patriarchal culture in which neighborliness was feminized, women were expected to bear the lion's share of the responsibility for establishing familial respectability (following Veblen 1967). Yet all of these women seemed to believe that neighborly alienation was a small price for them to pay for the feeling of upward social mobility, no matter how fantastic. The boundaries of these corner neighborhoods accentuated what would have been mundane in a larger world: themselves. Each made the best of what he or she had. Theodora Algermissen created her cultural capital on the basis of family ownership, while Lise Peters created it through her family's proximity to Protestant pastors. Their corner neighborhoods were larger than those of the previous examples, but they were still rather small: a handful of homes located on a single plaza or courtyard. Remarkably modern, these enacted neighborhoods enabled their residents to cultivate fantasies of social mobility in the face of an unresponsive social reality.

From her earliest memories in the 1920s, Theodora's home was typical for Hildesheim in that it had hot running water only in the kitchen and atypical in that it already had some appliances that ran on electricity instead of gas. The family had a telephone from early on, a shower instead of just a bathtub (or worse, a basin set up in the washing kitchen), and flush toilets instead of an outhouse. When I asked Theodora if her neighbors had hot running water in their residences as well, she replied:

The house next to us had no flush toilets and no bathtub. That I know. We had a good relationship with our neighbors and we children were really quite often around and about in the neighborhood, in the garden, and at the neighbor's house, which is why I know this [about their furnishings] at all. So we were actually very progressively equipped in terms of our residential circumstances. The neighbors not so much so. (G/1a R/240)

The Algermissen family lived in the back house of a larger property. With the exception of a short period of study in Berlin, Theodora resided there continuously until the 1960s. Purchased in the 1880s by her grandfather when the district was still considered outside of town, the property was developed into three apartment buildings on the street side and a backyard court around which they maintained their home, an office, a workshop, and a stall for her father's artisanal business. Her family sold two of the apartment buildings (street numbers two and three) over the years while her parents still managed and rented the third building (number four). Her house in the courtyard was also called number four. I asked if such duplicate numbering caused confusion with mail delivery. Her laugh suggested that I had failed to understand the nature of corner neighborhoods. Her family was sufficiently well known in this corner neighborhood that there could have been no confusion.

At first, Theodora defined "the area in which [she] lived" (*Wohngegend*) to include five streets surrounding her own. This neighborhood was bounded externally by two major thoroughfares, a local cultural institution, and a large, open plaza. Internally, the architectural style in this area was relatively consistent, Theodora explained, comprising buildings that had been constructed during the boom in housing production that followed the establishment of the Second Empire (G/2a R/70). Topography, aesthetics, and history seemed to define a coherent neighborhood for Theodora. In practice, the space in which Theodora behaved as a neighbor was much smaller. It included only a few houses on one side of her street. Theodora explained that the other side of the street had a corresponding set of houses. There did not seem to be any substantial difference in class, aesthetics, or history between the different sides of the street. Still, she did not know the other residents in the way that she knew those around her courtyard. And she did not know the residents of streets in the few blocks on either side, she explained, because these spaces were beyond her purview as a child (G/2a R/80). Yet Theodora lived in this home for forty years, and as an adult she was not so limited in her daily mobility. Indeed, the scope of her knowledge of her neighbors decreased as she grew older. These distinctions cannot be explained away simply by topographical features, such as brick walls or courtyards. House number five was adjacent to the east but separated from their courtyard (with its garden, play, and sitting areas) by a fence. House five was included in Theodora's neighborhood however, because the children climbed over the fence to play in that neighbor's garden.

Theodora's memories were bounded in the third dimension as well. Within the set of buildings two through five were fourteen households amounting to fewer than thirty people (including no other children). According to the local address books, the residents were mostly artisans, merchants, lower- to middle-level bureaucrats, and widows. Theodora correspondingly knew and remembered the area to be a middle-class neighborhood. Yet she knew and remembered the actual occupations and places of work more frequently if the residents lived on the ground floors (G/1b R/75). As in the case of the people across the street, she knew and remembered little about the occupations and places of work of those living higher up the stairs. This altitudinal boundary correlates with a class distinction. Apartments on the upper floors were cheaper. The only wage laborer in Theodora's corner neighborhood during her youth lived on the third floor of number two, and she did not know or remember him. Certainly a variety of considerations influenced this ignorance. Owners move less frequently than renters, and the upper floors are physically more removed from a child living on the ground floor. When explaining this to me in the interviews, however, she placed responsibility on the laborer for not making himself more known to her. She gave a similar account in terms of confession. Her neighborhood was socially mixed, as was all of Hildesheim.[1] Even her family was mixed: Theodora's father had been baptized a Catholic, while her mother was a Protestant. Yet Catholics, she claimed, lived in their own world and she knew of no Catholics in her neighborhood.

Topographic and social structures did not so much constrain Theodora's choices for neighbors as facilitate her self-cultivation. Using the circumstances given to her, Theodora shaped a corner neighborhood to match her desire for status and power. A restorer of church paintings, her father was as much artisan as educated middle class (*Bildungsbürgertum*), but Theodora cultivated her bourgeois identity through property. The residents of ground-floor apartments typically managed the buildings or owned them. Theodora was closest with the wife and sister-in-law of the owner of the house at number five, who also operated a sealing-wax factory in two rooms of their home. Theodora "had always watched and helped [her]. She was very nice. So I always discussed all of my problems with her—about God and the world" (G/1b R/90). Along with the wife of the owner of number three, she called these neighbors *aunts*. Theodora's corner neighborhood corresponded to that space in which her family (as she defined it) held local status as landlords, previous owners, and oldest resident family.

Ownership conveyed status and power in interwar Hildesheim. On the day of the housing census (16 May 1927), apartment complexes that contained more than ten units were very rare in Hildesheim, and only 9 percent of all residential units were homes in which only one family resided. Most (54 percent) Hildesheim households shared their building with several (one–three) other families, and the number of multifamily dwellings (with more than five residents) was on the rise (currently 27.9 percent as compared to 43.9 percent of planned construction). A total of 21.3 percent of these household units also had boarders living with them (individuals made up 9.7 percent, entire families 11.6 percent). Each of Hildesheim's approximately five thousand residential buildings had an owner, which meant that the vast majority of Hildesheimers rented. Financially, rent and food absorbed half of the family budgets (*SDR* 362/1: 36, 40, 51, 94 and 362/2: 22–23; see also Coyner 1975; on boarders cf. G/79a R/50, 160, 270, 330, G/79b R/245, G/81b R/395, G/82a R/30, 140, G/84b R/80). When it came to food, Hildesheimers could create a sense of independence from the capitalist system of wage labor by cultivating a garden and exchanging goods with neighbors and relatives, and therefore could gain a sense of control over their lives. By contrast, rent was paid in cash. Thus, landlords were different from other neighbors in that they held power through monetary relations and were potentially independent of control through neighborly reciprocity.

Theodora's family got to know her neighbors in these hierarchical circumstances. Summarizing her own commentary, Theodora described her neighborhood as inhabited by "those who are interested in culture, the middle classes" (G/1a R/250). She first defined her father's profession as an art historian; yet her family emphasized their power and status by carefully limiting whom they knew as neighbors only to other managers and own-ers of property. They created a corner neighborhood in which they were *primus inter pares* (first among equals) as prior owners of this courtyard community. Because they were no longer owners of all of these properties, to emphasize their distinction they had to know their neighbors *as if* they still owned the entire set of properties. Theodora's corner neighborhood was a creation of fantasy, though she produced it through habits enacted in her social reality. When asked if she identified with this part of town as her heimat, she corrected me, pointing to the map of her courtyard:

> Here too I must limit [my answer] to this district [*Bezirk*]. This was home for me, not what was around it. That was just the town and its surround-ings. This [courtyard] here—these external circumstances with the people who lived on the ground floor [here and] the ground floor [here].

Her courtyard neighborhood had provided her with a sense of security and integration as a child that she no longer required as a burgeoning adult. By her adolescence in 1932, she recalled knowing only her two "aunts" next door (G/3a R/360). Trying to resolve a tension between the process of exclusion in which she obviously participated and the experience of inclusion she desired, Theodora slipped into the deep history of self-cultivation without actually reconciling the contradiction. "Oh, Hildesheim was so small, you really knew everyone. *Those who could be considered at all*, they knew each other" (G/2a R/45, my emphasis).

Theodora did not create the economy and culture of ownership; she only created her identity in that context. Still, she did exclude certain irrelevant occupants from the list of relevant neighbors. By integrating *and alienating* her neighbors selectively, she preserved her family's status unchallenged in spite of actual shifts in ownership. Even if this community existed only in Theodora's imagination, her behavior vis-à-vis her neighbors was real, and it helped shape social relations in this corner of Hildesheim. Competitive identity production thrived in the neighborhoods of interwar Hildesheim: it played a significant role in extending the logic of formal power relations (like ownership) into informal social relations. But my interview partners still imagined themselves to be ordinary victims of circumstances (*Gegebenheiten*) beyond their control.

Lise Peters was born in 1903 to a sexton's family on one of Hildesheim's church squares. Later she informed me that her father was actually a gardener (G/139a R/185). Yet she described her childhood residence in terms of her father's church affiliation. "It was the old house of the former pastor. But then . . . another got built . . . and this is where the sexton lived" (G/139a R/50). Constructed in the sixteenth or seventeenth century, the building belonged to the local church community and her family lived in it for free. Their apartment took up the first and second floors of the building while the ground and third floors were set aside for community use. There was a room for the church wardens to hold their meetings, and the pastor also used this room to change into his gown before going to church. There was also a smaller confirmation room up top and a larger one built onto the ground floor. The latter was used for confirming forty or more children at a time as well as for meetings of women's clubs. During such events, Lise's mother set up coffee in the adjoining kitchen while the other women brought cake (G/139a R/70). That is, the Peters family lived in a semipublic building belonging to the Protestant church. By administering these spaces, they had direct access to resources and networks within that milieu. It is hardly surprising, then, that the Peters family used this religious milieu, with its center for meaning and status in the figure of the pastor, as the focus of their corner neighborhood.

Lise described all the last names and occupations for the families on one side of her home: the children had belonged to her play group. She also remembered storeowners and described shopping in their stores. Then her narrative turned to the topic of the Chodzinski family (a pseudonym) who lived a few doors down. "You must understand—they were Catholic. We did not have so many connections in that direction. This was strange. Back then it was like this: we Protestants did not have too many connections to the Catholics." This distance did not mean that the children did not play together: "but this was not always real friendship." The Peters did not let the relationship come to that. When I pressed her for specific differences in behavior, for different things she did with Protestants than Catholics, she could not find the correct words. Her parents did have small chats with the Chodzinskis on the street when they met by chance, and the children did play with each other if the latter were already on the church plaza. Still, circumstance and propriety rather than intention seemed to have brought them together. These groups of children never came to blows over religious differences; but Lise did not seek out contact with Catholics either. The Chodzinski's house evoked a disturbance in the easy flow of Lise's narrative of her corner neighborhood, a disruption that corresponded to her actual behavior as a child and young woman. "They also had many children, but how many I cannot say. But they, they were Catholic. Then that was like the end of it already, no? . . . There was a kind of a distance in between, no?" (G/139b R/00, 250). Lise could not express herself in specific words at this point, but her body narrative still reflected her sense that she had left her neighborhood when she reached the Chodzinski house.

Lise limited the scope of her corner neighborhood even more narrowly when she described the other side of her home, but her account was based on a similar habitual logic. Next to the sexton's house resided a cabinet maker with two daughters Lise's age, a shop in his backyard, and renters. "But as I said," Lise continued in a softer voice, "they too were Catholic and then one just kind of—I do not know how that came to be. Today it is different." Beyond them, Lise knew that there were other girls her age as well as a relative of the Chodzinskis who was an excessive drinker. "It was not so simple there," she explained. Lise could no longer remember the names of her neighbors beyond that site (G/139a R/80). According to local registration records (SAH 102/7427), the Chodzinski family lived on Lise's street quite consistently during her youth. (Lise herself got married and set up her own home in 1926.) Still, this cabinet maker's house marked the ontological boundary of her corner neighborhood. Her feeling of integration ended with them not only because they were Catholic but also because they were not obliged to respect the daughter of a Protestant sexton.

Lise's family had modeled their corner neighborhood on the cleavages of associational life. When asked whether her mother was well known in the neighborhood, Lise described her mother's sewing bees during the First War, occasions during which old clothes were collected, taken apart, and reconstructed for new use. "That was then the neighborhood—that the women helped each other [so] that the poorer [people] could get something to dress in." When pressed, Lise revealed that the poor were all from her parish and that this group of women belonged to the local Protestant Mother's Association (G/139b R/345, 375). As one of my oldest interview partners (b. 1903), Lise had direct contact with the generation of the *Kulturkampf*: the political struggle between the Catholic Center Party and the National Liberals fomented by Bismarck during the early years of the German Empire. Perhaps the confessional sensitivity of her parent's generation conditioned her perceptions of Catholics in her neighborhood more than was true of informants who grew up in subsequent decades. (Most of my interview partners denied the existence of any significant tension between the Christian confessions.) Perhaps it is also obvious that Lise's family kept its informal activities within the Evangelical milieu, given her father's occupation. But I prefer to read the shape of Lise's corner neighborhood as evidence that she and her family tried to maximize their status within the given circumstances of their neighborhood. In a town with four centuries of multiple confessions within its walls, her family chose not to get to know its Catholic neighbors. "We belonged in the sexton's house," Lise explained (G/140b R/180), as if she were making a declarative statement of objective reality rather than describing the way that they laid claim to status and power.

Lise's family's decision to extend the logic of milieu from church, associational, and family life into their neighborhood was perhaps to be expected, but it nonetheless required proactive implementation. As we have seen, women played a leading role in this process. When I asked Lise if her mother had had any friends, Lise replied that she had been content with all people—which really was to say that her mother had none. Whereas friends visited each other's homes, visits from the pastor and his wife, for instance, were "out of the question." During Lise's wedding, for example, her mother had restrained herself from inviting the pastor because Lise's mother was too simple: that was not her due (*ihr nicht zukam*). Yet the pastor and his wife were invited to her brother's wedding, a gendered distinction that Lise did not care to explain (G/140b R/110). Later in the interviews, she describes how the pastor's wife was actually invited to drink coffee in honor of her marriage but only together with a larger group of women, probably the Mother's Association (G/142a R/265). Lise could remember only one person who would come to visit her mother: the daughter of a retired pastor from a neighboring village. This woman had moved to Hildesheim to care for her father and his household in his old age. Upon the recommendation of their pastor, these two women became acquainted. They became sufficiently intimate that the children called her *aunt* and the adults spoke to each other in the informal (*du*; G/139b R/380, G/140b R/160). Like Theodora, Lise referred to her mother's affine in terms of fictive kinship and not as her mother's friend. As a young girl, Lise learned domestic skills in the home of a childless pastor and his wife (G/141a R/280) and even received a gift from the pastor's wife of a confirmation book that she proudly showed me in 1993 (G/142a R/240). With remarkable consistency, Lise's family constructed their status in networks centering on the pastor.

Attendance in church on Sunday was taken for granted for her family. After all, her father rang the bells that called worshipers to the service. When I asked Lise if she met her neighbors in church, she answered this question by drawing a map of the church interior, or more accurately, of her procession through the church interior. The line she drew through the middle of the paper was meant to represent herself, walking up the center aisle, around the altar, to the right of the pastor, at all times in full view of the rest of the community, which was represented by the blank page. "This is how we went into the church, and then we walked back here to a small corner behind the benches, and we walked this whole way up to here"—she repeated the drawing motion. "Father had his place in the last bench, by the altar, because he was always running down into the sacristy." The whole family sat together, across from the church wardens, with the altar between them. Conversations with the other church members seemed less than likely to occur. She defended her family's seating arrangements on the basis of tradition. "That was just obvious. No one felt anything strange about the fact that we sat apart up there" (G/140b R/35, 65). Still, her Sunday procession through the Lutheran community to the sacral space behind the altar distinguished her within that community. Her distinction meant little to Catholics in the community, who were not reminded of her status ritually every Sunday. Hence her family got to know only those neighbors among whom Lise stood out from the crowd. Given her eigensinnig way of interacting with her neighbors, it is no wonder that this church-dominated plaza remained a space of integration for Lise throughout the twentieth century. "When I walk by there today it is still mine, no? My home" (Zuhause; G/140b R/190).

Permanency mattered in the construction of Lise's status. Pastor and sexton held status within the bounds of their parish in part because of their long-term residency in their community. Lise did not know the names or occupations of the many renters who resided in the upper floors of her neighbors' buildings. According to the 1914 and 1920 address books, these neighbors were workers, widows, artisans, menial office workers, and the like. Given her description, I had assumed that the street came to an end with the house of the Catholic Chodzinski family to the south. Lise later corrected me, saying that there were two other large rental houses beyond that house. Slowly she recalled the name of one of the landlords, a baker. Of the tenants, she remembered only the presence of a homeopathic healer whom her mother trusted over doctors: again someone with whom they had business. Of the other renters of the apartments above the bakery or in the other building, she remembered "actually nothing at all" (G/139b R/55). Lise mentioned that her family had rented a room to a young female dental technician for several years in the mid-1920s. At times she even lived in the same room as Lise. Yet such transients were not narrated as neighbors. She mentioned this boarder only in a very different narrative context (G/141b R/10, 115).

Lise's family did not forget these neighbors because of class per se. When I asked her if there had been laborers in her neighborhood, Lise responded: "Yes that is really what they all were, people who had to earn their living somehow, but I cannot tell you where they went and what they were. I never concerned myself about that, no?" (G/139b R/170) Lise narrated the presence of renters as a group because their impermanence highlighted her relative stature, but those renters as individuals were absent from her memory of her neighborhood, just as she had not gotten to know them while they all had still lived there. The people immediately south of her home "also had a large house. . . . They also had some renters in the house, but I did not know them so precisely. And then there was the next house—"(G/139b R/20). Her family also did not own the building in which they lived; still, they did not rent per se. They saw themselves as a permanent and integral part of the Protestant community. Lise never knew her transient neighbors because they were not part of the world of this sexton's daughter.

Historians should not conclude simply that Lise was the member of the Protestant middle-class milieu and that milieu determined her neighborly relations. Such an explanation is convoluted in causation and disregards not only significant layers of status within these larger categories but also the idiosyncratic habits through which ordinary Hildesheimers imagined their ascent up the social ladder. The Peters family transposed the confessional logic of sociability (their formal membership in clubs and organizations) onto their conviviality (their informal social relations with friends and neighbors) so that Lise could retain the status she commanded in the church while she walked on the streets of her neighborhood. It is almost as if an invisible wall existed not far from Lise's home, on both sides. This wall was neither excused through the presence of bricks and mortar like Lotte's wall nor ignored as a resource like Theodora's fence. To ensure her continued relevance outside of formal social institutions, Lise marked certain families as the limits of her corner neighborhood.

Colleagues and friends could reside beyond the corner neighborhood. Lise knew of the presence of two old men who lived on the other side of the plaza. But she had nothing to do with them and did not know their names. Next door to those men was a family with seven children with whom she played. But these relationships were neither neighbors nor friends as such. This family was from the church community, and their boys helped her father in the care of the church itself (as *Opferjungen*). Their common responsibilities resulted in the two families being friendly, but no visits were exchanged (G/139b R/115, G/140b R/285). In her first description of that relationship, Lise used the phrase *mit denen . . . sehr befreundet,* an expression that does not connote *friendship* as much as *being friendly with* someone. When I referred to her relationship with this family in a follow-up interview as a *Freundschaft,* or friendship, Lise corrected me: "I cannot call that friendship, but it was a very good acquaintanceship, no?" The meeting house for the Christian Association of Young Men also stood across the plaza. Lise met her husband there through her father's activities as their gardener and her brother's participation as a member (G/139a R/185). Yet her vocabulary once again reflected a different style of interaction. *Friends* would come to visit, if there was money at all for such things, but not neighbors (G/139a R/220). *Friendly* (read: *collegial* or *comradely*) relations could transgress the topographical limits of the corner neighborhood, but neighbors whose identity as such was defined by spatial proximity could not transgress the boundary created by habitually amassed irrelevance. As a child, Lise did not even know that one of her neighbors who lived across the plaza was actually her cousin (G/140b R/285). Perhaps they simply never got to know that family well enough to realize their kinship.

Lise's weekly procession through the Protestant community to the sacral space behind the altar distinguished her within that community. It allowed her to lay claim to status, to cultivate an identity to which she subjectively aspired. This niveau required public enactment in the neighborhood: her claim to status was necessarily *conspicuous* (Veblen 1967). On the one hand, the very presence of Catholics in her neighborhood undermined her sense of self outside the church because they did not see her weekly procession within the church. At the homes of Catholic neighbors, her experience had shifted from integration to alienation. Hence it was at Catholic homes that her experience, her memories, and her narrative of neighborliness ended. On the other hand, Lise's status was, in the end, largely imagined. It could never be communicated openly to others without the danger of exposing her fantasy. Her agency in the cultivation of niveau had to remain hidden behind the veil of normalcy.

Comparisons

Insofar as all of this may seem strikingly familiar to the reader, this analysis has come close to representing some of the core elements of everyday life accurately. Nonetheless, it is precisely these kinds of naturalized customs of everyday life that require our critical reflection. In several ways, this manner of identity production was typical of modernity (of which interwar Germany is one archetype). Lise's experience corresponded to her desires for self-cultivation and therefore to a modern social order in which self-cultivation and upward social mobility was not only possible but ideal. She enacted that identity yet did not speak of it openly. Cultural historians characterize the fine arts during the interwar period in analogous terms. They speak of the challenge facing alienated individuals to express themselves in the face of hegemonic norms. They also identify a *great divide* between a revolutionary avant-garde and the dominant style of academic art from the nineteenth century. Lise understood herself not so much as a revolutionary but rather as a person who stood apart from the masses. To be sure, her everyday fantasies did not correspond to objective reality, but that dissonance was also typically modern. Above all, her astute, yet tacit, evaluation of her actual circumstances enabled her to violate that reality by letting her reinvent her self through willful acts of autobiographic elaboration and understatement. This ethos not only has characterized modernity in general (adapting Foucault 1978; Fritzsche 1996; Gebhardt 1999: 185–91; Harootunian 2000; Huyssen 1986; Jameson 1991; Peukert 1987). It also characterized the charismatic leader who would gain Lise's vote and commitment by the end of the 1930s: Adolf Hitler.

Comparing these six accounts, we see that there were a wide variety of options for self-cultivation in the corner neighborhood, not in spite of constraining factors but because of them. Lotte knew none of her neighbors, Frieda only Catholic nobles. Where Theodora knew only those neighbors who lived within a courtyard-neighborhood in which her family was *primus inter pares,* Lise knew only those neighbors who lived within a Protestant milieu in which her family could exploit their access to the pastor. These tactics of eigensinn cannot be reduced to the uniform definitions of class or confession implied by these aggregate categories; through eigensinn, each negotiated a better position within or between these institutionalized mass identities. Each of these corner neighborhoods was also surreal: based more on subjective desires than objective reality but nonetheless made real for them because they could inhabit their neighborhoods in those terms. Each Hildesheimer imagined the absence of those individuals who challenged their claim to niveau. Lena and Stella went so far as to isolate themselves entirely from all neighbors in order to imagine their superiority. Each Hildesheimer expressed a different sense of self through differently shaped corner neighborhoods, but seen analytically, all of these Hildesheimers sought a similar goal by imagining their corner neighborhoods in such small, homogeneous, and insular terms.

Analogous patterns could be worked out among my other interview partners, including many men. Like Frieda, Georg Brzezinski was also the child of Catholic entrepreneurs. He lived on the same street as Frieda in the Altstadt, knew other merchants, ignored the presence of the working class in the upper stories of the buildings, and experienced no real sense of neighborliness there. Theresa Stoffregen and Ulrike Volkmann commented that they did not know the residents of back houses in which lower-class residents often resided. By contrast, Stefan Nebe migrated to Hildesheim on his own. Between bouts of unemployment, he worked selling shoelaces and later as a taxi driver. At first he lived on a street known for its brothels. Later he rented a two-room apartment on Georg's street. Yet the only neighbor he knew was his landlord. It was all business people there, he explained, who had no time to talk to people like him (G/138a R/50, 280, 400). Günther Seidner created his corner of Hildesheim by knowing other teachers and in-migrants, for he was the son of a Protestant teacher and had immigrated in 1919 from Thorn in the so-called Polish Corridor. Ulrike Volkmann and Theresa Stoffregen's knowledge of their respective corners of the Altstadt (abutting each other) ended on either side of the same point: at an infamous apartment building nicknamed *The Flea Barracks* in which the anonymous poor resided. Daughter of a Nordstadt butcher, Thekla Mestmacher knew a wide variety of her neighbors, but not surprisingly they were also the same people among whom she had the power to distribute precious gifts of sausage. By limiting their knowledge of their neighbors, my interview partners each maximized their relevance in their corner neighborhood.

My point here is not to deny a role to class, confession, camp, and gender in shaping social relations but to demonstrate nonetheless that neighborliness in interwar Hildesheim was infused with proactive tactics of self-cultivation that corresponded to strong desires for upward social mobility. Interwar Germans were intensely status-conscious (Allen 1992: 144). The rules of neighborliness necessitated that one know one's neighbors, but the habits of neighborliness were flexible in defining who belonged to that category of proximate occupants. The actual process of neighborly interaction (including the extension of social distinctions from sociability to conviviality) therefore involved Hildesheimers marking invisible boundaries of relevance and directed attention inward, creating integration within its boundaries and alienation without. Not willing simply to accept their status as given, these ordinary Hildesheimers used what resources were available to them to dream of a better future. Those desires were typical of the interwar generation insofar as the bonds of social milieu were breaking down, while the strength of those fantasies only increased with the degree to which rigid social hierarchies and resilient social cleavages made them seem unrealistic (adapting Peukert 1987: 149–74; Weirling 1992: 84–85). That is, neighborliness did not transcend social cleavages to create a harmoniously integrated community across class and confession, but it did create fictive worlds of habit in which my interview partners felt integrated among some neighbors and veiled their role in alienating others.

In part, the Third Reich appealed to its supporters because it offered the prospect of an upward social mobility that was systematically hindered under previous political systems. Yet the evidence from Hildesheim suggests that this story began earlier and in surprising places. Relatively independent of political institutions and structural changes in the economy and society, ordinary people generated integration and alienation on the streets of their neighborhoods as part of the curiously self-sacrificial attempt to transcend formal structures through informal mechanisms. The Nazis played to these fantasies by excluding racial inferiors, but it was ordinary Hildesheimers who first got into the habit of ignoring their neighbors in order to imagine their own niveau. It is in this context that we should read Lotte's comment that neighborliness was "something completely normal." Her proactive role in creating alienation had to remain an open secret not simply so that she could preserve the romantic illusions of an integrated neighborhood where everyone felt they belong. She had to infuse conviviality with a culture of normalcy if she hoped to preserve her surreal fantasy from the incursion of the real—to prevent objective reality from shattering her secret, fragile hopes for self-cultivation.

3 | The Stroll

Ordinary Hildesheimers were not as insignificant as they liked to imagine. They used a carefully selected greeting to negotiate intimacy and distance, and a tip of the hat to balance their commitment to mutual respect with their desire for hierarchy and difference. They similarly developed a subtle way of knowing or not knowing their actual neighbors as a way to lay claim to status and power in the local public sphere without undermining their civil society. In this way, they balanced their contradictory needs for communitas and societas. Through this ritual process, however, they also subtly altered some customs of conviviality by commodifying, modernizing, and politicizing their informal social relations. Turning now to the culture of exchange relations, this chapter will describe the common practice among young Hildesheimers during the interwar years of taking a walk through the central business district. Rebelling against their parents, they experimented cautiously with both economic and sexual desire. Associated with both modernity and Jewishness, this custom of conviviality reflected critical elements of Nazi propaganda.

Walking Slowly

Like many of my interview partners, Theodora Algermissen distinguished between the group of friends that she developed in elementary school (ca. 1925 when she was seven years old) and those that emerged when she went to high school, the *Goetheschule* for (Protestant) girls, in 1929 (G/3b R/160). In the latter period, she belonged to a large group of friends with whom she rode bikes, went swimming, played sports, played music, did homework, and celebrated birthdays. She developed a few friendships with boys only in her mid-teens: they attended the (Protestant) *Andreanum* across the street. "We knew each other, greeted, chatted with one another, but these were not permanent friendships: it was more like comrades." Theodora had to explain that these relationships were not as close as I might have imagined because, for interwar Hildesheimers, the German word for *friend* (*Freund* or *Freundin*) has the connotation of a *best friend*,

68

boyfriend, or *girlfriend.* It suggests a more selective, permanent, and intimate relationship.

Theodora's first best friend was Inge, the daughter of a purchasing agent for an interregional grain cooperative who moved to Hildesheim in 1934. Theodora described this relationship in the terms that I later came to expect. She spent time alone with Inge exclusively. They talked about problems, shared feelings, and comforted each other without fearing that their secrets would be spread around as gossip. They had their share of disagreements but rarely over substantive issues. They learned to depend on each other and help each other out. Still, Theodora admitted—laughing—that it was usually she who helped Inge with her homework because Inge took longer to finish her assignments, was one grade below her, and was close to being left behind at school.

Inge and Theodora went to the same dance class in 1934 and attended its balls together. By 1935, they even shared ski trips to the Harz Mountains with young men. These male students became their first boyfriends. Some of the boys came from other schools and one was even a Catholic. I asked her how she got to know boys from other schools (G/3b R/370). "In such a small town," she responded, "you knew such things." In reality, the process was far more active. She described how, in the late afternoon (there was some disagreement over the precise hours: cf. G/9a, R/350), young men and women took a *slow walk* (*bummeln*) down Hoher Weg, the main business street in the center of town:

> During these hours, you walked up and down and up and down [the street], the girls on their own, the boys on their own, but sometimes boyfriends and girlfriends together, and you met each other and you greeted each other and said *good day!* and *how are you?* and chatted a bit, and got to know lots of people that way.

The interwar generation referred to taking the stroll as if it were an institution of sorts: as *The Stroll* (*Der Bummel*).

The stroll served purposes analogous to dance class. As Thekla Mestmacher explained, the overt purpose of the stroll was to meet old and prospective new friends, to see and to be seen, to be entertained (G/14a R/130; see also G/82b R/60). "No problems," Theodora concluded. Yet the stroll also represented an informal alternative to formal dance classes. On the stroll, young Hildesheimers could practice their skills at conviviality and courtship outside the controls of their elders (G/148a R/40, G/181a R/90). Thekla's parents—and her example was typical—insisted that she be accompanied on her way to and from dance class in order to preserve her respectability. Yet they allowed her to take the stroll on her own (G/14a R/170; see also 185). The stroll was thus eigensinnig in the sense that it offered a place for young people to cultivate their own identities in rebellion against parental authority. These young people transposed habits learned in dance class onto the street, and in the process, significantly altered the norms and social hierarchies inculcated in dance class.

The temporal framework for their memories of the stroll suggests that this eigensinn was directed against their elders. For instance, Theodora suggested that the stroll was only common between 1934 and 1936. Yet Heinrich Weber (b. 1903) recalled quite clearly that he courted his wife on the stroll (G/148a R/40), which dates it at least to the 1920s. Each of these claims is not historically accurate in terms of the dates themselves but as reflections of the historical experience of strolling. My interview partners remembered the stroll as the property of their cohort of adolescents in distinction not only to their parents and teachers but also to those young men and women who were just a handful of years older. Adele Jürgens (b. 1900) was not aware of the stroll as a preteen and was not permitted to take the stroll until she was sixteen. In contrast to Theodora, Adele drew the conclusion that the stroll probably emerged during the First War (G/30b R/350, G/31b R/00). Thekla (b. 1915) was only slightly less discriminating: she believed that there had been "a certain kind of strolling" (einen gewissen Bummel) during the Wilhelmine era, and guessed that it started perhaps as early as 1912, but suggested that it "really" began in the 1920s (G/14a R/120). In all likelihood, Hildesheimers did take strolls before 1912.[1] Nonetheless, each generation liked to imagine that they were doing something new that set them apart from their elders, and this consciousness of generational difference was particularly strong during the Weimar Republic (Peukert 1987: 25–32, 94–95). In this sense, the stroll was strikingly modern.

Adele tried to justify her eigensinn in terms of historical conditions. Throughout this period, Hildesheimer women who could afford such luxuries met friends who belonged to their circle for coffee, cake, and conversation on a rotating basis in the salons of their residences (gute Stube). During the First War, however, it became difficult to entertain guests in this way due to the lack of appropriate foodstuffs; and yet one still felt the need for conviviality. As Adele explained, the stroll was a viable alternative. In effect, she argued that the war forced Hildesheimers to leave their homes in order to entertain friends. Yet arguably, this behavior was considered inappropriately self-indulgent, as she revealed in her description of the custom: though she made sure that she looked her best before she went out into public, she did purchase a few candies, "spoiling herself in a small way" (kleine Verwöhung; G/30b R/325, G/31b R/00). Displacing conviviality from private to public spaces, the stroll made convivial consumption inappropriately conspicuous.

Several of my interview partners insisted that their parents did not take the stroll when they were the same age (e.g., G/14a R/120). For instance, Thekla's mother only sat at home, read, learned to sew or cook, and so on. Her parents even took dance classes only after they married. In contrast to her parents, "I was or became really quite deviant with respect to [leisure time] . . . All of us girls were actually. That is to say, we did not agree very much with them on this. Here again they were so conservative, too fussy" (*kleinlich*). Whether or not the Wilhelmine generation took the stroll per se, interwar Hildesheimers did so in order to revolt against the perceived style of their elders. Like Adele, however, Thekla followed this expression of eigensinn with a reassertion of the very norms of hard work and savings against which she revolted: she justified her parents' reluctance to participate in such leisure-time activities by explaining that they had only a few really good friends, had no vacations from their butcher shop, and were exhausted when they came home from work (G/14a R/120). Her parents were just as desperate to control their daughter's behavior. If Thekla came home from the stroll even fifteen minutes late, her parents immediately told her: "Tomorrow you do not get to take the stroll" (G/14a R/170).

The problem facing adults who were trying to preserve their authority in these informal spaces of neighborliness lay in the fact that young people had some legitimate reasons for being on the stroll, which the latter then used to disguise their eigensinn. Theodora's teacher used to allow her to leave school during instruction time two or three times a week to walk to the teacher's house and pick up the remaining exercise books from her sister, since they were too heavy for the teacher to carry to school in the morning. "And then I took my time [*bummelte*], I strolled," she exclaimed, and then laughed, "all the way there and back." I asked her to describe what she meant by the term *bummeln*. "Oh, I looked around at who was here and who was there, whatever was out there on the street to see. I did not have to [walk] all that fast since I would only have to go back to my reading and writing, so I took my time." She laughed again at her eigensinn (G/2a R/180).

Adele recalled a similar incident in which an acquaintance of hers had been spotted on the stroll by her French teacher who had been on the lookout for such infractions from within the Hôtel d'Angleterre on Hoher Weg. Though the older woman was herself a rather emancipated woman for her era, she nonetheless instructed Adele's acquaintance that it was inappropriate for a young girl to be out and about in the evening. Her father had to go to the principal in order to clarify the situation and remove his daughter from suspicion. A butcher, he had sent her to deliver a package of meat on his behalf (G/31a R/345).

Georg Brzezinski faced this problem on a regular basis and found an ingenious solution. His school, the Catholic Josephinum, strictly forbade its students to take the stroll. The problem was that he lived directly on Hoher Weg and frequently had to run errands down the street at precisely the same time as the stroll—at least, that is how he explained his presence on the stroll to his teachers. They challenged this explanation, asking *did his home not have a rear entrance?* to which he then responded, *No.* In the end, he was granted a partial dispensation permitting him to conduct errands on the stroll but only if he ran (*im Laufschritt;* G/93b R/115). Relying on young people to run their errands, adults reluctantly accepted the presence of adolescents on the street as a subversive, though necessary, element of modern life.

Children, or servants, were often sent to shop on behalf of their mother (G/7b R/20, G/9a R/350, G/22a R/95, G/96b R/135, G/134a R/425, G147a R/75, G/152a R/130, G/165b R/180, G/169a R/30, G/186b R/05; cf. G/169a R/40). This pattern surprised me in its pervasiveness among my interview partners. It suggested a tragic degree of social isolation for married women. In keeping with the bourgeois *cult of domesticity,* the women of Hildesheim were often confined to the private sphere because of excessive household responsibilities and their position as bearers of the burden of familial respectability (visually illustrated in Figure 7; see also Kaplan 1998). Yet requests for errands were not limited to members of the nuclear family: adult women neighbors and teachers could all make such demands of any child they knew. In response, young Hildesheimers did not always obey these demands so precisely: they took their time doing the errand, walking slowly.

This intergenerational struggle to control neighborhood streets is reflected in the archival record concerning pulp fiction (SAH 102/6670). In April 1920, the Town Schools Deputation joined forces with the Commission on Youth Literature, from the Teachers Association, to issue a "Warning to Parents!" It seemed that young people could be found "practically laying siege to" store windows, particularly of paper-goods stores, in order to view the latest editions of adventure literature, especially criminal and detective stories. "Greedily they glue their eyes . . . to the novelettes that lie in the window and depict scenes of murder and brutality in word and image." Critics felt that these deceptive fantasies brutalized the emotions, undermined the ability of young people to assess what was possible and impossible, poisoned their imagination, destroyed their natural sense for good and evil, and led ultimately to criminality and suicide. The root of the problem, they felt, lay in the inappropriate presence of young consumers on the streets of commerce, where they engaged in exchange relations amongst themselves. The novelettes were consumed too quickly ("before they even get to the street") and then were traded among peers: that is, outside of adult control.

This group of concerned adults responded to the eigensinn of youth with new strategies for herrschaft. They admonished parents not only to monitor the reading materials of their children strictly and energetically, but also to "attack this evil at its roots and forbid your children to shop in stores whose shop windows show this kind of trash and filth." They advised using physical activity to compensate for this abnormal "craving" to read (*Lesewut*) which they distinguished from a healthy "drive" to read (*Lesebedürfnis*). Specifically, they recommended small handicraft tasks and playing instead in the fields outside town used for annual festivals (the *Schützenwiese*): that is, anything but the stroll. The town administration, in turn, responded to this civic movement, which was also gaining press attention nationally, by collecting and distributing a list of bookstores that sold this kind of pulp fiction to parents, teachers, and clergy (Teilakte: Bekämpfung der Schundliteratur, 1920–22 in 102/6670). The representatives of the town and parent associations then visited these shops and pressured their neighbors not to make such books available to young people. Yet a public declaration of the disrepute of these stores was deemed to be unnecessary. The persistent faith of Hildesheimers in their informal strategies of herrschaft is revealed by the fact that by 1922, they considered parental and neighborly pressure to be sufficient.

This preference for informal mechanisms was also reflected in public art in Hildesheim. The *Huckup* statue (see Figure 9) depicted an avenging spirit that has mounted the back of a young man who has been caught in the act of stealing apples from a local orchard. Its inscription reads:

Boy, let go of those apples,	Junge, lat dei Appels sahn,
Or else the Huckup will get you.	Süs packet deck dei Huckup an.
The Huckup is a powerful imp,	Dei Huckup is en starken Wicht,
Who will pass harsh judgment	Hölt mit dei Steldeifs bös Gericht.
on thieves.	

The use of dialect (*Plattdeutsch*) for the inscription as well as the fairy-tale motifs in the narrative and design of the figures made this statue seem traditional. Yet it was built in 1905 and in fact addressed contemporary concerns. Representing precisely that circumstance in which formal institutions of authority were not functioning to maintain order, the Huckup promised swift and severe judgment on any adolescent who consumed inappropriately. On the one hand, *huckepack* means to carry someone or something on your back (as in *piggyback*). In a figurative sense, the imp riding the young man's back represents a none-too-subtle warning that the tactics of youthful eigensinn would face corresponding strategies of herrschaft—or at least that the

Figure 9. Postcard of the Huckup. Courtesy of: SAH 952/16/1/1.

adolescent would feel the burden of guilt when disobeying those rules. On the other hand, the statue dismissed that rebellion as just a youthful prank, just as the statue hid that warning in folklore. The statue was located at the intersection of Hoher Weg and Schuhstrasse, an appropriate place for the stroll to come to a dramatic halt under the shadow of the local fairy tale that disguised intergenerational conflict behind the veil of normalcy.

Desire

Thekla loved to shop, especially with her best friend Gertrude (G/21a R/105). That friendship derived in fact from common consumption because Gertrude's mother was the seamstress who made clothes for Thekla's sister. The women in the two families often went shopping for cloth together. Thekla and Gertrude continued this tradition yet revised its character significantly. They shopped for trendy perfumes, soaps, and clothing. One favorite store was Löwenstein & Freudental, a department store on Hoher Weg, which sold ready-made, mass-produced garments at lower prices. (The shop windows to a different women's clothing store are illustrated in Figure 10.) The girls often went there just to look around and try things on, even though they had no money to buy anything. "We wanted to take a look first."

Thekla proudly informed me that they were the first girls among their acquaintances to wear nylon stockings. Nylons were a new, somewhat taboo product in interwar Hildesheim. Thekla's mother wore socks made from Bamberg silk; they were thicker than nylons and could be darned if they developed a hole. Nylons did not fall down your leg like traditional stockings, but they had to be replaced entirely when they wore out. This attribute fit with the need of clothing companies to increase sales to match the rising scale of production; it also fit Thekla's desire for conspicuous, mass consumption. Nylons were available only through special advertisements "in the American style." They were considered "sinfully expensive" and of course revealed more skin than traditional stockings.

Because they could not afford to buy nylons, these ever-resourceful young women found ways to make it look as if they were wearing stockings when they were in fact bare-legged. They worked hard to find any possible way to get enough money to buy the real thing. For instance, they collected the money that their parents gave to them to buy stockings and bought nylons instead. Here, Thekla drew a clear distinction between this eigensinnig style of consumption, in which they could stoke their desires free from parental authority, and the act of going shopping "officially" with their mothers. Still, the two girls were often able to turn even the latter activity to their own interests. They convinced their mothers to go shopping

Figure 10. Shopwindow on Hoher Weg, ca. 1930 (D/77).

with them when they knew that a highly desired commodity had become available locally.

Young Hildesheimers took the stroll for much the same reason: in order to experiment with the modern culture of economic and sexual desire (cf. Benjamin 1968, 1978; Harootunian 2000). When Lotte Schohl needed something new and substantial, for instance, her step-mother bought it from stores in the center of town. But there were some things that Lotte did not need—something sweet, a new pencil, a headband "for decoration," or "other small items." She purchased those things in the center of town while on the stroll. Such indulgences had to be inexpensive, she insisted, because no one had very much money. Lotte received only a small allowance of fifty pfennigs. But even if one could not pay for these items, the stroll still promoted the desire for goods. I asked her about window shopping: "Yes, we did that of course: look at the display, and if we had to buy something, then we also [looked at the displays], but we really could not just go and buy something" (G/9a R/75). Jürgen Ludewig sometimes bought ice cream at the end of his stroll (G/106b R/180) and Gerhard Mock even frequented a café (G/117a R/105), but these were expensive exceptions to the norm. Almost all of my interview partners reiterated instead Lotte's pattern of large fantasies and small indulgences. They understood themselves as more ready consumers than their elders (G/22a R/25), and yet also stuck by and large to the bourgeois norms of self-restraint that they had learned from their parents.

These desires for new commodities were gendered though those distinctions were idiosyncratic. Karl Rudolph looked at sports equipment and clothing (G/183a R/110). Dietrich Vornfett shopped for clothes for himself and for stamps and coins for his collections (G/154a R/320) but on his own, whereas most of my female interview partners shopped with friends. Friedrich Rother claimed that the boys looked at books and watches while the girls looked at clothes, "but out of politeness . . . you also stood next to them when they were looking in [their] shop windows" (G/57a R/130). Clearly, boys of the interwar generation were just as interested in window shopping as girls. The open secret of the stroll was that sexual desire lay barely disguised behind these shared fantasies of mass consumption. Ulrike Volkmann claimed that she and her girlfriend took walks "on Hoher Weg, where the shops are. We looked at the stuff, but not with boys. We did not walk [with them]." Then she added: "Not that" (G/61a R/135).

Yet her identification with social norms misrepresented a more complicated past. Earlier in the interviews, Ulrike told me about a girlfriend who was *going with a boy* during her last year of school. This friend used to tell her parents that she was walking her dachshund with Ulrike, but this friend was in fact accompanied by a suitor. Ulrike played along until their teacher asked her to ask her mother to meet for a parent–teacher conference. Since her grades were very good, Ulrike suspected that the teacher had discovered their scheme, so Ulrike did not tell her mother about the teacher's request for two weeks. Finally, the teacher came to her house personally and talked to her mother. Ulrike was punished for not bringing the teacher's request to her mother immediately and was permanently banned from ever spending leisure time with this girl. Her mother then explained the whole situation to her friend's parents, who were also very appreciative. This girl later married her cousin, while the boy landed in prison for fighting and writing bad checks: he ultimately hanged himself (G/60 R/305). Ulrike recounted other, similar anecdotes whose moral lay in the severity of the punishments for girls who dared to take a stroll with boys (G/61a R/150).

Yet these same anecdotes suggest that some girls did so anyway. Even the well-bred Ulrike risked glancing at boys with "one eye" (as she told another interviewer: SAH 904–1/17b R/115, 35). Theodora came closer to historical reality when she admitted that her generation was really more interested in looking at the other young men and women, nodding their head at them as they passed, than in looking at the store windows (G/3b R/370). Gerhard Mock interpreted the stroll for me as a form of sexual display akin to a peacock spreading its feathers for a peahen (G/117a R/115).

Adult teachers monitored the stroll, and even distributed academic penalties to those young people caught on the stroll too frequently, precisely because they understood that the stroll offered young people an informal space outside adults' direct control in which young people could learn to flout adult authority and social norms (G/82a R/00, G/93b R/130; see also G/82a R/370).

The dynamic tension between economic and sexual desire is clearly evident in Helmut Rabitz's account of the stroll. He described it explicitly in terms of flirting, but when I asked him about shopping, he responded emphatically: "But that was the problem: we never had any money!" (G/52a R/225). Helmut admitted that it was common for young people to get an allowance, and most of my interview partners did receive one, but then complained that the sum enabled them only to buy small items (G/52a R/225). Both norm and necessity demanded that these young people restrict their purchases in keeping with their parents' principles of self-restraint, but as far as the children were concerned, they exercised their fantasies of desire far more than their parents did. They took the stroll day after day, walking back and forth along the same streets, imagining whom they could become intimate with and what new things they could buy, in opposition to the authority and in distinction to the (presumed) behavior of their elders. Not surprisingly, the interwar generation in Hildesheim was addicted to this particular form of surreal self-cultivation.

There is a long history of the association of economic with sexual desire, but the dynamic tension between these two factors reached new heights during the 1920s. The same short decade witnessed the emancipation of both sexuality and consumerism: that is, the legitimacy of desiring both, though many still lacked the means. The question here concerns how interwar Hildesheimers were able to make such dangerously powerful principles into a normal part of their everyday life against the opposition of those who still adhered to prior norms of self-restraint and without undermining a sense of normalcy. All of my interview partners dismissed the stroll as simply a prank of youth. Theodora insisted that she and her friends went to Hoher Weg simply because of tradition: "that was just the meeting place" (G/3b R/370; see also G/4a R/115, G/9a R/70). They were not ignorant of the disguised meanings, however. Martha Paul described how, if you took the stroll, "some people thought, we thought maybe, that you were *fast,* which was nonsense. We didn't even know what *fast* meant. And it was not done somehow. On the other hand," she admitted, "when you were fifteen, sixteen [years old], you would like to have that." She and her girlfriends even went so far as to construct fake packages so that her friends would think: "no, she is not taking the stroll, she just came from doing some shopping" (G/98a R/75). Clearly, interwar Hildesheimers were engaged in a complex series of contradictory self-delusions in which economic desire disguised and facilitated experimentation with sexual desire and vice-versa. They dismissed such contests as insignificant, even to themselves, in order for them to function as intended: as indirect mechanisms to lay claim to status and power.

Hildesheimers strolled, flirted, and shopped as if these were one and the same activity in part because they engaged in these leisure activities in the context of the same kinds of social relationships (friends) and with the same specific people (like Thekla and Gertrude). Thekla expressed this link most clearly: she purchased new items with the conscious intent of showing them off during the stroll. She bought her first pair of nylon stockings when she was seventeen years old, and she and Gertrude wore the trendy style of long-waisted, short skirts to show off their chic legs. "Oh, I was so proud of [them]. I would have preferred to have walked through the street wearing just [nylons]." She laughed again at her trick, for she knew full well that her mother disapproved of nylons (not to mention showing off her legs in public as seen in Figure 11). Thekla bought nylons with the intent of using them to construct a particular identity for herself among her peers and laying claim to status, perhaps even power, in the process. Her mother never learned that she had purchased and worn nylons because Thekla changed into them in the toilette or stairwell "ultra-secretly" (klammheimlich) on her way out of the house. Thekla laughed yet again. All the same, her eigensinn did not mean that she abandoned hegemonic norms entirely. Thekla insisted that her clothes were always in order: properly ironed, clean, and never with holes (G/16b R/20).

In this context, we should not accept at face value the claim of my interview partners that they were the innovators and that their elders were mired in tradition. While taking the stroll, young people both rebelled against, and embraced, their parents' norms of utilitarian restraint on consumption. This combination of tactics of eigensinn and strategies for herrschaft can be seen most vividly in the ways that young Hildesheimers got permission to take the stroll in the first place. As Thekla explained, "we always found some reason to get to the stroll, no? And they knew precisely that we were going to the stroll, no?" (G/14a R/120). It is relevant to mention that she gave this as her answer to my question about why her parents did not take the stroll themselves. In spite of the fact that they came from a different generation (her first explanation), and that "they never really understood why" she and her friends took the stroll (her second), she decided in the end that "they did understand when we said: 'I have just got to buy another sewing needle!'" The core principle of the stroll was thus the open secret itself: a shared set of contradictory truths and fictions whose entertainment value and eroticism lay in large part in the transgressive play they facilitated on all sides.

Figure 11. Women displaying stockinged legs, 1929 (D/900).

Dance class was designed to contain sexual desire within rituals of conviviality; by contrast, the stroll encouraged its release. To be sure, most of my interview partners insisted on their almost complete naïveté, particularly in contrast to the post-1960s generations of which I was a representative. "You are going to laugh," Friedrich said to me shortly thereafter, "when I came home after having gone out with a girl for the first time in the evening, and we kissed, I staggered my way home in fear that I could have a child. We were that dumb" (G/57b R/00; see also G/57a R/110, G/82a R/60). Yet such comparisons between them and me tended to efface the more relevant contrast between them and their elders. Like almost all of my interview partners, Theodora insisted that physical intimacy among her peers was very restricted prior to marriage (G/4b R/00; see also G/16b R/180). Friends kissed on the cheek and hugged as a form of greeting. Young heterosexual couples held hands, hugged, or at most perhaps kissed on the lips. In fact, some young couples dared to take the stroll arm-in-arm, and perhaps even walked to another location where they could have more privacy. Several of my interview partners could even recall examples of premarital pregnancies in which the young woman involved invariably left town (G/61a R/145), including Maria Rolf herself (cf. an extramarital affair: G/153 R/320, G/153b R/40). Yet the way in which these activities were avoided reflects the interview partner's attitude while these were still serious transgressions. Thekla was describing how boys and girls looked at each other and what they wore, "and when something really—." She stopped herself. She appreciated the way that the stroll facilitated cautious experimentation with sexuality, but balked at the verbal expression of this open secret. She continued instead in hegemonic terms: "Teachers also took the stroll. They observed. You were not allowed to walk with a boy together."

The best way to characterize these accounts is to note that my interview partners dynamically and frequently moved back and forth between eigensinn and herrschaft in order to recount these autobiographic episodes. Thekla gladly recounted tales of her hubris to me and just as readily disguised her experimentation behind examples of obedience to the rules. Thekla explained that when the teacher confronted her for walking arm-in-arm with a strange boy, she simply explained that the boy was really her cousin, which made the act legitimate. "Back then, we had lots and lots of cousins." The teachers knew full well that this was a trick, and Thekla obviously knew that they knew. For her own part, Thekla kept those open secrets during the interviews, just as she still relished her memories of her unpunished eigensinn (G/14a R/245).

By exploring desire, these young Hildesheimers challenged some of the norms of Wilhelmine society, so it is not surprising then that they conformed strictly to other ones: like the patriarchal principle of masculine sexual agency. Lotte insisted that young ladies waited for the gentlemen to make the initial approach, after being spurred into action perhaps by a friendly glance from one of the girls (G/9a R/50). This memory corresponds to her relatively protected childhood and "good" rearing. A particularly attractive young man (memorable in part because he was also an albino) asked Dora Pröbst to take the stroll with him using the following line: "Beautiful young Lady: may I offer you [my] hand and heart?" (G/124a R/265). She rejected him by simply strolling past him several times until he figured out that she was not interested. But this game was not yet over. According to Thekla, since girls looked past the boys as if they were not there, the boys sometimes threw a piece of candy towards them to get their attention—and candy never flew in the opposite direction (G/15b R/220). This pattern of informal courtship corresponded to the underlying principles learned at dance class: the boy approached the girl to request a dance. Yet the thrown bon-bon suggests that, even here, young boys were taking some liberties.

Even more rigid were the norms of heterosexuality. Almost universally, my interview partners claimed that they knew of no gay relationships among boys. Persistent questioning revealed not only an overtly gay neighbor (G/42a R/50, see Chapter 8) but also a pedophilic relationship between a teacher and a student at the Catholic Josephinum (G/182a R/290). My interview partners insisted all the more strongly that they had not even heard of lesbianism until after the Second War. The point here is that these young people gladly collaborated in the discursive assumptions of heteronormativity because their exploration of sexuality was legitimated within those bounds. For instance, girls could walk arm-in-arm and in pairs while boys walked in groups, never arm-in-arm. Thekla excused the former practice by saying that there was not enough space on the sidewalk, but that would have also legitimized the latter, which, my interview partners all agreed, simply never took place. Thekla described how the boys walked: "totally casual, hands in the pant pockets, their school caps a bit relaxed" (lässig, leger; G/15b R/220; see also G/57a R/110). Here again, young Hildesheimers took the customs that were formally socialized in dance class and adapted them creatively to the informal context of the street. The rigidity of formal dances was quite literally inverted into a casual style that conveyed status precisely because of its eigensinn, as seen in Figure 12. Yet the eigensinn of casual was contained within strategies for herrschaft as heterosexuals.

In the 1920s, the commodity most emblematic of mass consumption and the modern culture of desire was the cigarette. For one thing, it was a luxury beyond the financial means of most Hildesheimers (G/106b R/190). For another, advertisers associated tobacco with gustatory and sexual pleasure, women's liberation, and American culture, such that "back then it was

Figure 12. Portrait with cigarette, 1938–39 (D/824). Part of a storybook photo album *Comrades, Friends* (p. 24). The caption read: "As self-conscious and active as we are."

said that a German woman did not smoke," as Lise Peters explained (G/141b R/55). Still, many young Hildesheimers experimented with smoking, as seen in Figure 13. A poor Jewish immigrant from Poland, Bernward Nedderich began smoking as a boy. He and his friends collected cigarette butts from the street, placed the tobacco gleaned from them in a wooden pipe, and smoked their "peace pipe" as part of playing "Indian" (G/156b R/190): a game that was intimately tied to the very same adventure literature derided by the educated adults of Hildesheim.

To smoke their cigarettes, young Hildesheimers had to find places in which parental authority was less inherent. Bernward got his hands on cigarettes as an adolescent by mastering a game at the annual fair that rewarded the winner with cigarettes. He played repeatedly, and then hid his cigarettes under his mattress until his mother discovered them (G/156b R/230). Adolescents also tended to seek out the informal spaces and relationships of conviviality to smoke (G/45b R/160, G/52a R/235). Yet in the case of cigarettes, the stroll was not a viable option at first. Adult Hildesheimers strictly forbade young people to smoke in public. "You got the death penalty for that," Thekla explained. Parents and neighbors circumstantially monitored adolescent behavior on the stroll, but it was teachers who posed the most serious danger. They actively patrolled the stroll, looking for moral infractions among the students (G/14a R/245). Student received the punishment of bad grades in spite of the fact that these transgressions did not take place during school hours or on school property. That did not stop Thekla from trying cigarettes, but as she showed me with a photograph (D/908), she did so in the seclusion of her backyard garden rather than on the stroll.

The thrill of outmaneuvering adults on the cultural battlefields of everyday life in itself represented a significant motivation for engaging in such activities. An otherwise dutiful daughter, Lotte Schohl kept the secret from her parents that her cousins from Hannover had smoked cigarettes on Galgenberg, a forested hill just outside of town (G/9a R/370). Yet in contrast to smoking cigarettes or getting pregnant, the stroll represented a relatively modest expression of revolt: it was an act of eigensinn to be sure, but one that was more or less tolerated by the forces of herrschaft. Young Hildesheimers feared reprisals, but they also developed a realistic attitude about these potential punishments. As Dietrich Vornfett noted, there was no real way for adults to prevent them from walking back and forth on the stroll (G/154a R/25). Ordinary Hildesheimers used the stroll to reshape their society into a place in which they could cultivate the kind of self they desired. It was of only secondary importance to them that they modernized conviviality in the process.

Figure 13. Portrait with cigarette and cap, 1920s (D/512).

My point here is that these dynamic struggles for power and identity between the generations helped to make modern habits of conspicuous, mass consumption as well as public, sexual desire into part and parcel of everyday life. In itself, this pattern could describe many settings in the modern world (Harootunian 2000). Still, the scale of the stroll in Hildesheim was characteristic of German hometowns in particular, and is one quality that distinguished it from analogous strolls in the typical modern metropolis. Ulrich Gerke described Hoher Weg in these terms: "a beautiful narrow street [on which] one could always get a good look around from the sidewalks" (G/89a R/50). Hildesheim had its share of boulevards, like Sedanstrasse on which the so-called *upper 10,000* lived,[2] or the Zingel, which one used to get to the civic theater and concert hall. Yet the stroll as such was taken on Hoher Weg, a street reminiscent of the small frame of this provincial hometown, whose cityscape rejected the openness of a modern metropolis. Similarly, Dietrich Vornfett noted that strollers always walked only on one side of Hoher Weg in spite of the fact that the route was so narrow (G/154a R/340, G/154b R/00). Arguably, Hoher Weg was selected for the stroll precisely because the Altstadt framed innovation in insularity. Like the Huckup, the stroll disguised experimentation with modern habits of desire behind invented traditions of provincial German culture.

Shopping Spaces

I am not suggesting that interwar Hildesheimers accepted modernization without concern. Modernity posed a serious threat to their sense of normalcy, even among the younger generation. Yet they developed sophisticated cultural mechanisms to insulate themselves from that modernity even as they helped it penetrate the walls of their town. To appreciate this process, we need to understand first the particular cultural topography of exchange relations in interwar Hildesheim. My interview partners drew a surprisingly strong distinction between the *corner stores,* which they associated with neighborliness, and the stores in the business district past which they took the stroll. A close examination of their anecdotes about shopping will show that they demarcated the business district as a space of modernity apart from their neighborhood through subtle shifts in their customs of conviviality.

Hildesheimers purchased most of their consumable goods (i.e., groceries) from family-run, small-scale shops (e.g., G/65b R/285, G/66a R/40, G/67a R/100, G/67b R/65, G/91b R/270, 320). Defined as neighborly, the colloquial expression for them was *Tanta-Emma Laden* (G/12b R/100). I translate this as *mom-and-pop stores* in order to capture the sense in which these convivial relations were assigned qualities of fictive kinship. For instance, Günther Seidner explained that his baker serviced the people on his street and the two adjacent streets, but "that was it, because the next baker could be found close by" (G/80b R/120). This is not to suggest that all interwar Hildesheimers shopped for bread, meat, cheese, and vegetables in the topographically most proximate store. Jürgen Ludewig's family shopped at the market rather than at the closest butcher because the butcher's shop was too expensive, servicing really the wealthier families from the adjacent boulevard and not the far poorer residents of his street (G/106a R/00). Some Hildesheimers even regularly patronized village stores or master artisans that required a ride by train out of town (G/186b R/90). These "corner" stores (or even market stalls: G/91b R/270) were proximate in cultural terms: my interview partners made these shops into corner stores because they treated the shopkeepers as neighbors.

Any given shop became a corner store if Hildesheimers greeted each other by name and exchanged gossip about family, friends, or acquaintances. In the mom-and-pop store on Thekla's block, "you could always get completely oriented as to what was happening on the street" (G/12b R/100). Customers also experienced a sense of neighborliness in that particular store because the shopkeeper knew their preferences and perhaps even prepared their purchase in advance or had it ready for delivery. Years of reciprocal buying and selling meant that shoppers could also ring after hours to buy something forgotten during the day in spite of the fact that this behavior irritated the storeowner (G/85a R/220). In some cases, the keeper of a corner shop even spoke to regular customers in the informal (*du*) since they had been shopping there since childhood (G/179b R/75). If interwar Hildesheimers made best friends very sparingly, once they established intimacy, they rarely returned to distance.

This relationship should not be overstated or romanticized. My interview partners insisted that being a regular customer in a corner store did not enable them, for instance, to receive more than their share during hard times, of which there were many in the first half of the twentieth century. That prospect contradicted a deep-seated sense of fair, communal distribution that was based in corporate notions of representation, politicized during the First War by the concepts of *volksgemeinschaft* and *Burgfrieden* (peace in the castle) and reinforced by economic hardship. Although regularly shopping in a particular corner store sometimes did result in one family getting more than their fair share (G/73a R/210, G/90b R/160, G/92a R/100), this transgression of propriety had to be legitimized as an extension of the relationship into something more akin to friendship. Sofia Krumme recalled visiting the popular Italian ice-cream store, nicknamed *Ice-Onki*, on Kleine Venedig. Since her mother was fluent in Italian, they always got special treatment including extra servings of ice cream. But as she also explained, the merchant was her mother's best friend.[3]

Being a regular customer enabled you to purchase on credit (variously described as *anschreiben lassen, an Buch kaufen, auf Pump kaufen*). My interview partners almost universally insisted that they and their families avoided such practices at all costs. Buying on credit challenged the family's reputation among neighbors for autarky (self-sufficiency) and therefore called into doubt one's respectability. Interwar Hildesheimers preferred to send their child back to the store if they did not have enough money at that time (G/152a R/230), or to do without whatever goods they could not afford, particularly when it meant purchasing a more expensive commodity in town (G/147a R/30). Georg Brzezinsky's family permitted wealthy customers to pay on credit in their store, but forced artisans and workers to pay in cash (G/92a R/60). As many interview partner suggested, but often failed to mention explicitly, such circumstances led to unpaid bills and undesirable animosities. Those interview partners who admitted to such transgressive habits were very poor and developed complicated exculpatory mechanisms to justify their behavior (e.g., G/157a R/320). These principles played a significant role in keeping neighborly relations *neither too close nor too far.*

In some cases, the bond between regular customers and the shopkeepers of their corner store was reinforced by supplemental, reciprocal exchanges. For instance, one could exchange homemade goods like pickled vegetables, grown in the family garden, or sausages made from a pig slaughtered in the common courtyard. Yet when I asked my interview partners to describe specific examples of these kinds of reciprocal exchanges, more often than not they did not respond concretely or precisely (cf. G/190b R/165, G/73a R/190, 235). Rather, most Hildesheimers constituted the experience of neighborliness primarily by recalling symbolic acts of reciprocity such as the ritualized exchange of greetings. Symbolic reciprocity made possible the exchange of concrete resources, felt just as "real" but arguably not actually made concrete in most cases. Symbolic reciprocity, regular customers, and neighborly relations were woven together into the fabric of everyday life such that one acquired the moral character of the others without necessitating reciprocal exchanges of physical goods (cf. Simmel 1989: 2/308–16).

A significant exception was the case of small businesses. I heard many stories of how master artisans, shopkeepers, and even one insurance agent intentionally purchased reciprocally in the same stores whose owners shopped in theirs (G/67a R/170, G/67b R/100, G/91b R/320, G/148a R/315, G/152a R/125, G/180b R/170, G/181a R/100). Heinrich Weber's father, a master painter, could never have afforded to build his own home if he had had to pay for it. He was only able to do so gradually by exchanging services with a master mason and other master craftsmen (G/148b R/410). As Lena Turz explained: "one hand washed the other" (G/67b R/120).

Neighborly exchange relations also extended beyond the symbolic and into the reciprocal exchange of actual resources in the case of the loan of a durable good—but always with caveats. Lise Peters recounted a story of how neighbors temporarily borrowed their harmonium for a wedding (G/139b R/100, G/140b R/325). A wedding was by definition an exceptional instance, and the request seemed to imply inappropriate behavior in any case (see Chapter 8). When Hildesheimers borrowed a neighbor's telephone, usually from a shopkeeper or master artisan who had a phone for business purposes, they almost always paid in advance (e.g., G/143b, R/120, cf. G/123b, R/160). When I asked my interview partners if they ever requested a cup of sugar or an egg from a neighbor, they sometimes admitted that they could imagine neighbors pumping each other for such goods, but they personally neither did this nor witnessed it (e.g., G/29a R/305).

The only other circumstances in which neighborly exchange relations involved actual resources occurred at times of personal tragedy or emergency. Franz Meissner recalled a boy from school who had lost his father and whose mother ran an extremely small paper-goods business on an obscure little street. To help her out, the students of his class made a purchase at her store every time they passed by (G/166a R/140). Nonetheless, those interview partners who donated a bowl of soup to a sick neighbor, a sandwich to a homeless man, or a cake to the elderly implied that they stood only on the giving side of this exchange and that their giving was unsolicited (e.g., G/6b R/205, G/140b R/150; see also SAH 904-1/59a R/285). Sarah Meyer told me how her family sent her to give a basket of food to a desperately poor and starving Jewish family. She clarified that they were not Eastern but German Jews, a factor that only made their poverty all the more disturbing. She executed this task with great reluctance, as she was embarrassed by their squalor as well as by the awkward circumstance of giving another family gifts that could never be reciprocated. No wonder then that her parents sent a child to deliver these goods: for an adult, the action might have proven too humiliating altogether (G/176b R/170). In keeping with the same principle of autarky, families provided for themselves and asked no favors of neighbors.

Such acts of generosity were legitimate in interwar Hildesheim precisely because the residents conceived of neighborly reciprocity in broad terms. An exchange concerned the social relationship far more than the goods themselves: interwar Hildesheimers effectively effaced the distinction between symbolic and concrete exchanges so that a friendly greeting and a basket of food could be dismissed as fair and equal in value. Even the loan of a durable good was largely a social act because it was always temporary. Indeed, these exchanges focused ultimately on neighbors in general rather than on a particular informal social relationship. That is, one exchanged goods in interwar Hildesheim for the same reasons that one exchanged greetings: to show one's respect for the shared culture of conviviality itself. Voluntary, reciprocal exchanges signified mutual respect for human needs and reasserted the humanity of both neighbors; these were the priorities (following Simmel 1989).

The relationship between regular customers and corner stores should be understood as one part of a larger array of habits that my interview partners awkwardly described as *taking part in the lives of neighbors* (*Anteil nehmen*). Symbolic reciprocity laid real foundations for future reciprocal relationships that would involve more concrete resources. Dora Pröbst explained how the owners of a clothing store asked her parents if they would permit her to be apprenticed to them as a saleswoman because they had been customers for many years and had long known the family and inquired about them (G/123b R/200). Still, taking part in the lives of neighbors was more a matter of inquiring about life-cycle events of the family when you met on the street or in the stairwell (e.g., G/81a R/100) than it involved actual gifts or barters. Ritualized acts of neighborliness did not center on material products or personal gain: neighbors reciprocated even material exchanges with the far more significant gifts of dignity, respect, and concern.

In German, the term for groceries is *Lebensmittel*, literally *the means to sustain life*. In interwar Hildesheim, groceries were also the means of sustaining proper social relations. In a very real sense, by buying bread, meat, cheese, vegetables and the like from neighbors, Hildesheimers inverted the logic of commodification, redirecting exchange relations away from profit and back into human needs and human bonds; Karl Marx referred to this awareness as our *species being*. The bond between shopkeeper and regular customer facilitated long-term reciprocal relationships that resulted not so much in profit as in *a living* for both the shopkeeper and the regular customer. In their network of corner stores, Hildesheimers thus constructed a web of relationships in which they felt that their humanity was recognized. They did so by framing their relationships with particular storeowners in particular terms of neighborliness. To be sure, commodities (i.e., goods produced for sale according to their exchange value) still mediated local social relations and served as a mechanism for profit. Yet Hildesheimers effectively de-emphasized both when they removed them from their commodity context (Appadurai 1986) and focused instead on their use value for the physical and moral survival of that human community.

This economic culture makes all the more sense when we recall the degree to which the world's financial and commercial systems had fallen into chaos in the 1920s, particularly in Germany. Interwar Hildesheimers were confronted not only with the Great Depression after 1929 but also with the Hyperinflation in 1922–23, the economic burdens of the Treaty of Versailles, and the collapse of the Wilhelmine Empire more generally. Hildesheimers turned to informal social relations to survive these hard times. Though exchanges with those shopkeepers were primarily symbolic in nature, they generated powerful bonds that ensured the functioning of the economy on the local level, provided a feeling of community across boundaries of society and politics, and above all, restored a sense of control to ordinary Hildesheimers. From this perspective, making oneself into a regular customer of a corner shop was a pragmatic, if romantic, antidote to modernity. It took commerce to be an abstract process, as an end in itself out of individual control, and made it into a means to reinforce concrete, face-to-face relations very much within the scope of the agency of ordinary people. The point here, then, is not simply that the corner store provided a sense of insularity from a formal system of value and exchange that had collapsed into chaos. The culture of normalcy is far more sophisticated. Thanks to their multifaceted customs of conviviality, Hildesheimers simultaneously rejected the most insufferable elements of the modern system of commodities as alienating and reasserted their control over those that could be subjugated to local custom.

Shopping in the so-called *business district* felt different. Some stores had shifted their product lines to offer less expensive, mass-produced goods such as ready-made clothing, which were very successful in Hildesheim. These mass-produced goods only served to romanticize the more expensive handmade goods, available in adjacent stores or sometimes even in the same one. Still, even the upscale handicraft stores on Hoher Weg were now associated with modernity. They all tended to advertise aggressively through window displays and announcements of sales in the daily paper. They tended to offer a wider set of choices and often sold more expensive, durable goods as well as luxury items like porcelain, perfume and chocolate that were also sometimes "finer" in quality (G/186b R/35; see also G/90a R/270, G/90b R/00, 120, 140). Hildesheimers required large sums of surplus cash on-hand to make such purchases, or they had to pay on lay-away plans. Such purchases only seemed to entangle them in the very alienating system of financial and commercial capitalism from which they tried to insulate themselves by shopping in corner stores.

Some of the stores in this business district emphasized mechanization. The largest store for bicycles stood on the plaza at the north end of the stroll and was equipped with an asphalt yard in the back. There, Hildesheimers could actually mount this new contraption and take it for a test drive, receiving helpful advice from the shopkeeper. "That was really something exceptional," Heinrich Weber explained. "You could not find that anywhere else in Hildesheim" (G/144a R/20; see also Bergerson 2001). The business district also offered the largest public concentration of radios with loud-speakers (G/160a R/400). Some of the stores were themselves machines, such as Hildesheim's first "Automated Restaurant." It was not very success-ful, according to my interview partners, and only a few remembered it at all (e.g., G/106b R/280). Still, this business district served as one of the most striking emblems of modernity in Hildesheim.

On or near these same streets were banks, government offices, fancy ho-tels, and expensive cafés beyond the financial reach of most Hildesheimers. As in many larger cities, numerous sites of improper exchange relations—such as the bordellos on the Rosenhagen—could be found adjacent to this business district. Stefan Nebe also wandered these streets peddling shoe laces for one year (G/138a R/50, 110, 165, 280; see also G/160b R/330). The railroad station was located at the far northern end of this business dis-trict, and the streetcar routes that connected different areas of Hildesheim all the way to Hannover—i.e., to the larger world—crossed at the southern end of Hoher Weg (G/132b R/60). The business district was literally one of Hildesheim's gateways to the modern world. It seemed to be the entry point through which consumer capitalism invaded Hildesheim from Berlin, London, Paris, and New York (Lüdtke, Marssolek, and von Saldern 1996). It was even the space into which foreigners came to shop: Heinrich Weber told me how Polish seasonal laborers used to come to the business district, and his girlfriend from dance class got a bonus when she sold them a whole bolt of colorful cloth (*bunte Tuch aus Schuttenmusster;* G/144b R/130; see also G/14a R/130, G/145b R/290).

Many of these stores were run by families, and the store managers tended to know their customers personally (e.g., G/92a R/40, G/186b R/55). In contrast to the corner stores, however, exchange relations in the business district seemed to involve profit and growth more than human needs and relationships. Lise Peters found working as a saleswoman at the town phar-macy on Hoher Weg to be quite distressing. She began to work outside her parents' home during the Hyperinflation, and was saddened when elderly women who needed medicine could not pay for it and did not receive it. "I literally got sick from it . . . I could not go back. I could no longer tolerate watching as these elderly women were not able to buy [the medicines they needed] . . . That is the reason why I never became a business woman" (G/141a R/400, G/141b R/00). Dominated by the abstract rules of finan-cial and commercial capitalism, these shops seemed alien and inimical to neighborly relations of reciprocity.

Hildesheimers described going shopping in this business district as go-ing *into town* (*in die Stadt*): as if this were a space apart from their neigh-borhoods, even if the latter were topographically within the municipality of Hildesheim and just a few blocks away (G/60a R/40; see also Benjamin

1978: 36–40). Ulrich Gerke was born in 1920 to a poor, working-class family in the Nordstadt:

> To us, the center of town was *The Town*. One street was Hoher Weg. Back then it was called *The Stroll*. Young people met there and otherwise you did not go into town. What would one do there otherwise? We did not go to the bars, and were too young anyway, and shopping, yes, when mother or father bought something, they went on their own. (G/89a R/30)

It was therefore with considerable arrogance that Maria Rolf's father referred to Hoher Weg as *their* shopping street. They owned a store close by. They had business relations with the shopkeepers on Hoher Weg (G/71a R/70). And they had the income to shop in them as if they were corner stores. By contrast, Johanna Ernst's family produced their own food in the garden and courtyard, had bread delivered from village shops, purchased their remaining groceries from corner stores in their corner neighborhood, and bought only the fabric for clothing which was then made for them by a seamstress who came to their home. When I asked Maria whether she had any reason to go into town, she did not understand my question at first, but when I mentioned Hoher Weg in particular, she responded: "Yes, that was the stroll."

To fully appreciate the stroll then, we must locate it in this cultural distinction between moral exchanges conducted in corner stores and non-moral, or even immoral, exchanges conducted in the business district around Hoher Weg. Taking the stroll was understood as an experience of modern, urban living, almost as if participants were visiting a foreign city, though the area was safely and conveniently encapsulated within provincial Hildesheim. From the perspective of young Hildesheimers, the older generation came into town rarely and for purely utilitarian reasons: to purchase the more expensive yet relatively durable necessities of life. The younger generation went for very different reasons: to test the waters of desire, to explore their options for the future, perhaps to make small purchases or overtures, and to whet an appetite that few yet dared to satisfy. Akin to the way they adjusted their headdress, Hildesheimers cautiously experimented with modernity by weaving it into the seemingly ordinary act of taking a leisurely walk down Hoher Weg; and by distancing themselves from it once again by returning to their corner neighborhoods.

Jewish Hands

Heinrich Weber added an element to the distinction between corner stores and this business district: antisemitism. His family purchased their day-to-day groceries "here in the area." They bought whatever they "needed," i.e., shoes, suits, and household items, "on the main street, where the businesses [still] are . . . . These shops, they were concentrated in town. And these shops were mostly in the hands of Jews."

Heinrich recounted how he and his neighbors would visit the *Slipper-Cinema* (*Puschenkino*) on Goslarstrasse, so nicknamed because it was so near their neighborhood that they could visit it in house slippers. By contrast, he did not experience the other cinemas as corner stores. The Amerkanische Lichtspiele, in particular, played on common attitudes about modernization: that the United States was "miles ahead [of Germany] in every area." Located at the north end of the stroll close to the train station, this big cinema had a buffet where you could drink beer and eat cake, and though the latter was not very successful, the cinema itself was often so full that you had to stand. Heinrich's parents, like most Hildesheimers of the prewar era, had nothing to do with this symbol of modernity. If they had any inclination to spend money on such activities at all, they went to the theater (G/145a R/25). Like the stroll itself, establishments like the cinema appealed most to the youthful avant-garde. Heinrich insisted that he was not an antisemite, but he added that this was a Jewish establishment (G/146b R/275).

Heinrich explained the concentration of Jewish economic power in the central business district by the fact that Jews had not been permitted to be craftsmen and so had to work in commerce and banking, all of which boomed in the 1870s. After their emancipation in the mid-nineteenth century, the Jews of Hildesheim were free to live in any district of town, and by the 1920s, a fair number had moved to the business district, causing Jews to be significantly overrepresented there (Addicks 1988: 15). Several of my interview partners of Jewish or half-Jewish descent did, in fact, run clothing stores in the central business district. Herself Catholic, Frieda Stolzenberg lived on one of these streets in the main shopping district: "I have the memory that there were one-third Catholics, one-third Protestants and one-third Jews living in Hildesheim during my childhood. This cannot be correct. There were only five hundred Jewish families back then. But there were many in [our] area" (G/18a R/200). Jörg Schneider (1998: II. 11) has recently confirmed that Hildesheim's Jews were disproportionately represented among bankers, merchants (particularly: clothes, fabrics, furs, shoes, livestock, laundry), doctors, lawyers, and the rich. He argued that this dissonant socio-economic pattern not only ensured a certain degree of internal group cohesion but also provided fuel for the antisemitic fire.

When I asked Günther Seidner if there were any Jews in his neighborhood, he replied in the negative, explaining that they resided on the "business streets." He then corrected himself, saying that the wealthier Jews lived there while the poorer Jews (many being recent immigrants from Eastern

Europe) lived in the Neustadt (G/80a R/30). The large department store Alsberg "was in Jewish hands" (G/90b R/160). The Jewish Dux family ran a bank not far up the street, adding fuel to the antisemitic fire of an imagined world conspiracy of Jewish finance capital, in spite of the fact that most of the banks in Hildesheim were in fact in Gentile "hands." It seemed to some Hildesheimers that all of the stores in this business district, or at least the larger ones, were owned and controlled by Jews (G/80a R/90, G/101b R/230, G/186b R/60).

Dietrich Vornfett was born in 1907 to a well-to-do Jewish family who could afford to shop anywhere they wished in Hildesheim (or Hannover). Whereas his father had all his clothing made for him by hand every six months in the latest fashion, most of the time Dietrich purchased ready-made clothing. He had an account at Löwenstein & Freudental that he paid four times a year. He described shopping there in quite positive terms. "It was the largest clothing store in Hildesheim, had four floors and even a café, which was very new back then." One reason why he knew it so well was that his best friend worked there and he often visited him at the store. When he would arrive, the sales staff would tell him: "Mr. Vornfett, we have something new!" (G/152a R/150). In keeping with antisemitic stereo-types, several interview partners suggested that Löwenstein & Freudenthal sold inexpensive, mass-produced, ready-to-wear clothing on sale that were of "shoddy" (ramsch) quality. Some also presumed that the store only sold women's clothing (G/80a R/85; see also G/81a R/170, G/140b R/30, G/148a R/330) according to the antisemitic logic that Jewish men seek to lead Christian women astray. More than any other single establishment in Hildesheim, this store came to represent the Jewish quality of this business district.

The stroll stands at the core of a critical cultural distinction between a corner neighborhood and the modern world. Interwar Hildesheimers experi-enced the former as reliably concrete, reciprocal, integrating, and under their direct control: a *life world* that human beings could safely inhabit because it responded to their agency and met their needs. They experienced the latter as abstract, alienating, vaguely sinister, and vaguely Jewish: a *sys-tem* inimical and dangerous because it seemed so very unresponsive, espe-cially during the many recent crises (cf. Bergerson 2002a; Habermas 1981; Harootunian 2000; Schutz and Luckmann 1973). Here I do not wish to offer any legitimacy to this ideology of hate by reinforcing antisemitic lies about the Jews of Hildesheim: the center of town was not really Jewish or sinister. And given the fact that only some of my interview partners made this association explicitly, I suspect that many Hildesheimers ignored it when they went into town to shop or stroll. Nonetheless, I wish to suggest that antisemitic lies were able to crystallize and grow around that grain of experience shaped by the stroll. Ardent Nazis relied on a pre-existing cultural logic to make their fabulous antisemitic claims seem plausible.

This habitus predated and was relatively independent of Nazi barbarism. The reader may recall from the preceeding chapter that Frieda had mentioned annoying the little girl who lived above her. That family was not only fellow merchants in the central business district and the Stolzenberg's landlords; they were also Jews. Perhaps postwar sensitivity to antisemitism had inspired Frieda to depict this relationship as if it were only a prank of youth, thus giving her a way to disguise an underlying prejudice; but sensitive to this danger, Frieda reassured me that her teasing was done out of friendship (G/18a R/200). When I later asked Frieda what had happened to her Jewish neighbors, she responded curtly: "they disappeared." She then expressed general sympathy for the suffering of the Jews in retrospect (G/20a R/160), a telling shift from personal to collective memory designed to disguise the fact that she did not know the fate of these particular Jewish neighbors.

Perhaps Frieda, like many of her contemporaries, harbored latent antisemitism, feelings that were perhaps reinforced by twelve years of Nazi indoctrination. Yet ideologies like antisemitism cannot be artificially isolated from their cultural context in everyday life. Indeed, this study departs from a different point entirely. Whatever else they may have believed, what matters is what they habitually did: which behaviors they adopted and with what effects on their neighbors. The Stolzenbergs were not of noble blood, but they imagined their niveau through the careful selection of neighborhoods and neighbors through distancing themselves from the Jewish merchant-landlord "under" whom they lived in the central business district and moving to the Oststadt to live as pseudo-aristocrats. It is hardly surprising, then, that Frieda's family did not notice the deportation of their Jewish neighbors: they had already imagined the irrelevance of those same neighbors twenty years earlier.

Narrative interviews decades after the fact can hardly answer the question of whether antisemitism was latent or overt, limited or universal, in pre-Nazi Germany. But they do demonstrate the process by which ordinary people could make pre-existing customs of conviviality more overtly antisemitic. Frieda felt at home in the Oststadt, where her family mingled with Catholic aristocrats, not in the Altstadt, where they lived under Jews. When Heinrich Weber took the stroll in the central business district, he cultivated a Nazi identity. Rebelling against the egalitarian Weimar Republic, he laid claim to power and status in the new Third Reich. The stroll was thus one critical site at which local adolescents accustomed themselves to making antisemitic principles into antisemitic habits. Yet because Heinrich did so through conviviality, he could also nazify everyday life without disturbing his own self-understanding as an ordinary person. When Helmut Rabitz dismissed the stroll as "a harmless matter" (G/52a R/225), we should realized that he was speaking both as a self-identified, early member of the Nazi party and as an ordinary Hildesheimer, insistent on myths of normalcy. It is this kind of doublethink that made his eigensinn such a powerful tool for political mobilization in provincial towns like Hildesheim.

4 | A Moral Community

THE NEIGHBORHOODS OF interwar Hildesheim were spaces of transgression. Conviviality felt very personal and integrating. Friendship was by definition private and intimate; neighborliness shared in these qualities, to a lesser degree. Yet conviviality could also feel very alienating and political. Through friends and neighbors, Hildesheimers laid claim to power and status in the local public sphere. They also publicized their private affairs, challenged others with their political beliefs, and even tried to compel their neighbors to comply. In all its aspects then, conviviality bore the evidence that Hildesheimers shaped their lived reality. For good reason, then, interwar Hildesheimers associated the politics of neighborliness with dirt. This chapter will explore the more overtly political uses of neighborliness as well as the mechanism through which ordinary Hildesheimers restored moral order thereafter. Hildesheimers did not balk at using neighborly relations to actively promote their agendas for power and politics. Instead, they relied on cleansing rituals to purge the neighborhood of all memory of politicization and restore normalcy.

Street Politics

My interview partners suggested that politics was a matter for *those up there* while they were just *ordinary Hildesheimers*. They used the term *politizieren* to refer to the act of seriously discussing political issues. Some did so with very good friends or close relatives with whom they shared common convictions (e.g., G/12b R/110, G/148b R/140), but like the tables at local pubs where groups of men regularly met to play cards (a *Stammtisch*), these friends could discuss politics because friends tended to find friends who were like them. Self-selecting by definition, friendship actually insulated Hildesheimers from serious political disagreements.

Most of my interview partners denied having discussed politics with neighbors. In the atmosphere of civil war that permeated the Weimar Republic, direct forms of discourse about party politics could too easily have led to open conflict. In the atmosphere of economic uncertainty and status competition, even direct claims to power and status were too readily dismissed as false arrogance. For these same reasons, however, Hildesheimers felt the need to imagine a better status for themselves and make their political views known to their neighbors. The informal customs of conviviality were perfectly suited to accomplish these contradictory ends: to express the political self behind the veil of the everyday.

In recent decades, historians have expanded the definition of the political to encompass power relations, identity constructions, and cultural processes of everyday life. While most histories of Weimar street politics have tended to focus on the extensive, formal mobilization of the masses for politics or violence (Diehl 1977; Fritzsche 1988, 1990, 1998), in this study I consider instead the more subtle, informal style of symbolic discourse about politics and identity that permeated neighborly relations. My interview partners were very forthcoming about politics in this everyday sense. Categorically normal, it has been easy and convenient to dismiss semiotic politics as eigensinn rather than recognizing it as a means to herrschaft. Although the evidence is anecdotal and still somewhat limited, it suggests that Hildesheimers engaged proactively in a none-too-subtle form of street politics.

Hildesheimers knew a lot about their neighbors. Heinrich Weber explained that he knew to which Christian confession they belonged because each church held services at different times. Catholics left around 1:45. His father used to joke around lunchtime: "Right when I try to close my eyes for a minute, then [those church bells] start to jingle again!" Heinrich then remembered one family in particular. They left for church individually: first the children and then the parents. It was this "extended" departure, he explained, that drew attention to them and therefore to their Catholic confession. "Otherwise no one noticed who was Catholic or who was Protestant. That was of no significance to the children" of his corner neighborhood (G/144b R/30). He also knew their class: their father was a master artisan like his father. Later he added that Hildesheimers announced their class during neighborly intercourse through clothes, non-monetary exchanges, and the titles used while greeting. You could guess where men worked, Heinrich explained, because you saw their wives bringing them lunch every day (G/145a R/130). You could also draw conclusions about confession (G/135a R/55) and class from the school that one attended. Given these institutional differences, physical proximity was thus sufficient to ensure that Hildesheimers knew roughly to which milieu their neighbors belonged: working class, Catholic, or Protestant middle class. From this sociology, they could also infer the general political orientation of their neighbors.

And yet this process was not as passive as Heinrich implied. In large part, Hildesheimers knew the politics of their neighbors because their neighbors wanted to announce their private attitudes in the local public sphere. They did so by flying a flag or by wearing a uniform, of which there were many options in the 1920s. This was not a particularly new phenomenon. Hildesheimers had learned to publicly display their private affairs during the Second Empire. Back then, Hildesheimers had tolerated a diversity of public symbols as part of an historicist aesthetic of organic accumulation. Yet in the aftermath of defeat, revolution, and civil war, flags and uniforms expressed one's persistent commitment to won or lost causes. The presence of diverse symbols was disappointing only in comparison to romanticized memories of coordinated decorations from the Wilhelmine era. To be sure, flag-bearers and uniform-wearers hid their politicizing behind the veil of the everyday, but in the process they politicized conviviality.

Ulrich Gerke used to go shopping for several adults in his building, including for a widow who had lost a son in the First War. "To thank us she would let us in and we would be allowed to look in her closet." If she was well-tempered that day, "then she would say very softly: 'Shall I show you something beautiful?'" She would then lead them to her closet. "There hung the uniform of her fallen boy: a uniform of the Hussars. She was very proud of it. We *had to* take a look at the uniform." Since she presented it to Ulrich as something extraordinary, it was easy for him to remember many decades later precisely how it hung in her closet.

> Look and then go away. For the children [this was] *interesting.* [There were] no more colorful uniforms between the wars. In Hildesheim, there were just two barracks with men training to be policemen. For me, that was a historical experience: a uniform from the Imperial era. (G/85a R/455, G/85b R/00, my emphasis)

Ulrich described this experience alternately as a burdensome obligation ("had to") and as a pleasurable reward for services rendered ("interesting"). Ulrich thus reiterated in memory what he had experienced in history: her momentary and inappropriate claim to status, and perhaps statement of politics, was disguised as so much colorful history.

The custom of wearing uniforms as ordinary clothing has a long history in Germany, dating back at least to the Prussian monarchs of the eighteenth century. This kind of behavior certainly became more important during the reign of Wilhelm II and in Hildesheim probably after his ceremonial visit to town on 31 October 1900. Similarly, Heinrich Weber recounted how, during the first years of the new century, he and his friends had admired the soldiers in uniform whom they saw while drilling on the parade grounds and whose behavior they imitated (G/143a R/325). My oldest interview partners often showed me pictures of how they had worn military-style clothing as children, especially sailors' suits (e.g., D/1304). During the

First War, these kinds of symbolic, public announcements of private, political affiliations acquired cultic characteristics. Ulrich's neighbor had been able to gain public status by the fact that her son had walked the streets of Hildesheim in a Hussar's uniform. When he then died for the Fatherland, she most likely announced his and her sacrifice in the daily paper, at least in part as a means to lay claim to the prestige associated with her sacrifice. After the war, she could no longer gain prestige in such a straightforward fashion. She no longer had a son to wear the uniform, and in any case, the dramatic change of regimes and political culture after 1918 undermined her cultural capital, encouraging her to keep it locked in a closet. Under these circumstances, publicly announcing her personal tragedy became all the more vital to her sense of self.

At this stage, we should take notice of the curious position into which children were placed in interwar Hildesheim. In prior chapters, children loomed large in stories of neighborliness, and not simply as a result of the fact that my interview partners were mostly describing their childhood experiences. Children were the most readily visible inhabitants of these semi-private, semi-public spaces: they played on the street, greeted their neighbors, took the stroll, and so on. Able to cross into the private sphere of neighbors (through fences, past doors) with less sense of intrusion by the public, they served as the medium through which neighbors got to know each other better. Indirectly responsible for a certain amount of neighborhood solidarity (E. Anderson 1990: 145–46), they thus came to represent neighborliness as such.

Incompletely socialized, children often did not understand the stakes of political symbols and accepted the meanings of such things as uniforms in the terms provided to them by adults. Generational hierarchies thus made it relatively easy for adults to gain the kind of satisfaction they desired from a public display of their secret selves without running the risk of being challenged for their audacity. Because he was a child, it was unlikely that Ulrich would have criticized this widow for laying claim to status that did not belong to her properly, no less for being romantically attached to the Second Empire, or even for being insufficiently committed to democracy. No wonder, then, that this widow offered Ulrich hard-won glimpses of a beautiful uniform after he had fulfilled his neighborly service to her. As a child, not only would he have never dared to accuse her of inappropriate eigensinn but he also carried news of her status into the local public sphere on her behalf.

In effect, this uniform was functioning like yet another flag in a land filled with many competing options. Black, white, and red horizontal stripes stood for Prussian monarchists and German nationalists, while black, red, and gold stood for Weimar republicans. Red was used by some socialists and all communists while black, white, and red—in the arrangement of the swastika—was used by the Nazis. And then there was red and yellow, the colors of the town of Hildesheim, the flag of choice among some locals who wished to circumvent the contentious debate entirely by flying the flag of their particularist heimat. Each flag represented different political institutions and affiliations, and none held hegemonic legitimacy during the life of the Weimar Republic. When selecting one of these flags to hang from one's home, Hildesheimers were not only broadcasting their private political beliefs into the local public sphere but were also taking part in a largely symbolic, yet volatile debate with their neighbors about the nature of the German polity. Meanwhile, this chaotic multiplicity of flags flying in their neighborhood only served to remind ordinary Hildesheimers of barely contained animosities (following Stegge 1994): a German tragedy that they experienced as personally dangerous because it took place in their neighborhood.

Theodora Algermissen associated conflicts over flags with political radicals and street violence. She was the daughter of a master craftsman who was also a member of a veteran officers' association (*Reichsbund deutsche Offiziere*). Her father's politics were German nationalist. She claimed not to be so very interested in politics, though she did associate the Nordstadt with the communist proletariat. She found her way behind the train station from time to time because a girlfriend lived there. She could recognize the wage laborers because their clothes were old and their bodies hungry, because the boys wore school caps that revealed the school and class to which they belonged, and because of the flags they bore. She described how, by 1930 or 1931 in "some" areas, she saw members of the *Reichsbanner* (the republican, social-democratic paramilitary organization) bearing flags: "three arrows on a red flag . . . hanging from their bicycles and their windows, so it [their politics] was clear [*damit's aus und herum*]. The opposite party was the swastikas." For her part, Theodora flew the black, white, and red flag of the defunct Wilhelmine Empire from her bicycle, "because my father was German national." She laughed. "I did that for maybe a half of a year, then I got thrashed by a Reichsbanner." Theodora had been riding her bike in the Nordstadt with her flag mounted. "And there was a group of kids, some rowdies with bicycles and little Reichsbanner flags." Theodora was around twelve years old, these boys sixteen or seventeen. She presumed that they belonged either to a socialist or a communist organization. She heard them say: "Oh, here comes a Black-white-red!" One dismounted, asking, "Whatever gave you the idea?"—that is, of riding into their neighborhood with that flag. They ripped it from her bike, and she rode away. "They wanted to get physical [*doch recht handgreiflich*] because I defended myself at first." As far as Theodora was concerned, these boys attacked "because I had a different opinion than they did, which I announced [*dokumentierte*] with my black, white, and red flag." She then clarified, laughing, that she did not have any opinion in fact: she was merely following the opinions of her father. "It was just a game for me. . . . I believe it was not a game for them." After this incident, however, Theodora decided not to replace the flag on her bicycle (G/1b R/340).

Theodora's laughter broke the flow of her narratives about neighborliness in memory, just as civil war had been on the verge of exploding in them historically. In spite of customs of conviviality that praised civility, and in spite of her insistence that she had not been involved in politics seriously, she had engaged in a rancorous yet symbolic debate about the legitimacy of the Weimar Republic. She clearly knew that her flag announced her identity to her neighbors. She may have forgotten about its significance by the time she rode into the Nordstadt to visit her friend, but at the very least, she had chosen to mount a flag on her bicycle: out of a sense of non-conformity to the Weimar Republic, conformity to her father's politics, or both. More likely, this little flag was her (and her father's) way to lay claim to status and power in her neighborhood as well as being a semiotic substitute for direct political engagement. In the turbulent 1920s, such tactics of eigensinn easily led to verbal or physical conflict and, more significantly, undermined Theodora's sense of normalcy: her desperate desire to imagine that politics was just a game, that she was just an ordinary girl. So she acted as if that flag was only circumstantially present on her bike. Once the Weimar political crisis intruded violently into her lived reality, she chose to fly no flag at all.

Theodora's claims that she was really not very interested in politics, and that she hung this flag because of her father's convictions, are useful to historians not as an objective assessment of whether Hildesheimers were typically moderate in their politics (as they claimed) but as a window into typical experiences and ways of dealing with the contentiousness of Weimar politics. Theodora inhabited her neighborhood *as if* it were divorced from the kinds of political upheavals that ultimately destroyed the Weimar Republic. Most of my interview partners made it seem as if others had been the ones to introduce political contention into Hildesheim. This commitment to her own normalcy did not prevent Theodora from participating in politics actively, even when she was a little girl. Her strategies for herrschaft and tactics of eigensinn became undesirable only when that open secret was publicly challenged, which Theodora then experienced as the surprising intrusion of politics into her otherwise ordinary life. By hanging no flag at all, Theodora effectively retreated even further into that surreal fantasy of normalcy.

It is hard to tell from the interview data alone whether my interview partners were accurate when they described Hildesheim as relatively free from street violence during the Weimar Republic. Rather, it tells us more about the residents' perception of street politics and Theodora's all too typical response to it: they attempted to seek out normalcy. Theodora's self-imposed isolation from politics left that Republic undefended in its hour of need. Her contribution to the flag debate had helped to undermine the stability of the Weimar Republic in the first place. Yet thanks to the customs of conviviality through which both street politics and normalcy were negotiated, the problem of the Weimar Republic appeared to be a matter for political elites, not for ordinary girls like Theodora. Still, Theodora was not as naïve as she wanted to seem: she interrupted herself with surprised, awkward laughter when she noticed the contradiction between her claims to normalcy and her actual agency. Clearly, street politics in interwar Hildesheim was dirty business. It broke the rules of civility and normalcy by politicizing the neighborhood.

Running the Vote

Hildesheimers also engaged outright in dirty politics. They could and did use their personal knowledge of their neighbors to influence the electoral process. Closely linked to local traditions of corporate representation, these customs of conviviality walked a fine line of electoral propriety. They reveal the degree to which residents could make politics part and parcel of their daily lives without undermining their sense of being just ordinary Hildesheimers.

Consider the election of representatives from Moritzberg to the Hildesheim town council in 1911, the first in which the voters of the newly incorporated village could participate. As in other districts, a citizen's association (*Bürgerbezirksverein*) gathered at a local pub to discuss which two men should represent Moritzberg in the Hildesheim town council. Some Moritzbergers suggested that they should decide on one Catholic and one Protestant candidate in order to reflect the confessional composition of the neighborhood. Franz Engelke, a bricklayer by trade who was active in the Christian trade union, called for the election of a worker because no worker had yet been represented on the Hildesheim town council, even though two-thirds of the Moritzberg population belonged to the proletariat. Most were employed at the Wetzell rubber factory. After some complications relating to his police record, Engelke was elected to one of the seats and a master butcher to the other (Knott 1984); but the outcome is not as relevant here as the process. The three-way division of Hildesheim's political culture created a complication in an election for only two representatives.

Corporate notions of representation clearly had deep roots in Hildesheim. These Moritzbergers knew which camp their neighbors belonged to and used this knowledge publicly and instrumentally to negotiate what they considered fair representation of all elements of their community. That knowledge was so obvious to all neighbors that 31 out of 440 Moritzbergers (14.2 percent) placed their vote orally without sensing any invasion of privacy or loss of democratic legitimacy. On the grass-roots level, the only issues at stake were whether the local political body accurately represented this diverse social order and how to best realize that ideal.

According to liberal theory, political decisions were supposed to be a completely private affair, independent of local social pressures. Even under the old constitutional framework of the Second Empire, the state provided local municipalities with guidelines to preserve the fairness and secrecy of the electoral process. The magistrates admonished voting wardens on 2 January 1912 (SAH 102/84, "Nachdem wir Sie zu der am Freitag . . . ," p. 3) to organize the space of their voting area so that voters could place their ballots into an envelope in privacy, either in a separate room in which only one voter entered at a time, or at the very least at a table separated from the rest of the room by a divider. The Weimar Republic followed suit with additional guidelines designed to prevent electoral manipulation on the local level. In preparation for the elections of 1920, the *Reichsgesetzblatt* (93: 723–26, §47 Reichswahlordnung IV, Stimmabgabe, in SAH 102/87) made it clear that any voter could enter the voting room, but none was permitted to hold speeches there. Furthermore, only the voting wardens were to advise the voters about the business of voting. On 8 September 1930, the magistrates reminded voting wardens that posters and other forms of political propaganda were forbidden from the voting room (SAH 102/91, "Nachdem wir Sie für die am Sonntag . . . "). These procedures were supposed to enable voting wardens and their assistants to protect the electoral process from both the excesses of party propagandists and the prying eyes of neighbors.

In reality, there was a contradiction inherent in the electoral process at this most fundamental level. Those most interested in the political system and most attuned to the politics of their neighbors were also most likely to be those who served as wardens in their district, and the state relied upon their familiarity with their neighbors to ensure the smooth administration of elections. In order to verify that each person voted only once, voting wardens recorded which persons had voted. For the elections of 2 January 1912 and 6 June 1920, the magistrates and the *Reichsgesetztblatt* respectively advised voting wardens to demand identification from voters whom they did not know or "who had just moved in." If they suspected that the person was listed somewhere else, they were told to advise that person that "every voter can only vote once . . . and only in one voting district." These procedural safeguards presumed that voting wardens recognized most voters from their neighborhoods; for the rest, they were aided by voting cards. In large part, neighborly familiarity provided the very rationale for their office; but voting wardens knew more than was appropriate for neutral moderation. They knew the party affiliations of their neighbors. They also knew which neighbors had not voted in a given election. Putting these facts together, local party loyalists, who were likely to be serving as wardens, could pressure otherwise disinterested voters to cast their vote in the hope of giving their party a little edge.

As a child during the Weimar Republic, Franz Meissner (b. 1903) and his peers got used to the idea of political unrest because they read reports of street fights in Berlin, Hamburg, and Frankfurt, and because so many parties competed so publicly for votes during elections. "All the young boys" followed the results of elections "the same way we were curious to know about football matches." Curious, they also entered voting rooms to investigate the electoral process for themselves, even though they were underage. On the one hand, they were chased out by soldiers; "on the other hand, they · always tried to argue with us" (G/164a R/100). Trying to convince voters to support a particular political program or party while they went to vote was illegal and unethical. Trying to convince a neighbor to support a particular cause could instigate a civil disturbance. But these children were not voters, and were more readily influenced than their parents. A member of the quasi-fascist paramilitary *Stahlhelm*, Thekla Mestmacher's father stood outside the Martin Luther Church in the Nordstadt (where they and their neighbors voted) holding the black, white, and red flag of German nationalism. Opposite him stood his communist neighbors with their red flags. The latter then boycotted his butcher shop to punish him for his politics, though only temporarily.

While discussing her father's leisure-time activities, Ulrike Volkmann explained how her father had been an active leader in the Catholic Center Party. The *Zentrum* loomed large in her life as a result, even when she was a child. Voting in her district took place in her school, close to her house. She hung broadsides for the party before elections. During elections, she mobilized her neighbors as a *runner*. "You knew already, at least we knew in any case, who would vote for the Center party for certain in our parish. . . . Since we knew the area there pretty well, we each took one street . . . where we also knew all of the people." Shortly before voting closed, she ran to the homes of those neighbors, who belonged to this core constituency but had not yet voted, and urged them to vote. Ulrike's family took it upon themselves to enforce political participation among the Catholics in their neighborhood and used their position as voting wardens to lead their political party to electoral success. This dimension of neighborly relations perhaps helps account for the traditionally high levels of voter participation in Germany. As Ulrike explained, she did this because "we knew that we would lose a vote otherwise" (G/60b R/16, G/61a R/145). More to the point: running for votes influenced neighborly relations for their own sake. Ulrike's father served as warden not only of the electoral process but also of political respectability among his Catholic neighbors. By mobilizing convivial knowledge for political gain, he laid claim to power and status among those Catholic neighbors whose opinions he valued most. From the perspective of life in the neighborhood, runners politicized conviviality behind the veil of the ordinary.

Indirect evidence from the archives corroborates the likelihood of the increased use of neighborly relations in the electoral process in interwar Hildesheim. On 8 September 1930, town magistrates found it necessary to caution voting wardens not to evidence their own political persuasions in the execution of their duties: for instance, by wearing political symbols. The town reminded voting wardens that they must "enjoy the trust of the whole population" (SAH 102/91, "Nachdem wir Sie für die am Sonntag . . . ") On 30 December 1911, before the election of 1912, the names of the voting wardens and their substitutes had been printed, presumably at the request of the town administration, in the *Hildesheimer Allgemeine Zeitung* (HAZ 357: 11) next to the voting location for the elections. They repeated this procedure on 29 May 1920 for the election of 1920, in the same daily paper (119: 3). For the critical election of 9 September 1930, however, the *Hildesheimische Zeitung* (HeZ 209: 4) and the *Hildesheimer Volksblatt* (HVb 210: 3) did not print this information, again presumably on the request of the town administration. By making the voting wardens anonymous, town notables were perhaps trying to reduce the influence of informal social relations on electoral outcomes.

This shift in practice may also have been a response of a traditional elite to the threat of populism. Local notables had monopolized the role of the voting warden during the Second Empire, as one node on a local network of political influence and social prestige. In the 1920s, the lower classes learned how to use informal mechanisms of neighborliness for their own political purposes. They took their place next to notables at these posts as electoral wardens and their assistants (cf. SAH 102/84, 87, 91). The appeals to anonymity in 1930 may thus have been a response on the part of the traditional elite, who still played a significant role in the local bureaucracy, to reassert their control over the local political process and to reclaim status, now in the modern terms of the professional, governmental expert. Ulrike's father was a prime example of this challenge from below. An active Catholic, he was an assistant clerk at the post office. He used his subaltern role as voting warden instrumentally to create social capital for himself in his neighborhood, and he hoped, through the electoral success of his party, to affect the German political system as well. This interpretation also fits what we already know about the irregular growth of invasive government over the course of the Weimar Republic as well as the arrogance of the traditional German elite.

In one sense, running the vote corresponded to the multifaceted logic of conviviality. As a liminal space in which one negotiated the boundaries between public and private, it was easy for Hildesheimers to use one against the other. In another sense, it corresponded to the local political culture of corporatism. One could conclude simply that Ulrike's family used their public knowledge of political affiliations to ensure the fair representation of all members of the community. Yet Ulrike knew that there was something transgressive or dirty about this habit. When I asked Ulrike if other parties had runners, she responded that she was not sure: her family had little contact outside the Catholic milieu. Running for votes was an open secret among interwar Hildesheimers. It could not be conceded as a general phenomenon because that would reveal an unwelcome degree of conflict and self-promotion in their moral community as well as a degree of active participation in the political system that undermined the myth of Hildesheim's normalcy. For this reason, perhaps, adults gave the task of running for votes to children: their presence on the street evoked a sense of conviviality that masked the invasion of the private sphere by neighbors. The presumed innocence of a little girl gave vote-running a veneer of the ordinary.

Scat

Hildesheim's neighborhoods were dirtied by struggles for status, power, and politics. The classic interpretation of cultural pollution in German studies is *Life Is Like a Chicken Coop Ladder,* by American folklorist Alan Dundes (1989). He argued that Germans are only superficially concerned with cleanliness and order. In reality, Germans of all classes, and at least since the Reformation, have reveled in filth (e.g., 103). This collective anal obsession promoted the traits of inwardness, obedience to authority, violence, imperialism, and antisemitism. Dundes explained the paradox of the death camp in the same terms: as a sewage disposal facility for "the dirty Jew." He is not entirely off base in the latter interpretation; and it is also true that most interwar Hildesheimers bathed only once a week, usually on Saturday in preparation for church, and did so in the washing kitchen in the same basins used to launder their clothing (cf. G/96a R/95, G/96b R/70; Dundes 104). Yet the collective subconscious that Dundes allegedly identified decontextualizes folklore from the only sphere in which it can hold meaning: everyday life. Trapped in the folkloric stereotypes he claimed to be investigating, his "feces thesis" is a dangerous example of the *Sonderweg* metanarrative in which German neurotics are compared, implicitly or explicitly, to well-adjusted Anglo-Americans in order to blame the singular evil of the Nazi era on an identifiable group of perpetrators: the Germans (cf. Blackbourn and Eley 1984).

In her seminal work on contagion, *Purity and Danger,* anthropologist Mary Douglas (1966: 3, see also vii–viii) warns us against reading the cultural expression of anal eroticism as evidence of a population of anal erotics. She suggests as an alternative that every system of classification gives rise to anomalies: an object, idea, or fact that confounds or contradicts those cherished categories. Pollution serves as that readily identifiable label for those people or things that do not fit. Cleaning, in turn, represents a culturally sanctioned mechanism to discipline these dangerous things-out-of-place. It is the white magic that restores the pattern and its meanings. Cleaning evokes a feeling of order because it imposes systematicity over the inherently untidy experience of daily life. It puts people and things "back" in their proper place, preserving or altering social and power relations in the process. It re-establishes a moral community.

If cleaning is political, so too is politics dirty. Transgressive behaviors can seem contaminating, particularly those associated with conflict. Dirt is more likely to accumulate in those arenas in which there is a large scope for discrepancy between ideal and actual behavior, or where there are conflicting aims within the same culture (37–41, 97, 131). Moreover, people tend to focus attention on "free-lance benign contagion" in eras of rapid social change or when formal authority is weak, poorly defined, or being contested by rival segments (110, 114, 125). All this is usually the case in politics.

And it was particularly the case in interwar Hildesheim. Faced with the collapse and inversion of the formal institutions of the Second Empire, ritual cleaning offered an informal mechanism to restore a sense of moral order (see also V. Turner 1969: 160–68). Yet the neighborhoods of interwar Hildesheim were especially prone to the accumulation of pollution because of the way Hildesheimers behaved in the interwar years. As we have seen, the neighborhood was one immediate context in which ordinary Hildesheimers laid claim to status and power, cultivated imaginary identities for themselves, selectively integrated and alienated neighbors into their lived reality, challenged existing authorities, introduced modern habits of mass consumption, and even pressured their neighbors to take political action. Yet they acted as if they were just the passive pawns of grander kings.

Pollution was dangerous in interwar Hildesheim, then, because it attracted unwanted attention to this contradiction. The evidence of pollution undermined the open secret of normalcy. Moreover, eigensinn seemed like black magic insofar as it actually challenged the social and political order. Interwar Hildesheimers compensated for it, too, with rituals of purification. By cleaning up, they distracted attention away "from the social and moral aspects of a situation by focusing on a simple material matter" (Douglas 1966: 139, see also 95–114, 132, 162). The public, moral offense was the politicization of everyday life: the use of conviviality to lay claim to status, power, or politics, to reshape the given world into a selfish world. The simple, material matter was that this pollution had to be "instantly scrubbed out by ritual" (137). Privately orchestrated yet publicly supervised, ritual purges of the neighborhood erased all evidence of negotiation, transgression, and agency.

My interview partners all insisted that their street fronts were always clean, but this claim is impossible to verify; and in any case, it is culturally and historically relative (Douglas 1966: 2; cf. del Monte reprinted 1974: 19). Rather than being measures of actual cleanliness, their anecdotes about scat reveal the cultural logic of neighborliness in interwar Hildesheim. *Scat* (shorthand for those many forms of socially and biologically produced pollution) was indeed a matter of serious communal concern in Hildesheim, but not for the reasons Dundes suggested. By cleansing their front stoop, street, courtyard, and stairwell of its actual dirt, interwar Hildesheimers erased all cultural evidence that they too had tried to colonize everyday life. Cleansing served as an informal solution to the problem of the continual state of emergency that characterized modernity: to find culturally innovative mechanisms for managing the chaos (adapting Fritzsche 1996; Harootunian 2000). The Hildesheimers' concern for scat did not reflect a psychosocial dysfunction but its cultural-political function. It persisted not so much due to socialization from above as utility from below. Ever pragmatic, interwar Hildesheimers used their scat as a cultural medium for preserving normalcy.

The Stoop

Dirt accumulates. According to local police ordinances, homeowners were responsible for keeping the public thoroughfares in front of their property accessible to public traffic (Gerland 1908: 39–41; *Polizeiverordnung über die Regelung des Verkehrs* 1932: 44–53). If the owner did not reside in the building, the resident of the ground floor had to assume this responsibility. In particular, this meant removing any dirt, garbage, snow, ice, weeds, and so on from the sidewalk, gutter, sewer grates, and street or plaza up to the middle of the street or six meters into the plaza each morning without damaging that infrastructure. Snow and ice had to be removed from both immediately, or by the following morning if the snow had fallen at night. Should the stoop or street suddenly become dirty, it had to be cleaned immediately. Once a week, on Saturday or the day before a holiday, the street had to be cleaned more carefully. The specific hour by which this task had to be fulfilled changed over the years and during different seasons, but fell sometime between seven and nine in the morning and four to six in the evening on Saturday or a holiday. A supplemental phase of cleaning on Wednesdays, focusing more on the street than on the sidewalks, was added in the late 1920s.

The town assumed only minimal responsibility for cleaning public roadways and sidewalks. It did so only if neither owner nor resident existed, or if the street was neither cobbled nor paved (as if the property were located in the country). Sometimes public measures were misdirected. On 31 June 1931, a man working a sprayer accidentally drenched a woman chatting with a neighbor in her doorway (SAH 102/2997, 8784, 8786). More often, public measures were simply insufficient. Consider the issue of garbage. From 1910 on, the town collected and disposed of garbage while the owner provided a garbage container. These containers were brought out when the garbage was to be picked up and had to be brought back in within a half-hour of being emptied. Yet the collectors were not always efficient in their duties. "Back then, everyone swept their street," Käthe Stolte recalled. "I remember that every weekend, you know, or when the garbage people [had been] there, then my mother complained, '*Ach!* Today [they] were not at all careful. Now I have to sweep up half of the ashes again!'" Armed with the correct broom, Käthe's mother could get the street perfectly clean. Every one of her neighbors did this too. And "during the winter, when snow had fallen, then they also swept their sidewalks alternately" (G/185a R/60). In the end, the responsibility for neighborhood cleanliness fell to ordinary people.

Hildesheimers did not always clean as thoroughly as they should have. Police Chief Gebauer notified the Hildesheimer Aktienbrauerei on 4 January 1928 that town workmen had cleaned their street in the past by mistake and that the brewery had to clean the street in front of their property on their own or face prosecution. In 1925, the magistrates announced in several daily papers (such as: *HAb* 7 June, p. 1): "again and again, one can observe the bad habit of paper, the remains of fruit *per procura* being thrown onto the street." What is interesting is that in the 1920s, the state preferred to employ informal mechanisms of neighborliness to enforce propriety rather than formal modes of official authority. The town administration reminded its residents that the uncivilized act of littering was also illegal according to local police ordinances, and they threatened that the police would callously report offenders. As this threat implied, however, the state obviously preferred to rely on neighbors to monitor themselves. The same was true about cleaning the stoop. "It has been observed that street cleaning is executed unsatisfactorily at best. Here also the police have been notified to take close care in observing the street-cleaning stipulations and to report any defaults." In a version printed in the national-liberal *HAZ* on 6 June, the newspaper editor joined into the fray at this point. "Hopefully these measures will have the result that the face of our town, usually known for its cleanliness, will soon be friendlier again" (pp. 6, 12). Hildesheimers admonished their neighbors to abide by convivial norms.

Individual families were responsible for their individual stoops, but the act of purging the neighborhood of its pollution was both a community concern as well as a communal ritual. Theresa Stoffregen recalled that her family used to peel their potatoes in the courtyard behind their house, so they had to clean up the dirt afterwards. More precisely, her grandmother took care of cleaning up the dirt because Theresa's mother had other things to do in the home itself. Speaking of the sidewalk, Theresa said, "I swept it even as a child." Theresa laughed and then continued, "Back then, it was so cute around here. When the church bells rang Saturday evening at six, then everyone came out and swept. I thought that was so wonderful!" She laughed again. According to Dundes, the fact that interwar Hildesheimers described the collective rituals of communal purging as pleasurable reflects their anal fascination. There are better explanations.

For instance, these customs were pleasurable in part because they enabled residents to transcend their social differences within the neighborhood. Whereas most children played across confessional divisions in Hildesheim, Ulrike Volkmann told me that she (a Catholic) played with Protestant children only within the household community (where she held a position of authority as the daughter of the house manager) and not with those on the street. Similarly, her mother kept her distance from Protestant women. In part perhaps, this distinction was related to the fact that the Protestants living across the street were also socialists. At most her mother would greet those people who lived across the street, "and nothing else." Then again," she continued, "you did also meet sometimes." As an example of such a fortuitous encounter, Ulrike described sweeping the street. After I prodded her for more information, Ulrike admitted that women chatted while they swept, but only about everyday sorts of things, like how they felt that day (G/60b R/360). More like greeting than discourse per se, chatting while sweeping the street allowed neighbors to negotiate a proper balance between alienation and intimacy. During communal labor, when everyone was doing the same job, the potentially acrimonious cleavages of confession temporarily dissolved, evoking a community of neighbors.

These communal rituals of ablution revived the experience of volksgemeinschaft from the First War. On 19 January 1917, the *HAZ* criticized the town administration for not distributing sufficient quantities of ashes onto the snow. They preferred not to spread ashes on the streets because the process would only have packed the snow into ice. Due to the war, however, they lacked the manpower to clean the snow from the streets themselves. As a temporary solution, the town published an appeal in the daily papers on 12 February 1917 to parents to send their children into the streets to clear the snow, with privately owned tools if possible. This arrangement had the benefit of occupying the children who could not go to school for lack of fuel for heat, but the drawback that it kept some of the teachers and town bureaucrats busy watching so that they could supervise the children. Billed as a form of "helpful service for the Fatherland," this measure also reinforced the sense of an embattled community struggling collectively to maintain a moral order in a time of unprecedented violence (SAH 102/8360). Cleaning the stoop in interwar Hildesheim reinvigorated the civil peace of burgfrieden years after the foreign war had officially ceased—and the civil war had begun afresh.

Yet cleaning the street was also a mechanism by which one could lay claim to status and power in the neighborhood. Consider the issue of ownership. Heinrich Weber explained to me that street- and gutter-cleaning was the responsibility of property owners (G/146b R/255). Ulrike Volkmann told her account of sweeping the street (to another interviewer: SAH 904-1/17a R/470) just after she described the big, old house in which her family lived as managers. To be sure, it was often the landlords who concerned themselves with the neighborhood's appearance. Yet the issue at stake here was not so much a matter of property values, as property was not bought and sold as quickly in interwar Hildesheim as today: it was mostly transmitted between members of families. Rather, landlords commanded status among their neighbors. Arguably, they used their authority to enforce social controls not only to ensure the respectability of the corner neighborhood in which they held status, but also to reinforce and relish that status. From this perspective, cleaning the street was pleasurable for the owner or manager of the property because it gave them a rare opportunity to cultivate status in the neighborhood without seeming inappropriate. Käthe's parents took care of many such household duties for their landlords, even though they were not compensated for these responsibilities. "It was fun for them, no?" (G/185a R/60).

More accurately, interwar Hildesheimers made cleaning the stoop "fun" by using it as an opportunity to reinforce their herrschaft or undermine others with eigensinn. Consider the case of patriarchal power relations. Police ordinances that demanded punctual cleanliness presumed a patriarchal division of labor in which women, children, servants, or aged parents were available to conduct such duties while the male head of household worked for a wage. I got the sense that, befitting their relative isolation within the private sphere, women tended to do those chores that kept them physically within the home and therefore delegated these more public chores to other dependants when possible. In any case, Theresa suggested that women and girls were not the only ones who swept. "It depended on who wanted to. That is, it was mostly the old people who did this." It never came to conflicts, she continued, where the street ended up being neglected. But that was only the official narrative speaking. I had also asked Theresa if the neighbors chatted while sweeping. She explained that they did, but in an eigensinnig way: "It's your turn again?" and "Why does your brother not do this?" Theresa laughed again and then reiterated her typical reply: "He can do it also!" (G/191a R/200; see also SAH 904-1/17a R/470). Insofar as boys or older men sometimes took on the responsibility for ridding the private family of its share of public scat, it was in their capacity as a dependant of the male head of household, all of whom were feminized because of their dependency. Yet Theresa laughed while recounting this alternate narrative because she recognized all of a sudden the degree to which her personal memories of family life and neighborliness did not correspond to the official discourse of cooperative obedience.

An eigensinnig jibe helped make this chore into a pleasure. This was especially true in the case of public authorities. Even though they did not do the actual work, it was the police who ensured that the streets were *in Ordnung* (Lüddecke 1987): a German expression etymologically related to official regulations but connoting unofficial norms of propriety, cleanliness, and spatial organization (e.g., G/146b R/255). I asked Theresa Stoffregen what would happen had the streets not been swept. She explained that a policeman would walk through town to make sure that the streets were cleaned. "Back then, this would be punished. . . . But you had this cleanliness sensibility back then, no? Today people are indifferent" (G/191a R/235). Heinrich Weber argued similarly that, in his youth, Hildesheimers did not litter as they do today. "You would not believe the kind of orderliness that was prevalent here then. Oh yes! And you can well imagine all those who had been soldiers. They were trained in orderliness and cleanliness" (G/146b R/255). Littering was, in fact, illegal in town at least by 1932 (*Polizeiverordnung* 1932: 46). As in the example of familial patriarchy, however, we should not be distracted by this seemingly obvious, "typically German," identification with obedience, cleanliness, and public authority. This is only the official narrative. Heinrich Weber gets closer to the personal experience in this anecdote:

> Imagine for a moment what kind of power the policeman had on his beat. When he walked along the street, all the people opened their doors, brought out a broom and swept the street. That is how it still was, no? But the policeman, he just needed to turn around the corner for us. He came often in and out of our home because he sometimes had to clarify things that were probably not completely in step—what do I know, like cleaning the street for instance. (G/146b R/255)

The degree to which the state could use neighborliness to penetrate the private sphere was uncomfortable at best for ordinary Hildesheimers.

In response, many of my interview partners got to know their neighborhood cop personally. Käthe Stolte anticipated his timely arrival just as she knew the saleswomen from the blind-mission who sold her family their brooms for sweeping the street. Though she could not recall his name, she remembered one particularly large officer who had red hair and lived on Ottostrasse (G/185a R/60; see also SAH 904-1/17a R/470, G/146b R/255). Jürgen Ludewig found it "special" that the policemen and the residents of the neighborhood were so well acquainted. (He could not remember his name today, but he did recall that all of his neighbors had known that particular police officer back then.) Every afternoon, he walked down the street, and if you happened for instance to be sweeping your stoop when he arrived, he chatted with you: not just exchanging a greeting but taking part in your life. For instance, "if he knew that [you] had a sick dog, then, [he asked:] 'how is your dog doing?' That is how personal it was back then. Very beautiful" (G/103b R/30). Yet arguably the personal relationship with the neighborhood cop was beautiful only insofar as the officer stayed out of the private sphere. In this regard, the act of locating this officer of the state in a neighborly relationship is an eigensinnig response to the potentially invasive quality of herrschaft.

Having reiterated the norm of proper behavior, some of my interview partners then disclosed an even deeper history of conflict and eigensinn. For instance, Käthe Stolte's red-haired beat cop was well known, but he was also feared and challenged. "Whenever we saw him, we made a grumble [*Mucke*], you know. We made a grumble and then we ran away. Oh, that was so very dynamic [*so ganz energisch*]. And when no one had swept, then [the policemen] came and rang and said, "Who was responsible here for [this]?" (G/185a R/60). Heinrich Weber also claimed to disapprove of the "subordination mentality" (*Untertandenken*) that characterized the Imperial era. In another anecdote about the visit of his neighborhood cop to his home, he tried to prove to me that his family did not simply conform to the wishes of the police.

> We had a dog back in the workshop, a pointer, a black pointer. He often ripped the policeman's pelerina [cape] to shreds, you know. My father of course had to pay him for it. But [the dog] did not like him at all, and that carried over to the children. We also could not stand him. (G/145a R/250)

These tactics of eigensinn reinforced existing power relations at the same time that they conferred status and power on the rebels: the children who grumbled or the dog who ripped uniforms. That is, we must balance the fact that these ordinary Hildesheimers recognized and identified with state authority (even as it intervened up to the edge of, and potentially into, the private sphere) with the fact that they also relished every opportunity to challenge that same authority indirectly. Neighborliness allowed for both herrschaft and eigensinn, so long as you cleaned up the mess afterwards.

By knowing neighbors personally, the policemen could literally bring the authority of the state into the home. By knowing the names of the policemen, interwar Hildesheimers made their impositions seem less of an intrusion. Ulrike Volkmann's account of sweeping the street illustrated this contradictory amalgam of norm and deeds, rules and rebellions.

> In the morning, all the mothers would . . . sweep the streets. By eight o'clock, the sidewalk and the street had to be polished clean. Otherwise, the policeman who had that beat came through and opened the house door and called—especially when my mother—she was always punctual—when she had not swept and something was there [on the street]—he called "Mrs. Berthold! Eight o'clock!" Shortly before eight, we had to be in school, [so] I know that most [of the mothers] went out and looked at the street [to see] if everything was in order and they grabbed a broom if something was not in order. (*blank in Ordnung sein;* G/60b R/360)

To a different interviewer, Ulrike described these moments with a different emphasis. The policeman "came every morning at eight. My mother would get fidgety around eight, then she would say, 'I have to get out! . . . He will be by any minute!'" (SAH 904-1/17a R/470). Obviously Ulrike's mother was not always punctual, and as a result, the officers of the state were periodically able to invade her home. The fact that other neighbors could hear the policeman's cry was all the more reason for Ulrike to insist that her mother was in fact always punctual since the policeman thus made her indiscretion public knowledge. But whether she actually swept the street in time is not as significant as the cultural logic framing their behavior. Hildesheimers customarily swept their streets, and publicly demonstrated their propriety, to forestall the invasion of the private sphere by public authority, official or unofficial. Precisely because they sought to preserve family autarky, Ulrike and her mother participated respectably in the communal battle against filth.

Cleaning the stoop was not so much an issue of the dirt itself. Dutifully sweeping the street provided ordinary Hildesheimers with a mechanism to negotiate the conflicting demands of public and private, eigensinn and herrschaft. More essentially, it was also a cultural accommodation to the fact that eigensinn and herrschaft were themselves contradictory. In the process of sweeping the street, ordinary Hildesheimers cleansed this space of agency, transgression, contradiction, and negotiation. Figuratively, they erased all evidence of the cultural processes by which they shaped their lived reality. Sweeping the stoop was pleasurable for this reason: because it reassured Hildesheimers of their normalcy in precisely those spaces in which they most readily contravened that myth. Appropriately, children or dogs voiced rebellion, acting as the indirect vehicle of neighborhood transgression on behalf of full, adult members of society. It is also hardly surprising that, in the era of radical change, civil war, political instability, and economic chaos, the public demonstration of private respectability took on the character of a united moral community collectively battling filth.

Road Apples

The neighborhood was a contentious, liminal space: neither completely public nor wholly private. In the one direction, the private sphere extended well beyond the door of one's home: up to the middle of the street (which one was responsible for cleaning) and into the courtyard (where, as we shall see, one defecated). In the other direction, the public sphere often penetrated through the door of one's home: into the foyer (where policemen complained to housewives about their cleanliness), up the stairwell (where neighbors greeted and chatted about the weather), and into the salon (where guests were served coffee and cake). In this uncertain boundaryland, interwar Hildesheimers had to negotiate public identities based on private affairs and private defenses against public authority. Yet it was precisely this flexibility that left open the possibility of both herrschaft and eigensinn. Just as it facilitated political mobilization for elections, so did it open the Pandora's Box of how to properly distribute resources: based on the property rights of autarkic families or on neighborly norms of communal equity. Not surprisingly, the dirty business of balancing these contradictory principles of the local political economy had everything to do with scat.

Consider the problem of *road apples*. In German, *Pferdeäpfel* literally translates as *horse apples* but is a colloquial expression for horse manure. Thekla Mestmacher explained how impoverished neighbors sometimes took out credit at her parents' store and then sought inventive ways to pay their debts. She recalled how in order to make a few extra marks, they sometimes worked in her home as domestic servants. One man even collected road apples in a handcart and sold them either to family gardeners or to the factories of Senking or Ahlborn: producers of kitchen ovens and farm equipment respectively. In the latter case, these companies packed manure around dies to keep them warm after they were cast (G/12b R/25). This ingenious survival mechanism is related to the habit of *hamstering* during the First War: the way that families ran around the countryside identifying, gathering, and trading for groceries and fuel. In that instance, hamstering represented a rejection of the formal institutions that failed to distribute resources fairly to all members of the German volksgemeinschaft in a time of total war (Davis 2000). This self-help mechanism is also akin to the even more common practice of gardening that, particularly during the Hyper-inflation, enabled families to survive hardship as well as to preserve their independence from a monetary system in chaos. By contrast, collecting road apples reintegrated a poor entrepreneur back into the capitalist economy by letting him market a neighborly resource on the black market. The problem with this informal mechanism for promoting employment was that road apples fell onto the street and therefore fell under the auspices of convivial-ity. A neighborly resource, their fair distribution was caught between the dual premises of communal equity and familial autarky.

Jürgen Ludewig insisted that his corner neighborhood had felt "like a large family." Of course, you could not do anything you wanted: "there was still order after all." For instance, there was an ordinance against shaking dust, presumably from rugs or linen, out the window because it could land on people's heads. (And you would just have to sweep the street afterwards anyway.) Jürgen went on to explain how, under his neighbor's gaze, his family had to be sure that the streets were swept by nine in the morn-ing: "up to the middle of the street and in the width of their house, no?" Then Jürgen explained a curious consequence of the extension of familial responsibilities into the street. Every morning, two of his neighbors, who were farmers, led their horses out of town to their fields. The horses did not walk two hundred meters before they "tossed" their road apples on the street close to his house. "Everywhere it lay. It was a whole lot, you know." The owners were responsible for cleaning up their horses' mess. According to the 1932 municipal ordinance (46–47), "the dirtying of the walkways by dogs and other domestic animals is to be avoided." Moreover, a thorough cleaning and disinfection of the relevant area had to follow after the manure was transported out of town. Yet none of this was a problem for these two farmers because many of their neighbors had gardens outside town and used horse manure for fertilizer. They knew precisely when the horses passed, stood ready each morning on the sidewalk as they did, swept up the mess, put it into wheelbarrows, and took it out to their gardens. "Oh, they were hard on [the horses'] tails." When I asked if neighbors ever fought over the distribution of this prized resource for fertilizer, Jürgen replied: "Yes, yes, yes!" He recalled one incident in which two horses dropped "some pretty piles." One person came by to sweep it up when a window opened from the side of the street and a woman screamed at him: "Get! You get out of here! That lies in front of my door: it belongs to me!" Disregarding her, the man swept it up and moved on. "Of course" he took it with him, Jürgen explained. "She wanted to have it, only she looked out a little late, and he was already out of his house." Jürgen laughed. "That is how things were here: everything polite, everything peaceful, no?" (*schön, in rühen Frieden;* G/101b R/00).

Dundes explained that a large pile of manure in front of one's home was considered a measure of wealth in some parts of Germany (1989: 13ff). Yet the reason does not lie in an alleged Germanic anal fixation. Scat held real use value: for gardeners, manure could improve one's ability to survive in hard times. In an atmosphere of economic instability, manure reinforced the independence of the family. At the same time, scat held social exchange value: it reinforced the bonds of neighborliness. Like many of his neighbors, Jürgen's family made a deal with one of those same farmers. He owned a *Jauchewagen*: a steam-driven, cart-mounted pump for liquid manure. He parked it in front of their door, let it load up all the contents of their outhouse overnight, returned the next morning with his horse, and brought it all out to his fields as fertilizer. They did not pay him for the service, and he did not pay them for their excrement (G/102a R/225). Both parties benefited from this exchange in kind. The very definition of an a-social thing, even feces could be diverted back into exchanges that constituted neighborly relations. In the case of the human scat, this arrangement preserved both ideals without a sense of conflict: familial autarky and communal equity. The farmer and the Ludewigs both extracted use value for their families, while they also reinforced the bonds of neighborliness through the exchange.

The conflict over road apples was resolved less congenially. Interwar Hildesheimers could still use horse manure to improve the quality of their own produce and better provide for their families. Yet these resources were literally deposited in the middle of the neighborhood and therefore had to be distributed fairly in this still embattled community. The one neighbor claimed squatter's rights to the dung to ensure his familial autarky. The other applied the logic of street cleaning to claim property rights over all road apples dropped in front of her home, up to the middle of the street, or six meters into a plaza. At first Jürgen responded to these contradictions with laughter, but he then was able to frame the entire episode in the context of communal cooperation, respectability, and familiarity because ultimately these neighbors were just debating who had the right to clean the street. Purification rituals erased from memory precisely what was so disturbing about this incident: the prospect of fundamental contradiction and violent conflict in the neighborhood.

The Outhouse

At the start of the interview about neighborliness, I asked my interview partners to describe the physical environment of their apartments. When asking for descriptions of rooms, layout, and family use, I also inquired about the presence of specific appliances and utilities that entered their homes over the course of this period: electricity, gas, hot and cold running water, heating equipment, telephones, radios, and toilets. Some Hildesheimers claimed to have had toilets in their home that used water to wash away the excrement (*mit Wasserspülung*): such families were wealthier and lived in more recently constructed buildings. Most interwar Hildesheimers had closets with a bench that covered a pit into which excrement would simply drop. Called thud-closets (*plumpsclos*) for the sound made while using them, or drop-closets (*fellclos, fell-toiletten*) for the physics of the process (G/102a R/225, G/130a R/65, G/85a R/125), these receptacles were often located in the courtyard behind the home. Some thud-closets could also be found in the stairwell of the multi-family dwelling: halfway between floors and apartments (G/65a R/40). It was unusual for Hildesheimers to have toilets in their apartments, Georg Brzezinski insisted. He and his neighbors tended to have such conveniences because they lived on the main business street, where more modern sewage systems, telephones, and other amenities conducive for business had already been introduced. Yet, "there were still many streets in Hildesheim in this era where there was absolutely no sewage system . . . where, like, pits—" Georg did not finish his thought. He had approached too close to the scatological act itself and grew silent (G/90a R/240).

The reader should not misinterpret this silence: it did not reflect a lack of knowledge about or a neurotic obsession with scat. Hildesheimers knew precisely in what circumstances their neighbors defecated (G/79a R/70) simply because the act could not be ignored: most toilets were located in the semi-public spaces of the stairwell or courtyard. Otto Koch's family shared three outhouses with five other families in the courtyard behind his childhood home (G/41a R/45). Before the First War, Lotte Stolzenberg's family shared three to five thud-toilets that stood in the courtyard behind the house with four other families; they also shared a "washing kitchen" in the basement of the building next door (G/18a R/90). In Friedrich Rother's case, every two families shared a thud-toilet, and these three outhouses were placed next to one another in the courtyard. Their apartment building had several stories with large sets of stairs in between each one. One can only imagine the delay, and the publicity, in getting to the outhouse from the top floor during a physiological emergency. At such awkward moments, one hoped not to find it occupied by a member of another family (G/59a R/115). Stella Storch in particular recalled how demanding her father had been to her mother, keeping her so busy that she often had to hold her composure as long as she could. Only when she finally was bursting did she race through the garden to the outhouse. The Storch family, luckily, had their own toilet so she did not have to compete with the neighbors for access in such dire emergencies (G/26a R/50). But emergency or not, Hildesheimers could not help but notice what transpired in and around their drop-closets. The spaces of defecation were neither completely public, nor completely private, nor even completely sheltered from wind and rain (SAH 699/406: 6). They were semi-permeable. They were neighborly.

It was difficult for me to get my interview partners to describe how neighbors negotiated access to thud-closets; Hildesheimers often avoided discussing such matters directly (G/143b R/45). Again, this silence was not simply a matter of taboos concerning elimination; it also corresponded to the transgressive nature of these neighborly spaces. Dirt accumulated on the stoop and road apples in the street. In the courtyard, one could find stalls for animals and the communal kitchens where women cleaned clothing (G/190a R/75, G/25b R/50). As a public space in which private affairs were conducted, the courtyard transgressed both categories. All the more reason, then, for one to put a thud-toilet in these neighborly spaces. Hildesheimers obfuscated the act of defecating and its interpersonal context in narrative because the essence of this elusive sphere was hard to grasp and disgusting when one did. Because the subject was trapped in contradiction between the public and the private, interwar Hildesheimers grew silent when their narrative reached the spaces of personal purging.

By comparison, the process of removing and disposing of the collected fecal matter from the toilet was well known and easily narrated precisely because it resolved the contradictions in interwar conviviality. Hildesheimers clearly recalled the process of cleaning these facilities (G/1a R/235, G/25b R/50), and they also talked about the errant boys who pulled the plug on the sewage container after it had been filled to let "the brew" flow onto the street instead of into the fields (SAH 699/406). It is noteworthy that I did not ask about such procedures at first. The Hildesheimers volunteered these anecdotes after I posed a question about the kinds of toilets in their residences. It is also noteworthy that, in contrast to the categorical silence about individual moments of purging the body, they told stories of purging the communal outhouse in full detail. For this reason, Georg Brzezinski shifted his story of how individuals vacated their excrement *in flagrante* to how the pits underneath these toilets were emptied of their contents. "And then there was a company which had [a] mobile steam-engine and attached to it was a bucket car. And then they drove it in front and pumped out these . . . pits. This is still clear in my memory" (G/90a R/240). Georg's narrative replicated a habit from his childhood: in response to his public knowledge of these private acts of individual neighbors, he shifted his narrative to the communal act of voiding these installations. Arguably, the individual act of purging one's body of its wastes was akin to eigensinn: it expressed the self but could also offend. Both were also transgressive and therefore took place in the liminal spaces of a ritual process. Minus the physical evidence of eigensinn, the collective act of purging the neighborhood's outhouses re-established cultural order. No wonder, then, that Georg responded to the transgressive and contested character of neighborhood with a story of a ritual purge.

Voiding the neighborhood installations was also memorable for more obvious reasons. Günther Seidner recalled how most of his neighbors did not yet have water closets in their homes and how sewage trucks came by horse and wagon to clean the outhouses. He described that process succinctly: "everything smelled" (G/79a R/70). Ulrike Volkmann concurred: when the sewage-truck came by, it cost her father five marks and then, "it stank uncannily" (unheimlich; G/59a R/115). According to a local police ordinance (1932: 51, see also 46–47), "cloaca and liquid manure or other badly smelling and/or disgusting liquids" as well as solid waste products such as solid feces and manure could not be dumped in the streets, gutters, or public water systems but had to be transported out of town by tightly sealed containers at night. Only if the fecal matter could not be smelled did the town permit transportation during the daytime. Nor could manure and other "bad smelling things" be stored or emptied on private property, even temporarily, if it would "burden" the neighbors or passersby with bad odors. And again, a thorough cleaning and disinfection had to follow after it was transported away. Scat was not only sealed off in containers literally and avoided and voided narratively; scat was also figuratively contained by bureaucratic language of the worst kind. Yet these public ordinances succeeded neither figuratively nor literally in isolating Hildesheimers from their neighbors' scat. Both the initial act of defecation and the removal of its product had distinct and remarkable olfactory, ocular, and auditory components. Interwar Hildesheimers could not ignore this reality of everyday life. Private elimination and purification took place in full public view—or more accurately, in SenseSurround.

As usual, children were the critical medium for recording and transmitting such neighborhood information. The reader may recall that Theodora Algermissen's family had a water closet in their home during the 1920s but recognized that their home was "relatively progressively furnished: the neighbors not yet." She knew these scatological details of her neighbors' furnishings because, "we children spent a lot of time in the neighborhood, in the garden, and at the neighbors." She explained to me that these homes had all been built during the Gründerzeit (i.e., after 1871) when water closets were not standard. Instead, the neighbors had drop-toilets in their homes, a confession that evoked laughter from Theodora. To describe it, she compared the facilities available to her childhood neighbors to those in Finland: "You know, a wood frame, a throne, with a hole in it. That is where we sat and dropped everything into a pit. . . . And then came, I think about every quarter-year, a wagon. We kids called it the 'stink machine.'" Theodora laughed. "They came with long tubes and pumps and pumped out these pits. In the neighbor's house, as [you have] well noted, not in our house: but this was very interesting to us children" (*plumpsten*; G/1a R/220). Located in the narrative frame of good neighborly relations, taking part in the scatological lives of neighbors was both a practical reality and a customary practice, mediated in particular by the most frequent inhabitants of that area, children.

Neighborhood marked this in-between terrain in which public and private mixed almost by definition. Thekla Mestmacher complained sarcastically that one never added "please do not tell anyone" to a piece of news because everyone knew perfectly well that it would be "circulated" (*ausgetragen*) by the time one got to the next corner. Here, her expression suggests the notion of private affairs being brought into the public sphere where they did not belong (G/14a R/00). Earlier, she recalled particularly "entertaining" examples of this phenomenon. A married couple got into a squabble and the woman threw a bed, a suitcase, and the man's clothes out a window three stories above street level. Another woman beat her husband with a stick when he drank away his weekly wage (G/12b R/190). The neighborhood children loved these kinds of spectacles, Thekla explained. But the point is that they could hardly ignore them. Semi-permeable, neighborhood felt dirty almost by definition.

Here we should note the linguistic overlap between pumping out sewage and pumping a friend or neighbor for money or supplies. As mentioned already, *auf Pump kaufen* referred to purchasing on credit in a store. Most Hildesheimers considered these kinds of informal loans improper and to be avoided (G/143b R/325, G/147a R/30, G/157a R/320). This antipathy for credit made sense in the context of the era: it placed the family in a state of dependency within a monetary system that, especially since the First War, was not to be trusted. Adele Jürgens used the term *pumpen* when describing how one asked neighbors to lend a cup of flour or the like. It was done, but she preferred to do without (G/29a R/305). It makes sense, then, that these two terms are cognates. The pumping of credit relates both to the improper distribution of resources in the neighborhood and to a family's dependence on neighbors and a monetary system. The pumping of sewage re-established a fair distribution of resources as well as familial autarky. Figuratively, voiding the thud-closet purified neighborly relations of their contradictions.

It is in this context that municipal announcements about cleanliness should be understood: one needed to publicly air the uncanny evidence of scat in order to purge the neighborhood of its transgressions. On 7 June 1925 (131: 1), just before the May Prince Festival, the *Hildesheimer Abendblatt* complained about the "unbelievable condition" of the "donkey pits" as both a health risk and a sure way to hurt the local tourist trade. "An immediate remedy is recommended." A similar article appeared in the *Hildesheimer Volksblatt* the day before (129), titled *"Eine 'Sehenswürdigkeit,'"* which in German means both "a thing worth seeing" and a tourist attraction. The social-democratic paper mocked the cleanliness of public outhouses: "The public lavatory on Neustädter Markt still shines in its old 'beauty.'" It cynically reviewed the history of complaints to civic officials, official promises to renovate, and unfortunate delays. The paper also asked the town to remove this "ornament" immediately, even if it could not be replaced quickly, because of the many tourists that were on their way to Hildesheim for the Festival. "If it is your intention to leave this thing standing there much longer," they asked the town administration sarcastically, "then we recommend that it be considered for the new edition of the Hildesheim Guidebook." In keeping with the contentiousness of Weimar politics, the proletarian editors of the *Volksblatt* used this circumstance to embarrass their bourgeois opponents. Yet the fact that a similar complaint was found in a bourgeois paper makes sense only in terms of a style of interwar conviviality that crossed boundaries of class and confession. Filth was a concern of all neighbors, and the act of cleaning it was a means to resolve and efface conflict in the neighborhood, including political conflict. Hildesheimers of all camps admonished each other to take part in a collective cleansing of their neighborhoods. Just as policemen could remind the residents of his beat to clean without arousing suspicions of an invasion of privacy, so could citizens admonish town administrators to keep public restrooms orderly without seeming uppity. More to the point, Hildesheimers could demonstrate their unity before these many tourists only after they erased the memory of conflict, neighborly and political. Only through collective ritual purges could Hildesheimers restore their collective sense of normalcy.

No wonder, then, that some Hildesheimers resisted modernizing their toilets (G/85a R/125, G/190a R/75, G/130a R/65). "I remember still," Theresa Stoffregen said, "that grandfather avoided [installing a water-cleaning toilet] as long as he could. Old people always have something against renovation. And it also cost lots of money" (G/190a R/75). Ulrich Gerke explained that the costs for installation would be transferred to the renter (G/85a R/125). For his part, Heinrich Weber preferred the taste of water from a well, so he did not see the need for having running water inside, no less a water toilet (G/143b R/00). Thud-closets were more pragmatic: one could throw many forms of waste in them other than just feces. Cleaning up from his bachelor party, Otto Koch disposed of shards of glass (which had made it from the fourth floor onto the street) in the outhouse. He could not have done so in a flush toilet (G/43b R/40). Yet the most compelling reason for not modernizing had deeper roots in the culture of interwar conviviality. Water-cleaning toilets robbed interwar Hildesheimers of a precious commodity: their own feces (cf. Dundes 1989: 16). The thud-closet, Heinrich Weber explained, provided almost everyone on their street with manure for their gardens. His parents sorely missed that resource after they installed a water-cleaning toilet. "All we needed to do was to move the 'down-puller' as we boys used to say [*Runterzieher*: a toilet with a chain that one pulls to flush]. Then the water shot out and brought the feces away" (G/143b R/15; see also G/130a R/65). Only with the introduction of true water closets did human feces become *waste*.

The town insisted that its residents could not preserve their drop-closets just for the sake of their gardens (and Heinrich, the loyal town bureaucrat, defended the town's reasons in this matter). But there was far more at stake in this question than even the valuable fertilizer that the water-cleaning toilet stole from interwar families on which their gardens, and thereby their autarky, relied. Modernization also removed feces from the semi-public sphere of the neighborhood and isolated it in the home. Consequently, the proper distribution of feces could no longer bind neighbors into reciprocal relationships. Most significantly, Hildesheimers could no longer collectively purge their neighborhoods of the memory of dirty politics. For all its hygienic benefits, then, flush-toilets did little to inspire interwar Hildesheimers because these new appliances eliminated the very medium by which moral order had been reconstituted. Arguably, that left Hildesheimers feeling rather dirty.

Toward the Third Reich

Politics was never a purely private matter in interwar Hildesheim, just as neighborliness was never really a purely personal matter. Those neighborhoods were characterized by self-deception. Ordinary Hildesheimers cultivated an exaggerated image of themselves, laid claim to status and power, broadcast their political persuasions, and even tried to pressure their neighbors into political compliance: all in and through seemingly ordinary customs of conviviality that, thanks to regular ritual purges, insulated them from retribution for their eigensinn. In one sense, these informal mechanisms for political engagement paled in comparison to the formal processes of political mobilization and violence during the Weimar Republic. But in another sense, it was precisely this coordination of the formal and the informal that provided fertile ground for totalitarianism. Other scholars may wish to explore whether, in other contexts, other political movements relied on similarly dynamic combinations of revolution from above and below; but in interwar Hildesheim, as throughout interwar Germany, it was the national socialists who were most adept at this kind of coordination. That all said, this mechanism for political mobilization worked so successfully because, independent of the Nazi movement, Hildesheimers had already practiced and tolerated it as a normal aspect of neighborliness. Through their particular customs of conviviality, ordinary Hildesheimers had already accustomed themselves to the myths of normalcy behind which they could and did politicize everyday life.

The Nazis relied on these indirect mechanisms to, for instance, influence elections. On 30 March 1936, Gustav Hoppe wrote a letter to Hans Pasch, the codename for his contact in Copenhagen with the Sopade (the German Social-Democratic Party in exile). A transcription of this letter has been preserved in the police files of Hoppe's trial for instigating high treason (quoted from Schmid 1992: 152–53). Hoppe described the elaborate preparations used by local active Nazis to encourage people to vote in the recent plebiscite and to vote in support of the Nazi regime. Devices for mobilization included flyers, posters, films, torch-lit marches, propaganda wagons, and loud speakers on public squares as well as stickers on groceries and lockers at work:

> After three weeks of this kind of [propaganda] barrage, one was prepared for the most brutal forms of terror on election day. To be sure, SA guards stood in front of all of the voting locations, but they did not display any aggression. This was true for town as well as countryside. I was able to vote without any hindrance.

We must read this last comment as surprise: Hoppe was known in town for being an active antifascist resistance fighter. As a Hildesheimer, however, he should not have been so shocked that the Nazis preferred to use indirect mechanisms to compel complicity. Informal mechanisms to influence the vote had a long tradition in his town and were therefore more readily acceptable to locals than overt acts of fascist violence. The SA guards could pressure conformity simply by dint of the fact that they knew their neighbors and their neighbors' politics. In the process, they not only gained status in the eyes of their neighbors but also helped to create real political legitimacy for the Third Reich. Just the fact that the SA guarded the door to the election probably influenced some of Hoppe's less staunchly opinionated neighbors to behave as expected.

By assuming the seemingly traditional role of voting wardens, these SA were able to introduce fascist politics behind the veil of the everyday. In the end, however, their goal in monitoring these elections was not to mobilize votes within a legitimate democratic system, like Ulrike's family did by "running" the vote, but to shift the nature of that election towards fascist principles of Caesaristic legitimacy: of popular, public support for charismatic dictatorial rule. Hoppe suggests that local ardent Nazis wanted to go further, though he was vague in terms of how:

> Here in town, there are often attempts to get rid of secret elections through the so-called exemplary behavior of the Hitler loyalists, but in general, secret elections persisted in the towns. You could publicly see voters [*Abstimmende* (*sic*)] beside the window panes, on the window sills, and on tables.

In its propaganda barrage, the Nazi regime was behaving like a dictatorship, but it was the coordination of that from above and neighborly demonstrations of exemplary Nazi behavior from below that made this particular strategy for totalitarian herrschaft so effective.

Neighborliness was particularly open to this kind of misuse. It fused that part of the public sphere experienced as a personal matter with that part of the private sphere designed for public access. The neighborhood thus provided considerable precedents for the invasion of the private by the public: of neighbors legitimately monitoring neighbors for evidence of proper behavior. Thanks to the white magic of neighborly ablutions, however, my interview partners were able to ignore these tactics of eigensinn and strategies for herrschaft. After Jürgen told me his account of the fight over road apples, he shifted his attention to a seemingly unrelated topic.

> Things really swung around in that era, you know, with all the politics and everything. That never had any chance at all among us in the street, or even noticed somehow, you know. There were none, you know, who were some kind of Nazi, and there were none in the whole area, none at all [who] cared about all this politics. There was none of that down here. (G/101b R/30)

Actually, Jürgen himself joined the HJ in 1935, though he claimed he did so against his will; and he participated in its public parades, though he claimed that he was not affected by Nazi ideology (G/102a R/105; see also Bergerson 2004). Beating around this Nazi bush, Jürgen described the contentious politics of the interwar years in terms typical of the myth of normalcy: as if those uncivilized disruptions entered his world from the outside. Rather, his train of thought reiterates the function of neighborliness: to purge the memory of a barely contained civil war, not to mention the memories of his own exemplary Nazi behavior.

The second half of this book will take up this story in more detail. During the 1930s, ordinary Hildesheimers continued to negotiate the conflicting demands of eigensinn and herrschaft through these same mechanisms of conviviality, but in this later decade, they made Hildesheim fascist. By coordinating their informal customs of conviviality to fit the new racist–

fascist norms, ordinary Hildesheimers laid the foundations for the Nazi revolution on which Hitler, through formal mechanism of coordination, could build. Yet by colonizing the terrain of conviviality, they also polarized it into fascist and antifascist camps, and depending on one's perspective, criminalized it or politicized it. As a result, conviviality lost its functionality as an informal mechanism for negotiating power and identity, for disguising their agency and rejuvenating a moral community. In response to this crisis in conviviality, ordinary Hildesheimers turned increasingly to the Nazi regime to administer that new volksgemeinschaft on their behalf. Ordinary Hildesheimers thus encouraged the regime to apply increasingly formal regulations more rigorously, and that terrorist regime found increasingly violent solutions to social problems. Recognizing the new realities only reluctantly, some of the new outsiders responded to the shock of alienation by exiling themselves from the Nazi volksgemeinschaft. Yet most ordinary Hildesheimers preserved their sense of normalcy by locating the new order in a pre-existing cultural logic. During the interviews many decades later, most still refused to take cognizance of their central role in laying the foundations for the Nazi revolution, in large part by sticking defiantly to those same illusions about the everyday.

Part II
Herrschaft

5 | Coordination

An EXTENSIVE LITERATURE in modern German history focuses on the process of coordination through which the Nazi regime dissolved the vibrant diversity of formal institutions of civil society (newspapers, political parties, schools, and associations) that had been part and parcel of the different socio-political milieux of pre-Nazi German society. They sought to transform these multiple organizations into solitary units of the totalitarian party-state, subordinated to the will of the Führer. Meanwhile, coordination presumed social aryanization. The unity and homogeneity of Aryan organizations depended on the exclusion of Jews. As the political scientist Raul Hilberg asserts: "the isolation of the Jews in Germany was accomplished relatively early. Before the compulsory middle names Israel and Sara were decreed, and long before the mandatory star was instituted, Jews were already stigmatized and sometimes shunned" (1992: 196; see also Kaplan 1998).

Though critical of its racial elements, the classic accounts of this process suggest that, unintentionally, coordination helped modernize Germany and prepare the way for a democratic society. It wiped away the artificial restraints on upward mobility and self-cultivation that had kept most Germans in their place. The opportunities afforded by the Third Reich were often more a matter of status and consciousness than actual power and wealth (Dahrendorf 1965; Schoenbaum 1966; see also Arendt 1951; Berman 1997; Feldman 1986; Kaeble 1978; Lederer 1967; Matzerath and Volkmann 1977: 86–117; Parsons 1954; H. A. Turner 1975: 117–40; Wehler 1975). Coordination was also more limited than initially presumed, especially for the working classes and women (Mason 1972, 1976; Stevenson 1975), and it involved the local elite acting with relative independence of their political leaders as much as obeying orders descending from the political center of the Nazi dictatorship (Fritzsche 1990; Koshar 1986; Wagner 1998; see also Kershaw 1989). Still, the presumption remains that Germany was coordinated to fit Nazi principles, and thereby modernized, from the top down.

From the perspective of everyday life, Detlev Peukert questioned whether these changes were as radical as had been presumed. Viewed from the top

131

down, he hypothesized that historians exploring "perceptible, if not statistically provable, shifts in values and changes in social behavior" would be forced to conclude "that national socialism greatly loosened the previously firm hold of traditional social environments and systems of values." Viewed from the bottom up, however, national socialist policies of coordination adapted to long-term trends in socio-economic modernization rather than providing for a particularly powerful new thrust toward those outcomes (1982b: 181–82; see also 1985, 1987; Broszat 1985). The Nazi revolution did in fact provide a powerful new thrust towards modernization by politicizing, and thereby undermining, the previously firm hold of traditional customs, particularly in informal social relations. Yet the Nazi revolution also relied centrally on pre-existing dynamics of cultural negotiation.

This chapter will focus on Nazi flags, uniforms, and salutations. It will show that over the course of the 1930s, seemingly ordinary Hildesheimers coordinated their customs of conviviality to fit the principles of the Nazi movement. Some were motivated in part by Nazi ideology, but all were laying claim to status and power in the new order promised by the Nazis. Akin to David Schoenbaum, I will argue that Hildesheimers participated in this Nazi revolution in the hope that their real status under Hitler might finally correspond to their fantasies of niveau. Sometimes they acted in anticipation of political victory in 1933. Often, as Robert Gellately has argued, they acted independent of direct pressure from the Nazi dictatorship. To be sure, the coordination of conviviality depended on Hitler to seize power and implement policies based on Nazi principles. But equally, Hitler depended on ordinary Hildesheimers to coordinate conviviality to fit Nazi principles: to transform their friends and neighbors into Aryans and Jews.

This reinvention of convivial traditions (Hobsbaum and Ranger 1983), seemed to preserve old values but, in fact, created new ones. Because coordination challenged the normative authority of convivial forms of intimacy and reciprocity, it effectively opened the possibility for ordinary Hildesheimers to modernize their informal social relations. They could thus rid themselves of the traditional habits that preserved social hierarchies and, in the process, could open their society to self-cultivation. Also akin to the individual aspiration for niveau, this monstrous project in social engineering was modern in the sense that it was utopian (or rather dystopian, Bauman 1997: 80; Peukert 1982b, 1987). Above all, coordination presumed a typically modern correlation between the policies of a centralized political system and the practices of ordinary people in their manifold neighborhoods on the periphery. Talcott Parsons called this a *principally coordinated space:* a realm "upheld by uniform principles" and "maintained by the joint efforts of legislators and the armed *or unarmed* executors of their will" (1954, my italics).

To make Hildesheim fascist, a brown revolution was required in both the formal arena of high politics and the informal arena of friendship and neighborliness, as a result of orders from the Führer above and of the initiative of the volk below. As in Martin Broszat's *polycratic* model of the Nazi state (1981), this dynamic structure of everyday life took much of its direction from the leaders of the Nazi movement and its ideology: its antisemitism, its principle of leadership, its totalitarian claims on the individual. But the momentum for nazification derived from tensions inherent in the structure of everyday life itself. Broszat traces that dynamism of the regime to the competitive behavior of Hitler's henchmen; I trace the dynamism of everyday life to the competitive desire for self-cultivation that permeated conviviality just as thoroughly. As the first part of this book has shown, ordinary people regularly employed tactics of eigensinn and strategies for herrschaft to colonize everyday life in their own interests. The second part will show that, just as the Nazi elite disguised their innovations in German public policy behind the veil of obedience to the Führer and a bureaucratic culture (Arendt 1986), Nazi neighbors likewise hid their creative maneuvers in local public life behind their official status of being ordinary. Conviviality was particularly useful to the Nazi revolution because it enabled ordinary Hildesheimers to participate in it and benefit from it without losing a sense of their own normalcy.

The Swastika

Günther Seidner became aware of the impending Nazi seizure of power because, in 1932–33, his neighbors began to march around in a variety of Nazi uniforms: "the SA—and what do I know" (G/80b R/415). A certain margarine merchant in particular "was one of the first convinced people who showed their true character [*welches Geisteskind sie waren*]. That spread out more and more." This merchant "walked around in marching boots and carried the flag for the SA. I know that for sure." A member of the Young German League (*Jung Deutscher Ordnung*), Günther claimed to have distanced himself from the Nazis somewhat, but he also admitted that neighborhood adolescents watched the behavior of this SA man and some found his uniform "great." Right next to this margarine merchant lived a pious Catholic paper merchant who followed his neighbor to the "marching depot": he too joined the SA. Günther knew this paper merchant and his political persuasions because the Seidner family shopped in his store. When they made a political remark, the paper merchant would say coolly: "paper is patient." For Günther, this less ostentatious attitude made him preferable to the margarine merchant "who always carried the flag. He was a sporty guy with marching boots and marched there and believed that he was important.

Then he went into the service and carried the flag . . . marching in the rear but conscientiously" (G/81b R/00, G/80a R/305).

This anecdote tells us as much about Günther as it does about his neighbors. Though by and large a Nazi collaborator, Günther distinguished himself from ardent Nazis by withholding his enthusiasm for those few elements of the Nazi program with which he did not agree: in particular, racial antisemitism. In his caution, he was quite similar to the paper merchant. In any case, some ordinary Hildesheimers did use a Nazi uniform or swastika flag ostentatiously to lay claim to status and power among their neighbors. Their neighbors read this publication of private affairs as both a challenge and an affront. Yet rather than admitting an honest disclosure of intent, they hid similar claims behind the veil of the everyday. Whether Günther also did so for the Nazis is hard to say, but he certainly did so on behalf of the Young German Order.

The two central components of Nazi pageantry were flags and uniforms, items that shared the symbol of the swastika. In the early stages of the Nazi movement, these colors and symbols facilitated the public announcement of one's private political attitudes. Early in the Third Reich, they became a political confession of faith. A swastika flag or Nazi uniform conveyed one's willingness to collaborate with the new regime and challenged one's interlocutors to join up. Ordinary Germans contributed to the Nazi revolution in this way: through largely indirect, symbolic discourse disguised behind the veil of the everyday.

Georg Brzezinski revealed typically contradictory attitudes about the place of politics in everyday life. On the one hand, he often insisted that shopkeepers like his father did not make significant public statements about their personal politics for business reasons. His family therefore hung the town flag of Hildesheim or the provincial flag of Prussia outside of their home. The display of these flags preserved the family's status in the community while enabling them to avoid direct political confrontations with neighbors. On the other hand, he admitted that one did learn a lot about neighbors' politics by shopping in their stores and chatting with them briefly. True to form, Georg proudly explained (at other times in the interviews: G/92a R/210) that his father was an important player in town politics on behalf of the Catholic Center Party and that he often discussed local political matters on the street with neighbors.

As it turns out, Georg knew precisely, and could still describe, the identities and politics of various residents in the homes around the courtyard behind his. "And then here, there was an optician. That was a small half-timbered house. But we had no contact with him whatsoever. . . . He was a, a, a loner he was." Georg used the expression *Eigenbrötler* which translates literally to mean a person who breaks bread on his own or in his own way.

"He was kind of antisocial" (*abweisend nach aussen*), Georg annotated. "He was also one of the earliest Nazis in Hildesheim. There was no relationship there whatsoever, none whatsoever." According to Georg, they did not even greet each other in the 1920s. Georg then changed the topic to another neighbor (G/90b R/60), so I returned our conversations to the "loner" later in the interviews (G/92a R/240). Georg had been describing how, because his father was such a well-known figure in the town, Georg was constantly tipping his hat as he walked down the streets of Hildesheim, greeting all the neighbors he knew. I reminded him of the optician and I asked Georg how he knew that this neighbor had become a Nazi. "One noticed it in the fact that he participated in those parades. First a small group who marched through the street . . . and then one noticed also who came in and out his door and such and knew, 'Oh, he is also one of those!' no?" Clearly, ordinary Hildesheimers were highly sensitive to the politics of their neighbors. By subtly yet demonstratively adjusting their neighborhood décor, Hildesheimers indirectly engaged in a form of street politics without undermining their sense of normalcy.

Heinrich Weber offered a wider range of reasons why a shopkeeper might in fact break this rule of political neutrality to display some sign of Nazi support even though he was not personally committed to its ideology: "out of economic necessity, to prevent the Nazis from picking him up, [or] out of consideration for his customers" (G/148b R/140). Still, Georg insisted that this (alleged) public silence about politics forestalled all conflicts between neighbors on this issue. Politics was discussed at the pub among those who regularly met at a specific table (*Stammtisch*): that is, who knew each other and their politics sufficiently well to be able to carry on conversations without fear of conflict. But even then one's opinions could be "only hinted at cautiously." Coyly, Heinrich insisted that one did not know the specific party affiliations of one's neighbors. That all said, he nonetheless recalled one family. "This much I know: they were involved with the Nazis. That I know for sure, no? They were the first who unfurled the flag, no? Who encouraged the others." When money (*Brot*) was being collected for some event, like a visit to Nürnberg, these neighbors pressured Heinrich and his family. "But otherwise, our father, when he had to hang a flag out the window, just hung the Hildesheim town flag, until they ripped it down one day, no? So there was nothing further that one could do." It never came to open conflict with these neighbors, but the flag situation was also accepted as it had been "handed down" (*gediehnen genommen*) from the state in advance. "One wanted nothing more to do with such people. The least possible" (G/145a R/85).

Many decades later, Günther, Georg, and Heinrich could still recall these innovators for several reasons. An open secret, these early Nazis had announced their political persuasions in the flags they hung from their homes and the uniforms they wore as they moved through the neighborhood to and from the private sphere. In the context of the national-socialist movement during the Weimar Republic, this kind of incidental announcement of one's private political opinions in the local public sphere was an implicit challenge. Like other radical groups on the far right of the political spectrum, the Nazis claimed to be the most patriotic Germans. Günther had strong ties to the German East but a somewhat different vision of German nationalism than the Nazis. Georg's Catholic confession and Polish name (Brzezinski) placed his loyalties in question. And Heinrich had a strong desire to achieve more status than he had been awarded as the son of a master artisan. Consequently, each of them felt the pull of the Nazi challenge to prove their patriotism when these neighbors walked past. Each of them also suggested that their neighbors had joined the Nazi party not simply out of political convictions but in order to use this party affiliation to claim status and power in their neighborhood.

. These were textbook examples of eigensinn: self-expressive revolts against the Weimar Republic, and claims to status and power hidden behind the veil of the everyday. In response, these boys assumed a seemingly neutral position in a contentious public debate about the future of Germany. By hanging local colors, they could remain patriotic in their own minds while distancing themselves not only from Nazi extremists but also from the introduction of politics back into their neighborhood. In this way, they stuck to their myths of normalcy. As men many decades later, they preserved the same habitus: they insisted that they had not been the ones to introduce contentious issues into their neighborhoods. In this manner, these young men were simply behaving as proper Hildesheimers. As Heinrich explained:

> We never really trampled around about [national socialism; *da auch nicht darauf umgetrampelt*]. Our friends were our friends, and we [left] the rest alone. I have never known that one or the other of them packed up their backpacks and took part in one of those parades in Nürnberg. Not one of them. Me neither. None of us—no, its true, one of them wore a Nazi uniform. The other did not. . . . We all avoided [participating] until the going got hot, no? (G/148b R/155; see also G/54b R/55)

It was their neighbors who misused conviviality; they themselves were just ordinary Hildesheimers.

This anecdote makes sense only if we realize that Heinrich was narrating the past in the way he had lived it. Ordinary Hildesheimers used flags and uniforms subtly to jockey for status and power in the emerging Third Reich such that they experienced their own behavior as if it were innocuous. Only when other people did as much to them did they take offense. Heinrich even referred to one man who rented a flat from his father as the *Standard Bearer of the SA* because this man both held that position and pressured Heinrich to participate in Nazi educational evenings. Perhaps because he had more to fear from the Nazis as a social democrat, Otto Koch admitted openly that he had been able to guess his neighbors' politics.

> No one carried a sign around in front of them [*vor sich hertragen*], but you felt it about him and his behavior in a way that I cannot really describe. You sensed what was going on. And the Nazis, well, they made themselves loud enough. You could almost say that they wore [their politics] on their sleeve [*die tragen das vorher*]. They dressed appropriately: they wore uniforms and such, you know. (G/44a R/190)

Independent of the Nazi movement, ordinary Hildesheimers announced their politics to their neighbors, and read their neighbors' affiliations, behind a veil of the everyday.

National socialism was only one of many political positions that inter-war Hildesheimers announced with the intent of convincing their neighbors to join their cause. They laid claim to status and power should their cause win, and yet acted as if they did nothing of the sort. Yet the fact that residents found neighboring Nazis more memorable than followers of other parties, even communists, is only partially related to the Nazis' subsequent crimes. In quantitative terms, it reminds us that more than a third of all Hildesheimers voted for the Nazis in 1932 and again in 1933: more than any other single party. In qualitative terms, it suggests that newly converted Nazis typically announced their political faith in a more strident style. Local Nazis capitalized on the normalcy of conviviality by using friendship and neighborliness instrumentally to make Hildesheim fascist from the bottom up. National-socialist mobilization followed the contours of conviviality in much the same way that it did the networks of sociability (Fritzsche 1990; Kosher 1986). Through significantly reinventing the traditional customs of hanging flags and wearing uniforms (Hobsbaum and Ranger 1983), the Nazis of Hildesheim colonized everyday life. The fact that no shot was fired in Hildesheim in this process should not lead us to conclude that Hildesheim was somehow more moderate than the rest of Germany. Precisely *because* no shot was fired, Hildesheim is a model example of the Nazis' successful strategies for herrschaft.

Meanwhile, the Nazis also depended to a large degree on mass pageants for their political propaganda and legitimacy (Kershaw 1983a, 1983b; Mosse 1975; Theweleit 1987). The Nazis understood the emotional appeal of visual demonstrations of homogeneity and consciously applied them in posters, events, and parades to convey the sense of the German volk united under the leadership of their Führer. The rituals enacted during the party rallies at Nürnberg and the Thanksgiving Day festivals at Bückeberg transformed a diversity of German particularities, often named on banners or represented through völkisch costumes, into a German racial state. This process of coordination took place primarily in terms of aesthetics and ritual: visually through coordinated colors, flags, and uniforms, and physically through coordinated gestures, movement, and speech. The political significance of these mass, nationwide, carefully staged pageants can hardly be underestimated: they were the ritual enactment of the Nazi promise of communitas. Yet these formal rituals cannot be seen in isolation, as if they took place only on the parade grounds and simply as the product of masterful propaganda. Informal rituals were just as critical in evoking a coordinated volksgemeinschaft. Those Aryans who could not be physically present in Nürnberg or Bückeberg were supposed to be simultaneously listening to these events on their radios or reading about them in their daily papers (Bergerson 1997, 2001).

Presumably, they also decorated their neighborhoods with the same flags and uniforms. In Hildesheim, a cartoon appeared in the *Hildesheimer Allgemeine Zeitung* on 3 October 1936 (232: 6) that spoke to this expectation of simultaneity. Amidst articles describing national events in great detail, a cartoon depicted a man sticking his head out of his window to discover to his surprise that his street had been decorated with flags. The cartoon did not have to state explicitly that these were Nazi flags; it was most effective if it disguised this strategy for herrschaft as if it were merely a continuation of pre-existing custom. "Thankfully," his postman arrived in the nick of time and, accustomed to answering such everyday questions, the helpful government worker explained that the flags were in celebration of Thanksgiving. The resident responded to the news with surprise, "like a newborn babe." The postman advised his neighbor to "stick his head in some cold water from time to time" so that he would wake up to the world-historical events taking place in his neighborhood. The editors from the *HAZ* then reminded their customers to read the daily paper so that they will "not feel blamed" when they failed to demonstrate their support for the Third Reich with appropriate, public displays. The cartoon did not clarify who would chastise whom for failing to decorate their home with Nazi flags. They left the potential denouncer unspecified to leave open the possibility that neighbors would take on that responsibility for themselves (Gellately 2001). Aspiring to totalitarianism, the Nazi regime required not only formal control over the mass media and public festivals but also the informal contribution of ordinary Hildesheimers, decorating their homes and, whenever necessary, admonishing neighbors to do so as well.

To be sure, the Nazi regime provided Hildesheimers with the ammunition required to revolutionize neighborly décor. In the 1920s, Hitler had selected the colors black, white, and red for the Nazi party flag. Though the same as the colors of the Second Empire, he rearranged them into a new layout: a red background, with a circle of white in the center and the black swastika in the middle. The Nazi flag thus bespoke Hitler's claim that the Third Reich would be heir to the Second, yet also something new and different. Germans often referred to the different flags in terms of their colors, but the Nazi flag alone regularly acquired a different kind of appellation: one referred to it according to its central symbol, the swastika, rather than its colors. By adapting the colors of the Second Reich, Hitler made it easier for ordinary Hildesheimers to adopt the Nazi flag in their neighborhood décor as if it were just any flag (e.g., G/145a R/85). Yet its essential difference made it stand out among the symbols of many other parties in the Weimar spectrum.

For the Nazis, symbolic uniformity not only clarified the boundaries of the new volksgemeinschaft but also reduced the capacity for critical reflection among the German Volk. Yet Hitler did not order the coordination of flags and uniforms immediately. In 1933, he still stood in the shadow of Reich President Paul von Hindenburg; one could hardly imagine Hitler altering the flag of the Second Empire while the hero of the Great War still lived. So the Nazi regime issued only provisional ordinances concerning flags at first (Wördehoff 1990: 65–69, 71; cf. Busch 1954: 67). After Hindenburg died on 2 August 1934, Hitler became President (head of state) as well as Chancellor (head of government) and Führer (leader of the Nazi party). Shortly thereafter (15 September 1935), the Nazi-controlled Reichstag legislated some of the most essential points of the Nazi program. Collectively referred to as the *Nürnberg Laws,* because they were announced during the Nazi Party Conference in that city, they were in fact three different laws. The second and third were the Law for the Protection of German Blood and German Honor and the Imperial Citizenship Law. They fundamentally altered the basis for citizenship and participation in civil society in the Thousand-Year Reich. Race replaced citizenship as the basis for membership in the German polity. Thereafter, a hierarchy of races structured the interactions of people within and between these categories in civil society: for instance, German Jews were forbidden from having sexual relations with Aryans. These two laws were the first major, legal steps in a careful, long-term process by which the Nazi regime sought to purify the Aryan race for the sake of European culture. These laws presumed a fundamental reorganization not only of power relations within German society but also anticipated a fundamental reorganization of European borders and populations in keeping with these racial hierarchies. For good reason, then, Nazi legal commentators (Lösener and Knost 1941) as well as most postwar historians have been centrally concerned with the second and third laws, the subsequent ordinances based on them, and the way they were implemented. These laws served as a cornerstone for Nazi policy in Germany, Occupied Europe, and the Holocaust.

Yet it is significant to note that this first step towards the reorganization of Europe into homogenous and hierarchical racial units was prefaced by a law homogenizing German political iconography. The concise Imperial Flag Law changed the colors of Germany "back" to black, white, and red. It made the swastika flag into the official flag for both the German nation and German trade, with variations for the armed services and civil bureaucracy. Subsequent ordinances issued by the Reich Minister of the Interior in 1937 and 1939 (see Lösener and Knost 1941) clarified and expanded these laws. Private persons were supposed to fly the national flag only on "regular flag-hanging days," or on days in which flag-hanging was invited. The former days included seven specifically Nazi holidays; the latter left open the possibility for practically any day to fall under the scope of this ordinance. These ordinances prevented private individuals from hanging military, church, past imperial, or past state flags as well as precluded hanging even the national flag if it were hung in such circumstances unbecoming of its dignity: for instance, on the home of a Jew. The ordinances also made clear that the prohibition on flags included a prohibition of their colors as well.

Arguably, these regulations gave the corner neighborhoods of inter-war Hildesheim an appearance of uniformity that appealed to ordinary Hildesheimers on aesthetic grounds. It evoked memories of the way that neighbors had coordinated their décor for public holidays before and during the Great War. To be sure, the coordination of décor during the Second Empire did not yet imply the homogeneity of the Third. The dominant tropes of Wilhelmine historicism left open enormous scope for diversity, under the premise that these differences had in fact grown together in an organic process of development. Wilhelmine historicism tolerated aesthetic particularities precisely because it was designed to overcome political ones. Rather, the aesthetic appeal of homogeneity should be understood as a particularly fascist response to the memory of the embattled community of the Great War and the discord (semiotic and political) that followed during the Weimar Republic. The Nazi swastika and the black-white-and-red colors replaced the library of symbols that had expressed the many particularist identities in Central Europe since the Middle Ages. For the first time in German history, only one set of colors represented the German people. The swastika thus promised to remake politics on the basis of conviviality.

These various laws left Jews in an awkward situation. They were prohibited from hoisting the German national flag and its colors. The punishment for this act was identical to that for employing non-Jewish women under the age of forty-five in a Jewish household: a prison sentence of not more than one year, a fee not to exceed 10,000 marks, or both. In 1936, the Nazi regime further clarified that, should any Jews be living as part of a household or in mixed marriages, no Aryan flag could be hung from that home. However, if the resident Jew or Jews were only renting from Aryan landlords, the hanging of the national flag was permitted: an exception best explained in terms of bourgeois attitudes about ownership. The choice of alternate flags for the Jewish people was left to their own discretion: the Nazi regime suggested the blue-and-white flag of Zionism.

Yet the Hitler state relied on informal pressure to make coordination work as a mechanism to integrate Aryans and alienate Jews. For instance, Thanksgiving Day festivities followed closely on the heels of the Nürnberg Rally (*HB* 220: 1–2), and in preparation for the next event, the national-liberal *HAZ* printed an announcement on 2 and again on 5 October 1935 (both p. 5). These announcements described how the swastika flag would be the only flag flying from public buildings: even the old Imperial flag (black, white and red) as well as provincial flags (like the Hildesheim yellow-red) were no longer permitted. The Reich Minister of the Interior did not legislate what would appear on private buildings. Still, the text read, "it is to be expected that the population will join into this action and only show the swastika flag." It then reminded their neighbors: "it is only forbidden for Jews to fly the black, white and red flag." Clearly, the Nazi regime depended on neighbors to police their own neighborhoods: to make sure that local decorations were uniform and matched the principles of the Nazi movement. From the perspective of everyday life, the Nazi regime simply institutionalized what had been an informal mechanism of conviviality.

Thanks to this dynamic coordination of informal and formal policy, whenever a holiday required public decorations, Hildesheimers could identify those who did not wish to, or could not, participate in the volksgemeinschaft: Jews, philosemites, and any other assortment of political criminals from communists to Jehovah's Witnesses. We can now better understand why the second and third Nürnberg laws excluding Jews from the German polity and society were prefaced by the first law about flags. Seen in their everyday context, each law relied on the others for their functionality. Before Nazi bureaucrats gave Jews consistent, "Jewish" middle names (*Sara* for women, *Israel* for men), before they marked Jewish passports with a *J*, Jewish clothing with a yellow star, and Jewish arms with a number, ordinary Hildesheimers did not have formal tools with which to distinguish Jews from Aryans. The first Nürnberg Law enabled ordinary people to recognize these racial-political aliens within their midst. The Nazi regime designed its formal legislation to better facilitate what was initially and essentially an informal process of alienation: of neighbors treating their neighbors as Aryans and Jews.

Subsequent administrative measures radicalized this distinction, making it possible for the Nazi bureaucracy to better control, administer, and exterminate European Jewry. During the 1930s, however, the first Nürnberg Law still required the active collusion of ordinary Hildesheimers to make its provisions effective. Appropriately, antifascist agents relied on the same language of flags to monitor the degree to which their neighbors had succumbed to national socialism. For instance, Gustav Hoppe reported to Pasch on 30 March 1936 about the Nazi plebiscite in Hildesheim. As usual, the last days of the propaganda barrage "were marked by the special sign of hanging flags and illuminations in the windows." Yet Hoppe added, "the factory-cell leaders and block wardens were supposed to check and report on these matters." From the perspective of everyday life, the Nazi regime had simply formalized into state policy what had been an informal revolution in neighborhood décor.

Some Hildesheimers resisted the new aesthetic conformity. Even though he was a committed social democrat, Otto Koch had a good relationship with a Catholic family that lived in his neighborhood in the 1930s. They spoke to each other in the informal (*du*) and celebrated birthdays together while the air-raid alarms sounded. He felt badly for them because they could not hang their church flags out their windows in celebration of Corpus Christi (as much as they wished to do; the Nazi regime did not completely forbid Catholics to parade through town stopping at a series of altars as was the custom; their support was still too important to the dictatorship). Still, Otto explained, "Now it made no more sense" to hang their flags from their windows: "the flag itself also had no more meaning, I believe." In this, Otto was responding not just to the formal change in iconography but more to the informal homogenization of décor on his street. In a daring move, Otto did his neighbors "a favor": he borrowed their church flag and hung it from his window. "I knew what I had done. Then the Nazis, they knew—that was clear—they knew what I was or what I had been, no? and how I think." Not surprisingly, this flag "was very badly received by the Nazis." Otto hung this Catholic flag intentionally to anger his Nazi neighbors and please, or perhaps challenge, his Catholic neighbors. The latter responded at first in fear, warning Otto that he could be punished for this crime, perhaps with a reduced wage. Otto replied that it did not matter to him. "Let's see what happens. Something will have to come of it." Yet the Nazi regime preferred to use informal mechanisms to control Aryan dissidents. Otto was never punished for his eigensinn (G/43b R/240).

Still, Otto was exceptional. Most Hildesheimers responded positively to the new homogeneity of Nazi flags and the many public pageants at which they were displayed. Lotte Schohl recalled how many Nazi festivals there had been, and how she and her girlfriends had enjoyed them:

The first of May was celebrated and there were large parades and then in the evening it would pass through the streets with torches, and we thought that was all great. It was, so to say, a big *diversion* that was offered to us. There were many parades, [many times] when there was something going on in town. For instance, on Berghölzchen, that is where parades like these would end, with many uniforms, black and brown, and flags, and songs, and fireworks in the evening. And of course, this was well received by the young people. (G/9b R/220, my emphasis)

Nazi pageantry was appealing in itself as entertainment. The coordinated pageantry even seemed to help Lotte forget its very specific political messages.

My interview partners tried to place the responsibility for making Hildesheim fascist solely onto the shoulders of the Nazi regime. They described how the SA beat dissident Hildesheimers for disrespecting the swastika flag (G/46b R/20, probably the first time it was hoisted on the market square on 8 March 1933: *Verwaltungsbericht der Stadt Hildesheim 1936*: x; see also G/124b R/145). They argued that it was Hitler who began "the craziness" of ordering SS officers to be violent with forced laborers (G/84b R/325). Yet their personal memories of prior, independent acts of coordination on the part of their neighbors undermine these comfortable historical myths. The Nazi regime certainly desired and supported the coordination of neighborhood flags and uniforms to fit their claims to totalitarian herrschaft, but they relied on the creative eigensinn of ordinary Hildesheimers to colonize everyday life on their behalf.

By the end of the 1930s, Hildesheimers had by and large rearranged their conviviality to fit their ideal of a coordinated public décor. When one man celebrated his twenty-fifth anniversary of work in his factory, as seen in Figure 14, he framed his celebration in Nazi flags. What was true of collegiality was equally true of neighborliness. Figure 15 shows a watercolor that a schoolboy painted in 1936: when the street came alive with rows of flags bearing a consistent set of colors. The young artist had captured Hildesheim during one of the Nazi regime's plebiscites. He did not paint this scene because he was a convinced national socialist. Raised in a modern culture in which beauty was defined in terms of homogeneity, the pageantry no doubt impressed him for its scale and degree of coordination. By the late 1930s, conviviality was commonly framed in an impressively uniform Nazi aesthetic. While showing me two photographs of factory parties in 1938 and 1939 (D/640–41), Reinhart Oetteling responded to this new aesthetic with eigensinn. He exclaimed disingenuously, as if he had been caught red-handed: "Oh shit. There I stand directly below the swastika." Reinhart was far too cynical a person to try to mask the prevalence of the Nazi flag at these convivial affairs. He did not really try to hide his involvement in the Third Reich either. He just mocked his own bad luck to be caught in the act.

Figure 14. Twenty-fifth anniversary of working in the factory, 1941. (D/0632).

Figure 15. "Vote Yes on the 12th of November!" Heinz-Hermann Köhler, watercolor, Hildesheim, ca. 1936. Courtesy of: SAH 803/118/12.

Eve Rosenhaft (in Lüdtke, Marssolek, and von Saldern 1996: 132–33) has argued that although the Nazi paramilitary troops sometimes took direct, specific action against individuals or groups, more typically the Nazi regime used them to alter the atmosphere on the streets of Germany. As icons of power, discipline, collegiality, and hypermasculinity, the presence of the SA signified the repression of working-class organizations and offered a culturally legitimate alternative to them. Ordinary Germans used neighborly décor to much the same ends. The homogeneity of Nazi decorations on the streets of Hildesheim signified the destruction of the hated Weimar Republic, the transcendence of its political disarray, and a return to a new and improved "Third" Reich. From this perspective, ordinary Hildesheimers played a critical role in making Hildesheim fascist. They acted as grass-roots propagandists who exploited the specular culture of modern everyday life to express their eigensinn as Nazi rebels before 1933 and to assert their claims to herrschaft as the Nazi elite thereafter. To make their dictatorship truly totalitarian, the Nazis required precisely this kind of coordination of formal politics and informal power relations.

Yet they could also hide their agency behind the normalcy of coordinating their neighborhood décor. After all, the Nazis were not the first

Hildesheimers to insist on a harmonious aesthetic in the neighborhood. Neighbors voluntarily coordinated decorations during the Second Empire out of a sense of civic pride. In 1934 (pp. 22–25), Carl Saeger welcomed the fact that, as part of their solution to the Great Depression, the Nazi regime employed painters to redecorate Hildesheim's half-timbered homes with similar color patterns and encouraged homeowners to do the same. Saeger also insisted that painters should take care to ensure a sense of unity and coordination in color, a fact that suggests how Hildesheimers defined beauty in terms of the overall effect of the entire street rather than on the façade of any individual home. The Nazi appeal to visual homogeneity of flags in neighborhood décor during the Third Reich thus made perfect sense in memory of the Second.

Heil Hitler!

If the most obvious symbol of Nazi totalitarian aspirations was the swastika flag, the most obvious symbol of the Nazi volksgemeinschaft was the greeting, *heil hitler!* Otto Koch, for instance, had a relative who greeted his wife with *heil hitler!* every morning when they first got out of bed (G/48, R/280). Whenever a parade marched down the street, and there were many such parades during the Third Reich, observers were expected to greet the flag properly. Many a cover for historical monographs about this era bear photographic reproductions of precisely these moments of conjuncture between totalitarian state policy and enthusiastic popular participation (e.g., Benz 1990; Kershaw 1983; Peukert 1982b; Schoenbaum 1966). These moments epitomized the ideal to which the Nazi regime strove: of a united volk legitimizing the authority of its Führer in a demotic, public pageant.

Yet some Hildesheimers recalled these same conjunctures as stories of non-conformity to that totalitarian state project. Lena Turz was both a pious Catholic and a member of the Catholic Center party. Her husband felt pressure to enter the Nazi party because his painting business had relied on Jews and the town administration for commissions, but after 1933, the former stopped bringing in business and the latter turned fascist. Lena told me how, if she and her husband saw the swastika flag, they were supposed to greet it. Here too, Lena refused to conform. She and her husband would turn around whenever they saw the flag approaching and walk a different route along the narrow, winding streets of town. This way, they did not have to greet the flag with a *heil hitler!* (G/66b R/235). Gustav Hoppe was not so lucky, according to his letter of 30 March 1936 to Hans Pasch in Copenhagen. The fact that he failed to greet with *heil hitler!* at the end of a Nazi-orchestrated factory celebration got him fired shortly after he had returned to work.

Early research on resistance during the Third Reich, with its foci on the national-conservative assassination attempt on 20 July 1944 on Hitler and the organized socialist and communist resistance movements, had little to say about greeting; the topic was beyond the scope of its concept of resistance. In the last two decades, historians have expanded the definition of resistance to include more social actors and behaviors (see reviews by Fitzpatrick and Gellately 1996; Geyer and Boyer 1992; and Müller and Mommsen 1986: 13–21). Nonetheless, this scholarship tends to describe the relationship between Nazi state and society in terms of a range of essentially functionalist modalities: from *resistance* through *non/conformity* to *participation*. Their emphasis has been on determining those conditions under which passive dissent became active opposition to the Nazi regime. This generation of scholars concluded that resistance in the Third Reich was ultimately ineffectual. By implication, they devalued those forms of resistance that did not change this historical bottom line (Balfour 1988: 10–110, 253–54; Broszat 1983: 691–709; Kershaw 1983; Mann 1987). In the terms of this literature, Lena's decision to walk away from the flag would be considered a common but ultimately insignificant act of nonconformity. Hoppe's behavior perhaps constituted resistance, particularly when viewed in the context of his many other organized, antifascist activities, but he also paid the consequences for his overt gesture of non-compliance.

To his credit, Ian Kershaw (1983a, 1983b) did link the so-called *German greeting* to the issue of political legitimacy and dissent. He described how the *heil hitler!* greeting had been sporadically employed since 1923 and was made compulsory within the party in 1926. This outward expression of party unity disguised significant divisions within the early Nazi movement. Yet Kershaw also implied that the Nazi regime constructed popular acclaim in true totalitarian fashion. On 13 July 1933, Reich Minister of the Interior Wilhelm Frick made *heil hitler!* the compulsory greeting for all public employees and for all non-Party members during the singing of the national anthem and the Horst Wessel Song. Frick warned the German people that the absence of a proper greeting would be considered suspicious behavior. For Kershaw, *heil hitler!* was only one part of a larger state project centered around the Hitler myth. Through a collusion (untheorized in Kershaw's account) between popular participation and a propaganda machine, this state project by and large established legitimacy for the Nazi Party for the duration of the Third Reich. In propaganda events, on the street, at rallies and marches, on the radio, and in film and picture, the Hitler greeting allegedly provided mass support for the Hitler state.

Like the swastika flag, the use of *heil hitler!* was viewed as a measure of legitimacy for the Nazi regime among the Aryan populace by two major contenders for their allegiance: the Gestapo and the Sopade. Their respective situational reports cited the absence of a Hitler greeting as evidence of dissatisfaction with the regime. Taking these agents at their word, Kershaw sometimes interpreted these absences as political dissent. At other points in his narrative, however, Kershaw minimized the significance of these greetings in contrast to general political conformity. In the case of Catholic priests, he interpreted nonconformist greeting as "a minor, but symbolic, expression of political dissent" (1983b: 115). In the case of the middle classes of Augsburg and Munich, it was an expression of "ideological schizophrenia or utter confusion" (1983a: 132): that is, a form of self-contradictory false consciousness that bordered on the pathological.

Other historians associate greeting not just with the contradictions of everyday life but also with its mediocrity. As far as Michael Balfour is concerned, greeting forced public participation in the same manner as a display of the swastika flag, even from those Germans who were trying to "hibernate" through the Third Reich (that is, choosing inner exile). Though Balfour admitted that greeting with *heil schicklgruber* (the old family name before it was changed) was "highly dangerous" and some did refuse to conform in such matters, still he concluded that such acts of nonconformity were trivial (1988: 62). Celia Applegate also cannot make up her mind about the historical consequences of greeting. She shows that the "inspirational but casual" greeting, *wald-heil*, among heimat-hikers at the turn of the century helped create a convivial, populist alternative to the social organizations and power of the local elite; yet she calls greeting with *happy Pfalz, may God protect it!* instead of *heil hitler!* during the Third Reich a minor exception to the collaborationist norm (1990: 67, 202). Gerhard Binder circumvented the entire issue when he argued that the adoption of *heil hitler!* by the Archbishop of Vienna neither made him into a Hitler supporter nor prevented him from being associated with political opposition in other areas: this greeting, Binder claimed, was simply the style of the day (*Brauch*, 1968: 276–77). On one extreme, then, historians dismiss salutations as a quirk of everyday life: inconsistent at its best, vacuous at its worst.

On the other extreme, scholars use customs like greeting to measure the degree to which that society conforms to bourgeois-democratic norms. According to the classic modernization narrative, Germany developed unevenly. By the turn of the century, it boasted a "modern" industrial economy but was still plagued by "premodern" political and social structures. German society was patriarchal, militaristic, bureaucratic, authoritarian, and even "feudal," and scholars have isolated numerous manifestations of this "German" handicap to prove it. Among other "old-fashioned" traditions to which Germans clung, sociologist Talcott Parsons noted the excessive use of titles in greetings (1954: 112–14). This custom marked class, gender, and intimacy in rigid terms. Such excessively formalistic mores of conviviality limited, he believed, the full freedom of individual development and social mobility crucial for a liberal democracy and bourgeois society. "Down to Hitler's time," William Sheridan Allen argued, "Germany showed extraordinary status-consciousness: foreigners found few things more absurd than the German quest for and insistent use of titles as appendages to their names" (1992: 144).

Salutations cannot be summarily dispatched as a vacuous quirk of everyday life or evidence of ideological schizophrenia. Nor are greetings simply a functional tool in the hands of totalitarian state policy or the social control of traditional elites. More than any other single custom of conviviality, greeting had ensured a sense of normalcy in the neighborhoods of interwar Hildesheim, but that sense of normalcy disguised revolutionary bids for power and status. Even more so than hanging a flag or wearing a uniform, a salutation involved direct, ritualized communication. It reassured its denizens of a minimum of mutual respect as neighbors. But as Allen hinted, all this changed during the 1930s. By altering their greetings behind the veil of normalcy, ordinary Hildesheimers helped the Nazi regime to transform their civil society into a volksgemeinschaft.

This change was as profound as it was self-evident. What used to be a curtsy, a bow, a tip of the hat, a shake of the hand, an offer of the time of day, perhaps some questions about the lives of neighbors, now became *heil hitler!* As Figure 16 attests, this greeting literally and semiotically heralded the arrival of a new regime in Berlin and a new order in Hildesheim. Such state-sponsored propaganda cannot be taken as representative of everyday life in fact. Still, this dramatic change in greeting cannot be explained away solely as the product of a policy decision by a totalitarian state. Hildesheimers chose to alter their normal greetings (and not just in support of the Third Reich) relatively independent of German political elites and in some cases in advance of the Nazi seizure of power. What such photographs do reveal is how the valence of greeting had shifted back from pragmatics to semantics: from the fact that one greeted in general to the way one greeted in particular.

Heil is related etymologically to *salvation*: as in *ewiges heil* (everlasting salvation) and *heilig* (holy). As a modern greeting, it was closer in meaning to *hail* (Snyder 1976: 140). According to Prause (§72–73), *heil* had died out as a salutation by the twelfth century. It re-entered colloquial German in the first decades of the twentieth century in situations involving drinking (replacing *prosit*), and in coming or going (replacing *adieu* or *good day*). It was a common expression among youth, students, hikers, gymnasts, and the völkisch minded. In politics, it was associated with national socialists (*heil hitler!*) as well as with communists (*heil moscow*). Add to this list *adieu, auf wiedersehen,* and so on, and it becomes clear that there were many

Figure 16. Adolf Hitler in Hildesheim, 30 September 1934.
Courtesy of: SAH 951/7948.

Figure 17. First-year pub visit, Easter 1930 (D/1385).

options for greeting in Hildesheim in the decades before the Nazis seized state power. Yet *heil* differed from *good day* (and others greetings like it) in that it was more like a hat than a greeting. *Heil* announced something about your identity to your interlocutors: your political persuasions.

"For instance, here I have a picture," Günther Seidner began, and took out the image shown in Figure 17. Günther explained that when gymnasium students of the lower second class graduated to the upper second class (Günther was fifteen, almost sixteen years old), and formally became upperclassmen, they went to a pub to celebrate, sometimes with their teachers. "It was 1930," Günther explained, and "Adolf Hitler came in '33." Still, two of his classmates had already become convinced National Socialists. The group photograph captured the moment when, sitting together in a pub, drinking beer and talking in comfort, one (or perhaps both) of these "rascal" students lifted a hand in a Hitler greeting.

> This was quite typical. They [*sic*] wanted to make an example, so you could see. They were only individuals in 1930, still just a few individuals. He [*sic*] just felt he had to express his political convictions at this visit to the pub by showing the fascist greeting. (G/84a R/45)

In 1930, greeting was still a medium by which neighbors negotiated identities in their local public sphere, but the boys in Günther's class shifted its character. *Good day* had expressed the self through pragmatic meaning:

because all neighbors greeted in spite of differences, greeting effaced hetero-
geneity and conflict in the neighborhood. *Heil hitler,* by contrast, expressed
the self through semantic meaning: it drew attention to the words and
actions used to greet and thereby emphasized differences and conflicts.
While saying *heil hitler!* in typical interpersonal encounters, the greeters
were not submissive in demeanor, as one would be in bowing politely to
neighbors. By contrast, they stood upright, thrusting their right arms into
the interpersonal space. They no longer physically touched their neighbors
with a handshake; they challenged them. Instead of showing respect to
those customs of conviviality that established civility in this civil society,
their greeting now invaded the local public sphere and colonized it with
Nazi principles.

Käthe Stolte tells a similar story. Daughter of an officer at the railroad,
she lived her entire life in the Nordstadt, an area known for its proletariat
even though communists were actually very few in number and influence.
She remembered no overt conflicts between the communists and the Nazis,
or between the Stahlhelm (a paramilitary group on the right) and the Reichsbanner (on the left). "I only know that my father used to say, 'Leave them
be. They are communists. They will remain communists.' And you know,
that did not bother me. They were always very friendly and greeted, as it
were." Sometimes these communist workers would chat with Käthe's father
while he was returning home from work. Because he greeted and spoke to
them, they called her father "a very fine man." Likewise these communist
workers were always very orderly. "We children also played with their children, and I was never bothered by that!" (*juckt; G/187a R/100, 125*). The
ritual repetition of greeting ensured a minimal level of mutual recognition
by people of very different social standings and political opinions: a civil
society in practice.

Then times changed for Käthe. Her neighborhood became Nazi. "You
could see it—when they were in the SA. They wore SA uniforms." In the
quiet, still salon in which we were conducting the interviews, Käthe made a
sudden motion—the Hitler greeting, right at me—and I was startled. "Yes
indeed!" she added, as if to say that I should have been shocked by this new
salutation, that she too had been shocked. "And if you encountered them,
then you no longer said *good day* rather you said *heil hitler!*" So her father
told her, "OK, listen up. Times have changed. If they say *heil hitler!* to you,
then don't make a dumb face, but say it also!" Käthe said that her family
was forced to participate in Nazi organizations. Since her father's superiors
at the railroad were committed to the movement, her participation, too, was
deemed necessary. Yet Käthe associated the pressure to participate not with
these organizations as much as with this new kind of greeting. When the
Gestapo knocked on her door, such events would be full "of *heil hitler!* and

all of that whatever." Where the ritual repetition of greeting had repressed differences in the neighborhood, now it highlighted them. Greeting no longer evoked a sense of trust and equality but suspicion and alienation. Käthe summarized that "everyone got careful" after 1933 in her neighborhood (G/187a R/25, 70).

The dates that Käthe gives to this sequence of events are highly idiosyncratic, dependent on that first moment when she (or her father) personally felt the pressure to conform to new political circumstances. Other Hildesheimers, like the boys mentioned by Günther, began to challenge the logic of greeting years before the Nazi seizure of power. Yet the point remains that Nazi herrschaft in Hildesheim relied to a large degree on neighbors transforming how they interacted informally over the course of the 1930s. What began as a countercultural style of greeting that rejected the Weimar Republic became the hegemonic norm in support of the Third Reich. It is this quality of informal social relations that the Nazi regime sought to copy during Hitler's visit to town in 1934: a jubilant crowd voluntarily greeting with *heil hitler!* Salutations became a public demonstration of one's political faith *en masse,* as seen in Figure 16, but the formal enactment was supposed to seem like an informal insurrection as seen in Figure 17.

Whereas greetings had fluctuated in the 1920s, this shift to *heil hitler!* was more revolutionary precisely because it gave greater priority to the semantic meaning than to the pragmatic. As Heide Gerstenberger argued (1987: 41), the Nazi volksgemeinschaft "had been constituted first in that moment in which they enacted this comical gesture with their arm for the first time and added *heil hitler!*" By publicly announcing one's conformity to the new volksgemeinschaft, the Hildesheimers who first introduced *heil hitler!* into their neighborhoods altered the nature of the social for their neighbors. These early Nazi sympathizers did not act in a vacuum: the Nazi regime stood close by to enforce compliance with the threat of violence when required by law (Kershaw 1983a, 1983b). Yet no law mandated its use by all Germans during informal social encounters. For instance, when Gerhard Mock's family used to go strolling on Sunday with friends and met people they knew, they took off their hat and said *good morning, Mr. or Mrs. So-and-so.* It did not matter that his father was Jewish. Even Ernst Ehrlicher, the Mayor, exchanged proper greetings: *good morning, Mr. Mayor! How are you, Mr. Mock?* Gerhard believed that, had they run into Ehrlicher after 1933, he still would have greeted properly (though significantly, he did not recall a specific incident). Within a few years of 1933, however, many people had ceased greeting his family (G/120b R/140; cf. Arndt 1983).

In the 1920s, Hildesheimers had learned to insist on the ritual repetition of greeting among friends and neighbors. As children, they had faced possible denunciation from adult neighbors for an improper greeting. In the

1930s, too, ordinary Hildesheimers policed themselves and their neighbors. Because of the total claims of the Nazi regime, they experienced this informal social pressure as formal police observation, but that was more a product of coordination of conviviality than a result of specific Gestapo tactics. For instance, the Nazi seizure of power was discussed in Lotte Schohl's school. Fifteen years old in 1933, Lotte remembered "that there were lots of excited voices and also others, who behaved very calmly. And in our school, we knew precisely who was now for the Nazis and who was against them." Once again, it was a coordinated greeting that revealed one's political persuasions. "It was ordered that we should no longer say *good day* but *heil hitler!* Like this or this. And also if we went into a store." Yet Lotte did not clarify who gave that order. She also could not recall precisely if this shift took place immediately after the Nazi seizure of power or if it was a more gradual process, but she did remember the pragmatic problem she faced as a young woman. "If we said *good day,* then we stood out. Things were not all that easy then." Lotte then described the institution that loomed over these imperatives to participate: the Gestapo building on Gartenstrasse. Yet the threat of violent retribution by the Gestapo remained rumor for her. The social pressure to conform in school, in stores, and on the street was far more real than the Gestapo. She could immediately recognize which teachers approved or disapproved of the Nazis by how they greeted: either with enthusiasm or so that you could not understand what they were saying. It was in the greetings among neighbors that she noticed the presence, and felt the power, of the Nazi movement (G/8a R/00, G/9b R/230).

The state did not so much impose the new greeting on Hildesheimers as Hildesheimers used the new greeting, and the terror state that loomed behind it, to gain power over their neighbors. Günther Seidner described his father's colleagues at gymnasium as German nationalists and other "democrats" [*sic*]. But in 1933, one of his colleagues was denounced as someone who "thought differently." The director had made snide remarks about the Nazis during class. Two of his colleagues could not accept this and decided to get rid of him. So they denounced him. During his departing speech in the hall in front of the whole school, he said: "The denouncer is the biggest dog in all the land!" (*Der grösste Hund im ganzen Land, das ist der Denunziant!*) Regarding this incident, Günther commented: "So much courage he had had! Then he was gone." He was fired with only half pay and he moved to Hannover (G/80a R/450). By contrast, Günther's father was not denounced, Günther explained, because the school had prized him greatly. We cannot accept this excuse: surely the former director had also been a valued colleague. Rather Günther's father was not denounced because he had conformed. Prior to the Nazi time, when a teacher came into the classroom, all the students had to stand, greet him with *good morning,* and were told to sit by the teacher. During the Third Reich, "everyone stood up and shouted *heil hitler! And* the teachers had to shout also." Günther's father did not seem to have a problem with this for a decade: he shouted *heil hitler!* along with the rest. Only after Stalingrad did his behavior change. Only then did his father "always" have the courage to corrupt the Hitler greeting. He began by raising his hand as if to say, *heil hitler!* but instead let it fall, as if to tell the others to sit down. Indeed, Günther only learned about this aspect of his father's past through conversations with his father's pupils.

Günther used this story of nonconformity in the interview process, just as his father had used the original act after 1943, to distinguish themselves as German nationalists from ardent Nazis. Then Günther almost let the cat slip out of the bag: if his father could have been an antifascist rebel after Stalingrad, why had he not done so before? Recognizing this contradiction in his own story, Günther answered this question without my having to pose it. He described the punishment given by state authorities for such acts of eigensinn. When a column marched by with the swastika flag, Günther explained, those who did not hold up their hand in a Hitler greeting could get kicked in the backside or have their arm broken. "Then they shot their arm up fast" (G/84b R/325, G/80a R/365). This anecdote described one of the few instances when a proper greeting was in fact compelled by the Nazi regime. Yet he avoided alluding to the far more common case: when ordinary Hildesheimers met each other on the street.

Jürgen Ludewig told me a joke about the Institute for the Deaf and Dumb on Kesslerstrasse, the moral of which was very much the same as Günther's story: "When a division of the Hitler [Youth] or the SA came by with a flag, the flag had to be greeted. Everyone who stood there or walked by had to greet the flag. And then one day a young man stood there [and] when the flag came, he did this—." Jürgen made what seemed to be the greeting of the Communist Party. Continuing his joke, he explained that several Nazis pounced on this unfortunate man immediately. It turns out that this man did not intend an insult but, being "dumb," had confused the communists and the national socialists. In sign language, he had said: "I greet you, workers of the mind and the fist." But the Nazis neither appreciated his gesture nor, given their eugenic principles, did they sympathize with his handicap. Above all, they did not care if he understood what he was doing. They just wanted him to give them the proper German greeting. This off-color joke had been told to Jürgen by Erich Meyer, a Jewish boy who had lived on his street until he disappeared "suddenly" (see also Kaplan 1998: 58–59). Clearly, greeting was not a joking matter; and yet Jürgen dismissed the pressure to conform with eigensinn.

State power certainly reinforced the ritual repetition of *heil hitler!* during the Third Reich. As one historian writes, "every child was expected to say *heil hitler!* 50 to 150 times a day" (Snyder 1976: 140). The question is: by whom? The social expectation to greet neighbors in Hildesheim preceded the Third Reich, just as ordinary Hildesheimers introduced *heil hitler!* into convivial customs relatively independent of the Nazi regime. That is, Hildesheimers also greeted with *heil hitler!* when the SA were *not* marching past. Some Hildesheimers introduced Nazi habits for political reasons, some to gain power and status in the new social order, and some for both reasons. Günther admitted that he found much in national socialism with which he agreed: from the reconquest of the "German East" to forced labor (G/84b R/325). No doubt his father did too.

Salutations were neither solely a matter of Nazi dictatorship nor merely an act of ordinary interactions among friends and neighbors. Would-be Nazi rulers jockeyed for position in the 1930s with would-be rebels, making greetings into a critical, cultural battlefield on which the success of totalitarianism was decided. For instance, Gerhard Mock's family had a maid who had worked for them for many years. Her son had joined the HJ, but the adults had always been social democrats. One day, she came to Gerhard's mother crying. There had been a fight between the maid and her son, and the boy left the room in anger. His parting greeting was: *heil hitler!* His mother replied "Yes, why don't you throw him into this too [*Ja, leg ihn da mal hin*]!" Turning back, the boy threatened: "What did you say? Do you realize that you said that about my Führer! I am going to the HJ and report you!" (G/115a R/330). Historians would be shortsighted to interpret this greeting and threat of denunciation within the family simply as an act of political conformity or confusion on the part of the boy. It was also an act of self-expression in a power struggle between the generations, a struggle that Hildesheimers had been waging for years by wearing felt hats or taking the stroll. More accurately, his was both a strategy for political herrschaft as well as a tactic of generational eigensinn; but since it was "only" a matter of a greeting in either case, he could hide both behind the veil of the everyday. His collaboration was at once completely obvious and completely ordinary. What Kershaw called ideological schizophrenia made perfect sense on the streets of Hildesheim.

These absurd contradictions (Bergerson 2002a, 2004) were especially characteristic of the transitional years of the mid-1930s. Franz Meissner had been a convinced Zionist since before 1933. When he went to the Gestapo to make the bureaucratic preparations for his emigration to Palestine, the officer greeted with *heil hitler!* Franz replied, *good day!* The conversation continued: *heil hitler! good day!* and so on, until they finally decided to simply get down to the business at hand (G/160b R/70). A slightly different series of events took place one day in 1936 when Franz left his apartment to go out. He met a member of the SA on the street. This adult inquired about some address further along on the street, and Franz told him how to get there. Then, examining the boy's clothing, the adult inquired: "*Why are you not in the Hitler Youth?*" Franz replied: "*I am a Jew.*" "*Oh yes,*" the SA man answered. "Good day." Franz responded as well with: "Good day" (G/161a R/220; in *German* in the interview). Greeting with *good day* seemed to be the most ordinary thing for Franz to do at the time, or so he claimed. "What else would I have said?" Only in retrospect, after reading what happened in other places and times, did he realize how curious it was that a member of the SA greeted with *good day* instead of *heil hitler!* in the local, public sphere—and that he greeted a Jew at all. Yet Franz was also playing dumb: he obviously realized the significance of his eigensinnig greeting when he had met with the Gestapo officer three years earlier. Franz used the normalcy of greeting to get a jab at his oppressors, just as Günther's classmates had done in 1930 to challenge the Weimar Republic. Franz just hid his attempt to embarrass his neighbor behind the normalcy of greeting one's neighbor.

This example is not intended to evoke counterfactual thought experiments about what would have occurred had all Hildesheimers stayed true to the principles of their civil society. The factual point is that they did not. Some proactively changed their customs in anticipation of the Nazi regime's wishes. Others followed suit to avoid such awkward situations as these. In either case, ordinary Hildesheimers transformed neighbors into Jews and Aryans through this public, symbolic debate. This anecdote thus belies the claims of so many ordinary Hildesheimers that they were forced by the Nazi regime or even informal social pressure to coordinate their greetings to the principles of the Nazi revolution. In the case of this SA man, a representative of that Third Reich, it was the old habits of civility, not the principles of Nazi barbarity, that were still sufficiently powerful in the mid-1930s such that Franz was able to embarrass him into returning to the traditional *good day* instead of *heil hitler!* Ordinary Hildesheimers chose all-too-consciously between these options: they just tended to choose the latter over the former.

The agency of these kinds of Nazi collaborators corresponds to the model of the polycratic Hitler state. The Nazi leaders did not have to order ordinary Hildesheimers to change their salutations. Conscious of Nazi principles, they coordinated the customs of their informal social relations to fit Nazi principles. Yet even those who did not support the Nazi regime and had the courage to greet in nonconformist ways contributed to the Nazi revolution in everyday life. By insisting on an emphatic *good day!*[1] instead of *heil hitler!* Franz polemicized greeting just as much as this Gestapo officer had done. Both expressed their private political attitudes in the local public sphere. Both laid claim to status and power in imagined, future societies:

to herrschaft in the Thousand-Year Reich or eigensinn in the hope of its collapse. Both participated in a public debate that divided their neighborhood into fascists and antifascists. They kept this open secret even from themselves in order to protect themselves from retribution for their acts. During the interview process, they simply reiterated those same habits as ordinary Hildesheimers.

Coming to Terms with the Nazi Present

In this analysis, I do not seek to ignore the moral difference between conformity and nonconformity. And this process was not initiated by Jews but by their neighbors who were sympathetic to the Nazi cause, who were willing to use it to their own advantage, or for both reasons. Nonetheless, antifascist revolts against Nazi claims to herrschaft were also public declarations of political faith. If historians wish to understand how the Nazis achieved an atmosphere of totalitarianism in towns like Hildesheim, then we must recognize that the Nazis *solicited the aid* of their opponents and even some of their victims in this process (Bauman 1996; see also Kren and Rappaport 1980). This insight is absurd, but so was everyday life during the Third Reich. The absurdity of Franz's encounter with the SA man is precisely what made it so memorable decades later. Such anecdotes demand lucid, systematic investigation precisely because their implications are so disturbing (Bergerson 2002a, 2004).

The chronology of alienation from and integration into the Third Reich varied from person to person and depended on many factors (Kaplan 1998; Peukert 1982b: 243–99 at 244; cf. Hilberg 1992), but over the course of the 1930s, increasingly more Hildesheimers adjusted their conviviality to fit Nazi principles. Both Jews and Gentiles, Nazi sympathizers and skeptics found themselves in situations in which they felt that they were being asked to collaborate with the Nazi regime by excluding their Jewish neighbors or that they themselves no longer belonged. These were experiences of *disjuncture:* moments when their expectations based on habit memories did not correspond to present experiences.[2] It was in these moments of cultural alienation that some Hildesheimers recognized their social alienation from the new völkisch community and began to make concrete plans to rectify that situation. Arguably, they remembered these incidents so clearly, in spite of the passage of half a century, because these surprising moments of cultural contradiction saved their lives—and yet they were still trying to make sense of them (Bergerson 2004; Gerstenberger 1987: 41).

Perhaps Dora Pröbst so relished telling me about the absurd contradictions of life under Hitler because she lived so many of them personally. A Protestant woman, she had married Erich, a Jewish man, in 1934. She stubbornly refused to recognize the antisemitism in her community and country. For instance, Erich used to make dates with her by calling her on the telephone at the fire station across from her house, which her neighbors were happy to let her use. But increasingly, some of the firemen used this opportunity to insult her for dating a Jew (G/123b R/160). When she requested a pass for her imprisoned husband from a local Gestapo officer, he greeted her with *heil hitler!* and she replied with *good day!* According to Dora, this officer had studied criminology and was a Nazi by convenience not conviction; it was his boss in the Gestapo who was the ardent Nazi. Still, the fact that she greeted him with *good day!* while standing in the local Gestapo headquarters nearly caused him to fall off his chair in surprise (G/124a R/325).

Dora and Erich had become friendly with Gerdl and Ulrich Ossenkopp before the Nazi seizure of power. Gerdl worked as an apprentice in the same store as Dora on Hoher Weg. They spent much time together, both as two couples and just the men or the women on their own. They were all very close. As the Nazis gained influence in town (ca. 1932), they all spent more time together (G/125b R/60). These friendships helped to insulate her at first from recognizing how many of her fellow Hildesheimers were joining the Nazi party: friendship preserved a sense of normalcy for her. After 1933, however, the inverse was the case because now it was *her* friends who joined the Nazi party. Ulrich Ossenkopp worked across the street from Dora and Gerdl; Dora often ran into him on Hoher Weg. One day, she saw that he was wearing a swastika insignia. He tried to hide it quickly by slipping it under his lapel before she could see it:

> This happened a few times, and then . . . when I suspected that something like this would take place . . . then it was I who walked on the other side of the street so I did not have to walk past these people. He did not have to greet me nor did he have to hide his swastika because he felt embarrassed.

I asked Dora why she did this.

> Because strictly speaking I did not want to know so precisely that it really— 'Cause this Ulrich Ossenkopp and his wife . . . we were very close to them. We were of different temperaments, and my brother always said that he could not understand how we could be friends, but we got along well. We had lots of fun. . . . I did not want to admit to myself that things had changed. OK, I did not want to recognize the nazism, the antisemitism. I did not want to know about it so precisely. (G/123b R/250)

When Dora saw Ulrich with the swastika, she "had the feeling that very many people had become Nazis externally and internally were still—." In the 1990s, she still found it hard to admit that her best friends had become Nazis by convenience (G/126a R/40).

As sympathetic as Dora was to Ulrich's underlying motives, his swastika insignia functioned in the local public sphere in much the same way as a flag, uniform, or salutation. By adding an insignia to his clothing, Ulrich was publicly demonstrating his political conformity. Precisely because he was such a close friend, this particular swastika challenged Dora to recognize the spread of national socialism in her hometown. So when Dora guessed that one of her neighbors or friends might have been wearing a swastika or had become a Nazi, "then I simply walked on the other side of the street, then I let him or her walk down the street without me having to pass them and without saying *hello* and so on. All this resulted from the Nazi insignia which often disappeared under Ulrich Ossenkopp's lapel" (G/123b R/250). The more their neighbors showed their support for Hitler with public demonstrations of their political faith, the more Erich and Dora's friendship with Gerdl and Ulrich cooled off (G/128b R/140).

For her part, Dora knew that Ulrich, too, was not a Nazi by conviction but by convenience. Yet she blamed herself for placing him in a crisis of conscience.

> My husband was the Jew! You too [would] have avoided bringing these people into a circumstance [in which they would be forced to say:] "God, it is awkward for me to be together with you or to be friendly with you." So it got weaker and weaker, the friendship. (G/126a R/00, 40)

For his part, Erich still hoped that he could remain a Hildesheimer in the older sense in spite of the fact that he was Jewish. He insisted that they return to Hildesheim from a trip to the United States in the winter of 1937, anticipating that Hitler would soon be "gone from the table." By this time, however, Dora had already come to suspect that they would come to regret that decision. Erich drove himself to the Godehardi prison, where the Gestapo intended to incarcerate him, without concern. After parking his car in the prison's lot, he called Dora and reassured her: "Don't get excited. I will certainly be home by tomorrow. But pick up the car" (G/124a R/170, 225). She tried to persuade Erich to emigrate to the United States, and she thought that his imprisonment especially might convince him. But Erich still identified as a German and a Hildesheimer, and he refused to leave. All that she could do until he came around was attempt to lead an even more private life: that is, to emigrate internally. She finally persuaded Erich to escape to America in 1938 (G/129b R/120).

Salutations had long been the mechanism of choice by which interwar Hildesheimers negotiated integration and alienation in their local public sphere. The new Third Reich held meaning for Dora only when its principle of antisemitism was communicated to her through the medium of conviviality. She then adjusted her identity into the wife of a Jew by not greeting her best friends. Dora remembered this seemingly insignificant encounter with Ulrich so vividly half a century later because it was at that moment that she experienced a sense of cultural alienation: the subtle but revolutionary reinvention of conviviality. That disjuncture empowered her to take decisive steps to respond to the nazification of her hometown: the first step being as small an act as walking on the other side of the street. This choice was eigensinnig because Dora chose to alienate herself from her neighbors in indignant revolt against a situation that presented her with untenable options. Said in another way, hers was a courageous act of *Gegenwartsbewältigung:* of using local customs to come to terms with her Nazi present.

None of Dora's choices seemed viable. On the one hand, greeting in the new way with *heil hitler!* (as increasing numbers of her Aryan friends and neighbors were doing) was obviously unreasonable for a woman married to a Jewish man. On the other hand, she had been raised to show respect for her neighbors, her friends, and herself as a member of a civil society by greeting all of her neighbors with respect. Yet if she greeted with some form of *good day!* she would have alienated herself from her own community and marked herself as a potential victim of Nazi violence. Above all, an emphatic *good day!* did more harm than good since Dora wished more than anything else to preserve her sense of normalcy. Appropriately, she did not admit this desire to herself: that would have undermined the open secret that normalcy was in fact a myth. Instead, she projected this strong desire for normalcy onto her friends and neighbors. Taking part in their lives like a true friend and good neighbor, she avoided confronting them with such troubling, ethical choices entirely. She walked on the other side of the street.

Dora's story is highly idiosyncratic, but her choice is illustrative of the dilemma facing ordinary people during the Third Reich; it also shows how many people chose to cope with the situation (Henry 1984; Kaplan 1998: esp. ch. 1; Stolzfus 1996). Walking on the other side of the street enabled Dora to live as normal a life as possible as an Aryan woman married to a Jewish man in the Third Reich. In that inverted world, she salvaged her civil society and her sense of normalcy by removing its dissonant elements: her husband and her self. Yet in the process, she effectively helped her Nazi neighbors to coordinate conviviality in interwar Hildesheim to fit Nazi principles. Though acting clearly against her will (G/127b R/110, 130), she segregated herself and her husband into an alien subculture apart from the new volksgemeinschaft.

The Nazi regime took an active role in terrorizing Dora and Erich with defamation campaigns and false arrests. Throughout the 1930s, however, she responded to the taunts of the Gestapo and Nazi journalists with courageous acts of private and public dissent (G/124b R/230, G/129b R/120, 200). She even traveled to Gestapo headquarters in Berlin to demand her husband's files so that they could see what information they contained (G/124a R/225, 340, G/124b R/00, 85, 230, G/129b R/20, 120, 200). In itself, the Nazi regime could not succeed in sufficiently alienating her physically from her own community. What forced her change of consciousness was the moment of cultural disjuncture when she tried to greet her friend who was wearing a Nazi insignia. Arguably, she was able to lead her husband into exile only because she had already exiled herself. In this sense, she was behaving as a Hildesheimer *par excellence*. She used informal customs of conviviality to redraw the boundaries of membership in her neighborhood. This time, she just excluded herself.

Dora's trick of walking on the other side of the street was not unique. For instance, Gerhard remembered having had no conflicts with neighbors even after 1933: his was "a civilized neighborhood." Then he recalled his neighbor, the widow of Dr. Ohlendorf, who lived in the *twin house (das Zwillinghaus)* on the other side of his street. Gerhard believed that she was very lucky to have neighbors like his family because they restored their house and kept their garden in order, making the whole neighborhood look good. Her daughter was the closest of friends with his younger sister, so close that they used to crawl through a hole in the fence between the two gardens to play. "And then the Nazis came and much changed." The older Ohlendorf daughter had married a man who became the mayor of a nearby spa town after 1933. "And then Mrs. Ohlendorf did not seem to know us anymore." She no longer greeted the Mock family. "You just walked past each other." The Ohlendorfs looked away. "I also looked away." Gerhard's family was even alienated by neighbors whom they knew were still decent people, "but who were worried that others . . . could have seen them when they said, *Herr Mock! So how are you doing?*" So Gerhard did what Dora had done: he tried to not catch their attention. "It was too painful to play this little game."

To be sure, some courageous people still greeted the Mocks, even asking as to their circumstances. The neighbors across the way, the Neudeck family, still knew and greeted the Mocks and refused to give Gerhard "the thing." He raised his straight right arm to demonstrate what he meant, but refused to say, even in the 1990s (G/120a R/95; see also G/110b R/00, 140). In 1939, Gerhard recalled earlier in the interviews, he had tried to walk on the other side of the street to avoid a certain Mr. Pelz. Gerhard knew Pelz to be an upstanding fellow, but perhaps precisely for that reason, Gerhard tried "to help him out of this dilemma" by walking on the other side of the street. Like Dora, Gerhard tried to avoid forcing Pelz to publicly announce his antifascist beliefs simply for the sake of treating Gerhard with a minimum of neighborly respect. Pelz responded by crossing the street. "What is up with you?" Pelz asked Gerhard. "Are you running away from me?" Pelz told him never to do that again. "I want to talk to you," he added. Gerhard then disclosed his plans for imminent emigration to the United States via Lord Kitchner's Camp in England. Pelz responded to this news by saying: "I envy you." Referring to the Nazi revolution, Pelz concluded: "You can spit it out; we have to swallow it" (G/111b R/150). Pelz's humanity is noteworthy for its everyday heroism, but ultimately, Gerhard exiled himself from Germany in much the same way that Dora did. He too used the cultural logic of conviviality to come to terms with the Nazi present.

Ulrich Gerke recounted an even more tragic story about Eva Braun (G/86a R/220). He was referring to an attractive young woman with dark hair, the daughter of a master painter in Hildesheim, not to Hitler's consort of the same name; but this Eva Braun also fell in love with a Nazi: an SA man. In 1934, when he and the neighborhood all learned that Eva's mother was half Jewish, the SA man broke off the relationship and Eva jumped from one of the bridges over the train station. She survived only to spend the rest of her life permanently disabled. Nazi laws permitted quarter-Jews like her to marry Aryans if they received the approval of the regime. Yet she took it upon herself to adjust her relationship to fit Nazi principles. This tragedy of self-exclusion then further reinforced the norms of the new volksgemeinschaft as a story that was reiterated among neighbors.

Heinrich Weber corroborated this growing sense of interracial alienation from the other perspective. After several attempts, Heinrich finally replied directly to my question about whether Jews and ardent Nazis still greeted each other on the streets of his neighborhood during the Third Reich.

> *Ach was*! No one did anything to them. They were just required to wear their Jewish star. So you knew precisely that they were Jews. And then you walked out of their way or both people avoided each other, you know—as long as that could work in some way. (*noch einigermassen haltbar war*; G/146b R/50)

Heinrich was lying to himself as much as to me when he claimed that no one hurt local Jews, but his comment does provide reliable insight into how ordinary Hildesheimers (including town bureaucrats like him) were able to ignore the dehumanizing effects of their own daily behavior. Walking on the other side of the street was a powerful mechanism of social aryanization that enabled Hildesheimers to coordinate their neighborhoods and friendships to fit Nazi principles without sacrificing their sense of normalcy. By setting his story after 1941, when the Nazi regime first introduced the Jewish star, Heinrich was able to act as if the coordination of conviviality was imposed from above. Yet it was precisely the behavior of ordinary Hildesheimers like himself during the 1930s that set the stage for that public policy behind the veil of the ordinary.

By exiling themselves from the Nazi volksgemeinschaft, Dora Pröbst and Gerhard Mock saved their lives and the lives of their loved ones; yet they inadvertently aided Hitler in ridding Germany of its Jews. Heinrich Weber and the Ohlendorfs laid claim to status and power with their future prospects clearly in mind by proactively alienating and denigrating their Jewish neighbors. From the perspective of everyday life, then, it was not the Nazi regime as such that changed a civil society into a völkisch community, but ordinary people.

Modernization

In the 1930s, Hildesheimers had to make awkward, public choices about how to greet their neighbors. As requirements for any kind of subsequent interaction, these decisions were as public as they were personal, as disturbing as they were pervasive. Every day, throughout the day, Hildesheimers had to think seriously about how they should respond. Should they continue to greet their neighbors in any form even if it meant saying *heil hitler!* to preserve the experience of community? Or should they greet their neighbors with an emphatic *good day!* to preserve their civil society? The Nazi revolution was not a mysterious or silent process executed by agents of the Nazi regime while the rest of Hildesheim slept, as the burning of the Hildesheim synagogue is often depicted in postwar memory. To be effective, this revolution in social relations had to be executed in full public view. Here, then, is the open secret that haunts the memories of my interview partners: ordinary people helped make Hildesheim fascist behind the veil of the everyday.

Did they also modernize Hildesheim in the process? According to the classic modernization narratives in German historiography, Nazi coordination, terror, and racism eliminated barriers to self-cultivation in the long term by offering at most the possibility for upward social mobility, or at the least the illusion of greater status and recognition. When the brown revolution subordinated the Germans equally to a totalitarian state, it eliminated traditional social structures. Käthe Stolte vividly invoked the specter of the Nazi terror state within a longer narrative of totalitarian violence. First she explained how she was pressed into labor service at a local rubber plant. Then she explained how, when she rode back and forth for the midday meal between work in Moritzberg and home in the Nordstadt, the streetcar would stop in front of the Theater on the Zingel where the "big Gestapo house" was located. Once the Gestapo agents got on, "then it was deathly quiet in the streetcar . . . no one said anything." Normal conversation was replaced with "an enormous silence. Everything was quiet" (G/187a R/285, G/189a

R/130). In Käthe's account, it was the Nazi regime that not only made Hildesheim more fascist but also more modern. She clearly shared (or reiterated) this authoritative narrative of a totalitarian state atomizing historically impotent individuals. In order to better understand how systemic historical consequences could arise from the manifold activities of ordinary people, let us take a close look at two strangely inconsistent anecdotes, recounted by the same person but to two different interviewers, about the same everyday habit. This comparison will show that by engaging in semiotic debates over whether to nazify conviviality, ordinary people also helped modernize it.

As a child in the 1920s, Ulrike Volkmann covertly knew the politics of her neighbors and used this familiarity to mobilize support for her party during elections. As an adult during the 1930s, she once again learned which of her neighbors were Nazis according to how they behaved: she noted whether they used the German greeting. Her family responded with passive disobedience. "We held ourselves back. We did it as little as possible—when they did not notice it." As an example, she told me the story about how she and her brother had attended the funeral of a twenty-year-old woman. Afterwards, the woman was cremated and the coffin put in a wagon to carry it to the cemetery. "Everyone stood around [it], putting up their hands in greeting." That is, they made the Hitler greeting. "We still stood there in the door to the hall and, I will never forget it, my brother gave me a real jerk. 'Show me your handkerchief' [he said], and began to snort seriously. I was supposed to get out my handkerchief and poke [at my nose] so I did not have to do it." *It* refers to the Hitler greeting. Ulrike and her brother cleverly used their alleged sadness over the death of this young girl to avoid doing *it*. The Nazis interpreted not greeting as an anti-Nazi statement, but as she implied: one must wipe one's nose (G/61a R/125, 320). On the one hand, then, Ulrike proudly demonstrated that she could resist Nazi policy when it came to the Hitler greeting.

On the other hand, Ulrike also depicted herself as the passive victim and beneficiary of Nazi policy. In this case, she was discussing greetings with another interviewer, a native Hildesheimer then in his early thirties. To him, Ulrike admitted this about the Third Reich: "the only good thing was this greeting—that the men no longer had to take off their hats. Earlier, they all wore hats and then they had to greet properly. It was really annoying" (SAH 904-1/43a R/340). From this perspective, the Nazi regime modernized an outmoded greeting by foisting a uniform *heil hitler!* on ordinary Hildesheimers like Ulrike. The issue at stake here is not simply the burden of disrobing one's head at every social encounter but the social hierarchy that hats reimposed over and against the communal equality of the greeting itself. The new German greeting may have been offensive to Ulrike in the short- and medium term, but in the long term, it seems as if Hitler indirectly created a more open society by eradicating an old-fashioned habit that had only served to keep people in their place.

Both narratives made sense because greeting was a mixed bag for most Hildesheimers, as was the Third Reich in general. Ulrike resented the politicization of greeting because she was a Catholic, but she welcomed the change to *heil hitler!* because it rid Hildesheim of a bothersome, archaic ritual. These stories were narrated separately to two different interviewers because they explained two divergent experiences. In the first story, Ulrike boasted with eigensinn about her revolt against Nazi herrschaft in the 1990s for much the same reason that she did it in the 1930s: to feel the thrill of self-cultivation, to express her antifascist identity, and to lay claim to the status and power that came with it. In the second story, Ulrike presented herself as an ordinary person who had no meaningful influence over history. She was simply the indirect beneficiary when the dictatorship modernized traditional customs from above; and this policy from above removed an outmoded cultural hindrance to freer social interaction and the public recognition of fundamental equality. At the core of both stories lie the same greetings, but Ulrike could not narrate them together. Had she located her eigensinn in a larger story of world-historical change, she would have exposed the open secret of everyday life: that ordinary people like herself helped the Nazi regime both to nazify and to modernize.

Ulrike's eigensinn was not unique. There were examples of nonconformist greetings akin to her blowing-the-nose trick from all three German milieux. My interview partners told me stories about social-democratic workers who resisted nazification "up to a certain point" (G/48a R/125), Catholics who were "all a little imprudent" in the way that they related to the pressure of coordination (G/23a R/100), and even members of the Protestant bourgeoisie who added an ironic tilt of the head to the expected *heil hitler!* and continued it with *but otherwise, things are going well* (G/186a R/95). To be sure, one suspects that these kinds of non-conformist behavior were more likely among Catholics than Protestants and most likely among the socialist working classes. Nonetheless, Ulrike's blowing-the-nose trick was part of a mass movement of nonconformist acts that, along with the mass movement towards conformist acts, crossed the traditional social-political cleavages of modern Hildesheim. Indeed, they were often perpetrated by the same individuals. In order to begin to discuss the systemic consequences of these public debates, rather than trying to label individuals or groups in terms of resistance or participation, we first need to rethink these different kinds of behavior.

Historians have hitherto considered behavior like Ulrike's to be schizophrenic because she publicly objected to Hitler's anti-Catholicism through an inventive greeting while she also publicly applauded the fact that he had eliminated an outmoded greeting. Yet Ulrike was the same individual in the end: doing, or not doing, the same greeting. Her alleged confusion was also nothing new. In fact, the contradictions in her behavior are precisely what made salutations useful. Independent of the Third Reich, Hildesheimers had learned to greet all their neighbors flexibly and dynamically to balance their need for community and equality (which they accomplished by integrating themselves in a neighborhood) with their desires for hierarchy and status (which they accomplished by alienating their neighbors). They also did not relish seeing that open secret disclosed: that they, in fact, shaped their informal social relations to suit their needs and desires. So it makes perfect sense that Ulrike alternated between eigensinn and herrschaft when describing informal social encounters in order to protect herself from responsibility for her actions. Her narrative corresponded to her habits.

These different kinds of behavior in turn interacted in the local public sphere to give shape to the local society. Historians face an impossible dilemma if they seek to choose which of these two narratives was the single historical reality: to suggest, for instance, that Hitler alone or Ulrike alone changed greetings. Ulrike's choices did have historical consequences, just not the ones anticipated by her or by historians. She did not successfully overturn the Nazi regime with her antifascist statements, but she did participate in an informal, public debate on the principles and legitimacy of the Nazi regime—expressed through divergent styles of greeting.

During this debate, Hildesheimers faced a difficult choice among multiple and conflicting social expectations. They could greet with the time of day, by saying *good morning!* as they had in the years prior to 1933. During the Third Reich, this greeting should be understood as expressively *abjuring:* it meant refusing to swear the public oath of allegiance to the Nazi regime.[3] In Hildesheim, neighbors challenged each other on a daily basis to make public demonstrations of their political faith for or against the Third Reich. An abjuring greeting like *good day!* preserved the semantic integrity of prior customs and showed a tenacious respect for tradition as such. Yet it also put the future of the abjuring person at risk because they had publicly rejected the Third Reich. Alternately, Hildesheimers could greet with *heil hitler!* to show their support for the Nazi revolution. This *juring* greeting preserved or even improved one's status and power in the local public sphere, but it publicly challenged the integrity of greeting by altering it publicly, for political purposes, in the face of tradition.

The choice between these conflicting, yet compelling, imperatives divided Hildesheim. Günther Seidner explained that by the time Hildesheimers started hiding in bomb shelters (in the early 1940s), his neighborhood had split. There were those who "spoke about the weather whenever possible" and those, more commonly, who greeted with *heil hitler!* "and nothing else" (G/81b R/60; see also SAH 904-1/55b R/400). This public semiotic debate not only divided society into fascists and antifascists. It also effectively placed one's relationship to Hitler and the regime he represented at the center of convivial relations, intruding into all contacts between friends and neighbors as the measure of proper kinds of human interaction. Ordinary people thus helped to both nazify and modernize their informal social relations. Part of the same story of everyday life, tactics of eigensinn and strategies for herrschaft made conviviality into a primary medium for the Nazi revolution.

Nonetheless, these public debates were distasteful. They revealed the open secret of everyday life: that ordinary Hildesheimers manipulated conviviality for personal and political gain. Ever plucky, Hildesheimers tried to find ways to behave that could restore that undermined façade of normalcy. Günther recalled several neighbors who became active in the Nazi movement. He had to be careful to avoid making overtly political statements, but he still greeted them when they met on the stairwell or on the street (G/80a R/305). "You greeted each other, and talked about such things as health and what is going on, and [what is happening] on that day, and such things" (G/80b R/65, 305; see also G/79b R/105). It was never clear whether Günther meant a *good day!* or a *heil hitler!* in these various accounts. Yet this is precisely the point. Young people greeted, Günther explained, just as they carried newspapers for adults when asked. "Back then, you had respect for your elders. You just did it." Yet "just" greeting with *heil hitler!* meant pledging political support for fascist principles. By claiming "just" to be respecting local customs, Günther effaced the revolutionary reinvention of his traditions and his society to fit Nazi principles. In both of his anecdotes, the normalcy of a neighborly salutation offered Günther a prefabricated and legitimate tool to efface the disjuncture in conviviality. As was the case with walking on the other side of the street, the ritual repetition of greeting enabled him not to recognize the nazism in the neighborhood.

This desire for normalcy crossed both political and racial boundaries. Otto Koch told me how he had been sent to prison in Celle for resistance to the Nazi regime (Bergerson 2002b). When his guard brought him his food each day, Otto greeted him cheerfully. One day, the guard confronted him, challenging him to explain his curious behavior. After all, Otto was in prison, he should have been angry and unhappy. Moreover, Otto was on one side of the bars and the guard was on the other. That is, Otto was a socialist revolutionary and the guard was a Nazi policeman. Otto's response made no sense in the ideal fascist society desired by the Nazi regime, but every bit of sense within the Hildesheim he left behind: since the two men were going to be "working" together, for a while anyway, Otto suggested that they make the best of the situation and be friendly. Otto certainly had no intention of forgetting the political differences between the two of them; and even if he did, he would still have remained behind bars. Still, a cheerful *good morning* helped moderate what was an unpleasant and tense circumstance. Even in the face of a terrorist regime, greeting effaced social discord and resurrected a sense of normalcy in hard times.

Most of Hildesheim's Jews, however, were like Dora's Erich. They believed devoutly in their myths of normalcy and waited for Hitler to disappear from the table (see also Schneider 1998, III: 7). They were not confused by the mixed signals of friends and neighbors (Bergerson 2004; cf. Kaplan 1998): these multiple and contradictory expressions were part and parcel of everyday life. On the contrary, the more that Jewish Hildesheimers adhered to their traditional customs of conviviality—in spite of the Nazi revolution—the more they reinforced their sense of normalcy. They simply refused to recognize the disjunctures in the behavior of friends and neighbors, and continued to behave as if they still belonged in Hildesheim. This eigensinnig response to national socialism delayed their emigration, and those who never did leave were no doubt surprised when they were deported and fell into the Nazi's bureaucratic-industrial system of mass murder. Facing a far more radical experience of disjuncture, many of these people found it impossible to adjust to life in the inverted world of the ghetto or camp. Those not killed were then forced to adjust to their new identities only after they had been deported far from home, looking down the barrel of a gun. Thus, in addition to many other precarious circumstances, they now also faced a real cultural disadvantage. From the moment that they were removed from Hildesheim, they lost a critical tool that had enabled their neighbors to adjust their identities to, and to legitimately contest, Nazi herrschaft: their local customs of conviviality.

6 | Polarization

ALONGSIDE THE NAZI party's national strategy for acquiring political power quasi-legally through the electoral process, ardent local Nazis began the process of making Hildesheim fascist through conviviality. This latter strategy for totalitarian herrschaft was effective because coordination penetrated daily life and yet continued to preserve the veil of the everyday. Antifascists responded with eigensinn. Resisters needed to disguise their antifascist activities from the Gestapo to avoid retribution. Accordingly, they depicted their behavior as if it were simply everyday habits rather than ideological resistance. Once the Nazis destroyed the formal organizations of the opposition, which happened quite quickly in Hildesheim, conviviality represented one of the only legitimate loci remaining for resistance. Conversely, the Gestapo suffered from the success of their police efforts. After destroying the obvious cells of resistance in Hildesheim, they too found it necessary to explore the murkier realm of friendship and neighborliness for evidence of non-conformity. That is, both fascists and antifascists drew conviviality into politics in order to colonize this terrain for political ends.

In order to verify that ordinary people helped create and preserve the Nazi terror state, Robert Gellately has recently revisited judicial records from the Third Reich to show that Nazi police forces relied heavily on denunciations by family, friends, and neighbors to initiate investigations (2001). This case study of Hildesheim investigated conviviality further, in its own terms, and treated its cultural dynamics as a factor in its own right; as a result, it can piece apart the process that created totalitarianism in everyday life. It shows that resistance (from the perspective of antifascist rebels) and criminality (from the perspective of racist rulers) began as conviviality (in all its sincere ambivalence); that it was the struggle to control conviviality over the course of the 1930s that effectively polarized everyday life into the supporters and detractors of the Third Reich (in keeping with the principles of Nazi totalitarianism). This chapter will explore the activities and prosecution of a series of "resistance cells" from the perspective of both judicial records and interview testimony. These cells ranged from formally constituted organizations to informal gatherings among friends and neighbors. The one form of covert political mobilization was based in part on conviviality. The other became increasingly policed and politicized over the course of the 1930s. In the struggles of fascists and antifascists to control the terrain of conviviality, they ravaged it.

Shaving Yourself

Otto Koch described how he found himself in prison for antifascist resistance (G/47b R/90). Intermittently between 1933 and 1936, he received illegal printed matter from Czechoslovakia, England, or Scandinavia through a friend or acquaintance, sometimes in person and sometimes in the mail. Though he did not always know from whom such materials came, he gave them to friends whom he could trust, especially his best friend, Martin Engel. He did not pass such materials to neighbors, even when they were Catholics whom he knew were antifascists, because he worried that he could potentially endanger too many people. Similarly, such transactions did not take place at work or at the pub because he feared that a neighbor or colleague might see and denounce him and his contacts.

Otto said that the Gestapo arrested him in 1936 (though his trial records put the date in 1937). In retrospect, he felt that he had been quite naïve about the whole matter. He had stuck the letters that he had received from Berlin, with illegal materials in them, into the oven—but failed to turn it on. His wife even encouraged the Gestapo to look in the oven when they searched his house, presuming that it was empty. Otto figured that he was going to have to go to prison for at least two years as a result, so he decided to let the authorities (*Herrschaften*) know just where he stood. During his trial, the president of the Third Panel of Judges (*Senate*) in Berlin asked him whether he was a national socialist. He replied that he was not. The president asked, "So then what are you?" Otto replied "a socialist," throwing in "and a democrat" for good measure. The president screamed in reply that Otto was a dreamer, but Otto kept his head. With a heavy dose of eigensinn, Otto replied that screaming does not solve anything.

The pamphlet that got him arrested was a relatively famous one, seen in Figures 18 and 19. The executive committee of the Sopade in January 1934 inserted their Prague Program into a brochure for men on "The Art of Shaving Yourself" using safety razors, subtitled "new directions in masculine cosmetics." (Otto recalled the title incorrectly to have been "Instructions," *Anleitung*, for shaving yourself.) I held this minuscule text myself (5.3 cm in width and 7 cm in height, described in Gittig 1972: 125) at the Stiftung Archiv der Parteien und Massenorganisationen der DDR, a branch of the Bundesarchiv in Berlin (T783). It fits in the palm of your hand. Its size made it easy to hide and pass to someone else without notice, but Otto

DIE KUNST DES SELBSTRASIERENS

Neue Wege
männlicher Kosmetik

H. F. G. & Cie.
Hamburg-London-Paris-
New York

Figures 18 and 19. "The Art of Shaving Yourself." Sopade camoflage text, front and back pages. January 1934. Courtesy of: Bundesarchiv-Stiftung Archiv der Parteien und Massenorganisationen der DDR in Berlin/T783.

Die Höchstleistung

der Sieger

H.F. Gontard & Cie.

added half in jest that the brochure required a magnifying glass to read. Otto told the Gestapo that he threw it away after reading it. In truth, he had passed it on.

Transmitted between friends, this camouflage text (*Tarnschrift*) disguised resistance in everyday life. Metaphorically, it spoke of men caught in old habits by circumstance and implied the need to break out of them. Perhaps on the advice of "good friends," readers did in fact change those habits and now believed they knew something about "the art of shaving yourself": to prepare themselves, using dangerous tools carefully, for public engagement. Yet the writer assured the readers instead of their need to have expert advice from specialists on the "theory and practice" of cosmetics: a typically modern, though very subtle, appeal for the proletarian masses to be prepared to act on order from the revolutionary leadership in exile. Just before the story line from everyday life stopped abruptly, the camouflage text argued tongue-in-cheek that a man's "exterior appearance" is critical for his life, success, and self-consciousness. This camouflage text about preparing one's face for public display is itself a mask for instructions on how to prepare for antifascist resistance. Yet it is also a fable of sorts whose moral lesson described how to preserve one's internal commitment to social democracy while living externally the façade of everyday life in the Third Reich.

The "Struggle and Goal of Revolutionary Socialism: the Politics of the SPD" began in the middle of the third page (reproduced with exegesis by Lange 1972: 860–72). After surveying the tragic events of the first year of Nazi rule, the Sopade executive committee in exile advised their membership to create and preserve new local socialist organizations in order to prepare the ground for revolution. Unlike the German Revolution of 1918, however, this time the socialist leadership promised to immediately institute a long series of measures (described in detail for potentially estranged readers) to fundamentally eradicate the power of the traditional political and military elite whom they considered to be one of the major causes of the current dictatorship. To appeal to both social democrats and communists, they espoused a general socialist program and were cautiously ambiguous about the key differences between the two movements. The Sopade executive committee then reiterated its criticism of Nazi terror, violence, and plans for war, and encouraged Germans to give priority to antifascism over all other political interests. "The unity and freedom of the German nation can only be salvaged by overcoming German fascism" (p. 26 in T783; in Lange p. 870). Painfully aware that the Nazis exploited all divisions between their enemies, the Prague Program asserted its commitment to the Popular Front of all antifascist forces (though particularly among the working classes). In conclusion, they claimed grandly that this united socialist movement was the heir of the Western tradition of Enlightenment embodied in the English and French revolutions. The socialist masses, to whom this manifesto was directed, thus bore the responsibility of leading world history back towards its true humanist goals.

They then restored the veil of everyday life. With tongue back in cheek, this imaginary company thanked the reader for being able to "serve" them. Yet the convivial world in which ablutions took priority over politics was not divorced in fact from the system of Nazi herrschaft and the socialist resistance to it. "You must admit," they joked to themselves and to their readership, rich with double entendre, "would you ever have believed that so many relationships of a culture-historical, folkloristic and technical nature could be made to such an everyday and accustomed procedure?" (pp. 30–31 in T783). From its ancient history to today, the modern safety razor has come a long way, they asserted, but "it is the way of primitive experience to supreme, scientifically based, technical achievement." Indeed, "this small, elegant, sparkling apparatus that you take in your hand every morning to use according to our instructions, shows you how strongly your whole life, how all things in daily use around you, are filled with scientific reflection, for the genius of invention, from highly developed technological production methods." It closed with a polite request, in the language of bourgeois civility, for recognition of the "modest part" that they have played in this utopian historical development. Yet on the back cover, the text depicts the safety razor as a "great," almost historic "achievement of the victors."

This camouflage text provides us with a model for understanding antifascist eigensinn in provincial towns like Hildesheim. The normalcy of conviviality, akin to the safety razor, provided a kind of modern protection from being "nicked" by the Gestapo. Even during the Third Reich, everyday life itself seemed to contain disguised within it the promise of a better future, modern in both the technological and socialist sense, if only the reader could alter his or her everyday habits in keeping with the advice of experts. Disguising propaganda inside an advertisement was a typically modern form of eigensinn; disguising antifascist propaganda inside an advertisement for a safety razor seems especially appropriate as an act of rebellion against the violent yet technologically savvy Nazi regime. Above all, this propaganda device enabled an ordinary man like Otto, when caught, to feign innocence, as if he were only really interested in the advertisement and had not quite noticed that a declaration of war against the Third Reich was enclosed.

Conviviality was a disguise in this sense, but it was not *just* a disguise. Conviviality was a reasonable and viable medium for communicating ideas, especially dangerous and non-conformist ones about resistance, because these ideas were transmitted amid trusted relationships in which such resources and ideas had long been exchanged. Arguably, it was one of the rhetorical goals of the shaving pamphlet, built metaphorically into its text and literally into its shape and size, to encourage ordinary people to think critically about everyday life and, instead of coordinating their conviviality to the new Third Reich, to reshape their habits to help realize its collapse. From the perspective of everyday life, however, it is ironic that the writers chose the safety razor for this camouflage text. When men visited a barber as a regular customer, they bound themselves into relations of reciprocal exchange and trust. By enabling men to shave themselves, the safety razor in fact distanced them from these neighborly networks, modernizing them. In this sense, the camouflage text foreshadowed the real outcome of the struggle between the Gestapo and the Sopade to control the terrain of everyday life: it undermined the functionality of conviviality.

Organizational Cohesion

Gustav Hoppe was a typesetter from the Social Democratic Party (SPD) who had contacts with the Communist Party (KPD). He initiated the first, most significant resistance cell in Hildesheim. In contrast to "The Art of Shaving Yourself," the leaflet *Ran* was produced by and for Hildesheimers. Though this relatively well-documented case of resistance has already been thoroughly researched by historian Hans-Dieter Schmid (1992) on the basis of records available from the police and other court officers,[1] Otto Koch's interview account of these same events (G/47b R/80) from the perspective of everyday life suggests supplemental aspects of the story. Like the process of coordination, resistance to Nazi totalitarianism also began as conviviality.

Otto recalled that this mixed group of communists and social democrats formed in Hildesheim under Hoppe's leadership as early as May of 1933. (With the exception of my interview partners, these are all their real names.) They held their first two planning meetings at the home of Wilhelm Henze, a young car mechanic in the SPD with communist leanings, who spent entire evenings writing texts for the leaflet. Heinrich Bode described in his memoirs (written in May 1972) how representatives of the SPD and KPD met first in "Jungborn" at the gates of town. Schmid suggested that, starting in mid-July 1933, the editorial staff met at the house of Albert Reinert, a messenger associated with the social democrats who was also Hoppe's friend. Hoppe was the chief editor. August Lückgen, a mason in the SPD, was both an editor and an author. Erich Braun, a mechanic who was also a member of the council for the local branch of the SPD (and the son of a social-democratic town deputy), gave the finished stencils to Bode at a prearranged meeting point on the Hagentorwall and later distributed the 250 sheets, designed for the members of the SPD, to colleagues at Senking. Georg Roboom, the party secretary for the SPD in Hildesheim until

1945, got hold of the required 500 sheets of paper. Bode, a metal worker who switched affiliations between the SPD and the KPD, printed the flyers probably in a barracks in the vicinity of Hildesheim's main cemetery. Anton Lamek, a communist worker, distributed the 250 sheets intended for members of the KPD. Another conspirator was Heinrich Schaper, a communist worker who was already active as a courier distributing forbidden internal party reports.

The Indictment on 15 July 1935 and Judgment on 16 December 1935 of the Supreme Court (*Kammergericht*) in Berlin against Schaper (BA-P Z/C 13209) suggest that these adults also relied upon young boys to make arrangements for deliveries of newspapers like *Rote Fahne* (Red Flag) to distant locations, like Goslar, though the young boys and the carriers themselves may or may not have known what they were doing. This lack of knowledge may also have been intentional on the part of the conspirators so as to preserve as many people from harm as possible. Otto Koch recalled reading the first leaflet, but never saw the second. He believed that it never made it to the distribution stage: "They caught them while they were still carrying the bundles back and forth in their backpacks" (G/47b R/150, 205). The archival record disagrees: the Judgment on 7 July 1938 of the Supreme Court in Berlin in the case of Otto Eger (BA-P NJ 17762, pp. 2–4) refers to three editions of the leaflet. In any case, the Gestapo began to throw members of the *Ran* cell into jail as early as 20 July 1933. Sixteen of them were arrested on 24 August. The Supreme Court in Berlin convicted them in December to between six months and three years of prison time. Bode described this as the first "big" trial of the organized resistance in Hildesheim.

In his 1992 article, Schmid argued that Hildesheim represented a curious exception during the Third Reich. From the moment that the parties on the Left were declared illegal in 1933 until 1938, local social democrats and communists cooperated in their antifascist activities. Schmid called this a "Popular Front from below" (p. 100). The Nazi authorities agreed. As the Judgment against Heinrich Malessa on 14 November 1938 recorded (BA-P NJ 6783, p. 2), these leaflets had been "produced in Hildesheim by a community of communists and social democrats." In his memoirs, Bode confirmed that they accomplished a small but effective Popular Front (p. 1). To be sure, this community had its limits. It entailed cooperation in the production of flyers but not always in common texts. Bode reported that each party wrote its own articles. According to the Indictment of 13 September 1933 by the Supreme Court of Berlin against Heinrich Vorlob (VVNH NL Teich, pp. 12–13), Henze and Braun tried to make their own flyer because they did not entirely like the contents of *Ran*. Otto Koch confirmed that some local social democrats refused to cooperate with local communists (G/47b R/115).

Still, even this limited cooperation was a significant accomplishment, given the antipathy that existed between the main parties on the Left.

Schmid correctly suggests that party activism was a necessary condition for the formation of this resistance cell. Otto Koch concurred: these conspirators knew that their fellows were reliable because of their longstanding commitment to socialism. Yet ideological commitment was not a sufficient explanation for resistance. There were many other communists and social democrats who did not form cells. Schmid also notes in passing that these men knew each other personally: as neighbors and as acquaintances, within the same milieu of non-Catholic workers but across the political divide between social democrats and communists (pp. 107–108). Schmid described Hildesheim in the same expression that I also heard from my interview partners: *visible at a glance*. Such a risky endeavor required a pre-existing culture of reciprocity and trust: it was based on conviviality. Otto struggled to define these relationships precisely because they wavered along that fine line between the public and the private. He said that they were not close friends but acquaintances and colleagues; and even though they worked as a cohort, they had not previously been part of a distinct group. He imagined that they were just a group of acquaintances who decided, in conversations conducted in informal settings, that they needed to "do something" to help. They solicited aid from other trusted individuals, "and then a few, uh, illegal things took place, conversations, and then they set it all up, no? There was not much more to it" (G/47b R/140). Though subtle and evasive, the historical process by which legal activism translated into illegal activism was mediated by conviviality.

Since he was not personally present during these initial conversations, Otto's suspicions about the cell's origins would be a relatively unreliable source if it were not for the fact that documentary evidence confirmed them in these and analogous cases. In the Judgment against Hans Kirk (p. 9), the judge decided that the accused had made plans for illegal communist activities by chatting with his co-conspirators during common strolls. Otto's assessment is also confirmed by the fact that informal social relations facilitated their limited successes. The end of the leaflet held this appeal: "After reading this, pass it on to acquaintances!" The Indictment against the gardener Johannes Hesse by the General State's Attorney on 28 September 1933 (BA-P NJ 9662, Bd. 1) provides several examples of Hildesheimers who received small numbers of leaflets (from two to twenty-five) and distributed them further (see also Schmid pp. 105–106). In this most significant and well-documented case of resistance in Hildesheim, the cell relied on conviviality to mobilize human resources and communicate its ideas.

The more informal the group's resistance, the more convivial its foundations. Wilhelm Heitmann had been unemployed for a long time. He got a job as a molder at Senking in 1934, only to be permanently fired for refusing to participate in official afterwork celebrations organized by local Nazis. Starting around 1934, as many as fifteen social democrats and communists met at his residence on Triftäckerstrasse, a small home built on a garden plot at the rural edge of town. The core members of this group included Heitmann's wife, his parents, his children and their spouses, as well as his friends Willi Vetter, Hans Schipper, and Kurt Heinze, all from the communist union and the latter of whom stored potatoes in the cellar of Heitmann's garden house. They were indirectly linked to the *Ran* cell because Hoppe brought them copies of the leaflet to read. The Gestapo began to arrest them only in March 1937, which meant that they were active but largely unnoticed by the Nazi authorities for some four years.

Schmid described a similar group that emerged after Hoppe's release from prison in 1934, including Hoppe's wife Theresa, his brother-in-law Henry Graul, and Graul's financée Frieda Meyer. It also included Willi Vetter from Heitmann's group as well as Hans Schipper, Heinrich Malessa, and Johannes Hesse from the *Ran* group after they were released from prison. Malessa was also a close friend of Georg Heitmann, Wilhelm's son. According to the Indictment by the General States Attorney of the Supreme Court in Berlin against Malessa on 30 June 1938 (BA-P NJ 6783 p. 3), whenever Graul's fiancée questioned him about the legality of listening to Radio Moscow, he was accustomed to answering that it was allowed "among family and acquaintances."[2]

Most of the evidence about their activities comes from their arrest and trial records. According to the Indictment C of 16 September 1937 and Judgment C of the Supreme Court of Berlin on 31 January 1938 (BA-P NJ 1198), the Heitmann group listened to Radio Moscow, read and exchange illegal texts, and held treasonous conversations about political events. Judgment C (pp. 5–6) condemned Georg Heitmann for making vaguely critical comments about the failure of the Führer to do very much for the German worker. He also suggested the need for "an internal communist uprising" in the case of a war. Finally, he returned a *heil moscow!* to a *heil hitler!* All of this was not illegal per se but was used as evidence of his intent to commit and incite high treason. More seriously, all this took place "regularly in the presence of people who did not belong to the household" (*Hausstand*): that is, among friends and neighbors. Indictment B against Heitmann (p. 2) included the additional accusation that they celebrated May Day illegally in 1936 and collected money "to build an illegal organization." In Judgment A on 17 January 1938 against Gustav Voss (BA-P NJ 4973, pp. 9, 11–14, 20–21), the authorities argued that Heitmann attached loudspeakers to his radio so that all of his family and guests could listen to the broadcast at the same time. They concluded that his residence "is to be seen as a collecting point for Marxist elements." Heinrich Malessa tried to use the opposite argument in his defense according to the Judgment against him (p. 4): that Heitmann listened to his radio with headphones.

The so-called illegal organization mentioned in Indictment B against Heitmann referred to a collection fund created for the dependents of political prisoners (Schmid 1992: 122–27). It was approaching Christmas of 1933, and many of the men who had published *Ran* were still in incarcerated. So August Schwetje, a truck mechanic and driver, initiated a collection with the help of Gustav Voss and Georg Meyer. All three men worked for the same local coal company, Mehring and Krüger. They were often on assignment together and were all communists or sympathizers. They were also helped by Heitmann and Hoppe of the SPD as well as Hubert Schaare, the head of the local branch of the Independent Social Democratic Party. Meyer, Heitmann, and Hoppe were the most important collecting agents. They collected some forty to fifty marks for Christmas 1933. The collection for Christmas 1934 was even more substantial.

Josef Hesse, a machine mechanic, made a similar collection in the Senking factory among Erich Braun's former mates from work. Hesse and his wife had become friends with Braun and his wife in 1927, but this relationship cooled off after Hesse was unemployed due to lack of work. When he was rehired, he learned of Braun's imprisonment in the late summer of 1933, and immediately contacted Braun's wife, Minna. He defended himself during his trial with the claim that he had heard that they were in financial trouble, that Minna and her oldest child had gotten sick. Since he visited them in their home personally, he was able to see their dire living conditions. After the visit he had talked to his colleagues at work and organized the collection. After contributing ten marks himself, he was able to give her forty-two marks in cash as well as a package of groceries shortly before Christmas in 1934. He claimed that he only wanted to help the family, and that he believed such collections to be legal. The prosecution argued to the contrary that this collection was conducted secretly and, though Minna Braun did receive unemployment, she never reported any exigent circumstances to the official Nazi private charity. Although most of the money came from members of the union in Senking, of whom many were former social democrats, Hesse himself did not belong to any party. Moreover, though the collection was initially intended for this one family in particular, in the end the wives of Lamek, a communist, and Lückgen, a social democrat, also received five and seven marks respectively. (See Schmid 122–23 and fn. 75 as well as Indictment on 27 April 1938 of the Supreme Court in Berlin against Otto Eger, BA-P 17762, pp. 4–5.)

Wilhelm Heitmann continued collecting money in 1935. Theodore Schmalfeldt, Elfriede Läufer, Berta Engelke, and Karl Irrgang put together packages of groceries for the affected families (the latter two were the managers of the local consumer cooperative). In Indictment D against Heitmann for "treasonous activities" on 16 September 1937 (BA-P NJ 1215), the prosecution could show that some gave only pfennigs, some a mark or two, and only a few people gave multiple times and as many as three marks (pp. 2–7). According to Judgment D, they also collected tobacco for the prisoners themselves, though this charge does not seem to have stuck. By contrast, the Judgment against Gustav Voss mentions (p. 17) that Schmalfeld added chocolate to the baskets for Hoppe's children. Indictment B on 10 September 1937 and Judgment B on 18 March 1938 of the Supreme Court of Berlin against Richard Hartung (BA-P NJ 1268, pp. 4–5) adds to this list the factories of Ahlborn, Deutsche Leichtmetallwerke, and Senking as locations of collections.

Yet another collection took place in one of the large, local armaments factories, Vereinigte Deutsche Metallwerke, especially for Christmas but also throughout 1936. By this time, however, the collection had a more institutional quality that was also its undoing. Started in May 1935, the contributing members made regular monthly payments of one mark in addition to any other informal collections for existing prisoners. They had membership cards and received stamps when they made their contributions. Some had red cards, others had green cards, but not according to party: there were social democrats and communists in both groups. According to Indictment C against Heitmann, the red cards were for active members and the green for sympathizers (p. 2); according to Judgment B against Hartung, some cards were marked with a Soviet star (pp. 3–4). The leaders of this group of "eager Marxists" (pp. 3–4) met regularly starting in August 1936, had contacts outside of Germany, and even had plans to start printing leaflets again. Their political differences were too great (according to Judgment B against Hartung) for much to come of these other projects, but their collections did continue.

The judicial record confirms that these collections took place in a variety of different factories across town and across party affiliations. It demonstrates the existence of a limited Popular Front from below in Hildesheim. Yet it also confirms that the cultural foundations for this network of resistance lay in pre-existing customs of conviviality. An ideological commitment to antifascism cannot be separated analytically from the traditions of neighborliness and friendship through which these political goals were mediated.

Some degree of ideological conformity was certainly necessary for antifascist activism. In his commentary in the case against Heitmann (BA-P NJ 1215), federal attorney (*Reichsanwalt*) Dr. Giepel of the notorious People's Court (*Volksgerichtshof*) argued that "the theoretical differences between the KPD and the SPD were cleansed" during these meetings. These gatherings also served to educate participants in "the work of propaganda" (p. 8; see also the Indictment against Heinrich Malessa, p. 1). For instance, Elfriede Läufer had allegedly "taken photos from a concentration camp" (p. 10). When the officers of the secret police and people's court insisted on the political nature of these gatherings and collections, however, we must take care; these public officials are not neutral witnesses of history. It was their job to prove the presence of a treasonous organization. For instance, the grounds for conviction given in Judgment D against Heitmann were that he and his conspirators had tried to rebuild the eliminated socialist parties. "In Hildesheim, a communal group of KPD and SPD members was formed who worked towards the common goal of preserving an organization that stood ready to assist in a coup at the right moment" (*Gemeinschaftsgruppe*, p. 3; see also the Indictment against Heinrich Malessa p. 3). Arguably, these Nazi functionaries overstated the political content—and cohesion—of these cells in order to bolster their case. They mistook the degree to which these Hildesheimers would have welcomed a coup against Hitler for their intent to perpetrate it. Similarly, Hoppe brought the *Ran* leaflets to Heitmann's home for distribution, but that act does not imply that these were resistance cells to begin with. It suggests simply that antifascists mobilized resistance through informal social networks.

This was the expressed policy of the Sopade. As Hoppe admitted to the prosecution in his court hearing on 1 June 1936, he was instructed by his contact in Copenhagen to further distribute the illegal materials that he received from them only to "reliable, former SPD persons *or other persons* whom you trust without question" (BA-P NJ 15414/1, p. 7, my emphasis). As a result, resistance networks were typically self-selecting in terms of ideology but only partially based on former institutional affiliations. To risk antifascist resistance, the participants relied upon long-term relationships with comrades but also on family, friends, and neighbors with whom they shared reciprocity and trust (Hilberg 1992: 212–14). From this perspective, the Heitmann group shared illegal texts and listened to foreign broadcasts together only because it had been customary in interwar Hildesheim, particularly among those who could not afford subscriptions or radios of their own, to pass copies of the daily paper and listen to the radio among friends and neighbors (Bergerson 1997, 2001). Heitmann had already made his cellar available to Heinze for storing potatoes. The fact that they listened to the radio together fits this same pattern of reciprocal exchange relations. From the perspective of everyday life, conviviality was both a disguise for and a reality of the Popular Front from below, in keeping with the self-deceptive nature of eigensinn (Leber 1957: 70–71; Schmid 119–20).

Antifascist Hildesheimers located their non-conformity within the framework of conviviality to protect themselves from the Gestapo. In a situation report composed on 18 March 1935 for the Sopade, the author (probably Wilhelm Henze) wrote as if he were communicating with "his dear girlfriend." From exile on 19 August 1936, Willi Brandt, the future Federal Chancellor of West Germany from 1969 to 1974, similarly reported about a visit with Henze from Hildesheim (reproduced in Schmid 1992: 147–48, 159–61). After Henze had returned from prison in December 1935, Brandt explained, Henze had been meeting with small groups of Young Socialists who wanted to take action against the Nazis but did not know quite what to do. There was a certain amount of tension between the generations: as he was a young man, Henze considered his generation to be further to the Left and distrustful of the older party leadership. Loosely associated with similar groups of communists, their groups were most active in elementary political education: not so much in producing new printed materials but in obtaining that which was still found in their libraries and passing it around. They also listened to Radio Moscow, and Henze traveled around Germany by bike, visiting former camp comrades for the same purposes. Paraphrasing Henze, Brandt wrote: "Everywhere the Popular Front gets lively discussion among those friends who have remained stalwart." Henze also reported that discussions at factories were still quite open and sometimes even planned. At the breakfast table in his brick factory, workers openly described what they had heard on Radio Moscow the night before "and mentioned the source without concern" (p. 2). Like their Nazi counterparts, such reports by ideologically committed, institutionally affiliated socialists probably overestimated the integrity of the proletarian milieu. Still, we can trust the implication of these statements about everyday life in which Henze and Brandt were less invested: that antifascist resistance actually took place in convivial contexts, and that it was expressed through the medium of friendship and neighborliness to protect conspirators from the Gestapo.

As *eigensinn*, antifascist acts could be simultaneously resistance and conviviality. An elaborate code of everyday life is evident in Gustav Hoppe's correspondence with the social democrats in Copenhagen, according to the records of the Federal Prosecutor (*Oberreichsanwalt*) in the case against Hans Pasch for instigating high treason from 1935 to 1942 (BA-P NJ 15414/1). On 20 December 1935, someone who called himself Hans W. Arnold of Copenhagen sent a letter to his "dear friend" Hoppe. Writing "as a former war comrade," he offered him a small "Christmas gift" of twenty marks and asked for regular reports about the situation in northern Germany; Arnold wanted to know about "difficulties with food supplies, firing workers from armaments industries, terror against Jews" as well as government announcements, posters, reports, newspaper articles, and illegal leaflets. During the court hearing on 27 May 1936 (BA-P NJ 15414/1), Hoppe initially dodged the prosecution's questions about this illegal correspondence with Pasch by insisting that his most recent correspondence was a sympathy card after the death of Hoppe's wife on 9 January 1936. "It was the usual kind of letter with a black border." Similarly, a letter from someone named Karla Petersen of Copenhagen on 29 February 1936 was written entirely about families, vacations, and work at the hospital. In the hearing two days later (p. 3), perhaps after physical and psychological intimidation, Hoppe admitted that Arnold and Peterson were both really Pasch, and that he and Pasch had "had little to do with one another on a personal level" prior to their correspondence in the resistance. Nonetheless, Pasch got Hoppe's address through a real friend, Karl Rowold, and Hoppe refused to reveal the names of his co-conspirators in Germany, because he did not wish to betray them (pp. 4, 8). Conviviality was as much a real medium for resistance as it was a disguise for it.

It makes sense that conviviality involved such contradictory purposes because it had traditionally been used to those ends. Otto Koch annotated Figure 20 from 1942 as follows: "Around here it was actually defeatism that you heard, if not more." Yet he did not mention treason outright. He did not treat this convivial gathering as if it had been a resistance cell. The army uniforms of some of his guests remind us of the limits of this group's antifascist activities. During the interviews, however, he also explained that had the police overheard those conversations, the group members would have all landed in a concentration camp (G/47b R/250). It was most likely that Georg Heitmann made his remarks about Hitler and revolution in a similarly ambiguous and convivial context. The only difference was that Heitmann's gatherings caught the Gestapo's attention due to his indirect affiliation with the *Ran* group, while the gatherings at Otto's home escaped notice as just conviviality.

Though a committed socialist, Otto often disparaged his role as a collaborator. He admitted freely that he had worked in an armaments factory and had been too concerned with the welfare of his family to risk his life in really resisting Hitler. Otto compared his activities to those who smuggled people, weapons, or information across borders or published pamphlets themselves. "Now, you have to keep these things separate," he said, distinguishing non-conformity from resistance. He had various contacts with the *Ran* group, including neighbors, colleagues, friends, and family. They felt "they had to do something . . . something immediately." Because a family member had arranged an apartment for Otto with former neighbors, Otto felt even more pressure to participate according to the principle of reciprocity inherent in all conviviality. But Otto held himself back from such overt acts of resistance, as did his best friend Martin Engel. "What did they hope

Figure 20. Convivial gathering at home, 1942 (D/1029).

to achieve by this? I could not see anything useful in it." Also, he was put off by the new orthodoxy of a Popular Front, since it seemed to him to be only a tactical response to Nazi repression. Still, he read the *Ran* leaflets and passed them on to others. "There you naturally had to select people in whose hand one could place such texts. And that did not go very well for very long." Here, Otto was referring to the fact that the others got arrested so quickly. "Then things were quiet again. This story was over for the time being" (G/47b R/85, 150), he said, almost with relief. Otto knew that passing an advertisement for safety razors was a form of resistance, but it seems that, as far as Otto was concerned even many decades later, these were just acts of eigensinn, insignificant when compared to real subversion.

Otto captured the rebellious quality of such convivial gatherings with another story. He showed me a picture of a neighbor who was building a snowman with his and Otto's children (D/1033). This man lived across the courtyard, always fought with his wife, was a sergeant, and was also a "big Nazi." One day, he came home to find that his wife was not home. He went over to the Koch residence and began to scream for her. Otto's wife did not let him in the door, however. "Your wife is my guest," she told him, "and I am the housewife here!" She then closed the door in his face. It is perhaps hard for us to imagine the wife of a man, recently released from prison for instigating treason, slamming a door in the face of a Nazi officer during the Third Reich. Yet the normalcy of conviviality supported even such surprisingly expressive gestures of eigensinn.

The comparison between the various sorts of gatherings taking place at the home of the Kochs and those at the Heitmanns is instructive. At least initially, it suggests that these meetings focused primarily on conviviality and were structured according to those customs rather than on politics per se. Only gradually did informal conviviality become formal resistance. That process started perhaps when Hoppe first brought the *Ran* leaflet into an otherwise convivial gathering. Still, I suspect that even with such texts in hand, antifascists like Heitmann continued to use conviviality as the medium of choice to challenge Nazi herrschaft. Like the Kochs, they perhaps presumed that the veil of the everyday would continue to protect them from retribution for their eigensinn. In this sense, the conviviality of these gatherings was both a disguise and a reality.

The Gestapo followed precisely the inverse logic when uncovering, arresting, and convicting the participants of these gatherings as enemies of the state: the agents of the Nazi regime had to assert the criminality of conviviality. There were certainly many other undocumented evenings among friends and neighbors in which antifascist discussions took place, but the Gestapo redefined and prosecuted those "cells" that had the misfortune of being connected informally to the *Ran* group. In the process of discovering them, the Gestapo progressively invented these "resistance cells" as such in order to declare them destroyed. In their monthly situation report to Berlin on 31 January 1938 (BA-P St3/321, pp. 139–40, 149–52), the local Gestapo officers outlined their success in uncovering and dismantling the various resistance cells associated with the publication of illegal inflammatory texts and the collections for the dependents of political prisoners. They then claimed that women and young people were less antipathetic to the Nazi party and that there was no real danger that the workers of Hildesheim would revolt against the Third Reich. Even in a town that used to be a "center" (*Hochburg*) of social democracy, the workers had become too bourgeois. Rather, they blamed the sudden rise in illegal activities by Marxists that month on the many trials since mid-1937 that had "scared" the older generation of former SPD functionaries. They also claimed that the KPD, though never strong in Hildesheim, was trying to use the current circumstances to rebuild and extend its infrastructure. At least in the month of this report, however, these various organizational leaders had formed no new cells. Instead, the local Gestapo focused on "the discovery of illegal gatherings of groups of people whose activities [the oral transmission of radio propaganda] had already come to an end in Spring 1937." Faced with a largely coordinated population, the Gestapo had to extend the scope of its purview. In order to prove the vitality of the local Gestapo office to superiors, they looked for criminality in new places.

That is, pro-and anti-fascist Hildesheimers both redefined conviviality respectively as criminality and resistance. Both sought to colonize everyday life, as a tactic of antifascist eigensinn and a strategy for fascist herrschaft. Local resistance fighters were anxious to outmaneuver the Gestapo on the terrain of informal social relations, since this area was one of the only avenues still open to them after the destruction of formal institutions. And the local Gestapo, anxious to prove that they had identified and eliminated an enemy worthy of their time and effort, began to penetrate that same murky realm where public met private (with the aid of denunciation as per Gellately 2001). It was in the interests of both sides to reshape conviviality into a tool for political coordination for or against the Nazi regime. It made both of their jobs easier.

Consider the meetings at the Kapino house with acquaintances Georg Meyer, August Schwetje, and Adolf Berger, as described in Indictment C (p. 5) and Judgment C (p. 9) against Heitmann. Some of these individuals had passed along materials or had been seen glancing over an "inflamma-tory" text. When Elizabeth Borchers, a cousin of the Kapinos, was in town from the Netherlands, this quasi-cell met to arrange for contact with the émigrés living in Amsterdam. Borcher's relative Dorothea Piepenpott was similarly guilty by association (Judgment C, pp. 10–11). In March 1936, Dorothea visited Erich Braun, who had just been released from prison, to complain about her husband's punishment. She said that if people were not so cowardly, then much would be improved, but that it could not be long until the coup came, and that her husband would be out of prison in autumn. Here again, the evidence of criminality is not just their treasonous commentary or their reading of illegal texts on their own, but the con-vivial networks through which these revolutionary ideas and goods were exchanged in the local public sphere. Judgment C against Heitmann and his co-conspirators (pp. 12ff) made this clear:

> The organizational cohesion mentioned in the law does not need to be the illegal organization itself. A loose conglomeration of several persons for common education towards illegal endeavors is more than sufficient, even if this circle of individuals has not been incorporated into the solid framework of an illegal organization.

The group of people listening to Radio Moscow at the Heitmann home passed this very flexible measure of organizational cohesion. In a like man-ner, Fritz Henze was condemned in Judgment C (pp. 6–9) not just for reading resistance literature that he received from Georg Roboom but also for meeting with him in the first place. Judgment B against Richard Hartung, too, focused on his friendships with politically active Marxists (p. 8). These judgments were based on cultural premises about informal social relations: the presumption was that friends are alike and will support each other in all of their endeavors. The judgments also extended the definition of organization from formal institutions to encompass informal conviviality.

Arguably, the underlying problem for both the Gestapo and the Sopade was that the Nazi regime had already successfully coordinated the formal institution of sociability, so they had to turn to the informal networks of conviviality to justify their jobs and find a way to avoid, or penetrate, the other's organizations. The Nazi judicial system responded in turn to this dilemma by transposing the criminality of sociability into conviviality. It was not the organization itself that provided the initial impetus to participate in these resistance activities and condemned these Hildesheimers after the fact. Rather, the presence of the organization reflected a criminal state of mind while engaging in convivial activities.

Red Help

This process of redefining informal customs of conviviality as formal acts of resistance or criminality (depending on one's politics) is most evident in the case of Red Help (*Rote Hilfe*), the institution within the Communist Party for mutual aid under conditions of persecution. Here again, Schmid depicts the collection process as evidence of the strength of the traditions of the working classes, of the value placed on cooperation over programmatic unity, and as proof of "an actual example of a practicing Popular Front from below" in Hildesheim (p. 127). Although these factors are indeed part of the story, historians should not be so ready to accept the interpretation offered by the Gestapo and Sopade, themselves motivated primarily by politics, that the primary motives for resistance were political. Interview narratives, this time provided by Berhard Richeter, emphasize a different set of causes. From the perspective of everyday life, Hildesheimers took part in the lives of their neighbors. Particularly in moments of existential crisis, my interview partners insisted on providing symbolic gestures of support for families in trouble. It is this tradition of neighborliness more generally, rather than a particularly strong communist tradition of Red Help or any political commitment among the workers of Hildesheim to socialist unity, that provided the customary foundations for resistance.

Judgment D on 16 September 1937 against Heitmann described these events (pp. 6–9; see also Judgment A against Gustav Voss, pp. 6–9). Georg Meyer was able to convince Helmut Manthai, Heinrich Behrens, and Karl

Irrgang to contribute to the fund. Meyer claimed that Manthai, a small-animal farmer and carpenter who was also accused, had contributed three marks towards this collection for the family members of the political prisoners under the following conditions. Schwetje had already tried to get Manthai to donate when he met him on the street because "he knew him from before," but Manthai declined the request. Soon after, Meyer and Schwetje ran into him on the street while driving their company truck. "Manthai stopped them and let himself be driven for a bit. At this opportunity, Meyer went up to Manthai again and induced him to give something for the family members of the political prisoners." He contributed the large sum of three marks. Not only did Schwetje try to work his network of acquaintances initially, but Meyer also used the circumstance of doing a favor for his neighbor to compel Manthai to finally return the favor—with rich rewards for the families in question. Both men manipulated the expectation of reciprocity embedded in the customs of conviviality to political ends, and at the same time, they could both claim that they were just taking part in the lives of their neighbors.

There are many corroborating examples in the judicial record. In the case of Behrens, Meyer had delivered some of his company's coal to Behrens, but the latter could not pay immediately for lack of cash. Meyer came back on the following Sunday to collect (most likely, after Behrens received his wage that Friday). "At this opportunity, Meyer held out a collecting box." Behrens gave twenty pfennigs then, and another fifty pfennigs, comprising all of Behrens's tips, when Meyer met him again on the street some time later. According to Judgment A against Voss (pp. 6–9) however, Behrens claimed to have given fifty pfennigs at first, and because he thought Meyer wanted to get a drink. Meyer and the judges countered that Behrens obviously knew the meaning of the collection, and that the explanation was "an empty excuse."

Meyer and Schwetje used the same tactic with Ernst Schmidt and Heinrich Winkelhoff. As recorded in Judgment A against Voss (pp. 6–9), "just like Meyer, Schwetje used every opportunity to approach acquaintances whom he considered politically reliable for contributions for the families of political prisoners." A similar story can be told about how Wilhelm Heitmann induced Karl Irrgang to contribute to the Christmas collection in 1935. Heitmann knew that Irrgang would make money when they ordered packages of food to be assembled by his consumer cooperative, so he was able to convince Irrgang to give two marks. On Heitmann's recommendation, Irrgang also found himself adding goods such as bacon, lentils, and peas, each costing some two-and-a-half to three marks on at least two occasions in the spring of 1936. Consistently, these Hildesheimers were following the logic of conviviality that had shaped their relations long before the Nazis had emerged on the scene: one hand washed the other.

The political nature of neighborly contributions did not undermine their normalcy—at least not according to traditional customs. All of these favors were presumably reciprocal and ultimately symbolic in nature. As recorded in Judgment D against Heitmann (p. 20), the judges in the case of Wilhelm Heinrich Jürgens decided that he had agreed to make a contribution to the fund out of pity, not out of political conviction. Jürgens was well acquainted with Hoppe, Heitmann, and Braun. It seems that Hoppe convinced Jürgens with the explanation that he just wanted to bring Minna Braun a little joy. Jürgens' friendship with Hoppe also legitimized the fact that he gave money for Hoppe's children after the latter was arrested in 1936.

Here we should take note that such acts of charity were embarrassing for the receiver and, by projection, for the provider. In spite of the fact that they corresponded to norms of communal fairness and reinforced bonds of reciprocity, these gifts undermined a family's sense of autarky and therefore respectability. It follows then that Hildesheimers mostly organized collections for common baskets rather than giving money directly to families on an individual basis. For this same reason, and not because of some insidious communist plot, these friends and neighbors collected money as a group rather than individually and for the dependents of political prisoners rather than the prisoners themselves. The irony here is rich: the shame associated with the collection derived ultimately from the culture of conviviality rather than politics, yet they were arrested for political crimes in part because of the degree to which these gifts had been organized collectively.

Interview testimony confirms this reading of the archival sources. Bernhard Richeter described at length his exchange relations with a young Belgian law student forced to work in Hildesheim by the Nazi regime (G/38a R/240, G/38b R/00, G/39a R/40, 365, G/39b R/00). This young man had been convinced to come to work in Germany because he could no longer continue his studies. He had listened to a foreign radio station and discussed what he had heard in public in a group, only to be denounced by a German who overheard him. He consequently landed in prison in Celle and from there was subcontracted to do forced labor at the Bosch factory in the Hildesheim Forest, where he worked at the same double bench as Bernhard, who had similarly been forced to move to the Bosch factory from Senking in 1942. Since the student's German was excellent, they often talked, even though speaking was expressly forbidden. When Bernhard saw that the young man's feet were in very poor condition due to his bad shoes, he gave him a salve and some dressing material. However, the prisoners had to disguise their activities from the prison guards who had been sent to the factory to watch over them. On several occasions, Bernhard had seen the guards in action and realized that they were particularly brutal men. So Bernhard instructed the young man to go down underneath the work bench to bind his wounds. He said to the guard: "He has to find something under there." Hidden beneath the bench, the young student was able to dress or undress his wounds.

One time right before the end of their shift, a guard came over just as the young man was binding his wounds under the bench. The guard said: "What is he doing under there?" Quick-witted, Bernhard replied, "I am teaching him to be orderly." But the guard pushed him, asking for details. Since the workshop got swept every evening, Bernhard realized that he had to give some other excuse. He said: "At my bench, we clean not only on top but also down below." The guard replied: "That is correct." The guard then departed. Bernhard was glad that the guard had swallowed his lie. Still, when I asked Bernhard why he helped this forced laborer, he said nothing of his strong pro-socialist and anti-Nazi convictions. He said that he acted "out of pure, simple humanity. I felt sorry for the boy."

Here, Bernhard was not being completely honest in his reflections. His motives for these acts of charity were as much a matter of antifascist *eigensinn* as neighborliness. For instance, this forced laborer was also quite hungry because of the lower rations given to Latins as compared to Aryans.[3] Bernhard's family had a little extra in the way of groceries. His wife had been forced to work in a home for "hard-to-educate" children where she and her son could eat lunch, and they also had a garden that produced lots of food. So Bernhard's wife often gave him a little extra bread or an apple "for the prisoner." But this food, too, had to be passed under their common workbench, and the young man had to eat it "so that no one noticed." Bernhard enjoyed getting the best of these dumb-witted guards—particularly, I believe, because he was a worker and was acting on behalf of an educated law student. He also relished retelling the tale many decades later. Both in the historic past and in the interview present, these events were the medium through which Bernhard expressed his disgust at the Nazi regime's cruelty. At the same time, his under-the-bench trick was as much a tactic to avoid embarrassing both men as a way to avoid punishment for their crime. Arguably, Bernhard felt a sense of shame on behalf of this young man, who felt emasculated because of his vulnerability before the guards and his need for charity. Slipping him food under the table disguised such ulterior motives as much from Bernhard and the Belgian as from the guards. Their shame was part of the open secret on which *eigensinn* relied for its success (Otto Koch recounted similar stories; see G/48a R/180).

In Judgment D against Heitmann (pp. 10–14), the judges concluded that the purpose of the collections for the dependents of political prisoners was not simply to help friends and neighbors in their economic need but also to prove to those families, and the incarcerated men, "that there are still people around who share their opinions and will stand up for them."

The problem, therefore, was not simply that informal arrangements such as this collection group tended to, and actually did, lead to more formal organizations, like the one at the Vereinigte Deutsche Metallwerke. Insofar as the act of charity itself served to reinforce the Marxist convictions of all of the involved parties, they were promoting the purposes of communism and instigating treason:

> It is therefore in no way necessary [to prove] that the criminal was somehow linked to an organization, rather one need only test to see if his behavior was suitable to promote or support the endeavors of the KPD or SPD. Supporting the dependents of political prisoners, clothed in the form of charity, sufficiently satisfies these conditions.

In this case, I agree with the judges that these Hildesheimers knew at the time of these collections that they were supporting antifascist resisters. Still, I also believe that they disguised this fact from the authorities, and arguably from themselves, by treating their contributions as a normal part of taking part in the lives of neighbors. My point is that having such a collection was probably not a crime at the time of the collection. Only in 1937–38, when the collectors and contributors were "discovered" by the Gestapo, betrayed by their co-conspirators, and framed by the prosecution in the context of a "treasonous organization," did the normal quality of neighborly reciprocity acquire a pernicious quality that the judges could then condemn as criminal and abnormal.

This retrospective criminalization of conviviality was instrumental. In their investigations, indictments, and judgments, the Nazi functionaries exaggerated the institutional quality of these meetings and networks in order to divorce these customs of conviviality from the sense of normalcy that impeded prosecution. For instance, one key witness for the prosecution was Frieda Meier, who provided names and detailed accounts of the criminal activities of friends and neighbors to the Gestapo (e.g., Judgment D, 16 September 1937, against Heitmann, pp. 6–9). Heitmann tried to argue that she was unjustly accusing him in revenge for the fact that Heitmann's wife had once said something negative about her. In their Judgment (pp. 5–6), the panel of judges in the Heitmann case had to dismiss this excuse if they were to successfully distance these acts from their context of neighborliness and dignify them as resistance.

The inverse was true of closer relationships: they emphasized friendship with the wrong people in order to find evidence of treason. In Judgment A on 17 January 1938 against Gustav Voss (BA-P NJ 4973, p. 4), the judges viewed Schwetje as a leader of the resistance in part because of his "friendly relations with communists as well as socialists." Judgment C viewed Fritz Henze to be "in no way a friend of the national socialist regime" because of the simple fact that he was friendly with and visited with other social democrats, some of whom had been convicted before of treasonous behavior (BA-P NJ 1198, pp. 7–8). If Heitmann could not prove that he was being framed because of old neighborly conflicts, Henze was guilty of being a good friend and neighbor. After Hoppe was arrested in May of 1936, Adolf Berger discussed with Hartung (the accused in Judgment B, pp. 8–9; see also Judgment against Voss, pp. 24–25) how they could best warn Hoppe's friends in Copenhagen to cease the flow of illegal texts. Berger decided to write to one of his own friends, Hansen, saying: "Friend in Hannover had an accident. Correspondence is useless." These were real friendships in part, but friendship had also been conflated with politics.

It was international connections that were their ultimate undoing: that is, the degree to which these forms of neighborly cooperation and friendly engagement in the locality did in fact become linked to international networks of political resistance. It seems that the Gestapo used letters to and from socialist activists abroad to lead them to the membership records associated with collections. Through interrogations of turncoats like Meier, they could then expand their investigations retroactively beyond the familiar figures of the *Ran* cell in order to infiltrate the more informal networks of those who simply contributed funds to the collection, shared newspapers or radios, or met in homes to talk and share each other's company. More accurately, both the Nazi regime and its antifascist enemies redefined long-standing customs of neighborly compassion and friendly communication as resistance or criminality. They did this for sound political reasons, in keeping with their own purposes. Yet ultimately, relationships that had been relatively fluid precisely because they were left to individuals to negotiate in informal social circumstances now became formal categories measured entirely in terms of one's relationship to the Nazi regime. In this way, ordinary Hildesheimers on both sides of the political fence colonized the ambiguous yet strategic terrain of everyday life in their political interests.

Winter Help

Most of the people involved in these stories, on both sides of the law, were adults born sometime during the Second Empire (1871–1918). Young people were also active in collecting for the needy through the Hitler Youth and Association of German Girls. In these Nazi organizations, young Hildesheimers took part in the lives of neighbors in the broader sense of members of the Aryan community through the dechristianized and centralized program *Winterhilfe*. Though it antedated the Third Reich, under Nazi rule Winter Help became an annual charity collection that helped to finance the official Nazi private charity (Rosenstrauch 1988: 56; Schmid 2002; Snyder

1976: 381). It substituted for both Red Help and pre-existing neighborly exchange relations that crossed racial and political boundaries, and yet it was modeled on both.

A member of the HJ, Ulrich Gerke recalled collecting for Winter Help every four weeks. They walked door-to-door in their neighborhood, asking for small donations and encouraging contributions with this slogan: "Live like the Führer, plainly and simply! Make a sacrifice on One-Bowl Sunday!" The idea was that each family would prepare a single, less expensive soup for their Sunday meal so that they could contribute more to the Aryan cause. According to Ulrich, this policy was ingenious. Hitler "did not have to raise taxes. He sent his boys out into the street" (G/87b R/330). Winter Help functioned as an efficient mechanism for making Hildesheim fascist because it was implemented by ordinary people and was grounded in pre-existing customs of conviviality.

Heinz-Hermann Köhler depicted Winter Help activities in two water-color paintings of street life. Given the fact that he was young (in the sixth grade of the Agricultural School), we can consider these images to be relatively accurate representations of everyday life. In one (D/0454), he painted an advertising column. At the top right was a poster asking neighbors to "Give to Winter Help," with a woman giving a set of groceries to what was most likely an HJ member. This poster admonished Hildesheimers to coordinate their informal social relations to fit Nazi principles. Winter Help was no less a routine affair to the artist than were advertisements for a puppet theater, cigarettes, or a cleanser. After all, Hildesheimers took part in the lives of neighbors. In Figure 21, Köhler reproduced or imagined a scene on a farm, perhaps similar to the countryside whence he came. (He had been living with his cousin in town so that he could go to school.) There was no work and nothing to eat for the family. The viewer was therefore encouraged to give to Winter Help. Appropriately, the viewer was addressed in the informal plural: i.e., as friends, neighbors, or acquaintances.

In effect, Winter Help coordinated and increasingly worked to aryanize neighborly exchange relations. Prior to the Third Reich, Hildesheimers exchanged greetings and sympathetic inquiries into the health of the family. If material goods were exchanged at all, they too were largely symbolic in nature: a small gift in times of emergency. It was also very likely that a child served as the mediator of informal charity between neighbors (though adults collected too; see Gellately 2001: 43). Although that same child (or sibling) was now collecting for Winter Help, he or she was nonetheless much harder to refuse since the power of the Nazi state stood behind his new uniform. Resources were now redistributed not through informal networks of neighbors but through a charity tied to the Nazi regime. The Nazis also forbade Aryans to engage in exchange relations with forced laborers: the

Figure 21. "W. H. W." (Winter Help). Heinz-Hermann Köhler, Watercolor, Hildesheim, ca. 1936. Courtesy of: SAH Best. 803/118/04.

former giving the latter food out of sympathy or the latter sharing food with the former out of appreciation (G/48a R/250). Though money was collected from both Aryans and Jews, Nazi welfare programs gave increasingly more funds to Aryans and less to Jews, though the choice to aryanize local charity programs was left to the initiative of local bureaucrats for most of the 1930s (Grüner 1995; Kaplan 1998; Rosenstrauch 1988: 49–68; Schmid 2002). That is, the Nazi regime concretized and institutionalized what had been a largely symbolic and informal set of exchange relations and then directed it towards political ends, promoting not only its ultimate, racist goals but also the regime's immediate fascist claims to totalitarianism.

But to redirect neighborly exchange relations in this way, the Nazi system first had to get control over them. Ordinary people played a critical role in that process of internal colonization. Historians have come to recognize that the Nazi seizure of power over the formal institutions of German state and society took place far more gradually than the propaganda of the Third Reich openly conceded (for Hildesheim, cf. Knott 1978; Politz 1971; Schmid 2002; Thimm 1999). The Nazi dictatorship did not arrive suddenly in 1933 but was strengthened step by step over the course of the period from 1930 to 1938. Yet the politicization and criminalization of conviviality preceded the policy decisions of the Nazi regime to create a police state from above (cf. Gellately 2001: 47–50). Gradually over the course of the 1930s, pro- and anti-Nazi factions polarized friendship and neighborliness according to their political agendas as they discovered the formal organizations and legal terms through which to mobilize and criminalize these informal social relations. This transition in the nature of "Winter Help" was captured in Bernhard Richeter's description of the events surrounding the Christmas collection for Erich Braun's family in 1934 (G/37b R/275, G/38a R/00, G/39b R/195; cf. Indictment of 27 April 1938 and Judgment of 7 July 1938 of the Supreme Court in Berlin against Otto Eger, BA-P NJ 17762).

Bernhard had been unemployed for three years before returning to Senking. His family was on welfare and had little money for food: during the summer, they ate only a little bread, tomatoes, and cucumbers. He and his otherwise corpulent wife were starved thin. Then, thanks to new orders for field ovens and other military-related products, Senking began to hire again.[4] Bernhard had to watch in frustration as Nazi party members were selected for work before him, regardless of their qualifications, for he patently refused to join the Nazi party. Bernhard was not actively involved in formal resistance activities and never read the *Ran* leaflet. He even falsely presumed that Braun was a communist because of his active resistance. Still, Bernhard had worked near Braun, even with him at times, and saw the Gestapo arrest him.

His description of the conversation between potential "conspirators" conforms closely to Hesse's testimony before the court:

> "We have really got to get his wife a little something."
> "Like Christmas, so that she has something to cook at least."
> "Yes, let's do that."

The foundations for this Christmas collection lay in many years of convivial interaction. There were Nazis in his workshop, but Bernhard explained that the men all knew each other and had worked together for years. They were all in the German Metalworkers Union and most of them had been in the SPD. They knew exactly each others' attitudes, and knew who had gone over to the Nazis out of ideological conviction and who had joined the party to get a job. With the former, one talked about one's garden or fishing. With the latter, one could still play jokes on the Nazis without fear, because such acquaintances were still linked in long-term convivial relationships. For instance, a person would state an intentional lie and laugh as the gossip passed around town. Still, they made sure that they discussed this Christmas collection for Minna Braun secretly and only among those whom they could trust.

Bernhard personally gave Hesse some money for Minna Braun. He falsely believed that the Braun family was receiving no financial support at all. True to the thesis of a Popular Front from below, Bernhard was very proud of the fact that social democrats went to the assistance of "a communist."[5] But he seemed most affected by the fact that Minna Braun was overjoyed that she had some food for Christmas. Then Bernhard's story turned sour:

> We made a mistake. We created a list. Not I [but Hesse], the one who took responsibility for the job, he created a list. Everyone entered their name and how much and why, no? We even said why! Hesse said that it was protection for us. He put himself at the very top and gave five marks [sic], and five marks was wages for five hours of work back then, no?

In reality, Bernhard explained, Hesse was trying to pressure his colleagues to give larger amounts, like two or three marks, and the collection was large as a result. Right at that moment, however, a Nazi colleague looked up and saw the list. He was not a bad man as far as Bernhard was concerned. He was just a little dumb and often the butt of their jokes. He walked over to them, and it was too late to let the list simply disappear. So they explained that they wanted to collect some money "for Braun's wife since he had been locked up." "Ach," the man replied, "the communist!" "Yes," one of them countered, "but it's not his children's fault that he did something wrong." The "conspirators" talked to their Nazi colleague in this way until one of them dared to ask: "Will you also add a little to the pot?" Bernhard described this as *the Alpha and Omega*: the question that put the entire scheme on the line. The man replied that he would not give any money, but that he would contribute something to the bag of groceries. Thus an ardent Nazi gave a box of sausages and a big bag of cookies that his wife had baked to the dependents of an anti-Nazi resistance fighter. "I told you that he was a little dumb!" Bernhard mocked.

Clearly, such collections began as much a result of proper neighborly relations as a result of politics. But they did not stay that way. Sometime later, this Nazi colleague got elected to join the new Nazi-ordained Factory Council (*Vertrauensrat*) that required membership in the Nazi party. Perhaps to prove his usefulness and loyalty to the Party, he gave the list to the Gestapo. They arrested the first three men, perhaps the first three names on the list. Throughout the interrogation, however, all three men stuck to their story that they had only wanted to help the children. The fact that the Gestapo did not get an admission of guilt lies as much in the fact that the Gestapo did not resort to their usual methods of excessive violence as in the local culture that disguised their resistance as conviviality.[6] After three days in the cellars of the Gestapo office on Gartenstrasse, these men were back at work.

For Bernhard, the stakes at the trial were high. Had the initial three men been convicted, the Gestapo would then have arrested and been able to convict the rest of the contributors and "ship" them to concentration camps for re-education. The list was almost their undoing. Yet during the court hearing in the County Courthouse (*Landgericht*) on the Cathedral Square in Hildesheim, and again in 1938 when some of these same individuals were indicted by the Supreme Court in Berlin, these men still insisted that they did not think anything of this collection: they just felt sorry for the family. Conviviality on its own was probably not sufficient for their acquittal by 1938 since judges were already treating informal gatherings as evidence of treasonous intent. Their best defense instead lay in the fact that the "arch Nazi" (*Edelnazi*) from Harsum had also contributed to the fund. The three "conspirators" were able to argue before the judges that they had nothing against the Nazi party, or why else would they have included a party member in the collection? The ardent Nazi could have given money elsewhere, but he also chose to give through their fund. The judges could not get around this argument, so they acquitted the contributors. "Winter Help" for the dependents of political prisoners was a completely appropriate act, according to local customs of conviviality. The men had "simply" been taking part in the lives of their neighbors.

This list was, as far as Bernhard was concerned, "the biggest act of stupidity," but his judgment is harsh and anachronistic. Bernhard came much closer to historical reality when he located such lists in their pre-existing customs of conviviality:

> We were so accustomed [to making such lists] long before the Nazis came. If there was a wedding, a list would be made and then everyone wrote down their name and the amount of money. Then a gift would be purchased. If someone died, a list was made, and everyone wrote down his contribution—for good management [*zur Kontolle*]—just how much, then a wreath would be purchased, or flowers, no? And that is how we did it in this case too.

The fact that these contributors always made such lists shows the degree to which bourgeois civic virtues had permeated German society, even on the informal level (Blackbourn and Eley 1985). Yet this group was far too informal to be called a club. Rather, Bernhard and his colleagues got themselves into hot water because the Gestapo was fishing for victims in the largely uncharted waters of conviviality, and because new waves of resistance-like activities spread into informal social relations once the Gestapo had successfully destroyed the cells of formal resistance. Bernhard and his colleagues were not really aware of these ramifications at first because, to them, collecting funds for the family of political prisoners remained a normal element of reciprocal exchange relations among colleagues. Or at least, to calm their fears of being caught, they liked to imagine that such actions were still ordinary.

Historians should not take sides in this debate and decide, for instance, that the donators were really resisting (and that they lied during the trial) or that they were just being neighborly (and that the Gestapo ensnared them). We should instead base our analysis of everyday life during the Third Reich on those contradictions. When faced with compassionate donations for friends and neighbors, the officers of the court were often hard pressed to determine reliable metrics by which they could measure intent on an individual basis and therefore render judgment. The courts, like historians today, found it hard to determine intentionality empirically. As a useful proxy for state of mind while providing assistance to the families of political prisoners, they looked instead at the defendants' memberships in formal organizations. This was an arbitrary measure, but it served the Nazis' purposes of laying claim to the critical terrain of conviviality.

Once again, the testimony of interview partners helps us to read the archival sources for their everyday character. Otto Krüger, too, was excused for making a donation (Judgment D against Heitmann, p. 18). He gave the judges the impression that he was a "simple and not very spiritually active person." He believably insisted that it was his compassion for the families in trouble that motivated him, for he knew from experience how hard it was to survive on welfare only. The fact that he had become a member of the German Workers Front (*Deutsche Arbeiterfront,* the Nazi "union") did not hurt his case. By contrast, Irrgang obviously knew the criminal purposes of the fund, as far as the judges were concerned, especially given his "political background." Yet his claim, that he gave to the fund because Heitmann and Schmalfeld accused him of "half-heartedness" and he simply wanted "to be rid of the collectors," seemed true to the judges. Here again, the fact that Irrgang had joined the SA proved to them that he was in the process of changing inside. Perhaps the judges were also influenced by the fact that he had been a member of the Ehrhardt Brigade, the Freikorps that stormed Berlin on 13 March 1920 as part of the Kapp Putsch against the Weimar Republic. In both examples, misbehavior in terms of conviviality was excused as so much eigensinn so long as their sociability, which conformed to the Third Reich, verified their true state of mind.[7]

More interesting is the case of Heinrich Baedje's contribution to this informal fund for "Winter Help." He insisted that he had "made his gift of money to help his acquaintances but not to promote the treasonous purposes of the collection" (p. 20). The judges excused him because they found evidence of an internal shift towards the Nazi movement in the fact that he had externally changed his social activities: he had joined the local branch of the Nazi Brotherhood of Plumbers and the German Workers' Front, and had attended the Thanksgiving Day Festival on the Bückeberg. Significantly, he had also collected for the official form of Winter Help. Beadje shifted the nature of his neighborly reciprocity from contributing to a fund for the families of political prisoners to collecting for Aryans on behalf of the Third Reich. Within the context of this trial, a seemingly insignificant custom of conviviality served demonstrably political purposes. No doubt outside the courthouse, however, Baedje could imagine, like my interview partners, that he had only been carrying on a local tradition of helping his neighbors.

For the judges, the goal was not so much accuracy in judgment as Nazi herrschaft. Yet we should read Judgment B against Hartung almost with a sense of frustration on the judges' part: "A former membership in a Marxist party or an affiliated organization is not punishable in itself but generally informative about the attitudes and opinions of the accused, especially when he had been active as a functionary" (pp. 20–22). The judges were trying to find the right measure for the ambiguous environment of conviviality in which the existing categories did not seem to hold much validity. It was obviously distressing to the Gestapo when the three men associated with the Braun collection walked free because they claimed only to be trying to help the families out of compassion. But the Gestapo must have been truly dismayed by the judges' reasons for acquitting some of the social democrats. Judgment D against Heitmann explained that since there was no Red Help in the SPD, then these individuals could not have been intending to promote a criminal organization (p. 15). In effect, one's formal party affiliation made the same act criminal in some cases and neighborly in others.

By contrast, Adolf Heitmann (Wilhelm's son) was acquitted in effect because his friend and co-conspirator was a Nazi. Adolf drove Hoppe to Goslar in order to warn a co-conspirator that their mail was being opened, but he used a motorcycle that he borrowed from his friend, Franz Kohlenberg, who was also a *Sturmführer* in the SA and Nazi party member. In court, Adolf Heitmann admitted his collaboration openly but claimed "that he had not been aware of the implications of his actions and only wanted to do a favor for his father and Hoppe." He had nothing against the Nazi state, he insisted, and proved this by the fact that he had wanted to join the SA but had been prevented to do so by his father whose criticism of the Third Reich had always been "hard" for him to hear. This story was then verified by his "Nazi" friend Kohlenberg, whose testimony the judges accepted without question (Judgment against Voss, pp. 24–25, 31–32).

The officers of the court were using sociability as a measure of intent in the far more ambiguous contexts of conviviality: to chart the newly discovered terrain of conviviality in order to colonize it on behalf of the Third Reich. At times, however, they stumbled along the way on their own assumptions about the normalcy of conviviality. Judgment B against Hartung (pp. 9–10) asserted that Friedrich Rausch knew Hoppe from their days in the Reichsbanner, the republican paramilitary group. Rausch "lived as a subletter" with Hoppe for a time and regularly interacted in Hoppe's family life. Since he was acquainted with Frau Hoppe, he met Hartung, Schwetje, and Berger at her burial in January 1936 and helped Hartung that spring with his garden work. In July 1936, Berger gave five marks to Rausch for Hoppe's children, Rausch added three marks to this, giving it all to Heitmann, who then gave it to Hoppe's sister who was caring for his children after his imprisonment. What had been symbolic gestures that insulated ordinary Hildesheimers from world politics now convinced Nazi officials all the more that these Hildesheimers intended to instigate high treason. Yet the Nazi authorities were nonetheless convicting these Hildesheimers in effect for being good neighbors.

The authorities seem to have considered it an even worse offense when these Hildesheimers added something of their own to the packages purchased using collective funds (as Schmalfeld did for Frau Lamek and Heitmann did for Frau Kirk in Judgment against Voss, p. 17). Worst of all, some Hildesheimers actually made packages of their own means entirely. In Judgment B against Hartung (p. 11), we read how Heinrich Winkelhoff brought Frau Wunstorff a package of groceries from his own means for Christmas in 1936 and admitted that he did so because he knew her and knew that her husband Paul had been condemned to two years of prison time for instigating high treason. According to the Judgment against Voss (p. 14–15), Berger did much the same to an anonymous woman on Alter Markt, a street with particularly poor people. Aware that this woman's husband had become a political prisoner, he purchased groceries out of his own money, created a basket for them, and brought them to her for Christmas in 1935. Berte Engelke spent some fifty marks on a similar package. Here, we see cases of informal "Winter Help" that were not at all associated with an organization. Though arguably still political, they represented individual acts of human kindness all the same. Here is the clearest evidence, then, of the proactive politicization and retroactive criminalization of neighborliness, so long as that human sympathy was directed towards the dependents of the enemies of the Nazi regime.

Nazi law-enforcement not only destroyed the "organized resistance" of Hildesheim by placing the ringleaders in prison, concentration camps, or exile. In the process, the local Gestapo also developed a new degree of sensitivity to signs of treason in conviviality. For some of those who were acquitted, the brush with the law probably reinforced their proper behavior in the appropriate Nazi organizations. For their friends and neighbors, these trials served as a warning to coordinate social relations, formal *and informal*, to fit Nazi policies and principles: to restrict one's human sympathies to Aryan neighbors and to do so by voluntarily participating in formally constituted Nazi charity programs. And just in case one did not know the affected persons directly, the results of arrests and trials were announced in the daily paper (e.g., *HAZ* 19 December 1933, 15 May 1937; see also Gellately 2001).

Towards Social Engineering

In interwar Hildesheim, neighbors had shared radios and newspapers, exchanged greetings and gossip, shopped in neighborhood stores, and even brought over small gifts for the sick and needy. They continued to do so during the Third Reich not only for political reasons but also because they had established these bonds and habits of reciprocity long before the Nazis had arrived. It was easy for some to fall into antifascist resistance by continuing this reciprocity: sharing printing presses, and, when husbands were arrested, sharing groceries among dependents. The latter became an offence that threatened the Nazi volksgemeinschaft only retroactively once the battle for and against the Third Reich extended beyond the formal institutions of social and political life and into the informal realm of convivial customs. Speaking in the language of friendship and neighborliness, the Nazi regime in turn made powerful claims to have resurrected the embattled community of the Great War: fairly redistributing resources between Aryans through such programs as Winter Help and One-Bowl Sundays. Once Hildesheimers learned to restrict their human compassion in this way, however, it was not a far step to ignore the suffering of the enemies of the volksgemeinschaft entirely.

As one might expect under totalitarianism, sharing resources with convivials became a dangerous affair (e.g., Judgment D against Heitmann and his conspirators, p. 10; Heinrich Bode 1972 and "Ein Leben . . . "). Suspicion soon permeated otherwise sincere forms of human compassion. Once, when the young Belgian man was repairing Bernhard's bag, he took a piece of fruit. Bernhard confronted him about this, and the student began to cry. He begged Bernhard not to denounce him to the guard, fearing that the guards would beat him up. Bernhard knew that these guards were indeed the kind of persons who would take any excuse to get violent. It was not Bernhard's style "to report a pair of stupid apples to the guard," and anyway, it had been his intent to give food to the student all along (G/39b R/20). In spite of Bernhard's former acts of compassion, however, the fear of denunciation still poisoned their relationship.

Other Hildesheimers chose to remove themselves from relations that might endanger others. Dora Pröbst made this point explicitly (G/124b R/330). A proper Hildesheimer and good neighbor, her father-in-law often visited her sick mother. Yet Dora feared that the firemen, who had accused her of defiling the race, could have seen that a Jew was visiting the home of Christians. She worried that her mother could be incarcerated for this infraction of racist norms. As it turns out, the firemen did not say anything to the Gestapo, but the fear was now present: that is, of her neighbors more than the Gestapo per se. To help me understand, she asked me to imagine that her family and mine were friendly prior to Hitler, "and suddenly this [monitoring] begins, and a great fear arises. . . . Now, I married a Jew and I come to your house to visit . . . and [my name] was besmirched. I come now to you and talk to you—and I [inadvertently] draw you into it too. This I refused to do." To protect her family and friends, Dora had to cease making public contact across the Nazi divide.

Yet it would be a mistake to overgeneralize the decline of compassion and the rise of alienation as a result of denunciation and racism (Gellately 2001; Henry 1984; Kaplan 1998). The Nazi revolution did not contribute to a secular trend from community to society in any straightforward manner. While on a visit to Copenhagen in August 1935 (as disclosed to the prosecution during his court hearing on 29 May 1936, p. 4), Hoppe complained to "Arnold" (Pasch) that resistance activities in Germany were extremely limited "because you cannot trust your best friend." This was hyperbole for effect. Hoppe did trust those friends who shared his convictions, and relied on them for much of his antifascist activities; he just did not trust his other friends and neighbors. It was much the same for Otto (G/47b R/70). Bernhard obviously continued to try to share food with his Belgian workmate in spite of the danger and suspicion. Gerhard Mock preserved a longstanding friendship with a non-Jew in spite of the Third Reich. The Nazi volksgemeinschaft did not leave its outsiders wholly isolated from friends and neighbors; rather, the choice to create intimacy was now always evaluated with reference to the Nazi regime. The totalitarian centrality of the Nazi regime to informal social relations was also evident among many ordinary Hildesheimers who felt perfectly integrated within the Nazi volksgemeinschaft. They participated in formal institutions of sociability in part because the new Nazi institutions seemed to transcend the old hatreds between Catholics and Protestants, bourgeoisie and proletariat (Bergerson 2004). They participated in informal customs of conviviality, in acts such as making a small donation for suffering neighbors, in spite of—or because of—the fact that the Nazi regime reinvented these acts in fascist–racist terms. The alienation of Jews, communists, and the like helped many other ordinary Aryans feel at home in the Third Reich.

So we need another metric to evaluate everyday life under the Third Reich since ordinary people across the political divide both preserved and lost friends. People felt so alienated from many neighbors but so reassured by others. A more global appraisal would suggest that the struggle between strategies for fascist herrschaft and tactics of antifascist eigensinn over the course of the 1930s did not so much transform their convivial community into a mass society as colonize conviviality for political purposes. The more that informal social relations were measured in terms of formal institutions and memberships, the more conviviality acquired the rigidity of sociability and politics. That is, the Nazi revolution not only shifted the categories by which ordinary people created alienation and integration in their neighborhood to fit its ideological agenda. It also made these distinctions more rigorous and systematic. The Nazi revolution constricted the scope of conviviality to a considerable degree, but more essentially it constrained the flexibility that had been a hallmark of friendship and neighborliness. It undermined the degree to which ordinary people could independently determine the membership and character of their moral community.

The struggle between herrschaft and eigensinn so undermined the functionality of informal social relations that the regime assumed responsibility for managing them instead. As the next chapter will show, the Nazi regime stepped into this vacuum, taking on the task of policing the local moral community. Though they based their policies on conviviality, and many ordinary Hildesheimers welcomed their administration of the local moral community, their increasingly bureaucratic measures translated informal mechanisms of negotiation into formal procedures for social engineering. Like the Nazi revolution itself, the momentum driving Nazi managerial "solutions" to social problems derived in part from cultural dynamics in everyday life.

7 | Administration

For MANY YEARS, a technician at Senking had rented an apartment from Heinrich Weber's parents. This man wore a large party insignia with an extra rim to show that he was an old party member. He was also literally a Standard Bearer for the SA: the man who carried the flag when the group marched. As soon as Hitler took power in Germany, the Standard Bearer also assumed command of the building. As the owner of the house, Heinrich's father was still the house manager *de jure,* but the Standard Bearer assumed this role *de facto.* The Standard Bearer "pushed himself in the middle of everything" in the neighborhood. "Suddenly, you no longer complained to the owner of the house about something." The Standard Bearer had to know about it first. When Heinrich's father wanted to rent an apartment to someone, the Standard Bearer decided first if the person was acceptable, and he based that decision on whether the prospective renter was a sufficiently good Nazi. "Not in this house," he would say. "I will lay claims here."

The Standard Bearer justified his minor coup by citing the Nazi maxim that placed common good over personal property (*Gemeinnutz geht vor Eigennutz;* see also Allen 1992), but it was his connections in the Nazi party that gave his bark its bite. The head of the local party organization, who determined which people got which local party offices, lived literally next door. Increasingly over the course of the 1930s, ardent Nazis "called the shots in almost all areas." The prime movers here were not the Nazi regime as such but individual neighbors proactively laying claim to status and power, conscious of the power of the regime behind them but relatively independent of it nonetheless. Appropriately, Heinrich depicted this revolution in neighborly hierarchies as a usurpation in keeping with the analogous story of the Nazi seizure of power.

Over the course of the 1930s, the Nazi regime and its neighborhood officers increasingly assumed the role of watchdog over the local moral community (Gellately 2001). Yet ordinary Hildesheimers also placed the Nazi regime and its local representatives in this new position of moral authority in order to keep themselves ordinary. The archival data here is scanty due to the destruction of Nazi era records on 22 March 1945 by Allied bombs, but that which survived, when combined with testimony from interviews, will show that the coordination of conviviality to fit Nazi principles in fact undermined the functionality of neighborliness as a medium to communicate and negotiate identities. As seen in the case of hats, salutations, flags, and uniforms, this contradiction hindered the construction of a moral community more generally and made ardent Nazis insecure about the state of the volksgemeinschaft in particular. For both reasons, ordinary Hildesheimers relied increasingly upon the Nazi regime to manage from above what had been negotiated through conviviality from below: the scatological boundaries of the moral community. Encouraged by ordinary Hildesheimers to clean up the neighborhood of pollution, the Nazi regime proceeded to actually engineer social relations in keeping with its totalitarian image and for purposes of racial hygiene. Though based on informal customs of conviviality, this formal administration of the local moral community proved to be far more brutal and inexorable. Intertwined in all aspects of everyday life, this racist system presumed the collusion of ordinary people. Yet because Nazi policies were based on pre-existing habits, they could act as if this violent, racial order was perfectly normal.

Hat Tricks

In his neighborhood, Heinrich Weber had a reputation for being a reluctant Nazi—at least in his memory. He tried to avoid Nazi activities, but this was not easy for a town bureaucrat, even in a lower position. "You can imagine that a state scribbler like me would have been a welcome addition to the local party group—to organize all the written junk, you know." The Standard Bearer in particular tried to pressure him to get involved a bit more regularly. "The best possible response was to avoid him." Take for example the so-called educational evenings: these were meetings designed to inform those Aryans who demonstrated an insufficient understanding of, or support for, national-socialist doctrine. Heinrich's father attended them because he feared that the Nazis would call for a boycott of his painting business if he did not. But Heinrich found them to be an inconvenient waste of time: he preferred to work in his garden. Ever resourceful, Heinrich showed his face at the sessions but made sure that he went "without a hat or a cap" so that, when he stepped out "to wash his hands," he could disappear quickly. Had he worn a hat or cap, he could hardly have taken it with him to wash his hands, but he also did not wish to leave it sitting on the chair after he left. Leaving his hat at home prepared him socially for anonymity and culturally for political escapism.

This hat trick was only one of a series of tactics that Heinrich used to avoid undesirable forms of participation in the Nazi system. He did so not because of his moral or political convictions; he gladly worked for the Nazis in the local bureaucracy. Rather, he rebelled against these educational evenings in response to the totalitarian claims of the Nazi regime on his private time as well as to the inverted state of power relations between his property-owning family and his standard-bearing neighbor. Yet, the Standard Bearer eventually figured out Heinrich's hat trick and denounced him for truancy to the local party leader, who in turn reprimanded Heinrich. The party leader told him precisely which events he should attend "as a prospective Nazi" (G/147b R/20, G/148b R/160, 365). Heinrich could no longer use his hat trick to escape participation in Nazi activities.

The Nazi regime increasingly determined who wore hats and when. On Kristallnacht in November 1938, Lotte Schohl saw Jewish men and boys who had been forced out of their homes improperly dressed: without adequately heavy coats for the cold November temperatures and without their hats (G/9b R/360). The fact that she noticed the latter is particularly appropriate because this event marked a turning point in Nazi policy towards increasingly bureaucratic solutions to the so-called Jewish Question (Bauman 1989). Lotte was shocked by the fact that her neighbors were now being treated as Jews, but their alienation was communicated in simple, symbolic terms: their hats were absent. This police action also made sense in part because Jews had always represented dangerous anomalies with regard to the local customs of headdress. Catholic and Protestant boys wore caps that revealed confessional identities that were otherwise disguised by a polite greeting. By contrast, Jews wore a headdress that disguised their identities: the school cap of either a Catholic or a Protestant. The same was true of homosexuals and Jehovah's Witnesses, two other sets of Nazi victims. From a communicative perspective, these groups were all dangerously subversive (following Bauman 1992: 56–60), particularly for those who had already been attracted to ideologies of antisemitism and homophobia. These groups all abused the language of caps by using them to disguise what they should have revealed: racial-moral deviance behind a façade of propriety. By removing the hats of Jews, parading them down Hoher Weg, and then removing the Jews themselves, the Nazis were claiming, in the language of conviviality, to have uncovered disguised transgressors within the neighborhood.

Gerhard Mock was one of the Jews who had been forced to walk down Hoher Weg to witness the burning of the synagogue on Lappenberg. Deported thereafter to Buchenwald, he recalled a game that the SS often played during his four-month incarceration in that concentration camp. If the guards grew lonely or bored, they called over one of the prisoners, asked him to remove his cap, and said: "Throw that cap—see how far you can throw it." They then told the prisoner to get it, but when he ran for his cap, the guard shot him dead for trying to escape. Gerhard did not succumb to this hat trick because his hut leader told him not to obey the guards. "They will kill you, if you do" (G/115b R/110).

In Hildesheim, neighbors had recognized their mutual membership in a civil society by exchanging greetings. The hat reasserted their different identities in terms of class, confession, age, and gender. Hildesheimers could hardly imagine a grown man walking the streets of their neighborhood without one. It was far too dangerous a proposition: without hats, self and society might very well dissolve entirely into a faceless mass. Yet this was precisely what these concentration-camp guards did to Jews. By removing the prisoners' hats, the SS communicated their new status and power in the inverted world of the concentration camp. The guards made clear that they were Aryans and their prisoners Jews in a society based on racial hierarchy. The removal of the prisoners' hats also marked the first, cultural step towards murder. By inverting the rules of civility, the SS guards ritually initiated barbarity.

The Nazi regime based its inhumane policies of social engineering in part on local customs of conviviality. Similarly, ordinary Hildesheimers turned increasingly to the Nazi regime to administer a moral community whose boundaries had been managed formerly by friends and neighbors. The shift towards bureaucratic solutions to everyday situations was motivated in part by a contradiction within conviviality of which ordinary Hildesheimers and ardent Nazis only gradually became aware. The failure of Heinrich's hat trick to protect him from totalitarianism hinted at it: the more that ordinary Hildesheimers and ardent Nazis used greetings, flags, and uniforms to lay claim to status and power in the new Third Reich, the more they undermined the functionality of those symbols to communicate and negotiate identities.

The Nazi greeting, the swastika flag, and the SA uniform provided the means by which Hildesheimers could announce their support for the new political system. Of course, the Nazi regime mandated proper behavior in certain cases and formally orchestrated Nazi pageants that included all of these symbols. Yet they hoped, in fact, that ordinary Germans employed these symbols of their own accord and throughout their daily lives because this voluntary demonstration of support for the Third Reich was far more effective than official regulations to pressure the reluctant into conformity. In the absence of democratic elections, such populist demonstrations were also the best measure of the success of their brown revolution. German historians have struggled to determine how many people greeted with *heil hitler!* and hung the swastika flag out of conviction and how many did so out of convenience. Yet we cannot ever resolve this conundrum after the fact, for the same reasons that the Nazis and their opponents were so obsessed with these acts at that time.[1] By homogenizing their neighborhood symbols, ordinary people undermined their utility as a means to accurately express and assess something true about themselves and others.

Consider the example recalled by Margarita Averdieck. Her husband finished his training as a mathematics and biology teacher in 1933, but he found it difficult to find a job. He had several offers, but then the local leader of the town party organization ruined his chances by investigating his political background with their peers in Hildesheim. His reputation was conveyed to the party leader of the other town, and he was accused of being too much on the Left, though Margareta denied that this was true. "My husband was also in the Party; he had joined up. If you were not, you got no position at all." The local party officer in Hildesheim commended him for trying to change his ways, but at that time, Margareta explained, "they were taking only those who were 100 percent Nazis." One town in East Pomerania offered the post to a competitor who was also a more committed Nazi, who had appeared at his interviews in a Nazi uniform. In the end, her husband was indeed offered a job (G/77a R/60), perhaps because the "100 percenter" had accepted a different post, perhaps because Margareta's husband was more Nazi-oriented than she wished to admit. In 1933, Hildesheimers still tried to illustrate their political convictions by hanging a particular flag or wearing a particular uniform. But increasingly, those of less staunch political convictions could rally to the Nazi flag or uniform for quite pragmatic reasons *as if* they were really convinced Nazis.

This pragmatism undermined the function of such public displays. Interwar Hildesheimers had found the diversity of public iconography distasteful during the Weimar Republic because it signified the lack of consensus among neighbors on fundamental political principles. The uniformity achieved by the Nazis satisfied some, as a sign of the brown revolution accomplished, but challenged them all. Residents began to wonder whether neighbors were disguising their true political beliefs under the veil of totalitarian uniformity. The irony of this situation was not lost on interwar Hildesheimers. Dora Pröbst recalled how her husband visited a customer in the late 1930s who had hung a Nazi flag from his roof. Erich, a Jew, said to him: "If the communists took over the ship then you would have a hammer-and-sickle flying up there!" His customer laughed and replied: "You are probably correct about that" (G/126a R/60). By the end of the interwar period, greetings, flags, and uniforms no longer accurately expressed one's private political beliefs.

This confusion stuck with Dora over the intervening years. She explained that her husband Erich continued to do well economically in spite of Nazi antisemitism. After they returned from a vacation to the United States in 1937, they found many who joined the Nazi party, "but they were not really [Nazis] in their essence. For instance, the son of the owner of an aristocratic estate used to stand around in an SS uniform [while he] looked over [Erich's] horses and bought some." Despite his SS uniform, she implied, he was not a Nazi to his bones. She then gave me an example of the inverse case of a seeming philosemite who became "a really big Nazi": the chauffeur whom Erich hired to bring customers to town and who took a liking to his Jewish mother (G/129b R/60). Dora told me these anecdotes to emphasize the enormous risk that she and her husband had run by returning to Hildesheim in 1937, but she measured this danger in terms of how difficult it had become to distinguish dangerous Nazis from mere collaborators.

Over the course of the 1930s, ordinary Hildesheimers collaborated with ardent Nazis to officially create the homogeneous semiotic landscape for which some had longed in the 1920s. Yet homogeneity destroyed one critical function of greetings, hats, flags, and uniforms: to express self and society behind the veil of the everyday. As a result, Hildesheimers of all sorts became obsessed with determining the degree to which their neighbors, colleagues, family, and friends actually supported the Nazi regime as opposed to those who simply adopted the styles of the period. It is significant that Dora concluded our final interview with this paradox. She had learned how to deal with antisemitism in her neighborhood in part by distinguishing between committed and less committed Nazis. Yet when less committed neighbors flew the same flags and wore the same uniforms, even if out of convenience, those signs lost their ability to subtly communicate one's private political convictions. The Third Reich had finally become too disorienting, even for the courageous Dora.

Cleaning Up

This communicative crisis was self-induced, but it was also one main reason why, over the course of the 1930s, ordinary Hildesheimers turned increasingly to the Nazi regime to formally manage what neighbors had previously negotiated informally: the integrity of their moral community. The Nazi regime responded by adopting more direct methods of administrating convivial relations, though they conducted these formal procedures in a manner befitting informal customs. This correlation enabled ordinary Hildesheimers to imagine that the new Nazi policies of social engineering were still perfectly normal. And precisely because this shift from convivial process to bureaucratic procedure was designed to efface the collaboration of ordinary Hildesheimers, this story has everything to do with cleansing rituals.

Neighborliness was a dirty affair. In its semi-public, semi-private spaces, ordinary Hildesheimers laid claim to status and power, struggled to preserve their independence from invasive social and political forces, made Hildesheim fascist, and yet hid their eigensinn behind the veil of everyday life. These open secrets undermined the moral credibility of the community. Pollution, analogously, was a neighborly affair. Neighbors shared in the experience when individuals purged their bodies just as they collectively purged their street and outhouses of accumulated muck and dirt. The ritual cleansing of these semi-public, semi-private spaces served pragmatic ends: providing valuable resources for families in the form of manure. They also served ritual functions: erasing the memory of conflict, transgression, self-cultivation, even historicity. To restore their moral community, inter-war Hildesheimers ritually wiped clean the slate of convivial relations and started afresh by cleansing the stairwells, stoops, courtyards, and streets of physical pollution.

In the early nineteenth century, private homeowners had been responsible for paving the street and sidewalk for the length of their property and up to the middle of the street. This informal system led to such poor road conditions that the town organized a public till in 1851 into which each resident would contribute and out of which the town would draw for paving. The condition of the sidewalks and streets improved as a result. The town administration still considered street pavement to be primarily the responsibility of private citizens, but clearly, they had begun to facilitate its satisfactory execution. A cholera epidemic in 1867 further inspired the town to build a sewer system (Gebauer 1950: 159, 170). On the one hand then, official responsibility for neighborhood sanitation grew in keeping with the steady march of state power.

On the other hand, Hildesheimers gradually grew to expect more of their civic administration, as can be seen by comparing complaints about street-cleanliness in 1912, 1928, and 1936 (SAH 102/2997, 8784, 8786). On 29 May 1912, the owners of the large hotels on the train-station plaza notified the local tourism association that the plaza was often dirtied by wagons, some carrying manure, which did not provide a pretty picture for locals or tourists sitting in front of their hotels. The residents of Judenstrasse wrote a similar letter on 10 September 1928. Located adjacent to the old market square and its architectural masterpieces, they worried about the response of tourists when they came to look at the Wedekind-Haus and the Tempelhaus and found the street covered in dove droppings. In contrast to 1912, however, they sent their letter of 1928 directly to the town, asking for sprayers to be sent through their street on a regular basis to clear away the scat. Clearly, some citizens had begun to believe that the town had a larger responsibility than it claimed for public order. Still, the town contested their presumption and wrote a report on 25 February 1929 in which they concluded that residents were still responsible for cleaning up most of the dirt on their streets.

The town changed its tune a few years later. In a letter dated 24 July 1936, a similar group of shopkeepers complained to the town that the latter did not send the spray-machine through the streets of town with sufficient frequency to keep them clean. In contrast to the two previous complaints, this time the town admitted fault and promised to pay closer attention in the future. The transition to this new attitude about the state's responsibility for public cleanliness probably took place during the Great Depression. According to the civic report of 1936 (*Verwaltungsbericht der Stadt Hildesheim:* xiii, 10, 16, 24, 25), the town hired unemployed workers in 1932, when local unemployment figures were at their highest, to clean up the debris that collected on the streets near the Innerste dike, to repair sidewalks, bridges and streets, and even to build new ones where necessary. Between 1928 and 1937, the town also purchased several large trucks for garbage and street cleaning. In 1937, the municipality assumed responsibility for cleaning those streets that had heavier traffic. These policies reflected the growth of the interventionist state in the interwar period in general.

They also characterized the Third Reich in particular. The Nazi movement came to power in part on a platform of law and order in response to the exaggerated threat of communist revolution (Gellately 2001; Hamilton 2003). As Heinrich Weber insisted, orderliness "was closely observed under the Nazis at any rate. Cleanliness and orderliness, etc. After all, they built [their movement] on these old Prussian virtues, [so they insisted] on sticking to them" (G/148b R/285). Friedrich Rother said that "everyone believed that there was order on the streets. That was one of the few good sides of the Nazi era. Criminals were punished back then, and there were fewer of them" (G/58a R/00). The Nazi regime claimed to be willing and able to re-establish order in Germany. As true modernists, they also claimed to be able to do so expertly and efficiently. To preserve their legitimacy then, fascists had to keep the streets clean in fact.

Those claims should not be misinterpreted as success. In 1936, Douglas Chandler, a "German-friendly" American journalist, visited Hildesheim to see if he and his family would want to live there for a year. The Hildesheim bureaucrat who recorded their meeting (SAH 102/8784) noted that Chandler had been invited to attend the recent party congress in Nürnberg and had a generally positive evaluation of the Third Reich. Yet he did not have a similarly glowing assessment of Hildesheim. Whereas nearby Goslar was "a clean town," Chandler "rebuked Hildesheim for its dirty streets and especially the paper lying all over the place. He apologized for having to say that, although he knew all of Germany including the East, he believed that he had never seen such a dirty town as Hildesheim." Chandler found the train station to be "very unclean" and "that paper and road sweepings get thrown over the wire fence and that creates an unprepossessing picture." Chandler's critical assessment of Hildesheim in 1936 was fueled by his otherwise strong identification with German fascism and culture (Edwards 1991: ch. 4). Yet precisely because he was enamored of the brown revolution, the civic bureaucracy in Hildesheim was all the more sensitive to his comments, insisting that the police take more care that their beats were cleaned on schedule. The mayor realized that "the execution of street-cleanings by the town is not possible at this time," but since the streets could get dirty in between the two cleanings scheduled per week, he increased the number of times to three per week: on Monday, Wednesday, and Saturday. The police also still had provisions for ad hoc cleanings should the streets get especially dirty. At least in principle, the town administration recognized its increasing responsibility for cleaning up the streets, in keeping with popular expectations for Nazi hygiene.

Meanwhile, Hildesheimers associated Jews with both illicit forms of commerce and pollution. Theresa Stoffregen recalled that Jews owned smaller stores on the margins of the business district and in the Neustadt. Her family did not purchase items there, but she nonetheless heard about them from relatives who lived in that neighborhood. "There was a porcelain store—Jews." They were all engaged in "truck and barter," but that kind of commerce had an indecent quality. Because her father could negotiate well while shopping, she used to say: "You are half a Jew!" In her opinion, the Jews' neighborly behavior also had a subtly immoral character. Even as a child, she explained, one could tell that they were Jews: not just "from their appearance" (as one might expect during the racist Third Reich), but also from the fact that "they always sat in front of their door and sunned themselves." The stoop was a space of neighborliness, but Hildesheimers were supposed to clean it, not inhabit it. "These Jews always sat outside." A public nuisance, Theresa concluded: "they were not very clean, and the shop was not very clean" (G/191a R/65, G/191b R/115). A young girl during the Third Reich (b. at the very end of 1929), Theresa reiterated these prejudicial perceptions as a matter of fact.

Theresa did not mention who was responsible for preserving moral order—a silence for which there are various interpretations. Arguably it was not simply a matter of post facto repression. During the Weimar Republic, the communal police had been a local institution under the authority of Hildesheim's mayor. During the Third Reich, Jürgen Ludewig was not sure whether the police took their orders from party or state. This confusion corresponded to the polycratic nature of the Nazi regime in which conflicting and overlapping authorities competed for power and status within the Nazi hierarchy by trying best to fulfill and anticipate Hitler's policies. From the perspective of an ordinary Hildesheimer like Jürgen, however, such policies came "from up there to down here" (G/103b R/40; cf. Lüddecke 1987; see also Lüdtke 1992). An ordinary person, Theresa did not mention who was responsible for moral order because she had learned to leave it to the authorities to clean up the Jewish mess.

Prior to the Third Reich, a single officer used to walk Jürgen's neighborhood; he knew the inhabitants on his beat often by name as they did him. The anticipation of his presence at a specific time each week was in itself sufficient to motivate the inhabitants to clean their stoops: to preserve their respectability among neighbors and insulate their family from state intrusion. By sweeping the street, they did both—and erased all evidence of the contradiction. During the Third Reich, anywhere from two to eight policemen now packed into a troop-carrying vehicle, usually open but sometimes covered with a tarp during bad weather. This *surprise-attack detachment* (*Überfallkommando*) was responsible for restoring moral order through far more direct mechanisms. "If something was up, then they raced up in this truck." Part paramilitary organization, Jürgen explained that Nazi policemen used this tactic to break up union meetings on the Goschenstrasse (near his home in the Neustadt) and to beat up social democrats (see also Thimm 1999: 23–30). Jürgen described various other police actions in the neighborhood that ended in brutality and deportations.

Yet Jürgen also saw these Nazi thugs simply as ersatz neighborhood policeman. "Obviously," Jürgen continued, these fascist police forces also used these troop-carrying vehicles to patrol the streets in general: "to care for order." Jürgen slipped at times and almost called this kind of unit a *mobile killing squad* (*"Einsatzkommando"*): the name for those troops responsible for segregating and shooting Jews on the Eastern Front. Jürgen couched the murderous colonization of everyday life by the Nazi regime in the pre-existing context of conviviality, as if Nazi social engineering were simply a matter of keeping the neighborhood clean. The association in his memory reflects his historical experience. The Nazi regime interpolated totalitarian terror into traditional models of moral order, while ordinary Hildesheimers tried to preserve their normalcy by framing this expanding state into the pre-existing cultural framework of neighborliness.

Ulrich Gerke also claimed to be just an ordinary German in extraordinary times. Born at the start of 1920, he reacted strongly when I asked if he had played with Polish children as a child. Of course they had, he argued. Racial hatred was unknown to them as children. Racism was introduced by the Nazis. He claimed to be neither antisemitic nor responsible for the Nazi revolution in social relations that laid the foundation for the Holocaust. The Nazi regime was solely responsible for both. To support this claim, he recalled that he first experienced racism when the Nazis removed his Jewish neighbors, the Nussbaums, in 1934. Before then, he knew that certain doctors or bankers were Jewish, but the distinction was not there as such (G/86a R/170; see also G/84b R/190). Ulrich remembered this incident with the Nussbaums because it was a moment of disjuncture: when a civil society changed into a volksgemeinschaft, when neighbors became Jews and Aryans. Yet this anecdote should not be read for its overt content, as if the Nazi regime were really solely responsible for introducing racism into Hildesheim, but for the habit memories at its core. Ulrich remembered this incident because it was at this moment that he first became addicted to a bad habit: to behave among neighbors like an Aryan, for whom the Jewish Problem was a matter best left for the Nazi regime to manage.

This dependence on the Third Reich for moral order (see also Browning 1998; Gellately 2001; Kaplan 1998) can be seen in terms of the stroll. Prior to the Third Reich, adults, parents and teachers had policed the stroll to prevent young people from engaging in illicit forms of desire, economic and sexual. During the Third Reich,[2] the HJ took on this responsibility—and altered its nature. They considered smoking, swing dancing, and sexual affairs not just inappropriate for young people but also degenerate in the physical and psychic sense. The HJ therefore tried to dissuade adolescents from engaging in these activities for eugenic reasons. In this way, the HJ not only undermined the traditional authority of parents by introducing peer-based social control in its place but also substituted a formal Nazi organization in the place of an informal mechanism for preserving the integrity of the moral community. When some of my interview partners described how they smoked, danced, and had sex nonetheless, they were remembering eigensinn directed at both parents and Nazi peers, finding support for their revolt against the one in the other (G/93a R/140, G/98a R/300, G/135b R/60).

Meanwhile, adult Nazis also did their part to police the stroll and restore moral order to this core site for experimenting with desire. The boycott of Jewish stores on 1 April 1933 took place primarily in this central business district with SA guarding the doors to Jewish stores to intimidate or physically prevent people from entering; the night before, the shop windows of many Jewish stores in the central business district had been broken. Within just a few years, Jewish incomes and standard of living declined dramatically because fewer Gentile customers shopped in their stores, sought out their professional advice, or hired Jewish clerks. The Nazi regime certainly promoted the aryanization of shopping habits through acts of violence. Their policy at this stage was to promote Jewish emigration by making Jewish lives in Germany untenable. Yet most of the antisemitic legislation excluding Jews from economic life was implemented after 1938. Initially, the systematic pressure behind economic aryanization lay in the informal pressure of neighbors (Kaplan 1998; for Hildesheim, Schneider 1998: III, 6–10; Teich 1979: 107). On 11 April 1935, Deputy Führer Rudolf Hess still had to remind party members "not to shop in Jewish stores and to avoid personal interaction with Jews." His order (*Anordnung*, reproduced in Rosenstrauch 1988: 38) also asked party members to help rearrange (*anordnen*) German society informally by "dealing with" those who refuse to abide by the new racial principles.

The Nazi regime began to make "sweeps" of the streets of Germany to remove "asocials" only in 1937, around the same time that they began to revive their antisemetic policies (Gellateley 2001). Still, the regime in Berlin left it to local Nazis to plan how best to execute the Kristallnacht of November 1938, and the latter did so in keeping with local culture. In Hildesheim, they conducted their ritual purges in precisely those spaces that the moral community was most threatened: the central business district characterized by unrestrained capitalism, consumption, sexual desire, modernity, and Jews. Jewish men and boys were marched through town in their pajamas, towards the burning synagogue in the Neustadt, along Hoher Weg. Some were deported directly to Buchenwald the next evening, and most of those who remained were resettled into a half-dozen so-called Jewish houses: buildings owned by local Jewish foundations, confiscated by the Nazi regime for this purpose, and located away from the stroll (Schneider III, 11; Thimm 1999: 52). Though adults had always monitored this dangerous space for youthful transgressions, the Nazis punished these alleged transgressions more aggressively (see also G/195b R/105). Local Nazis forced the Jews of Hildesheim to take the stroll down Hoher Weg one last time in order to demonstrate to them and their neighbors that the economy was no longer *in their hands:* that is, as a ritual prologue to their physical deportation, concentration, and murder. Proceeding to many other streets as well before reaching the burning synagogue, this forced march through town was a public spectacle designed as much for Gentile consumption as Jewish persecution (Friedlander 2003). As Otto Koch reported, they even made sure to drive their trucks, on which sat the Jews scheduled for deportation, through the streets of town "so that everyone saw what was up, no?" (G/48a R/90).

In the language of conviviality, the Nazi regime was in fact promising to restore the moral community when it promised to cleanse Hildesheim of its Jews. According to the same cultural logic, antisemitism worked best as public policy when that purge remained anonymous, if ordinary people did not have to recognize those Jews as former friends and neighbors: that is, insofar as ordinary people colluded in laying the cultural foundations for alienation, deportation, and murder. At one stage during their forced march through town on Kristallnacht, Gerhard Mock recalled that he and a crowd of some seventy-five to one hundred other Jews had been lined up in front of the Gestapo building. Another group of non-Jewish Hildesheimers stood watching from across the street in the windows of the Chamber of Commerce. Some of these Aryans were amused, particularly by the fact that some Jews were dressed only in their pajamas. Then Gerhard recognized one of the young women in the window. Daughter of a postmaster in a village near Hildesheim and a friend of Gerhard's sister, she had gone to tanzstunde with Gerhard in 1931 and had even been his Dance Class Lady. She too was standing there to see what was going on and seemed amused at first. Gerhard concentrated hard to catch her gaze, and "it worked. Suddenly her expression changed, and grew very serious, and she turned away and left the window" (G/11a R/270). To be sure, some Hildesheimers were distressed when they witnessed their daily habits being transformed into a violent public policy, not because they disagreed with this policy or even the violence itself, but because the presence of their friends and neighbors disclosed their collusion in that violence.

Kristallnacht was too direct for local tastes, habituated to open secrets. In effect, the Nazi regime had not yet learned how to navigate the contradictions of local culture. In the case of Kristallnacht, they gratified secret desires for niveau through public rituals, but they did not do so behind the veil of the everyday. Nor did they restore it as such afterwards. Just as they were reluctant to accept street-cleaning responsibilities in prior years, so did the town administration take its time cleaning up after the pogrom. The debris from the synagogue languished on Lappenberg for several months before it was removed (Schneider III, 11). Nonetheless, the purpose of the pogrom was obvious to the ordinary Hildesheimer: to purge the local public sphere and to restore morality to their community.

The lack of grace with which the Nazis perpetrated Kristallnacht only further encouraged both the regime and ordinary Hildesheimers to search for a better way to restore moral order in provincial towns like Hildesheim. They sought a method that satisfied the ideological commitment to antisemitism at the same time that it preserved the cultural commitment to normalcy. Between 1939 and 1941, the Nazi regime developed that solution which took the form of increasingly bureaucratic management. Although still based in informal customs of conviviality and dependent upon the collusion of ordinary people, the Nazi regime increasingly assumed direct responsibility for the moral order.

Volunteer Helpers

The shift from informal to formal mechanisms for establishing a moral order transformed the lives of all Hildesheimers. It made it far easier for ordinary Hildesheimers to imagine their normalcy, and left those who did not belong to the new volksgemeinschaft literally at the disposal of the Nazi regime. This latter stage in the Nazi revolution is difficult to recover in the most significant cases of the Jews and the Roma/Sinti of Hildesheim, because those who experienced this process of segregation and annihilation most explicitly—the victims—did not typically survive to tell their stories.

As for the perpetrators, many Hildesheimers were directly involved in the system of mass murder, as soldiers, factory and railroad workers, party officials, bureaucrats, and so on. As one would expect, however, my non-Jewish interview partners were rarely willing to speak openly and honestly about deportations, camps, ghettos, executions, or experiments. Here we encounter some of the real limits that face oral history as a methodology: there was no way that I could force my interview partners to describe overtly criminal activities against their will, nor conjure stories from the murdered.

Yet ordinary Hildesheimers did have a surprising amount of contact with forced laborers and prisoners of war, and they had a startling amount to say about those relationships. Though racism in and around Hildesheim proper lacked the horror of the death camps in Poland, it was nonetheless quite deadly. More significantly, both emerged from the same shift within the Nazi revolution from conviviality to bureaucracy. Ordinary Hildesheimers turned to the Nazi regime to insulate themselves from moral responsibility for their own everyday behavior; the Nazi regime responded with administrative procedures for social engineering.

In the 1940s, the Nazi regime imported foreigners into the town and countryside of Hildesheim and forced them to work in the war economy to fill positions vacated by Aryans and new positions created by these expanding industries (Notzen-Hillman 1989; Schmid 2002; Teich 1979; Thimm 1999: 65–72). Hildesheim had relatively fewer foreign laborers than surrounding towns and industrial regions such as Hannover, Braunschweig, and, most notably, the Hermann-Goering-Werke in the "Volkswagen Town" of Salzgitter. Some statistics of uncertain worth can be reconstructed on the basis of the correspondence of the Bishop of Hildesheim (for Italians, see correspondence Nr. 8545–6, 9086–70, 9900, 4376, 4443, September 1938, 4458, May 1940, BAH GII [neu] 827; for Ukrainians, see the letter to the Apostolic Visitator, Berlin, 6 March 1942, BAH GII [neu] 828). The more reliable Trade Surveillance Office (*Gewerbeaufsichtsamt*) counted some ten thousand forced laborers in the town of Hildesheim by 1942. This sum comprised one-seventh of the total urban population. An additional three thousand lived in the immediate countryside, and the total rises to over 26,000 if one includes nearby Peine, Holzminden, and Alfeld (SAH 808–1/22; cf. Notzen-Hillmann 1989: 131–38; for more on the Trade Surveillance Office, see Eichhorn 1985: 393 and Jeserich et al. 1984: 3/244, 4/795–96). Reports suggested that more forced laborers were on their way (SAH 808–1/22 Kleebach 1943), and the relative presence of forced laborers was even higher if one also takes into consideration the large number of enlisted men missing from town during this period.

These forced laborers came from a large variety of European countries: mostly Italy, France, Poland, and Russia; other nations included

Belgium, the Netherlands, Ukraine, and White Russia. There were also some Germans who had been forced into service, or who were being punished for criminal activities. Some seven hundred (in this case, all Italians and French) were military personnel, while the vast majority were civilians, including three hundred women and thirty-six children. These figures are neither systematic nor accurate: they combined various reports concerning individual factories over the period 1943–45 (SAH 808-1/22). The backgrounds of the 2,400 forced laborers in the largest single factory were not described in detail. These records probably underreported the actual number of foreign laborers in Hildesheim in the early '40s, but they do provide a qualitative sense for the scope of forced labor in Hildesheim. Bernhard Richeter described the situation for the Bosch factory in the Hildesheim Forest. In the mechanics division alone, where he worked, there were two hundred Germans out of an employed population of three thousand (G/39b R/250, 300). "In brief," Bernhard summarized, "there were few Germans employed down here. I believe, at most a third. And the others were all foreigners, from all of the surrounding countries" (G/39b R/75; see also G/39b R/300; Teich 1979: 65).

Ethnic diversity in itself was nothing new to Hildesheim. Polish seasonal workers, Roma/Sinti street musicians, beggars and vagabonds, students and tourists, as well as German and pseudo-German migrants from ethnically mixed regions had long since made Hildesheim their home or passed through on their way to other places. Still, the Nazi racial war had made Hildesheim more cosmopolitan, and more overtly so, than ever before in its modern history. Moreover, this ethnic diversity posed a serious challenge to a local moral community based on permanence of residence and cultural homogeneity. Yet the real challenge lay in the fact that Hildesheimers used to decide for themselves which neighbors belonged or did not belong to their moral community. Dynamic customs of conviviality had enabled them to make some strangers into neighbors and to ignore the others, so that they could imagine their own respectability while also absorbing considerable shifts in population. They now left such matters to the Nazi regime.

My interview partners were of different minds about the degree to which the Nazi regime permitted racial mixing. Otto Koch recalled that, at the Senking factory in the Nordstadt, forced laborers could not go into town (G/48a R/180, 220). By contrast, Friedrich Rother reported that their situation improved over time: they received a little more food and the freedom to go into town (G/58b R/40). Here, the facts of their stories are not as important as the assumptions that the Nazi regime set these rules. Bernhard Richeter recalled the situation in the Bosch factory in the Hildesheim Forest:

They were internees, civilians, yes? They all had a band on their arms so that you could recognize them. And when they went out walking, the Russians all had on their jackets, they all had a sign on the back, Russians, Poles, everyone, they were all marked. . . . They had some kind of letter on their arm on the band or on their back. (G/39b R/85)

The Nazi regime had only just purged the center of town of its Jews. Befitting their claims to racial hygiene, they manned the new boundaries of ethnic diversity in the local moral community. As much as possible, they protected Aryans from contact with the biological bearers of pollution. Insofar as they permitted the latter to penetrate into the center of Hildesheim at all, the Nazi regime now garishly administered these differences with marks on clothes.

Historian Ulrich Herbert (1985; see also Gellately 2001) has shown that the Nazi system of forced labor developed from a combination of racist ideology, emergency responses to wartime necessities, and a tradition of German imperialism in the East. It was also based on the traditional logic of conviviality. For instance, the Wetzell plastic factory in Hildesheim-Moritzberg used a house on the Steinberg (southeast of town) to create a camp for forced laborers. It was selected in part because it could be easily isolated and linked to their factory (SAH 808-1/22 Wetzell, 1944)—that is, for proximity, security, and control. It also made sense to place these forced laborers in the same barracks that had once housed seasonal laborers. Käthe Stolte had also been requisitioned to work in the office of the Wetzell plastics factory, which functioned as an armaments factory during the war. When I asked her whether there were Poles or other forced laborers at this location, she ignored my question at first, and described her own forced labor. On further questioning, she told me that Hildesheim had forced laborers from France, Italy, and Holland (she was not correct: most came from the East not the West), and mentioned that they were housed in barracks on the Pferdeanger. "Once a real long time ago, the Gypsies all lived there" (G/188b R/240, 270). Similarly, most of the over 2,500 forced laborers engaged at the Vereinigte Deutsche Metallwerke either lived in barracks on the property of its factory for semi-finished products or on the Lademühlefeld where the "Gypsies" (Roma/Sinti) had also once camped. Pragmatic considerations as well as local cultural traditions led Hildesheimers to place forced laborers in the spaces that had been inhabited by earlier generations of strangers.

To be sure, the Nazis did not house forced laborers only on the topographic perimeter of town. Other barracks for workers at the Vereinigte Deutsche Metallwerke could be found all over town (SAH 808-1/22, BAH GII [neu] 824, G/134b R/275). Within the walls of town, however, they were often housed in buildings already associated with immorality. Ninety-two forced laborers lived in a pub on Steuerwalderstrasse known as *The North Casino*. Lena Turz remembered this space as the regular bar for glass blowers. They were a "unique variety of human being." They were communists. It was also the regular bar for her landlord, a worker at Senking who was a drunkard and with whom her family had as little contact as possible. Lena's Catholic parents kept her far from the North Casino (G/65b R/215, G/66b R/110). Curiously, Lena had gone to balls there for tanzstunde, always accompanied by her mother, but Lena remembered this space in disreputable terms. That forced laborers now lived in the same building was neither surprising nor disturbing.

Precisely because the system of forced labor was deeply integrated into daily life (Gellately 2001; Herbert 1985), Aryans could have undesirable degrees of contact with those who were officially their racial inferiors. In the aviation shop just outside Berlin in which Jürgen Ludewig worked during the war, they "had had just one or two old Italians, you know, who swept the hall and brought [us drinks for] breakfast." (There were also many inmates from the local concentration camp, but he did not mention them at this stage.) In the foundry, there were even more foreign workers. Yet he never heard of nor saw any brutalities—not a single event (G/107a R/50; cf. G/39b R/85, 155). At stake here is the presumption that the Nazi authorities were managing these foreign populations properly. Reinhard Oetteling explained why Flemish forced laborers chose to stay in Hildesheim. Reiterating Nazi racist propaganda, he suggested that some of them were recruits. "They were Flemings after all. . . . Not Latins but Germans in contrast to the Walloons who also lived there in Belgium" (G/134b R/275). I asked Reinhard Oetteling if he had seen Nazi officials mistreating them, and he cautioned me that this was "another issue." The Flemish and Dutch were recruited to work in Hildesheim, he insisted again. "Of course, they did not have the same rights as the German workers," he admitted, "but they felt very comfortable here." By contrast, the Nazi regime housed, "more or less in barracks," those so-called *Hilfeswilligen* whom they had relocated to Hildesheim by force, including Poles, Russians, and Czechs (G/134b R/285). Reinhard used sarcasm when referring to this latter group of forced laborers as *volunteer helpers*, but he nonetheless reiterated the fundamental hierarchy of the Nazi racist society. He not only presumed that the Nazi officials managed these moral categories with due efficiency and probity but also normalized that racial hierarchy in convivial terms, as if these forced laborers ever felt comfortable in Hildesheim.

Racist distinctions were both common knowledge and common practice. Otto Koch described how Italians at Senking were given more freedom than Russians and Poles (G/48a R/180, 220); and foreigners in general were given harder labor and worked under worse conditions than locals. On 1

March 1943, the Vereinigte Deutsche Metallwerke in Hildesheim requested the permission of the Trade Surveillance Office to institute a night shift for German women with the understanding that they would be given easy tasks, "while foreign women would be given the heavy labor and obviously also the night shift" (quoted from Notzen-Hillmann 1989: 136). Similarly, the new racially based working classes were given the dirty job of street cleaning. The dependents of the male head of household had always been the ones responsible for neighborly cleanliness. A division of labor that used to involve Aryan women, children, and elderly parents now included racially subordinate forced laborers. This policy, too, fit the logic of local conviviality.

So the Nazi regime did not insulate ordinary Hildesheimers from these new neighbors so much in physical as in cultural terms. When Ulrich Gerke came home from fighting with the German army on leave, he learned that the factories of Bosch, Wetzell, and Senking "all had POWs as forced laborers, or abducted Poles." Yet his family, he insisted, never had any direct contact with them. "First of all, they were housed in barrack camps and they were also guarded—watchmen running all around" (G/89a R/130; see also G/105b R/190). Other Hildesheimers dissented. Reinhard Oetteling insisted that these "were lodgings, not concentration camps precisely" (G/136b R/330). In the case of the Bosch factory in the Hildesheim Forest, Bernhard Richeter similarly insisted that there were guards inside the workshop only when there were prisoners there from Celle. "They were more carefully watched, no?" To watch the forced laborers, there were just a few guards from the factory outside the workshops. He was less certain about the situation at night in their camp. Bernhard explained that in their free time, such as on Sundays or Saturday afternoons, these Russian and Polish forced laborers could travel into town and take walks in the forest. "That is how much freedom they were given." He knew this to be true because he saw them loading onto the bus in front of his home near the factory. "So they also got some money, otherwise they could never have traveled on the bus" (G/39a R/340, G/39b R/105; cf. Teich 1979: 65–68). Here again, the point is not the contradictions in their accounts but in the similarities of their assumptions: ordinary Hildesheimers presumed that the Nazi regime was responsible for the whole matter.

The freedom to shop in town did not entail an opportunity to escape. As Bernhard Richeter explained, "you try running away in such a country where there is someone on every corner who watches out" (G/39b R/110). Given that he saw only a few guards on the shop floor, his comments suggest that it was ordinary locals who identified and denounced Poles and Russians as resident aliens. Yet as much as the Nazi regime relied on the denunciation of neighbors to prevent these forced laborers from escaping, their foreign-ness was "immediately identifiable" thanks to the Nazi regime.

As was reported in 1941 in the *Homeland Letter of the Hildesheim Civic Administration*:

> There they went: the figures like vagabonds with a blue *P* on a yellow background and odd characters who speak languages to one another with which one cannot imagine that normal human beings could ever make themselves understood. On top of that there are the French and Walloon prisoners of war. On the street, we sometimes feel quite international. But only there. In pubs, cinemas, and theaters, we are amongst ourselves again. (Quoted in Thimm 1999: 69)

Repeatedly in its propaganda, the Nazi regime proudly announced the successful aryanization of the local public sphere (Gellately 2001; for Hildesheim, see Schneider 1998). Precisely because ordinary Hildesheimers played a critical role in that process of dehumanization, expropriation, and alienation, they welcomed the opportunity to let the Nazi regime take the credit for it.

Anticipating the proper management of these subordinate, alien populations, ordinary Hildesheimers were shocked when they encountered them in the middle of town and unmediated by the Nazi regime. Lotte Schohl described this experience:

> You saw forced laborers first during the war. That was when the Poles and Russians and foreigners came, who had to work here or who were imprisoned even, and you saw them all right. For they . . . had to wear a badge on their jackets where a *P* on it was for Poles and an *R* [was for Russians]. They were immediately identifiable.

One saw them in town while shopping, she explained. "It arose right out of daily life, precisely as one goes into town today to get provisions and take care of whatever errands. That was how it was back then as well." Lotte neither knew where these foreigners lived nor did she ever see any brutalities. Then she added,

> Just once I saw a group of Russian women, I can tell you, who probably were very hungry and fell upon a vegetable stand [on the Schützenallee] and bought heads of cabbage which were laid out there, and bit right into them. And that really shook me up. (G/10b R/240; cf. Kaplan 1998: 157–60)

Hildesheimers' sense of normalcy was disturbed only when the regime failed to shield them from the inhumane consequences of their racist society. The challenge to normalcy was all the more disruptive insofar as those Slavic vagabonds were shopping, speaking unintelligible languages, and starving in the central business district in which the Nazi regime had only just recently restored moral order.

Appropriately, the Nazi regime tried to find better ways to manage the lives of these alien populations to prevent future breaches in the façade of normalcy. As of 6 November 1941, the Nazi regime restricted Polish forced laborers from access to German cultural, convivial, and religious establishments as well as from standing in line for tobacco goods and using German barbers: that is, from entering into neighborly exchange relations with Aryans as if they were locals. Additionally, Hildesheim's mayor expressly forbade Polish forced laborers from walking along the streets of the central business district from five to nine o'clock in the evenings on weekdays and at all on Sundays and holidays (Thimm 1999: 69). In effect, they were prohibited from taking the stroll. During an inspection of the Trillke factory in Hildesheim-Neuhof by the Trade Surveillance Office on 25 May 1944, Russian workers complained that their daily meals were insufficient. Russian women therefore spent all their limited free time and effort walking to town, "running from shop to shop and purchasing hundreds of bottles of yogurt-milk per day, and bringing them back to the camp" (SAH 808–1/22). The company and the inspector tried to negotiate a weekly supplement of yogurt-milk to be delivered from the town dairy. Their stated intention was to limit the black market in the barracks and improve worker efficiency. Their tacit intention was to limit informal social contact between German locals and Russian foreigners through proper administration, and to purge the recently restored moral community of its polluting foreign elements.[3]

That the Trade Surveillance Office as well as local Hildesheimers had little sympathy for the actual well-being of forced laborers can be illustrated with reference to a recently rediscovered collection of burial certificates (SAH 102/9211). These related to some three hundred individual graves created for forced laborers in Hildesheim's main cemetery between March 1941 and March 1945. The vast majority of these deceased came originally from Eastern rather than Western Europe, providing indirect evidence that Slavs were treated worse than Latins. A little more than half of these individuals lived within the town of Hildesheim at the time of their death. The remainder had resided in the region around Hildesheim, from as far as Goslar, Wolfenbüttel, Sarstedt, and Alfeld. (Most died while living in camps near large, industrial factories, most frequently in the northwest of Hildesheim: but some died while employed in private homes, in small businesses, or on farms.)

Two-thirds of these corpses had been male, and a full half of them died at the young ages of seventeen through twenty-three. Almost a third of them died violent deaths related to Nazi persecution (12 percent) or the conduct of war (17 percent). The causes were (alleged) suicides, hangings, broken skulls, and Allied air raids, the latter of which affected them more than locals because they lived, worked, and were incarcerated in close proximity to the targeted factories. The brutal methods of interrogation used by the local Gestapo suggest that many of the broken bones were intentionally inflicted as part of Nazi terror (as per numerous reports from 23 May to 14

August 1947 to the Criminal Police in Hildesheim, BA-K Z42 VII/1851).
The doctors who were responsible for filling out the death certificates were
clearly complicit in this violence. Gustav Hoppe reported that he had been
so heavily beaten with bundles of keys, metal cords, and other hard objects
that his head was bleeding and his hands and back were swelling. Yet the
doctor approved further interrogation. That all said, half of the victims
were simply worked to death under inhumane conditions. Aryan doctors
identified the causes of their deaths as various forms of tuberculosis (33
percent), exhaustion/weakness (9 percent), or infection (6 percent): that is,
the diseases of exploitation. Again, these statistics probably underreport the
number of deaths. For instance, the Bistumsarchiv in Hildesheim preserved
records of the burial of some fourteen forced laborers in a mass grave on 16
April 1945 in the St. Godehardi parish, yet many of the other parishes failed
to make a report. Other reports are almost certainly missing (GII [neu] 823;
cf. G/134b R/275). Nonetheless, these death certificates illustrate that the
pattern of life and death in Hildesheim in the 1940s corresponded roughly
to Nazi racist principles.

To be sure, the Trade Surveillance Office made detailed inspections of
the barracks in which forced laborers resided. They evaluated the amount
of space available to each person, the cleanliness of their environment, and
even the working hours. In cases in which the barracks did not meet proper
standards, the inspectors forced the company to correct the circumstances.
For instance, they found overfilled sewage pits, no toilet paper, lice, and
two women Eastern Workers (*Ostarbeiterinnen*) sleeping in one bed (e.g.,
Annahütte, 1943; Mölders 18, 22, and 26 May 1944; Jacobi, 4 September
1943 in SAH 808-1/22). Yet the goal of industrial oversight in these barracks was not to prevent diseases of class exploitation (like tuberculosis and
exhaustion at the age of eighteen) among the foreign-"subhuman" population of Hildesheim. Rather, they sought to prevent the spread of infectious
diseases to the local Aryan population of Hildesheim. In his letter to Kasper
& Co. on 12 October 1943, the inspector, Dickebohn-Rhotert, described
the barracks at Rosenhagen:

> *The camp is overfilled and totally failed during the investigation to meet
> the specifications which must be demanded. The washing and lavatory
> facilities are also completely insufficient.* Because of the war, everything
> cannot be so furnished as one would wish it; still one must definitely make
> sure that the minimum of hygienic demands get fulfilled. By not meeting
> these requirements, dangers also become not unthinkable for the German
> people. I therefore beseech you to fulfill the minimal requirements con-
> tained in the enclosed paragraphs as quickly as possible. (SAH 808-1/22;
> his emphasis)

Dickebohn-Rhotert insisted on improving the working and living conditions of forced laborers in order to protect locals from foreign corruption. Moreover, this "camp" was actually close to the heart of the Altstadt: it could be ignored by most Hildesheimers only because it was located on the street known for its bordellos. Cleaning up the foreigners fit logically into the local tradition of policing and marginalizing local prostitutes. Properly managed, there were only a few cases of typhus among the local population.

Formal administration was all the more necessary now that locals had become more intimately involved in the lives of forced laborers. In earlier decades, seasonal laborers were mostly engaged in agricultural employment in the countryside. During the 1940s, however, local companies now provided services to these inmates. They constructed, maintained, and inspected their barracks, emptied their sewage pits, did their laundry, and guarded and worked with the workers in factories (e.g., G/48a R/160; SAH 808-1/22 Zuckerraffinerie, 17 May 1944). Foreigners shopped on their streets and sometimes even lived and worked in their homes. Käthe Stolte recalled cordial contact with the foreign workers in Wetzell: "No one said anything about it and that was also very nice. That was not just with us, at Wetzell. I know also, that was also [the way it was] in the other large factories." Käthe described these relationships as more collegial than friendly (G/188b R/280), but there was considerable informal contact nonetheless. Reinhard Oetteling reported that the Flemings working at the Wetzell plastics factory were quartered in an upper story of his parents' home. He described them as "solid people" but insisted that he got to know them only briefly when he was on vacation from the "Nazi" military (G/134b R/255). Friedrich Rother described his interaction with forced laborers in a similar tone: "Back then, everyone had to get involved somehow. Everyone was called upon to participate." Since he had always been interested in languages, he opted to teach German to a group of Russian forced laborers in the Senking factory who were "at first, still behind barbed wire." It was not a problem that he could not speak any Russian, since the point of the exercise was to teach them German. Moreover, "they were supposed to learn only enough so that they could recognize the signs for tools, so they could work together." Clearly, ordinary Hildesheimers were in close contact with forced laborers, but that contact consisted of civilizing them—as much as possible in wartime conditions and befitting their supposed racial inferiority.

To be sure, the results of this forced acculturation was "variable." According to Friedrich, some learned "a few expressions," others were "completely dumb-witted," and still others "were highly intelligent" and "learned unbelievably quickly." Russians, he explained, "are very talented in music and languages." Yet the more he thought about these forced laborers as individuals, the more he recalled the racist circumstances under which they lived, which raised the question of his collusion in their oppression and murder. Friedrich hinted that some particularly clever girls from the Crimea were "taken away violently." He recalled one of their names. He even admitted that some of the workers were very young: only fifteen or sixteen years old. "The Nazis drove buses into the villages there and invited all the people to come to Germany as workers." Friedrich insisted that even though the conditions were pitiful at first, circumstances improved over time, and that, at least by him, they were treated as human beings (G/58b R/40). Yet just as Friedrich shifted his story to the Nazi administration of forced labor when he began to recall the violence inherent in this system, so too did he rely upon the Nazi regime to shield him from the racism in his hometown.

Those who could not behave like Germans had to be removed. My interview partners condemned them to this fate in narrative. Since Reinhard Oetteling's father worked at Wetzell plastics, I asked if he had heard of any personal relations between Germans and the Russian forced laborers. Reinhard categorically denied that this could have been possible, since the presence of guards at the barracks and at work prevented such relationships. The fact that other interview partners denied precisely these kinds of rigid controls suggests that Reinhard had internalized the distinctions of a racist society. Not a moment later, he described a relationship between a local boy and a Polish girl. Son of the factory master Bode, this boy was almost totally blind. He "walked around with a magnifying glass"—a behavior that Reinhard then physically re-enacted. The Bode boy was forced to work at Wetzell though "he was half-dead already. Ok, not dead, but he could not see, could not work." Then he made friends with a Polish girl from the barracks. After the end of the war, when the forced laborers were all freed, he went back to Poland with her, "and we never heard from him again. Probably they slaughtered him there in Poland, no? I don't know" (G/137a R/70). Reinhard's story transformed this boy's handicap into a fate of alienation, exile, and murder. In the Eastern territories that had been newly colonized by the Third Reich, Reinhard presumed that such a transgressive love affair ended in death at the hands of indigenous barbarians, even after 1945.

Indeed, the "nice" thing about life during the Third Reich was that barbaric foreigners simply disappeared from the public view. I asked Käthe Stolte how many years a Gypsy woman had come to her door. "Oh, she came for a long time. Then suddenly, during the war, I would say, as soon as the wartime had begun, about '38 or '39, then that automatically stopped. Then practically no more beggars came either, no?" (G/185a R/100) Käthe knew abstractly that the Nazi regime had deported Roma and Sinti to concentration and death camps, but Käthe never mentioned this fate. Relying upon the Nazi regime to take care of her personal "Gypsy problem," Käthe no longer had to concern herself with it.

In the final pages of his history of *German Home Towns* (1971: 427–30; see also Applegate 1990), Mack Walker suggests that the Third Reich translated and expanded hometown values into aspects of national politics. The customs of interwar Hildesheim verify this hypothesis. The Nazi regime transformed what had been neighborly custom into bureaucratic procedure. Yet ordinary Hildesheimers also turned to Hitler to preserve the moral order more efficiently and more directly than they had ever done on their own. It took the bulk of the 1930s to make this shift from informal acts of symbolic violence to state-organized procedures for industrialized violence, but a very different set of expectations about the role of government was in place by the start of the Second World War. Like the communal rituals of cleanliness on which they were based, the bureaucratic purges of racial "inferiors" cleansed Europe not only of "dirty" people but also of all memory of the collusion of ordinary Hildesheimers in that racist system. By abiding with the logic of local customs, local administrators seemed to promise ordinary Hildesheimers that no matter what cruelties the Nazis inflicted, the local authorities would be there to clean up afterwards.

Hildesheimers were protected by local bureaucrats even after death. The latter continued to employ administrative measures to contain the corruption of foreignness. During the warmer months of 1941, the few forced laborers who died were buried next to the other residents of Hildesheim. Then, a new policy emerged after the death of two Russians in the POW camp in Drispenstedt on 7 November 1941. The local Garden and Cemetery Office decided to designate a special section of the cemetery for foreign forced laborers and POWs (there already was a special section for fallen Aryan soldiers). These strangers were wrapped in oil-paper, sometimes identified on their burial certificate only by a number or a racial label (*Pole, Eastern Worker,* etc.), unceremoniously laid to rest, and in the case of POWs, often buried by fellow prisoners (SAH 103/8941). Like the so-called Final Solution to the Jewish Question that was being developed at the same time in Eastern Europe, these policies arose from the ingenuity of local bureaucrats responding to an admixture of the exigencies of wartime, racial ideology, and the desire to fit local policies to the principles of the Third Reich. In this case, however, officers of the Nazi regime also isolated foreigners from locals in death in the same way that they had been separated in everyday life. By November 1941, the Hildesheimers who ran the Garden and Cemetery Office took it upon themselves to ensure that local Aryans were not buried near "sub-humans," that grieving locals did not have to hear or see any evidence of degenerate foreigners in Hildesheim—neither their hard lives nor their tragic deaths.

Over the course of the 1930s, ordinary Hildesheimers coordinated conviviality to fit Nazi racial principles, changing neighbors into Jews and Aryans. Yet the more that Hildesheimers turned to conviviality as an alternate site for their struggle to colonize everyday life in their interests, the more they undermined its traditional functions of preserving moral order. To accommodate, Hildesheimers invited the Nazi regime to formally administer what had been informally negotiated through convivial customs: the local moral community. Kristallnacht in 1938 made sense in these terms, but did not satisfy, since it disturbed the open secrets of everyday life. The Nazi regime began to deliver on its promises only during the war, when they took conviviality more directly in hand and actually managed racial interactions. Ordinary Hildesheimers now looked to the Nazi regime to insulate them from the racist system in which they were now intimately involved, by managing those victimized populations, so that they could continue to imagine that they were just ordinary Hildesheimers. Once these alienated groups were exported beyond the realm of the ethical or the relevant, ordinary Hildesheimers tolerated, and even expected, a barbaric end to their story.

The Pole Joseph

The Allied victory over Nazi Germany in the spring of 1945 inverted interethnic power relations in Hildesheim. Stefan Nebe's sister had moved to Rheinhausen because of the air raids. When the Allied Occupation Army found the family's apartment empty, they requisitioned it for Poles. When Stefan arrived home and opened the door, a Pole confronted him. "What do you want here? Get out!" the Pole said. "So I had to get" (G/138b R/255). In the absence of the Nazi regime, the moral community seemed to collapse. Bernhard Richeter told me that as forced laborers were returned home from other locations, those remnants left in Germany were brought to Hildesheim. They did not work anymore, and the Allies provided them with food, but they lived in Hildesheim in increasing numbers. The Allies even set up a church for Polish services in the Hildesheim Forest. Bernhard also described how the Poles and Russians fought amongst themselves, sometimes with violence (G/39b R/120). Rather than seeing these conflicts as a consequence of dire circumstances, ordinary Hildesheimers labeled them in terms of the barbarity associated with foreigners. Reinhard Oetteling felt it less likely that forced laborers physically attacked Germans, but he claimed otherwise about the Poles, "who had been brought here earlier and then were freed, no? They then permitted themselves a few abuses, and then probably hauled [stuff] away, and more like that" (G/136b R/330). Friedrich Rother exclaimed: "they suddenly felt so strong!" Friedrich accused them of plundering the parsonage of St. Godehard, but then admitted that only a handwagon was in fact taken, and from a private home (G/58b R/100). To be sure, German Hildesheimers admitted to black-market exchanges and even to stealing in the wake of the destruction. One had to ensure the family's survival in any manner necessary (G/78a R/280). Yet Hildesheimers believed that theft on the part of a German was a moral act, on the part of a Pole it was not.

Such accounts refocus attention onto German victimization in order to ignore the more obvious suffering of the forced laborers. One Hildesheimer recalled the following scene from the old market square in the final weeks of the Third Reich (Meyer-Hartmann 1985: 72; see also Gellately 2001: 239; Thimm 1999: 79–80; cf. *HB* 15/73: 2):

> I see gallows on which people are hanging, four men close together. One has black hair and a yellow-brown face. His head is hanging in the noose; his eyes are closed. A sign attached to the cross beam contains just two words: "They plundered." Next to the gallows, laid out in two rows, I noticed the corpses of twenty people who had perhaps been hung already. They were lying on their backs.

During the collapse of the Third Reich, it became easy to focus feelings of anger, fear, and betrayal onto forced laborers. Otto Koch thought he had befriended a certain Russian forced laborer because he had even given bread to him illegally. When the Russian man accused Otto after the war of being just the same as the other Nazis, Otto was both hurt and disappointed (G/48a R/180). Likewise, Bernhard Richeter longed to re-establish contact with the Belgian student with whom he had worked and whom he had also given food illegally (he never did: G/138b R/30, G/139b R/145). Ordinary Hildesheimers anticipated the loss of respectability and the challenging ethical questions that would be posed once the Allies liberated the concentration camps and forced-labor installations.

Once "liberated" from the Third Reich, ordinary Hildesheimers related to their former racial subordinates with a mixture of fear and guilt. This typical experience had everything to do with the fact that the Nazi regime no longer protected Hildesheim from its own barbarity. It is readily illustrated by Theresa Stoffregen's account of the Pole Joseph. Even Hildesheimers as young as Theresa (b. 1929) could recall having used the Nazi regime as an excuse to punish moral infractions in racist terms (Gellately 2001: ch. 7). In the absence of Nazi administration of that moral order, she had to deal with dangerous memories of collaboration.

Theresa's father came from Ahrbergen, a village some ten miles northwest of town, near Sarstedt. Every first Sunday of the month, her family would get together with their paternal relatives there, regardless of weather or sickness. "That was tradition" (G/190a R/195). When she began her year of service in the summer of 1944 at the age of fifteen, her parents sent her to a farmer in Ahrbergen. She learned to care for children in the town where her grandmother still lived by watching over this farmer's three girls, aged five, three, and newborn (G/194a R/205). Meanwhile, the farmers of Ahrbergen had been ordered to make room for two soldiers in their farmhouses. These were the last reserves, very old and very young men from Bavaria. When I asked if she had had any relationship with these men, Theresa explained that she had had long braids when she was a girl. One of the older men always used to say, "Girl, I would like to watch when you braid your hair. For I have a daughter your same age." It was not clear to me how Theresa dealt with the sexual implications of an older man from a different family living in the same house watching her braid her hair. Theresa quickly stifled any innuendo by eliminating the person who threatened her propriety from her narrative. She explained how she later learned that these soldiers did not survive the war. The whole company was wiped out, she explained, because they were just taught how to shoot and were send to the Eastern Front improperly trained for war—the fault of the Nazi regime.

This anecdote makes more sense when we realize that the event described was not the only time that Theresa had to deflect a man's sexual advances. This same family also had two foreign laborers on their farm, an elderly Russian woman and a Polish man of unspecified age. Theresa had known of no Poles in her neighborhood, but she did know that Polish seasonal workers could be found in Ahrbergen harvesting potatoes (G/191a R/55). When I asked if she had any relationship with them, she explained that she did not speak with them because they spoke very little German. Also, they did not eat at the table: they ate in the kitchen, while the family, with Theresa, ate in the living room (G/194a R/220). Forced laborers may have been an economic benefit for the farmer, but they were a moral threat to a town girl like Theresa. Sometimes a sausage was missing and she presumed that they must have taken it and either eaten it themselves or given it to other forced laborers. Whereas the Russian woman slept in a room in the upper story near Theresa's room, the Polish man slept in a barrack that housed all the (presumably male) agricultural workers. As in town, these Polish forced laborers were free and unsupervised in the evenings (G/194b R/00, G/192a R/390).

"The Russian woman was already very old," Theresa explained, "but the Pole—I don't know if I should tell you this." Theresa laughed uncomfortably. It was the last of four days of interviews, Theresa was my final interview partner, and I had accumulated almost two hundred hours of taped oral histories. If something remained unspoken, both Theresa and I wanted it to be revealed at this point. "Please do," I said. Theresa told me about "the Pole," Joseph:

He was really quite fond of me. And we had outdoor toilets, so we had to go through the stables. And then he laid in wait for me. There he stood in the horse stall and wanted something from me. Something like this had to be reported immediately. I told the farmer's wife about it and she reported it further, and then he was—we got a different one. He was called away. But at first we did not know to where, where he ended up, and what was up with him. (G/194a R/230)

Theresa did not state explicitly that he had actually attempted to rape her, just that he "wanted something" from her. When I later asked Theresa if she had denounced him, she then gave a slightly different version of the same story:

He held me tightly by the arm. Then I called, called for help, and then the farmer's wife saw what was happening, and she reported it immediately. I was still very young. And I could never ever have defended myself against this strong, large man. He could have tried it again perhaps. I don't know. (G/194a R/290)

He seems to have used force on Theresa, though only in the second version of the story, when Theresa felt the need to justify the fact that she had denounced him.

The Pole Joseph committed an immoral act on many counts. His advances transgressed proper relations between Aryans and Slavs, farmers and their seasonal laborers, older men and younger girls; perhaps also he abused his strength. Yet there were other adult male strangers residing in her home who were dependent on the generosity of the farmer. The German soldier could show Theresa attention, even bordering on the sexual, without his actions being interpreted as overstepping the bounds of propriety. The contrast between these two anecdotes illustrates how easy it was for Hildesheimers to conflate earlier traditions of conviviality and Nazi categories. Theresa differentiated between good and bad men on this farm in keeping with racist codes of conduct.

Because the latter were framed within local customs of conviviality, she could imagine that she was doing nothing out of the ordinary. Nonetheless, Theresa relied on the Nazi regime to preserve her moral community by literally expelling the Pole Joseph for his crime. Theresa repressed the question of who actually denounced the Pole Joseph precisely because her convivial customs now held such radical implications. At stake here was not simply the fact that she had repressed the memory of an attempted rape. Already while this history was being created, Theresa drew this distinction between the fatherly intimacy of the German soldier, tragically soon to perish, and the violent intimacy threatened by the Pole Joseph. In the civilized neighborhoods of town, she had learned to disarm the threat of illicit intimacy from flashers and prostitutes with a subtle *good day and good bye*. In the countryside beyond its walls, she learned that blatant accusations of illicit intimacy from a Polish forced laborer could make that foreigner disappear entirely thanks to the timely intervention of the Nazi regime. Accordingly, she also relegated the memory of him and his disturbing advances into oblivion. Theresa responded to questions about Nazi violence by claiming that she did not know anything about the concentration camps, "or that this Pole ended up there either. We heard about this only afterwards, when he came back, you see? . . . He was simply gone. He was gone." She never presumed that he had been sent to a concentration camp. "No, I believed that he was sent to another place, no? where [he] was unknown" (G/192b R/30). She (or the farmer's wife) had invited the Nazi regime to preserve local respectability by banishing the Pole Joseph from their community.

Unfortunately, the Nazi regime did not keep its promises. In the spring of 1945, the war came to an end and the Third Reich was destroyed. Theresa's year was over, and she was no longer employed on the farm. She still lived in Ahrbergen, however, because her family had lost their home in Hildesheim during the air raid of 22 March 1945. One day, she was told: "Theresa! The Pole Joseph is coming, with a shaved head, and he is looking for you, with two others as well! You have got to hide!" His shaved head marked him as a survivor of a concentration camp. Probably he had been released recently by the Allies. For three or four days, the Pole Joseph and his comrades "rioted" around the village, drunk, while Theresa hid in an underground bunker. Finally, she was told that they had moved on and she could come out. "I don't know if he wanted something from me or if he wanted to revenge himself, or whatever. But they were all concerned for me. That's how it was" (G/194a R/230, G/192b R/45). With her community behind her, Theresa still believed that she had done the right thing when she had reported him a year earlier.

Arguably, Theresa never really clarified what happened between them in part because she herself was never quite sure. "Perhaps I could never have gotten rid of him. He always said, 'You beautiful girl!' and such things. They could not speak much German, no? Talking with him, conversation, was not possible. They never really tried anyway, I don't think, and did not want to understand" (G/194a R/295). Theresa accused this Polish forced laborer of misconduct, but by the end of her account it was no longer clear if he had tried to force himself on her at all. She no longer explained the incident as the threat of rape. His transgression was now linguistic, moral. Theresa translated the physical barbarisms of this rural Pole (closely linked to inappropriate sexuality and an inversion of personal status) into the man's unwillingness to speak High German properly. It was the Nazi regime who punished the Pole Joseph for a failing that was, in their opinion, eugenic, and they did so with bureaucratic efficiency rather than convivial subtlety; but they did so on her behalf, if not at her request. So she was deluding herself when she felt surprised to learn that he had been deported to a concentration camp. More accurately, she relied on Hitler to keep herself naïve.

Theresa depended on the Nazi regime to preserve her niveau and to administer moral justice. When she used its terror to remove the Pole Joseph for his presumption, she further tied her respectability to that of the Nazi regime. As a result, she could avoid responsibility for his suffering only as long as that regime preserved its authority. Theresa felt vulnerable to the revenge of the foreigner once the Third Reich collapsed because her moral order had depended on it. Personally familiar with the racist system under which forced laborers suffered, she anticipated revenge and hid in a bunker to avoid this confrontation. In the summer of 1945, ordinary Hildesheimers thus set a precedent for both dealing with the Nazi past and with interethnic relations in the postwar era. As a matter of course, Theresa's Aryan neighbors sympathized with her as the victim of Polish aggression in spite of the fact that her narrative of German victimization grossly misrepresented cause and consequence: who treated whom inhumanely first and foremost. They hid their collaboration from full public view figuratively just as Theresa hid herself literally in the cellar.

Even after the collapse of the Third Reich, ordinary Hildesheimers continued to rely on bureaucratic administration to preserve the moral community, setting cultural precedents for postwar Germany. In 1947, the Garden and Cemetery Office still kept separate statistics for different kinds of graves: normal residents, soldiers, "victims of the air war," "foreigners," and Jews (SAH 102/9210, 9212, 103/8942). Unfortunately, the evidence of local racism refused to stay buried underground. In November 1947, the British ordered the Garden and Cemetery Office to exhume, identify, and where possible, return the physical remains of dead forced laborers to their respective homes. When they exhumed several-year-old corpses, gravediggers were given cigarettes and brandy. Alcohol and nicotine was intended not simply to dull their senses but also to dull their wits: to help them ignore the physical proof of how badly Hildesheimers had treated their foreign "guests," how they had helped make Hildesheim fascist in the first place (as per correspondence from 20 November 1947, 17 January 1948, 18 February 1948, 3 March 1948 in SAH 103/8941; see also Browning 1998; Thimm 1999: 81). After 1945, actuarial statistics and consumer drugs were designed to reinforce what yogurt-milk deliveries and different burial plots had supported before 1945: the ordinary-ness of Hildesheim in extraordinary times.

8 | Epistemologies

Erich Bruschke had been a member of the local socialist resistance. In a quasi-autobiographical report to the criminal police in Hildesheim on 23 May 1947 (BA-K Z42 VII/1851), he described the brutality of a particular Gestapo agent, Wenzel, who had been active in the anti-Marxist unit. Bruschke then warned the police against any attempt on Wenzel's part to whitewash his past. "If Wenzel claims that he did not know anything about the deportation of Jews, then I would like to point out that every child in Hildesheim knew about these procedures, even if Mr. Wenzel in the Gestapo House itself insists that he did not see anything of it." Heinrich Bode drew much the same conclusion in the autobiographical memoirs that he wrote shortly before he died in May 1972 (VVNH, NL Hans Teich, p. 5):

> In the May days of 1945, I arrived back in Hildesheim and one by one also other surviving comrades. And then we experienced a wonder: there were no more NSDAP (Nazis), they knew nothing about the crimes that were committed and could no longer recall the burning of the synagogue, the boycott of Jewish businesses, and the murders on the marketplace in Hildesheim—in which a well-known Hildesheim businessmen was supposed to have taken part as hangman and yet is still a free man today. They also did not know anything about what happened to the sick people at the sanatorium in Hildesheim when they were put on transports. Even today, one does not speak willingly about this past and consciously protects the guilty.

In the wake of the Second World War, Holocaust denial enabled Hildesheimers to rebuild and re-establish a sense of normalcy. They seemed neither aware of, nor responsible for, the tragic events of world history. Yet as Bode suggested, this kind of selective knowledge dated as far back as the very first years of the Third Reich. "Already in 1933," he wrote, "the simple, lower functionaries of that era's resistance movement [like us] knew what [others] did not see or did not wish to see."

Holocaust denial is still alive and well in our global public sphere (Evans 2001; Lipstadt 1993; Petropoulos 1998b; Schermer and Grobman 2000).

234

In its extreme version, this neo-fascist litany denies that the Holocaust ever existed as such. In its subtle version, it argues simply that ordinary people did not know about the crimes of the Third Reich and therefore cannot be held responsible for them. At the core of the latter claim stands an ambiguous admixture of antisemitism on the one hand and an unwillingness to face the prospect of industrial-bureaucratic mass murder on the other. The latter claim is also epistemological (Kren and Rappoport 1980) in two ways. It not only posits the existence, during the Third Reich, of a specific regime of knowledge and ignorance about the Holocaust. But our academic analysis of the Third Reich also rests on the myth, part and parcel of a modern culture of normalcy, that such regimes of knowledge and ignorance are imposed on ordinary people by exogenous forces. Challenging Holocaust denial, therefore, is not simply a matter of documenting who knew what and when in response to those murders, but also the contemporary task of reflecting critically on our analytic models, with the goal of more lucidly understanding how the epistemology of an ordinary existence anticipated and helped facilitate those murders in the first place.

This study of ordinary Germans in extraordinary times cannot conclude without considering this latter aspect of Holocaust denial: the persistent and pernicious attitude of incredulity in the face of Nazi crimes against humanity, then and now. This chapter suggests two alternate epistemologies of the Holocaust. It argues that those open secrets were culturally constructed in a typically modern way by ordinary people, who were cultivating a self and society that corresponded to their fantasies of niveau. It also defends the use of narrative interviews to reconstruct everyday life in the shadow of the Third Reich. It shows that my interview partners did not invent the trope of normalcy out of whole cloth after the fall of the Third Reich, but rather elaborated on a dynamic culture of normalcy that preceded national socialism—and helped promote it in the first place.

People in the Neighborhood

Most historians who study the issue of popular knowledge of the Holocaust in its own era tend to limit their investigation to objective knowledge about the so-called Final Solution: how and when information about the death camps reached ordinary Germans, the Allies, Jews, and so on. In terms of propaganda, Robert Gellately has shown that the Nazi regime openly publicized its system of concentrations camps, its purges, and the extended scope of police justice. By showing that it was fulfilling its promise to restore moral order with firmness and determination, the Nazi regime hoped to win the allegiance of the remaining reluctant segments of the German populace (2001). In terms of reception, political scientist Raul Hilberg has argued that the effectiveness of the messengers who carried news of the Holocaust depended, among other factors, "on the extent to which their listeners were prepared to absorb and accept the substance of the information itself" (1992: 217). With the benefit of hindsight, scholars often write with this same sense of incredulity that more people were not willing to believe the report and act effectively upon it (Bankier 1992; Gilbert 1981; Kaplan 1998; Laqueur 1981; Lipstadt 1986; Morse 1968; Wyman 1984). Yet if the Jewish minority itself was reluctant to accept the truth about annihilation (Henry 1984; Hilberg 1992; Kaplan 1998), it should not be surprising that the Gentile majority, who knew perfectly well about Nazi antisemitism and concentration camps in general, were all the more willing to discount specific reports of mass murder. Some recent works of scholarship continue to veil the Holocaust in shrouds of incredulity. In his book, *Neighbors* (2001), Jan T. Gross tells the story of how ordinary Poles destroyed the Jewish community of Jedwabne. Yet contradicting the purpose of his own scholarship, he also claims that the origins of such inhumanity are by definition incomprehensible (see also Kaplan 1998; Kren and Rappoport 1980). If we wish to insist that ordinary people should have been able to comprehend these events as they were happening, then we surely cannot maintain a posture of incredulity in hindsight.

Part of the challenge for scholars lies in the fact that it is hard to draw general conclusions from the many and various individualized epistemologies of the Holocaust: the idiosyncratic way that each individual chose to know, and not know, about Nazi crimes against humanity. Dora Pröbst hinted at this problem during our interviews (G/124b R/160). She had emigrated with her husband to the United States by 1941. Dora remembered that "you could not overlook" the brown shirts guarding signs in Hildesheim that read: "Don't Buy From Jews!" She recalled seeing such signs "all over." In a garden on a predominant street in the southern section of Hildesheim with large villas, she recalled, there was a gigantic board that read: "Jews walk on this street at their own risk" (see also Schneider 1998: III. 7; Teich 1979: 109). To be sure, some people remembered everyday life in Germany differently. Her dentist in the United States insisted, "It was not true that Jews were not allowed to walk on the streets or did so only at their own risk. I never saw that." As was her wont, she replied sarcastically: "Yes, I believe that of you. The signs, they were turned around."

Dora admitted to me that most signs of this antisemitic propaganda really did disappear during the Olympics in 1936. The Nazi regime actively promoted policies of deception that shielded those who did not wish to see the darker side of their regime (Schäfer 1982). These policies ranged from perpetrating most of the antisemitic violence outside the German Reich proper (most of the deadliest camps were in occupied Poland), to the attempts made in the final months of the war in 1944–45 to erase all evidence of mass murder before the invasion of Allied troops. That is, the regime announced its accomplishments in social engineering for those who wished to view those policies as progressive: its concentration camps, its forced labor programs. Nonetheless, Dora's sarcasm suggested that she understood the necessary corollary of these state policy—many of her neighbors, each in their own way, also chose on their own not to see that which they did not wish to see.

This kind of self-induced blindness is not unique to the Holocaust. All human beings proactively demarcate the limits of their consciousness: we give our attention to different objects at different moments in our lives. As sociologists Alfred Schutz and Thomas Luckmann argued (1973), every person constructs a shifting *horizon of relevance* that constitutes inside of it the *life world*: the lived reality of that human being, the microcosm of perceived, known, and relevant information for that person at that point in time. As structuralists, Schutz and Luckmann tended to focus on the exogenous forces that determined the boundaries of the knowable beyond the control of ordinary individuals and therefore facilitated this kind of focused attentiveness. These boundaries were defined by the limits of time and space, biology and psychology, politics and society, gender and class, and so on. As a poststructuralist, I have instead emphasized the way that individual agents construct that life world dynamically in response to those given circumstances, and yet proactively through cultural processes that manipulate contradictions in those circumstances and therefore help to shape history. Selfishly, we construct the boundaries of what—and who—we know in order to cultivate a particular kind of identity in our social environment. We do not shape that lived reality independent of constraints, but we do it ourselves.

This epistemology of everyday life disarms the claim that ordinary Germans did not know about Nazi crimes against humanity simply because they were ordinary. Historically, prior to the Nazi revolution, ordinary Hildesheimers knew the biographies of some neighbors, making those lives part of their own history, while ignoring the fates of others. Analytically prior to ideology though never independent from it (cf. Goldhagen 1996), the minimal goal was the cultivation of status and power that was only possible by imagining that those who could challenge those claims were absent. In this way, Hildesheimers increasingly imagined the absence of their Jewish neighbors over the course of the 1930s, making the Jews subtly but demonstrably irrelevant. Empowered to purge the moral community, the Nazi regime then translated this fantasy of niveau into murderous reality by actually deporting, concentrating, and murdering these local aliens. Nonetheless, it was ordinary Germans who laid the everyday foundations for these antisemitic policies by treating them like Jews, and not like neighbors, in the first place (cf. Kaplan 1998).

This history is best studied as memory—or more specifically, as habit memories. When encouraged to present the story of their lives in narrative, my interview partners arguably re-enacted those same habits by which they cultivated their identities in the first place. At times, they re-enacted these behaviors physically, as when Käthe Stolte show me how to greet or when Reinhardt mocked the boy who was wearing "magnifying" glasses. At times, their narratives reiterated an ingrained cultural logic in discourse, like when Georg Brzezinski suddenly interrupted his story about outhouses when he had to describe the scatological act itself. These were body narratives: accounts of habits creatively enacted. Most of the time, Hildesheimers simply excluded from their contemporary narratives the same people who undermined their sense of self in their past neighborhoods. This way of cultivating identities in the local public sphere constituted a bad habit, but one that held rich psychological rewards for them. Arguably, they stuck with these habits to preserve the illusion of a coherent sense of self in spite of real changes in their ways of life, in keeping with changing historical circumstances. These habit memories also hold rich rewards for historical analysis. The habitual correlation between self-cultivation in the past and self-presentation in the present enabled me to reconstruct their roles in the early stages of the Holocaust. From this perspective, ordinary Germans still deny their knowledge of Nazi crimes against humanity in the present because they first denied their knowledge of it in the past.

Consider the case of Lise Peters, the sexton's daughter who paraded down her street in much the same manner that she proceeded down the aisle of her church, and who imagined her niveau by limiting the scope of comparison to other Protestant residents of the parish. A Jewish butcher lived at the corner of Lise's street, but on the far side of one of the Catholic families. Lise's language here is telling. Rather than *neighbors* (*Nachbar*) as such, she described this Jewish family as *people in the neighborhood* (*Nachbarleute*). At no point in the interview process did she refer to this family by name. Lise claimed that she also did not know what became of these neighbors during the Third Reich. She clarified her relationship with the Jews in her neighborhood in this way:

No, no, no, no. That is, I would never have had any kind of contact there. 'Cause here we, we were more concerned with ourselves [*auf uns eingestellt*]. . . . I mentioned already that, at the corner, the butcher, that he was a Jew. I never heard about it, that they were taken away. That is, something like this—as I said, I really had enough to do by myself, no? (G/142b R/345)

When this Jewish family heard that Lise had received a harmonium as a confirmation gift from her grandparents, they asked if they could borrow it for the wedding of their eldest daughter. Such a request stood on the edge of the appropriate according to neighborly exchange relations in which one gladly offered but never asked for assistance. To be sure, the Peters' family behaved like proper neighbors and generously complied, but Lise reiterated that they had no other instances of contact with them. "We knew them only from, as people in the neighborhood. Nothing further. We were never—I was never in their house, no?" They did not play on the street together. They were older, she explained. Also, "they probably kept their distance from us and we from them." Significantly, Lise associated them with contagion. "Look," Lise added, their son fought in the Great War and "came back with a sexually transmitted disease" (G/140b R/325).

For good reason, historians have been skeptical of the claims of postwar Germans that they did not know about the barbarities of the Nazi regime, particularly those directed against Jews. And there is good reason to believe that Lise was simply lying. Her entire family and her circle of friends had been active Nazis. Some had already joined the party in the 1920s. Perhaps they were also directly involved in antisemitic violence. Yet Lise remained an unreconstructed Nazi even in the 1990s. For the turncoat who "suddenly changed his shirt" after 1945, Lise has only scorn. "I have to say this: *first give hosannas and then crucifixes.*" She did not praise Hitler in the 1930s only to denounce him after 1945. But "that's how it was then. And that is beyond my comprehension. I did not participate in anything like that" (G/140b R/375). Lise was quite willing to express her Nazi sympathies to me despite the conventions of postwar political correctness.

For this same reason, I was less willing to presume that she was lying (cf. Goldhagen 1996). Her claim to a coherent sense of self denies personal memories of disruption resulting from collaboration with Nazi crimes against humanity (Benjamin 1968; Ostovich 2002). It also represents an eigensinnig revolt against the many betrayals and disruptions of modern German history. Yet the Nazi movement itself embodied and politicized the same kind of eigensinn. Lise's style of interacting with her neighbors seemed remarkably consistent throughout her life, and she had good psychological reasons for sticking to those ingrained habits, as they preserved the illusion of coherence for her identity. From this perspective, it should not surprise us that she did not know much about the Jews residing on the far side of the boundary that marked her corner neighborhood, the microcosm in which she imagined her status. In spite of topographical proximity, she had always treated those Jews as if they belonged to a wider, alienating society rather than her smaller, surreal community. Lise's antisemitic attitudes explain her involvement in the Nazi movement to a large degree, but they alone do not explain why she did not know her Jewish neighbors. For that explanation, we must turn our attention to her antisemitic habits. Those habit memories are disturbing, even to her, because deeds have direct consequences in ways that attitudes do not, and the Nazi regime had offered Lise a radical, violent confirmation of what had initially been only her idiosyncratic and secret fantasies of niveau.

Though oral history has a longstanding tradition as a methodology (Botz and Weidenholzer 1984; Herbert 1983; Oliver 1975; Niethammer 1983a, 1983b, 1985, 1988, 1992; Passerini 1985, 1992; von Plato 1985; Thompson 1972, 1978; Siebert 1992; Wierling 1992), it still faces considerable skepticism as an academic epistemology and for what it claims about epistemology more generally. In presenting my research to colleagues, I have been challenged on the acuity of the memories of my elderly informants because of the physical degradation of their synapses. This issue is part of a larger debate about what any individuals can know of their own psychological processes. This study departed from the different premise that knowledge, which mediates both power and identity, is culturally constructed. This study, therefore, sought to recover not so much Lise's objective reality as her subjective experiences. Her interview testimony provided rich evidence for the dynamic process through which she made sense of and helped shape her world. Precisely those memories are more vivid for the elderly, who may otherwise be incapable of remembering factual details or recent events.

Another common concern is the likelihood that people's memories have been altered, on their own to avoid recrimination, or due to intervening, authoritative narratives of remembrance. The danger of romanticizing the past or of instrumental self-presentation seems particularly relevant in the case of the Third Reich. The tragic enormity of Nazi crimes against humanity seems to necessitate that perpetrators—and perhaps also victims—would lie about their past for personal gain in the present. Even some historians of everyday life see in this a grave limitation to the reliability of autobiographical narration as an accurate representation of past reality (Gebhardt 1999: 50–65; Stern 1992: 39–42). The present context in which one narrates one's life story shapes that narrative, but rarely out of whole cloth. Inside these narratives lies the same style of self-cultivation by which one shaped that identity in the first place.

By definition, that process includes reflection on self and society. Human beings are always part of and engaged in social life: they do not inhabit some ideal realm outside human subjectivity. All historical sources, public and private, presume a human audience and are therefore intersubjective in nature (Gebhard 1999: 57–58). Within the context of this implicit public sphere, individuals try to make sense of their own lives by linking their experiences creatively and dynamically to larger patterns of meaning. By definition, also, that process of reflection always involves a comparison of past and present. For it is the function of memory to use past experience as a flexible guide to contemporary behavior. Oral history provides an opportunity for ordinary men and women to narrate how they used past and present to make sense of the world. As historians, we can then investigate the impact of those creative habits on self, state, and society.

In the modern era, individuals added to these universal attributes of self-cultivation an astute sensitivity to their own historicity, even though they often tried to deny their role in grand narratives of historical transformation and to insist on their normalcy. Precisely because they had to change those identities to fit changing circumstances, modern individuals also tried to maintain the illusion of a coherent sense of self, as compared to relatively stable senses of self in less volatile societies. This project for the self was not in vain. Most moderns succeeded in responding to those changing circumstances with eigensinn and by developing a basically consistent, if idiosyncratic style. Most moderns also added an autobiographical component to any historical event even as it was taking place, to make sense of that event in modern terms of turbulent change and resilient continuity. That is, they shaped their identities as much historically (by developing particular tactics for responding to circumstances) as autobiographically (by framing those events in a meaningful story). This dynamic process of cultivating identities was particularly relevant to Germans born and raised in the first half of the twentieth century, precisely because their world was changing so rapidly, so frequently, and so violently. Insofar as they all responded to similar conditions however, those idiosyncratic styles shared similar essentials. This was particularly true of those habits through which they interacted with each other, which were collective by definition. For this reason, then, autobiographical narratives about conviviality are reliable sources for historically accurate insight. As interpersonal encounters between acquaintances, narrative interviews reveal the interpersonal process by which individuals negotiated their identities among friends and neighbors.

So one need not make a liar out of Lise in order to prove her culpability in the early stages of making Hildesheim fascist. She admitted to supporting the Third Reich. After all, Hitler, as if omniscient, had seemed to gratify her secret desire for niveau. She simply adjusted her customs of conviviality, insofar as any adjustment was necessary at all, to fit Nazi principles. In return, she helped Hitler change her neighbors into Aryans and Jews (or perhaps only to shift a non-person by dint of religion to a non-person by dint of race). Since she cared to know the biographies of only some of her neighbors before the war, it is hardly surprising that she knew the fate of only some of them during it. She then held fast to these habits of self-cultivation, in spite of the degree to which they incriminated her, because they alone promised to keep a lid on her disruptive, personal memories of collusion in history and fragmentation in identity. My request for interviews simply gave her the opportunity to narrate the same eigensinnig habits of self-cultivation that she had used to construct that niveau in the first place.

Wandervögel

Otto Koch was born in 1906, and like Lise, he grew up on one of Hildesheim's church squares. His family rented a small, cramped, dark apartment on the back side of a house. In the kitchen, the only windows were too high up to look out of and offered little light. The buildings next to the house were stores that opened onto the adjacent shopping street and were extraordinarily tall (G/41a R/50, 230). The only window that opened onto the plaza and offered sunlight into their flat was thirty centimeters long. In Hildesheim, apartments were often built into the backs of buildings or in courtyards removed from the street because space was cramped, especially in the older parts of town, so Hildesheimers were wont to describe their homes in terms of the size of their frontage. Yet it was with self-mockery that Otto's parents boasted that they had a "thirty-centimeter-long frontage" onto the plaza.

This expression can serve as a metaphor not only for Otto's relationship with his neighbors but also for the general relationship between the working classes and the middle classes in interwar Hildesheim. Hildesheim's wage laborers glimpsed social life, communal integration, financial benefits, and political influence in interwar Hildesheim, but they did not feel that they had full and equal access to that bourgeois-dominated world. They responded by creating a workers' subculture with their own newspapers, publishers, clubs, party, cooperatives, and so on. Yet they were still kept in their place by an inflexible social structure in education, income, and custom. In the short term, Otto responded to his inferior status by participating in "ringing tours" with other neighborhood children: youthful pranks that created a sense of belonging across class and confession (described in the appendix). In the long-term, however, he developed a personalized way of cultivating his identity among friends and neighbors that rejected the bourgeoisie just as they had rejected him.

The evidence here was difficult to recover because it was more habitual than linguistic. Lise found it hard to express the difference between degrees of familiarity within her neighborhood between Catholics and Protestants. Similarly, Otto found it hard to communicate to me in words how his bourgeois neighbors expressed their sense of superiority. Instead, he told me a story about a fancy hair salon on the main shopping street around the corner from his house. Otto's family could not afford such expensive services; they, by contrast, got their hair cut at home or in a barbershop. The family that owned the salon was also very arrogant. Otto recalled how the son had several aquariums and had invited Otto to see his fish. Otto then remarked, "I am also going to buy I some fish" (*Ich kaufe* ich *auch mal Fische*). Otto explained to me how it had been common in the rural dialect of the countryside around Hildesheim to switch the direct object (me, *mich*) and the indirect object (to me, *mir*). This adult neighbor made fun of Otto's poor German. Indeed, he often heard the remark that the children who went to upper schools were smarter than he was (G/41b R/410). To illustrate the aspirations of this salon-owning family to superior status, Otto turned to a habit memory. He put his hands on his sweater as if it were a suit jacket, showing me how they acted: as if they were something special (*Hetapateta*; G/42a R/15).

Given his family's reception among the middle classes, it is no wonder that the Kochs interacted primarily with neighbors *like themselves:* as he called them, the *little people.* Like Lise, Otto excluded those people from his neighborhood who undermined his sense of self. He also cultivated his identity proactively in that same context. Otto later joined the Social Democratic Party, resisted the Third Reich, landed in prison, and even sat on the town council after the war. Seen in the larger context of his biography, his childhood memories were still so vivid to Otto in the 1990s because they had been the crucial experiences through which he had molded an identity that lasted a lifetime. What the Evangelical milieu did for Lise, the social-democratic milieu did for Otto. Associational life did not become the model on which to base their neighborly relations automatically. Rather, that identity, cultivated in terms of both formal and informal social relations, provided each with a way to pry himself or herself out of a specific clinch. Lise and Otto made the best of what they had.

Otto's tactic was to outflank bourgeois claims to niveau, with which he could hardly compete, by treating them as degenerate. The Heine family lived on the corner of the main shopping street and the plaza, literally on the margin between bourgeois and proletarian life worlds. Otto recalled one of the Heine boys: "What was his first name? He was always teased for his name. He was somewhat of a lightweight (*eine leichte Heini*), a wimp. I believe he was homosexual, a fact revealed only much later. But already as a kid—." Again, Otto stopped narrating and acted instead. He held his hands and arms together, and made a "sweet" face as if to say *this was how the boy behaved* (G/41b R/440). Later in the interviews I asked him again about the boy's effeminacy. "Yes, everyone [noticed] it because he really was this way, no? It was his whole way of being. He was not nasty, you could not say that, but you suspected that something was different there, no?"

(G/42a R/50). In spite of the fact that Otto's family and the Heine family lived very close to each other, their relationship was less close than was the case with Otto's other neighbors.

An otherwise sympathetic man, Otto found a variety of excuses for the fact that he teased this effeminate boy. Everyone noticed how the boy acted. He really did behave that way. They were only stating a fact. His name also lent itself to such abuse: *Heine, Heini*. Yet Otto also resented boys like the Heine brothers who could live on the fancy shopping street, who could afford to attend upper schools, who could afford to have fish as pets. And Otto had been taught, through bitter examples of public ridicule, that such boys considered themselves his betters. His narrative moved directly from explaining how one noticed this boy's sexual deviance to how his elitist neighbors deprecated Otto for being born into the underclass. Otto's response was to strike back using his only available weapon. He could not assail boys of this class for having the sophistication he lacked, but he could deprecate this particular boy as a representative of the bourgeoisie for being "sweet." He did to this boy for being gay what the bourgeoisie had done to him for being undereducated and poor.

This tactic of eigensinn worked for Otto: it validated his sense of self in response to an unforgiving social hierarchy. So when he encountered a similar circumstance a few years later, he fell back on this reliable tactic for survival. After graduating from middle school in 1920, Otto joined the *Wandervögel,* which translates roughly as the *Hiking Birds* and refers to the bourgeois hiking club for young people. In 1924, however, he switched to *Vorwärts* (*Forwards*), the proletarian gymnastics club. At first, Otto left the reason for his departure vague, claiming simply that the Wandervögel was not for him (G/42b R/290; see also SAH 904-1/20-21). He explained his return to the socialist milieu in terms of politics: "Once the völkisch ideas and the swastika emerged, then it was over." When I pressed him about his reasons for leaving, he disclosed a more telling body narrative: "We had a conference at the house of one of the members, and as I was welcomed at the door, he hugged me and kissed me. Blech! That was so disgusting to me, no? That was it! That was just not my style" (G/42b R/290, 320). This kiss so tarnished his experience of the Wandervögel that Otto rejected the whole movement a few months later.

Even now, Otto had not disclosed the whole story of how this experience laid the foundation for a lifelong habit that shaped his relationships with friends and neighbors. Seamlessly, he moved on to explain that it was at this point that he met his future best friend, Martin Engel. "We were of the same mind, no? We became very good friends. Fundamentally we were cut from the same tree, if I could say it in this way." Not only did Otto and Martin see their friendship as a unity, as a meeting of minds and hearts in politics as well as everyday life, but they were also perceived that way in the public eye (G/42b R/380, G/45b R/220, 300, G/46a R/40, 110, 200). Otto explained that their mutual friends did not dare speak their suspicions outright—that Martin and Otto were suspected of being gay lovers. They simply said: "You know, with those two, something is not right there." Otto explained to me that this suspicion existed "because we were so tightly knit, you know. But both [of us] also had had this experience that I have already reported to you, how the Wandervögel hugged you" (G/45a R/200). Thus Martin and Otto became friends and joined a socialist gymnastics club where they in turn met their future wives. Safely heterosexual, true proletarian comradeship emerged through the rejection of degenerate bourgeois homoeroticism. This deep, fulfilling, lasting friendship was made possible precisely because it had emerged from the common experience of rejecting the bourgeoisie for its sexual deviancy. This behavior pattern constituted Otto's style of self-cultivation: what began when he was a boy was continued when he was a man and, throughout his life, was tied to his most intimate personal relations. Otto and Martin then reinforced this habit in ever-new circumstances: like when Martin encountered gay men in the workplace, or when I prompted Otto to tell me about his friends and neighbors.

The habits of self-cultivation are addictive. As Otto faced new circumstances in which his imagined status was challenged in particular ways, he transposed a habit proven reliable in analogous circumstances before. As external circumstances changed radically over the course of modern German history, he learned to rely on those embodied habits as the measure of his identity. Those habits provided a sense of coherence even in spite of actual changes in the definition of his self: for instance, as he moved into and out of the Wandervögel, the antifascist resistance, the Nazi war effort, and so on. On an interpersonal level, however, those styles of self-cultivation created an insular world that excluded homosexuals by definition (even though those styles are strikingly "queer": see Jagose 1996, esp. chs. 7 and 8). No wonder, then, that Otto claimed that he knew nothing of the fate of this boy during the Third Reich. He knew abstractly then that homosexuals were being persecuted, and he demonstrated attentive concern for other victims of Nazi terror, such as the family members of political prisoners. Though an otherwise engaged antifascist, he did not directly take part in the lives of gay friends and neighbors, no matter what the Nazi regime did to them. He omitted these victims of Nazi terror from his purview because he still had to protect a fragile sense of self from the ridicule of the bourgeoisie, and because he had long since addicted himself to this particular way of being and behaving.

The interview process from intellectual curiosity to published narrative does not offer an objective window into the past. It represents an intersubjective, ethnographic encounter between a researcher and a cohort of witnesses. Therein lies its strengths, not its weaknesses. In the neighborhoods of their past, my interview partners were confronted with similarity and difference. With the help of customs of conviviality, they learned to negotiate these treacherous waters. By developing a personalized set of tactics for handling particular, challenging situations, they even survived with a sense of self intact. During the interviews, we were likewise confronted with our similarities and differences, and once again, my interview partners had to negotiate these interpersonal circumstances. The stimulus to revive their habit memories was no longer their Jewish or gay neighbor, but a young American for whom little about everyday life during the Third Reich was self-evident. For reasons unknown to them at first, I asked probing questions about such unorthodox issues as relations with neighbors who were Jewish or gay (I offered to answer personal questions about myself only after the interviews were concluded, but few took me up on this offer, since most were quite content to talk about themselves). They told stories about the way they handled such sticky situations in the past, often as if providing advice. And those stories of herrschaft and eigensinn were precisely what I wanted to hear.

Their self-presentation in the present rested on habits of self-cultivation that they had developed in the past. The more we focused our attention on those moments when they first developed those habits, the closer the interviews came to historical reality. Otto and Lise stood on opposite sides of the political spectrum, but their styles were similar in this respect. Both cultivated their identity by alienating specific neighbors whose very proximity to them threatened to undermine their insecure sense of self. That everyday process framed what they knew about the Holocaust because, prior to national socialism, Jews and gay men were not abstract ideas but actual neighbors. The Nazi regime implemented its antisemitic and homophobic policies on the basis of this earlier form of denial.

Books

Some scholars read the consistency between Nazi principles and the habit memories of ordinary Germans very differently. Rather than as a cause, they see this similarity as a consequence of twelve years of Nazi totalitarianism. In this model, Germans describe Jews in impersonal terms, and themselves as ordinary, because a dictatorial regime taught them to think in those terms (e.g., Stern 1992). I argue the opposite, on the basis of the consistency with which my interview partners described conviviality outside their relationships with Jews and Nazis, because it was the allegedly normal world of friends and neighbors that served as the starting point of our interviews, and because of their own tendency to rely on habit memories to preserve a coherent sense of self. Like Otto and Lise, Heinrich Weber told me stories of how, independent of the Third Reich, he resolved the contradiction between envy and imitation of the educated middle class on the backs of his next-door neighbors. Also like them, Heinrich's particular style of self-cultivation shaped what he knew about the Holocaust. This neighborhood epistemology not only led to Holocaust denial in its classic form but also made the Holocaust possible in the first place.

Born in 1903, Heinrich learned the habits of respect for authority from an early age. He helped his father, a master painter, to distribute wages to his journeymen from his office, a room that Heinrich otherwise did not enter without a sense of awe and restraint (G/143a R/140). He identified so strongly with this position of power that he could still remember precisely how much each worker earned, how many hours they worked, and when they received breaks. He could also recall those neighbors who, through reciprocal gifts or payments of rent, reinforced his status as the son of the landlord and skilled craftsman. The first major anecdote that Heinrich offered during our interviews was the story of how he used to have to enter his father's office with his report card: a nervous experience for him as a child because he was never a very good student. Still, he desperately wanted a bicycle for his birthday. All of the other boys had learned to ride and had bicycles that they rode around on the plaza in front of the barracks. His father purchased a bike one Christmas and had his apprentices open it in front of Heinrich, only to then tell them to pack it up again because Heinrich was "not worthy" of such a gift given his performance at school. His father's motto was: "He who does not want to learn in school does not need to ride a bike." Still, Heinrich did get his bike the next year for his birthday by moving from the twenty-eighth to the ninth seat in his class (in Wilhelmine Germany, one's physical location in the classroom corresponded to one's level of accomplishment.) Because he had a bike, Heinrich explained, he then had a whole pile of friends and was the center of attention of the many children who played on the plaza in front of the barracks (G/143a R/170).

Many of Heinrich's anecdotes had this fable-like quality either about being shamed by authority figures for poor performance or about receiving rewards for dutiful collaboration. The boys on his block used to play *soldier* on the plaza while the enlisted men of the 79th Battalion drilled. "Eyes up! Fingers long! Take down your weapon slowly!" The boys with their wooden rifles could perform the drills better than the men, Heinrich insisted, especially the recruits. To show me how the men practiced their aim, Heinrich once again physically aped the soldiers of the Kaiser during the interviews, obeying the commands of long-since deceased noncommissioned officers or lance corporals (G/143a R/220). And when the men could not perform their drills correctly, the neighborhood boys were placed in front of them to perform so that the men could see: "The boys do it better than you!" (G/143a R/370).

Heinrich desperately longed for upward social mobility. He wanted "a career with a collar." Yet he lacked the background, which he understood to include not only a gymnasium training but also a degree of sophistication that he associated with the educated middle classes:

> The niveau and spiritual prerequisites were lacking for [gymnasium], what the children from other households had already learned. They practically brought that with them [to school] from their homes. They sucked it along with their mother's milk. And we had to work hard to produce all of that after the fact: la-bor-i-ous-ly. And that was hard! (*müh-sel-ig;* G/148b R/240)

After leaving middle school, Heinrich applied to the civic bureaucracy and was hired in the final months of the First War. Ironically, he met his old "comrades" from the Steingrube again. Heinrich laughed at the irony. After their twelve years of service, they moved to the postal, rail, or other positions in the civic administrations as military observers. Suddenly Heinrich found himself working alongside the same non-commissioned officers whom he had aped as a child. "You have to imagine," he insisted, "how that went off," a fifteen-year-old apprentice among these "mighty men" with their Kaiser-Wilhelm mustaches (G/143a R/290, 360).

Heinrich recounted these stories to provide me with insight into the events that shaped his personality. His laughter could barely contain his self-satisfaction. The interviews simply offered him yet another circumstance in which he could reiterate his habit memories, like "Eyes up! Fingers long! Take down your weapon slowly!" Through these body narratives, he tried to justify his life choices to a young American (Bergerson 2002b).

Heinrich struggled throughout the 1920s in this style: to compensate for his mediocre education by taking night courses so that he too could qualify for a higher position. But in spite of his hard work, Heinrich was hard pressed to ignore his socially inferior position in his neighborhood. Whenever Heinrich encountered the daughters of the educated middle classes on the street, his grandmother would tell him that he had to greet them properly while standing in the gutter to let them pass:

> She meant that, since we were a class lower, since we did not go to an upper . . . school, that we owed them something. This was still this subordinate thinking typical of that era. It had been so imprinted on the older people, you know, that many could not kick the habit. When some important person came by then they stood in the gutter to let him pass.

Heinrich laughed when he told me that story, as much at himself as at the situation. "Yes, yes," he exclaimed, "that is how it was, oh yes!" (G/144a

R/230) Clearly, Heinrich resented the class location into which he was born but not the hierarchy of his society as such. He repeatedly took control over the direction of the interview from me by narrating a series of anecdotes that legitimized a mode of self-cultivation that combined resentment for established authorities and collaboration with them (see also Bergerson 2004). So I was not surprised when he told me that he resented the new Nazi authorities for having forced him to join the party, to learn about Nazi ideology in his leisure time, and to join the army; but that he nonetheless did as he was told in order to continue to work his way up the ranks of the civic bureaucracy. Out of fearful respect for authority as much as to get his fair share of respect from others, Heinrich collaborated.

Lise, Otto, and Heinrich all came from strikingly similar social circumstances: the Protestant petty bourgeoisie, endangered by proletarianization, desiring upward social mobility, yet incapable of bettering themselves owing to economic uncertainty and a persistently rigid social structure. Trapped in a circumstance in which they could not respect themselves, each made the best of what he or she had in order to preserve a sense of hope for the future. Each enacted a surreal neighborhood that maximized status within its imaginary boundaries and indirectly but effectively alienated some of the neighbors. To preserve their sense of normalcy, they then acted as if these limits on knowledge had been dictated by circumstances beyond their control. Depending on their choices, the residents cultivated identities that landed them in dramatically different positions vis-à-vis the Nazi regime, from collaboration to resistance. Their political action was certainly influenced by their milieu, but not predetermined by it. Heinrich and Otto explicitly insisted that their parents had not forced them to adopt a political position or join a specific party. Both master artisans leaned, in fact, towards the social democrats but permitted their sons to make their own decisions. Heinrich's father instructed: "You have to run your own life. I can neither advise you nor help you. . . . You know best [what to do]. I don't want you to blame me afterwards that I forced you into some profession or whatever" (G/145a R/100, G/146b R/220). These young Hildesheimers did not fashion their identities free from constraints, but shaped their lives of their own free will because they had to enact those identities in everyday life if they were to make them real. Meanwhile, Heinrich himself recognized that elderly people could hardly kick old habits, particularly when they played a central role in cultivating their identities over the course of their lives. When asked to recount his salient memories in autobiographical terms, Heinrich appropriately provided me with stories of those critical moments in which he first learned to behave like himself.

He did not mention the teacher from the local grade school when he first reconstructed a map of his neighborhood, but realizing his oversight, he added the teacher's name and profession along with the label *Jew* (G/144b

R/60). He immediately answered what he presumed would be my next question: "Only the devil knows where they ended up. No man can say." He then proceeded to explain to this young American about everyday life during the 1930s. "You must imagine that there were a large number of Jews in town. Every second or third store was in Jewish hands, you know." Heinrich put out his hand and grasped at the air, demonstrating the aspirations of the so-called Jewish world conspiracy. "No one would have complained if the Jews"—he did not complete his thought because what he was thinking was politically incorrect to state in the 1990s. Nonetheless, the way that he narrated his relationship with these neighbors was revealing because his story followed the same contours of habit with which he had cultivated his identity among his neighbors in the first place.

He started again from a less condemning position: "They had a completely different mentality than the other *people's comrades*." *Volksgenossen* is the Nazi term for the members of the new racial community. "They were more supple: out of the experiences they had had, they were much more restrained" (*anschmiegsamer;* G/146b R/70). Here again, this description of this Jewish neighbor tells us more about Heinrich than it does about them. To be sure, Heinrich insisted that he had not been antisemitic, that it was the Nazi propaganda machine that had introduced such elements into social relations. Still, Heinrich described his next-door neighbors in unflattering terms. The wife of this Jewish teacher, he continued, was a "curled up" woman. True, his two sons went to gymnasium, but Heinrich used to see this grade-school teacher run out of the house "with his Koran or Bible or whatever else he had under his arms." To show me what he meant, Heinrich again used body narrative. He acted as if he was carrying something large. "It was such a batch of books!" he exclaimed. This Jewish teacher then raced off to school by walking along the gutter. "*That* is how I know him" (*So kenne ich ihn;* his emphasis).

Heinrich tried to recall the names of the two boys who lived there. He remembered only the one that had a very Germanic name but forgot the other who had some "Jewish" name. "But it does not matter. In any case, I lost sight of them. Whether the teacher—." Again, Heinrich briefly silenced something that could not be said and began elsewhere: "For they carried him off. Where he ended up, I do not know." He then insisted that this Jewish family isolated themselves by and large from the rest of the neighborhood and trafficked instead in Jewish circles. To be sure, Heinrich knew precisely when *Pesach* or *Sukkoth* took place (Passover and the Jewish equivalent of Thanksgiving respectively) because he watched all of the "curious" rituals that took place in their home and backyard. After all, throughout the interwar years until this Jewish teacher was deported by the Nazis, this family of Jews lived literally next door (G/144b R/60).

The fact that Heinrich did not know what happened to this Jewish family during the Third Reich is suspect for several reasons. As he finally admitted, they lived right next door to him, and he made a point of looking into the semi-private spaces of their backyard to observe them. Moreover, he worked in the town administration during the deportations. Still, Heinrich's particular form of Holocaust denial must be understood within its biographical context. Long before 1933, Heinrich knew this Jewish neighbor purely in pejorative terms: as a man who still walked in the gutter in spite of his education. He cultivated this prejudice for highly idiosyncratic reasons: as a fascinating inversion of his own shame of being ritually subordinated to the educated middle classes. No wonder, then, that Heinrich approved of the "sudden" disappearance of Jews from his neighborhood, to which he admitted later in the interviews. He even bemoaned the fact that they had not disappeared sooner: those that did not take advantage of the opportunity to exile themselves stayed in Hildesheim, in his opinion, "to their detriment." The Nazi regime offered Heinrich an administrative solution to his neighborly dilemma: how to resolve the tension between being jealous of, and wishing to emulate, the educated middle classes. Only later, Heinrich explained, were the remaining Jews of Hildesheim deported to concentration camps for work and "so they would not disturb" anyone. Only later and suddenly, Heinrich insisted, did the idea arise "that the Jews would have to disappear entirely! They had to be gassed, you know. The [German] people did not know anything about that at first" (*Das hat das Volk erst gar nicht mitgekriegt;* G/146b R/80).

Obviously, Heinrich was more antisemitic that he was willing to admit, but it is easy to both over- and understate the role of ideology in the origins of the Third Reich. On the one hand, my argument here differs from that of Daniel Jonah Goldhagen (1996) who insisted that ordinary Germans were Hitler's willing executioners: that they participated in the Holocaust because they were motivated by a pervasive "eliminationist antisemitism." The degree to which Lise, Otto, and Heinrich collaborated with the Nazi state was not predetermined by an ideology. Each showed various degrees of support for different elements of national socialism, and took part in the regime's policies on an active basis in keeping with his or her convictions. Still, their crucial and earliest contribution to the Nazi system of terror was the fact that they chose to alienate their Jewish or gay neighbors in everyday life. They behaved this way prior to and independent of national socialism. On the other hand, their neighbors were not simply scapegoats for their upward social mobility, real or imagined. Just as my interview partners chose to follow some of their neighbors' biographies and ignore others, they were able to select from a panoply of attitudes in their culture in order to leverage their way out of their clinch. They chose to apply tropes of antisemitism and homophobia to their neighbors. Their contribution to the Nazi revolution was that they chose to make hateful ideas into hateful habits.

To be sure, Heinrich denied any direct participation in Nazi crimes against humanity, and conveniently, little archival evidence remains to serve as proof of these subsequent crimes since the Allies bombed and destroyed most of the relevant civic archives on 22 March 1945. Still, because I encouraged Heinrich to narrate whatever habits of self-cultivation that he had used to construct his identity in the first place, his interview testimony became a reasonable vehicle through which I could reconstruct his initial, informal malfeasance from which later, formal collaboration stemmed. It is clear from the interviews that Heinrich was accustomed to making his Jewish neighbors irrelevant long before 1933. He looked in on them in order to be able to look down on them, but he never got to know them. He could then rid himself of his shadow-self and transcend his own internalized self-hatred after 1933 by allying himself with the new Third Reich. Heinrich adopted Nazi vocabulary like *Volksgenosse* and *lebenswürdig* (G/143a R/40), and used the concept of *volk* as if it applied only to "Aryan" Germans and not to Jewish Germans, not simply because of the educational evenings that he was compelled to attend but to cultivate the niveau he wished to acquire. To this selfish end, he helped make Hildesheim fascist not just as a member of the town administration but as a neighbor and ordinary person. His persistent claims to have not known about the Holocaust in memory follow with the tragic logic of this same bad habit.

Conclusion: Dangerous Deeds

THIS BOOK HAS tried to integrate multiple layers of modern German history that are often treated as distinct. In the big picture of state and society, this study has revisited the story of the origins of the Third Reich and the Holocaust. It shows that the Nazi revolution from above depended to a large degree on a parallel, relatively independent revolution from below, a transformation in everyday habits that simultaneously disguised its historic traces. In the hallways of the regime, as on the streets of the neighborhood, not-so-ordinary people struggled to colonize everyday life through tactics of eigensinn and strategies for herrschaft. Remarkably modern, the Nazi movement relied upon the proactive cultivation of the self, just as Nazi ideology pointed the internally competitive structure of conviviality in the radically destructive and fundamentally inhumane direction of fascist violence and eugenic engineering. Rather than seeing political ideologies and personal claims for power and status as analytic alternatives, this book has attempted to demonstrate the revolutionary consequences when *intentional* and *structural* factors reinforce each other. My narrative certainly stresses a polycratic society over a polycratic state, but I emphasize the story of new manners only because historians are already so familiar with the story of the new regime. The point is that the formal institutions of Nazi society and its informal customs shared essential similarities; the momentum of the Nazi revolution derived from their dynamic interaction.

That said, it is in the small picture of everyday life that these grand historical questions of German state and society are best demonstrated. An interdisciplinary debate about the historicity of *cultural practices* has likewise posed the question of the role of ordinary people in co-producing inhumane systems of domination and destruction—for which the Third Reich is an archetype. This book has tried to show that Hildesheimers, convinced of and dedicated to their own normalcy, nonetheless collaborated in the world-historical Nazi revolution. As much as possible, it has tried to redirect our attention to their deeds so that we might better comprehend how new manners not only legitimized a new regime but also drove the revolution forward.

253

Summarizing that story, ordinary Germans laid claim to status and power through customs of conviviality that veiled those agents in normalcy in order to preserve their scope for maneuver. Building their new manners on this foundation of habitus, ardent Nazis led the way in introducing fascist and racist principles into everyday life. They did so by initiating a public, though largely symbolic, debate about the nature of self and society. Implicated in those very customs that constituted normalcy, these deeds were dismissed as pranks. Yet that debate was in fact quite serious and necessarily engaged everyone across social and political barriers because it was located in conviviality: in those ritual acts through which public intercourse was initiated. In the short term, the Nazi seizure of power from above overshadowed cultural practice; yet it was made real and realized by ardent Nazis in their own neighborhoods. That dictatorship provided the neighborhood Nazi with considerable additional leverage in these moments of interpersonal engagement; that analogous seizure of power from below gave the Third Reich an immediate and increasingly totalitarian atmosphere.

Yet it was the medium-term consequences of the Nazi revolution that arguably surprised Nazi detractors and supporters alike: the way that cultural practices undermined their own functionality. Ideally, the Nazi regime hoped that ordinary Germans would adopt its racist and fascist ideas out of conviction. Practically, they realized, what mattered simply was that the German people grew accustomed to fascist and racist habits. Both strategies for Nazi herrschaft and tactics of antifascist eigensinn placed Hitler and his movement at the fulcrum of informal social relations. As the Nazis fought (and won) the major battles with the organized resistance, as antifascists turned increasingly to informal social relations as a means to continue the good fight, this dynamic structure of everyday life acquired a momentum of its own, ravaging the terrain of conviviality. Ordinary Germans could no longer judge their neighbors by looking at their neighborly behavior. In the absence of informal cultural mechanisms for negotiating social relations, ordinary Germans turned increasingly to the Nazi regime to administer conviviality using the formal mechanisms of bureaucracy. In this way, ordinary Germans helped transform a cultural process into public policy.

The macrohistory of the Third Reich thus shares essential similarities with the ritual process in microhistory. In the interwar period, the Nazi movement placed many of the elements of communitas at the core of its political ideology and cultural practice. These elements included its populism and its pageantry, its critique of existing institutions and its promise of utopia, and its dynamic energy as a movement rather than a party per se. This was herrschaft based on and depicted as eigensinn—and it could not last forever as such. Yet the key question here is how precisely the Nazi rebellion against the Weimar system during the late 1920s transformed into institutionalized murder by the early 1940s. Arguably, the act of purging each and every community across Germany of its polluting elements stands at the symbolic core of the Nazi project to restore moral order to Germanic civilization. The Nazi regime was content for most of the 1930s to rely on informal mechanisms to accomplish this goal of resurrecting the moral community; even its legislation was designed primarily to encourage Germans and Jews to adjust themselves to new conditions rather than forcing them all to comply from above. But the more that ordinary Germans adopted Nazi manners, the less such symbolic acts revealed about their inner convictions. No longer functioning as a means of communication, nazified customs of conviviality proved less functional as a means to negotiate identities among friends and neighbors. The less that informal mechanism of conviviality served to mediate actual social relations, the more that ordinary Germans turned to the Nazi regime to administer them formally. Like any ritual process, the very success of the Nazi regime in creating a politicized communitas encouraged a shift back to societas. Yet in this case, the newly re-established hierarchy had changed fundamentally from a civil society to a fascist, racist volksgemeinschaft.

The bureaucratic quality of the so-called Final Solution to the Jewish Question as well as the many other programs for social engineering executed by the Nazis between 1938 and 1945 did not follow automatically or necessarily from this cultural dynamic at the heart of the Nazi revolution; but it did follow from that cultural logic, and it consequently made "sense" to ordinary people. From their semiotic system of colored triangles, middle names, and tattooed numbers to their schemes for physical relocation, incarceration, and murder, the Nazi regime increasingly administered informal social relations to meet a need for moral order that the Nazi revolution itself had generated because of the totalitarian way it colonized everyday life. From this perspective, the alleged "willingness" (Goldhagen 1996) of ordinary Germans to participate in Nazi terror and genocide was based not fundamentally on their commitment to Nazi ideology per se but on the degree to which they had grown accustomed, and perhaps even addicted, to Nazi habits while still living at home. For this reason, it is appropriate to speak of *ordinary Germans*: not to prevent us from considering how other ordinary people participated in the Nazis' inhumane system of mass destruction, but to remind us that the everyday foundation for this particular Holocaust was first made in Germany.

Thanks to the myths of normalcy, my interview partners were able to publicly ignore the inhumane consequences of their behavior in everyday life, but their private memories were far less cooperative. Ultimately, they remembered all too well their seemingly ordinary deeds that changed friends and neighbors into Aryans and Jews. These deeds were dangerous in that the

memory of them threatened to undermine the very normalcy on which self
and society were based. My interview partners were committed to keeping
this open secret long before the Nazi regime developed its Final Solution to
the Jewish Question. Postwar politics of memory only reinforced that open
secret. It follows, then, that we can come to terms with the Nazi past only
insofar as we are willing to invert that open secret: to abandon the notion
that ordinary Germans ever really existed as such and yet pay close attention
to the way that they naturalized those myths of normalcy in everyday life.
It also follows that dealing with the Nazi past in the present is a challenge
only because self-styled ordinary Germans refused to come to terms with
the Nazi present during the past. Their memories have been politicized and
romanticized, but at their core lie real historical experiences in the context of
which they shaped their identities. The challenge of everyday life during the
Third Reich thus lies not in the unreliable memories of ordinary Germans
but in their all too reliable memories of actual deeds.

Appendix: A Ringing Tour

THIS APPENDIX FURTHER describes my theory and method, defines some of my key terms, and surveys the scholarly debates to which I hope this book will make a contribution.

Theory

The first generation of postwar histories about the Third Reich tended to focus on the German political elite, their ideologies, and their public policies. A typical example was *Die nationalsozialistische Machtergreifung* written in 1962 by Karl Dietrich Bracher, Wolfgang Sauer, and Gerhard Schultz. The history of the origins of the Third Reich is unthinkable without an accurate account of high politics. But this *intentionalist* approach to the troubling questions of historical and ethical responsibility tended to reduce the question of collective guilt to the motives, plans, and policies of the officers of the Third Reich. In this sense, it served the postfascist interests of self-styled ordinary people, not to mention the Cold War interests of the United States. Some scholars of this first generation were more sensitive to the unintentional results of public policies. In David Schoenbaum's study of the modernization of German society, *Hitler's Social Revolution* (1966), we first learned that the Nazi regime afforded Aryans the opportunity for upward mobility, if not in concrete terms then at least in terms of status. By breaking down the traditional institutions of German politics and society, the Nazi regime indirectly laid the foundation for a modern democracy and mass society after 1945. Hannah Arendt also shifted our attention away from motive per se. Her landmark study of Adolf Eichmann in 1961 first raised the problem of what she eloquently called "the banality of evil." In the classic case of the Nazi bureaucrat who simply followed orders, she suggested that the Holocaust was based not so much on antisemitism as on normalcy. These studies still focused primarily on the policies and culture of the Nazi elite, but they nonetheless raised the prospect that the pursuit of power and status might have played a critical role in the Nazi revolution and the Holocaust, particularly when acts of individual self-cultivation were veiled by the everyday.

A second generation of research expanded the range of categories for historical agents to include active and passive collaborators, conformists and non-conformists, bystanders, and so on. This new trail was blazed in 1977 by a team of scholars led by Martin Broszat studying *Bayern in der NS-Zeit.* Ian Kershaw's *Popular Opinion and Political Dissent in the Third Reich* (1983) has since served as a model for many German historians, just as Raul Hilberg's monograph *Perpetrators, Victims, Bystanders* (1992) does for scholars of the Holocaust. These studies provided far more precise terms for the historical and ethical responsibility of ordinary people. Still, they tended to only hint at the processes of everyday life that lay hidden behind these otherwise static categories, often ignored the contradictions in their subjects' behavior, and as a result tended to downplay the essential absurdity of these circumstances (Bergerson 2002a, 2004). In his controversial synthesis from 1989 *Modernity and the Holocaust* (see also Kren and Rappoport 1984), Zygmunt Bauman suggested instead the possibility that this culture of normalcy represented a critical component of modern ways of life more generally and even that Nazi victims contributed to their own victimization by sharing those habits.

This generation of excellent scholarship proved more willing to criticize intentionalist models for reducing process to motive. In his classic study *The Hitler State* (1981), Martin Broszat coined the term *polycracy* in an attempt to better account for the way that the Nazi regime developed the so-called Final Solution to the Jewish Question (*Endlösung;* see also Bessel 2003; Fraenkel 1969; Geyer 1987; Mommsen 1983; Neumann 1942). He showed that the various leaders of the formal institutions of party, state, and society faced overlapping competencies. They competed for the same resources and to accomplish the same goals. They were encouraged with both the carrot and the stick to voluntarily adapt their behavior to fit Hitler's goals. These Nazi subalterns each tried to out-perform the others to win Hitler's favor. From this perspective, the Holocaust was not so much an ideologically motivated policy decision as a systemic consequence of each subaltern taking the initiative to find better solutions to existing administrative problems. Nazi ideology, particularly antisemitism, provided the overarching orientation for their murderous policies, but the competitive structure of the Nazi regime gave that revolution a momentum of its own.

This *structuralist* approach[1] offered a critical corrective, but it still focused analytic attention primarily on the ruling elite. Increasing numbers of scholars studied the contingent and variable process by which the local elite implemented the Nazi revolution on the ground. William Sheridan Allen's landmark study of the Nazi seizure of power in Northeim from 1965 is still taught in many classrooms in the United States and is used as a model for new scholarship (e.g., Wagner 1998). In most cases, however, scholars simply extended their definition of the state without changing their definition of the political; or they transposed the paradigm from the center to the periphery without developing a model based on everyday life itself (cf. Maier 1988; Sheehan 1981). Robert Gellately, on whom I repeatedly rely in this book, broke new ground with his research into the Gestapo precisely because he recognized that the Nazi regime relied on the active denunciation of kin, friends, and neighbors for its system of terror (1988, 1990, 2001; Fitzpatrick and Gellately 1996; see also Mallmann and Paul 1994; Mann 1987; for Hildesheim, Schneider 1998: III. 7). Still, his archival sources rarely afford the opportunity to give informal social relationships the same analytic emphasis as the formal institutions of state.

Two notable exceptions were Detlev Peukert and Frances Henry. Peukert's excellent book *Inside the Third Reich* (1982) studied everyday life in its own terms without losing a sense of connection to the grander questions of German state and society. I turn in my book to many of his excellent arguments about the Weimar Republic and the Third Reich, particularly those concerning modernization. Whereas Peukert never offered a coherent, synthetic model of everyday life, Henry's ethnographic study of "Sonderheim" did provide a systematic model for ethnic relations before, during, and after the Holocaust. On the basis of oral history, she discovered that, in spite of formal barriers to integration, and in part due to latent antisemitism, Jews and Germans had in fact learned to live together in relative harmony as friends and neighbors. The evidence from Hildesheim verifies this conclusion, but it also explains this kind of accommodation in more detail, for conviviality facilitated integration and alienation, collaboration and resistance, civility and barbarism. Concerned with group dynamics rather than individual acts, Henry never considered how ordinary Sonderbergers actually negotiated these contradictions. More seriously, she never penetrated the veil of the everyday. Challenging what she called the "myth of complicity," she ended up reiterating the myths of normalcy that helped generate the Holocaust in the first place.

The question at stake here is not so much collective guilt as the precise nature of the agency of ordinary individuals in the public sphere. We cannot legitimately hold them responsible, or irresponsible, for any historical event or process if we have not theorized how, precisely, the daily behaviors of ordinary people help shape world history. There is no question that ordinary people respond creatively to circumstances beyond their control, but do they also help to shape them? Given the extent of Nazi crimes against humanity, the stakes in this question are high. Given the way that the Holocaust is often used as a model for comparison to slavery, colonization, and genocide, they are even higher.

An emerging third generation of postwar scholarship is concerned with this question. Daniel Jonah Goldhagen has argued that an ideology of *eliminationist antisemitism* inspired ordinary Germans to willingly execute

Hitler's orders for the mass extermination of the Jews (1996). Yet Goldhagen only transposed a relatively simplistic version of the intentionalist model from political elites to ordinary Germans (see also Gross 2001). Reducing process to motive, his account cannot help us see how antisemitic words became antisemitic deeds (van Rahden 2000), how ordinary Germans first made fascist violence and racial hatred into a way of life. Christopher R. Browning had already studied the same set of perpetrators in his book *Ordinary Men* (1998). His social-psychological analysis offered a more complicated, and more satisfying, story of the process by which ordinary men became mass murderers (see also Kren and Rappoport 1980). Like Goldhagen, however, he is interested primarily in wartime crimes, and the debate that these scholars initiated about genocidal warriors does not investigate, in its own terms, the earlier cultural process by which these ordinary men, not to mention women, first accustomed themselves to racism and fascism while still living at home near Jewish neighbors.

Robert Gellately and Marion Kaplan moved us back in that direction in their most recent books; and my research confirmed many of their insightful conclusions. Gellately's version of this history, *Backing Hitler* (2001), condemns ordinary people not simply for knowing about Nazi crimes (since they were repeatedly informed about them by a regime obsessed with popular opinion) but also, in effect, for actively supporting Nazi totalitarianism: by initiating police investigations and by approving of its police actions, particularly when the latter re-established a sense of moral order in the local community. Gellately (and Browning) point to the period from 1937 or 1939 to 1941 as a key era of transition: when the Nazi regime dramatically increased the scope for arbitrary police action, when the war engendered a revolution within the Nazi revolution. Yet in spite of the fact that Gellately's research hints at a far more dynamic process of state and society, he explains this process of radicalization primarily in terms of public-policy decisions initiated from above. Kaplan's version of this story, *Between Dignity and Despair* (1998), similarly treats the contributions of ordinary people to the Nazi revolution on an interpersonal level analytically distinct from the policy decisions of the Nazi elite. She also describes in rich anecdotal detail how friends and neighbors played a key role in establishing racism and terror in everyday life before this shift in public policy, but like all of these scholars, she describes friendship and neighborliness in commonsensical terms—as if conviviality did not have its own structures, meanings, affects, and effects that demand critical investigation. Failing to theorize everyday life and its contradictions, these otherwise excellent forays into the Nazi revolution fall short of explaining how ordinary people in the broadest sense (not just genocidal warriors) helped create the Nazi system of mass destruction.

In spite of its flaws, Goldhagen's almost gratuitous reiteration of case-after-case of sadism on the part of the reserve police battalions reminded us that the questions of the historical and ethical responsibility of ordinary people for the inhumane crimes of the Third Reich, not to mention broader questions of autonomy under fascism, remain largely unresolved. Robert E. Herzstein made this critical point in his review article for *The Journal of the Historical Society* (Winter 2002; see also Bergerson 2004). Moreover, Herzstein noted that Goldhagen's work revived critiques, evident in the German public sphere since at least 1979, that the "dense prose" that characterized German historiography rarely "put a human face" on the Nazi revolution (p. 114). In the case of ordinary people during the Third Reich, we must take special care that ethnographic data does not excuse their deeds. Yet ethnographic history based on rich anecdotal evidence can help us to humanize ordinary people and uncover the logic of everyday life (e.g., Frykman and Löfgren 1987; Ginzburg 1980; Gross 2001; Hunt 1989; Kaplan 1998; Medick 1995; Sabean 1984).

This book revisits these nagging questions about ordinary people. It uses the theories and methods of ethnographic history to construct a systematic, critical model for everyday life analogous to and complementing that of the polycratic state. Instead of focusing on the ruling elite, it grounds this model in the behavior of ordinary people themselves. Ordinary Germans have never been universally antisemitic (Graml 1992; Kaplan 1998), though a large minority was ideologically committed to racist ideals and many more became increasingly indoctrinated over the course of the Third Reich. They have never been particularly obedient (Blickle 1998; Davis 2000), though they did cooperate with Nazi policies in critical ways, and even those who opposed the Nazi regime often indirectly contributed to its goals. Still, ordinary people undermined their own civil society, divided German society into Aryans and Jews, and taught themselves new manners of racism and fascism. They did so proactively and relatively independently, by coordinating their customs of conviviality to the principles of the Nazi regime and by matching the polycratic Nazi system with an analogous contest for power and status in everyday life. Since we know quite well the story of the Nazi revolution from above, this book emphasizes the story we know less well: the Nazi revolution from below.

I approach that question through the history of everyday life (*Alltagsgeschichte*): a popular, if marginalized form of remembrance that emerged in Germany in the 1960s (Amann 2000; Brüggemeier 1983; Crew 1989; Davis 2000; Eley 1989; Gerstenberg 1987; Lefebvre 1971, 1987; Lüdtke 1982, 1986, 1993, 1995; Medick 1995; Niethammer 1983a and b, 1985, 1988, 1992; Peukert 1982; Röhr 1995; Sheehan 1981). A form of microhistory (Ginzberg 1985; Lepore 2001), it is often criticized for limiting its focus exclusively to local phenomena. Yet like cultural anthropology, whence it takes much of its epistemology, this style of ethnographic history is at its best when it tries to explain the dynamic relationship between micro- and macrohistory (Comaroff and Comaroff 1992; Harootunian 2000). Just as it reads world history from the subjective perspective of ordinary people, so too does the history of everyday life interpret the actual agency and experiences of ordinary people in terms of their impact on world history. As a result, the history of everyday life is uniquely situated to reconstruct how ordinary people helped implement the Nazi revolution.

At the core of the history of everyday life lies the problem of *normalcy*: i.e., what gives everyday life its everyday qualities. Consider how Otto Koch described the Kapp Putsch in Hildesheim: "No, that lasted only a few days, let's say eight, ten days. Then life was normal again [or] whatever one means by normal: the usual life, let us say" (G/46b R/280). As I use the term in this book, normalcy refers neither to Otto's sense that daily life seemed usual (repetitive, homogenized, plebeian, traditional) nor simply to a category of shared values (common sense, official norms). It refers to the very distinction that Otto drew between the world in which he lived and the grand narrative of history: to his feeling that he was only one of *the little people* whose actions and opinions do not seem to matter, that he felt alienated and dominated by *them up there,* those elite decision makers who directly influence policy and shape world history (cf. Althusser 1996; Auslander 1996: 3; Benjamin 1968, 1978; Bloch 1962; Certeau 1988; Gramsci 1971; Hammerich and Klein 1978; Harootunian 2000; Kaplan 1998; Lefebvre 1971, 1987; Lukács 2002; Marcuse 1960; Schutz and Luckmann 1973; Smith 1987: ch. 3; and Trommler 1992). Normalcy is related to the apolitical attitude of many Germans during the Weimar Republic who preferred local social life to national mass politics (Koshar 1986) and to the claims of Wilhelmine public figures to stand above politics (van Rahden 2000). Yet normalcy presumes a view of the world from the perspective of the ordinary person rather than from even local notables.

Normalcy does not preclude political activism. Otto participated in and sometimes even led workers' associations (social, economic, political)—but he still understood himself to be ordinary. Normalcy is therefore more than just a divided, segmented, desensitized, or rationalized consciousness (Diner 1990; Kren and Rappoport 1980; Schäfer 1982; Trommler 1992). A matter of experience rather than belief, of customs rather than plans, it has a demonstrably passive feel. It is imbedded in daily habits and embodied in physical beings. Normalcy has been particularly challenging for historians to theorize for this reason. It consists of a categorical rejection not only of one's immanence in the grand narrative of history but also of the kind of intentionality that motivates classic historical actors. By removing themselves

from the subject position of history, the culture of normalcy insulated ordinary people from any sense of ethical or historical responsibility for the
turbulent and often tragic crises of the first half of the twentieth century.
Yet it required doing nonetheless, and those deeds held consequences.

This argument requires careful theorizing in order to avoid getting
caught in analytic dead-ends. During the vituperative *Historikerstreit* (Historian's Conflict), intellectuals and academics debated the legitimacy of
historicizing national socialism (e.g., the exchanges between Broszat and
Saul Friedländer in 1985, 1987, 1988; see also Augstein 1987). This debate
gave rise to the question of whether the Third Reich was in fact normal or
has simply been normalized in memory (e.g., Gerstenberger and Schmidt
1987; Kren and Rappoport 1980). One alternative to both methods is to
historicize normalcy, to trace the cultural process by which people imagine
themselves as ordinary. One can study normalcy without presuming its condition to be harmless, but instead to demonstrate the dangers of that illusion
(Peukert 1987: 2). This epistemological move takes seriously the critique
that postmodern epistemologies cloud the question of responsibility in the
case of the Holocaust (e.g., Himmelfarb 1994), yet offers a critical alternative that incorporates many of the insights of postmodern theory.

My model of everyday life focuses on two ways to lay claim to status
and power in everyday life: strategies for *herrschaft* and tactics of *eigensinn*. First and foremost, herrschaft refers to the formal, macro-institutions
of power and politics: national elites in control of party, bureaucratic and
industrial machines, their subalterns at all levels of these organizational
structures, as well as local power brokers exercising control through voluntary associations and production sites. Modern German historians command a relatively detailed appreciation of the nature and history of Nazi
herrschaft understood in these terms: the way that the Nazi party came
to dominate Germany and much of Europe politically. Yet herrschaft also
refers to those informal micro-structures of power so embedded in the
habits of everyday life that they are taken as natural. Herrschaft in the former sense of political institutions relies centrally on herrschaft in the latter
sense of power relations (following Althusser 1971; Elias 1978, 1982, 1988,
1996; Foucault 1978, 1980, 1984; Gramsci 1971). Both, in turn, depend
on a culture of normalcy. Established authorities hope that power relations
become so much a part of everyday life that they are taken for natural. They
also preserve their authority best when ordinary people do not challenge
those presumptions—or those challenges are not publicly recognized. In this
sense, normalcy is a by-product of strategies for herrschaft.

By contrast, historians do not yet fully understand the nature of Nazi
eigensinn, in no small part because it is multiple, contradictory, and self-
deceptive. First developed by Alf Lüdtke in a series of articles in the 1980s

(translated into English in the 1990s), I use eigensinn to refer to those stubbornly persistent habits of everyday life through which ordinary people expressed themselves publicly in revolt against established authorities. In terms of genre, eigensinn most frequently takes the form of jokes, pranks, or parody. Like herrschaft, eigensinn also presumes, and thereby generates, a culture of normalcy (Bergerson 2002a, 2004).

Consider the example of Otto Koch, the son of a proletarianized master artisan. He described with relish one "cool thing" (dolle Sache) that he and the neighborhood children used to do. For instance, he told me how they went on a "ringing tour" of the neighborhood. After the girls checked to see if the coast was clear, the boys pressed the doorbells on their neighbors' homes, inserted a match in the corner to make it stick, and then snipped-off the end of a match in the corner of the bell so that it kept ringing (G/45b, R/180). Lüdtke explored the role of horseplay among workers in promoting class consciousness; these youthful pranks promoted friendship and neighborliness instead. For ethnographic reasons alone, eigensinn is a useful category when trying to reconstruct past forms of conviviality (of which eigensinn is a significant, though not the only, mode). Yet eigensinn also contains inherent contradictions that make it hard to pin down. Those contradictions made it particularly useful for ordinary people to negotiate the unevenness of everyday life (Harootunian 2000). They also make eigensinn useful for historians trying to reconstruct the contradictory process of living that everyday life in general, and conviviality in particular as a site for negotiating those contradictions.

In colloquial use, adult Germans often refer to uncooperative or stubborn children as eigensinnig. Appropriately, the ringing tour was in large part an act of rebellion against existing authorities. Children annoyed adult neighbors, mocking their power and status. It was fun for Otto and his fellow conspirators for this very reason. It gave power temporarily to an underdog. Eigensinn carries the connotation of the willful, obstinate non-conformity. The ringing tour, in turn, generated a sense of integration among its participants. The children of Catholic and Protestant, middle-class and working-class families, of whatever sex, played together in Otto's neighborhood. I presume that they also played jokes on their adult neighbors ecumenically (though specific choices here would have revealed more about the nature of neighborly relations). In any case, Otto took part in the ringing tour, at least in part, to belong.

The cultural logic of eigensinn corresponded closely to the ritual process. According to Victor Turner (1969), rituals begin with the existing status hierarchies and power relations of societas (society). Rituals invert them temporarily to create a state of anti-structure, or communitas (community) in which the low can mock the high and both groups can feel a sense of liberation, equality, and belonging. But as the ritual process comes to a close, so too does anti-structure concede its place back to structure. Insofar as the disempowered were able to criticize their betters (as in the case of carnival) or actually change ranks (as in the case of an initiation), the ritual closes by reasserting those hierarchies of power and status. In this example, it is likely that the ringing tour evoked a feeling of neighborliness even for the adult victims of these youthful pranks—but perhaps only after they restored their authority and dignity by punishing Otto and his friends. If seen through this functionalist lens, eigensinn offers a brief window of opportunity to publicly make a mockery of herrschaft, but does not challenge it fundamentally. A more accurate assessment would suggest that eigensinn is regularly dismissed as just a prank of youth in order to isolate that critique into the liminal space of ritual *as if* it were *not* a fundamental critique: that is, to preserve a sense of normalcy. But that does not mean that the actual system of herrschaft remains the same.

Eigensinn also has a second set of connotations in colloquial German: it can refer simply to a sense of oneself. Putting the needs of the self above those of others, eigensinn provides a rush of self-gratification. In a status-conscious society, however, this kind of public expression of the self can seem dangerously self-absorbed, as if one were claiming more than one's due. Otto reveled in that ego-satisfying confirmation of identity at least twice: by participating in the ringing tour as a young child and by telling me that story as an elderly man. Over time, eigensinn molds identities. After a few experiments with it, to determine what works best, Otto soon discovered that particular tactics afforded the most viable means to survive everyday life with the desired self in tact, perhaps even to promote it.[2] Accumulated over the course of his life, these experiments gradually became habits: highly individualized *modus operandi* for everyday living that were addictive precisely because they confirmed the kind of person he hoped to become, because they preserved that façade of false coherence. Because they were developed in the process of cultivating the self, these idiosyncratic habits themselves came, in the long term, to define that self. By telling me this story, Otto was trying honestly to do his part for the interview process: to describe those critical moments in his biography when he worked out his identity.

Like the everyday life it seeks to circumvent, eigensinn is fundamentally and necessarily contradictory. It is clearly instrumental, though not in the classic sense of atomized individuals making explicitly rational choices to maximize their own benefit. It seeks to reshape society into a context in which a desired self could thrive, and does so by cultivating that self as if society already confirmed it. Eigensinn in this form is classically modern. It expresses a desire for social mobility without suggesting a real prospect or plan for it. It responds to a rapidly changing environment that is potentially if not explicitly resistant to reasonable human agency. Eigensinn is still a form of creative agency, for it involves human beings acting meaningfully in the world to reshape that world. Yet it can never be agency in the classic historical sense of willful, self-conscious intentionality. Self-deceptive, it is all too aware of its impact on the world and yet acts as if that outcome had not been planned in advance or intended as such. Eigensinn is a *slave's trope* (Gates 1988): it tweaks the nose of more powerful authorities, and then plays the fool or innocent to shield itself from retribution. From this perspective, both eigensinn and herrschaft give daily life its everyday quality. Both require normalcy to function properly.

Eigensinn is only one mode of behavior in everyday life, conviviality is only one site where it is applied, and Nazi eigensinn is only one application of that technique. There has never been much doubt that forms of Nazi eigensinn existed (though they have never before been studied as such). My contribution is to suggest that Nazi eigensinn actually shaped and drove that Nazi revolution. (I discuss the question of ethical vs. historical responsibility for Nazi eigensinn in Bergerson 2004.) In 1988, Lutz Niethammer framed the history of everyday life by applying an oft-quoted assertion of Rosa Luxemburg from 1913: "people do not make history of their own free will, but they do make it themselves" (p. 11).[3] Scholars have long struggled to determine how to apply that concept in practice (e.g., Lukács 2002). To be ordinary, by definition, means that the scope of one's agency feels constrained by circumstances out of one's control. Yet everyday life is filled with multiple and often conflicting circumstances. A form of contingent agency, eigensinn manipulates these circumstances to create a limited degree of autonomy. Thus the exigencies of everyday life simultaneously circumscribe and facilitate its impact on history. In order to reconstruct how ordinary people negotiated the particularly challenging circumstances of the Third Reich, then, we need to focus on the historicity of cultural practices. By studying how ordinary people changed their customs, we rediscover how they changed history.

On the one hand, this historicity is hidden from discovery by the fact that eigensinn tends to be lodged more in bodies than in discourse. My interview partners found it hard to explain in words how they negotiated the absurd contradictions of modern life. Yet the historical process of cultivating these particular kinds of selves left residual evidence embodied in those same cultural practices and the stories that relate to them. Rather than concentrating on narrative in isolation, I looked instead at the artifact of habits buried in *body narratives*: stories about habits creatively enacted. Moreover, the subjects' behavior during the interview process often mimicked the original act: they raised their hand to say *heil hitler!* or looked both ways before listening to a foreign station on an imaginary radio. Often, they laughed awkwardly when the interview process forced them to reflect in discourse on the contradictions between the ideal and the real, the body and consciousness (see also Benjamin 1968). On the other hand, this historicity is hidden from discovery by a culture of normalcy. Officially, eigensinn was an *open secret* (Sedgwick 1990). Everyone knew but no one wished to think critically about it, because those cultural regimes of knowledge and ignorance facilitated everyone's maneuverability in everyday life. When they laughed, we had come close to the indecent: to publicly speak about the essence of eigensinn. But that habitual response also dismissed eigensinn as mere curiosity, returning it back to the body with a ritual act.

In the example of the ringing tour, it would be easy to conclude that eigensinn only inverted existing power relations and cultural norms temporarily, that it ultimately served to reinforce herrschaft once the ritual process had concluded. Victor Turner in the 1960s did not see much in the way of historical consequences emerging from the Franciscan revolt against the medieval church or the contemporary hippie revolts on college campuses including his own. Since the 1960s, however, an interdisciplinary body of scholars has struggled with these questions in particular: the historicity of multifaceted forms of everyday revolt. Cultural anthropologists and historians began to explore how such anti-structural inversions could transform culture, by reinventing traditions, for example, with the return to structure (Hobsbaum and Ranger 1983; Sahlins 1985). Trying to balance synchronous culture with diachronous history, Pierre Bourdieu (1989) proposed the notion of *habitus*, a mediating cultural logic that gives meaning to experience, is enacted through regular ritual acts, and yet is flexible in terms of how and when it is applied.

It took longer to theorize how cultural practices could alter or overthrow a social, economic, or political system; a difficulty which emerged because most of these scholars were looking for an unlikely outcome: a social or democratic revolution against colonialism, capitalism, or authoritarianism. Dick Hebdige's study of British *Subcultures* (1979) presumed that the revolutionary threat of the Punk habit of wearing safety pins as jewelry was reabsorbed by capitalism in short order (see also Hall 1980; Hall and Jefferson 1976). Michel de Certeau's study of *The Practice of Everyday Life* (1988) found no revolutions against company mangers or city planners emerging from white-collar petty theft or jaywalking. *Tactics* for everyday survival could only negotiate circumstances set by the *strategies* of established elites; tactics could not alter those circumstances themselves. Bourdieu explicitly limited the causes of revolution in habitus itself to exogenous forces of historical materialism beyond the scope of the agency of ordinary men and women. In the German context, Lüdtke similarly circumscribed the potential of horseplay to generate social revolution among the working classes.

This book frames the disciplinary questions of German historians about everyday life during the Third Reich in this interdisciplinary, cross-cultural debate on the historicity of cultural practices. This approach takes as its frame of reference neither "the representations that men give of themselves, nor the conditions that determine them without their knowledge, but rather what they do and the way they do it: that is, the forms of rationality that organize their ways of doing things . . . and the freedom with which they act within these practical systems, reacting to what others do, modifying the rules of the game, up to a certain point" (Foucault 1978). It "does not try to raise fundamental secular change to a level detached from human agents, occurring behind their backs, as it were. Rather, historical change and continuity are understood as the outcome of action by concrete groups and individuals. Human *social practice* is shifted into the foreground of historical inquiry" (Lüdtke 1995: 6, his emphasis; see also Apter 1992; Comaroff 1992; Harootunian 2000; Lan 1985; Lukács 2002; van Rahden 2000; cf. S. Turner 1994). As a paradigm, practice theories offer a way to integrate the still disparate stories of ordinary people and the Third Reich.

Conversely, German history once again offers a model venue to explore a theoretical paradigm precisely because of its historical uniqueness (Blackbourn and Eley 1984). The typical studies of non-conformity under Hitler (Balfour 1988; Broszat 1983; Kershaw 1983a; Mann 1987; see also reviews by Fitzpatrick and Gellately 1996; Geyer and Boyer 1992; and Müller and Mommsen 1986) disclaim the historical significance of non-conformity because they know only too well that, ultimately, the European resistance movements did not succeed in overturning the Nazi regime. In keeping with the trend in more recent literature (e.g., Fritzsche 1994, 1998; Gellately 2001), this study suggests instead that, even though eigensinn did not result in a systematic and successful resistance movement against the Third Reich, it did generate a systematic and successful revolt against the Weimar Republic. That is, the dynamic cultural practices of everyday life did result in a revolution: it was just fascist and racist in orientation.

Engaging both these interdisciplinary and disciplinary debates, this book tries to demonstrate more precisely how ordinary Hildesheimers helped *enact* and thereby *implement* fascism in the first place (Lüdtke 1995; Sewell 1992). It argues that the dynamic struggle between the tactics of eigensinn and the strategies for herrschaft provided momentum for the Nazi revolution from below. To refer to these behaviors as *resistance* and *participation*, as is often the case in the literature, makes sense in political-ideological terms, but it obfuscates their relatively independent existence in everyday life. The boundary between tactics of eigensinn and strategies for herrschaft also begins to blur once we introduce historicity into cultural practice: as tactics of Nazi eigensinn during the Weimar Republic became strategies for Nazi herrschaft during the Third Reich, as strategies for republican herrschaft became tactics for antifascist eigensinn. We should therefore consider these cultural practices not simply in terms of their political objectives but also as part of a largely symbolic debate in the local public sphere (Gerstenberger 1987; Negt and Kluge 1993; cf. Calhoon 1992; Frazer 1990; Habermas 1981, 1989; Johnson 1993; J. Peters 1993). Since these same acts are expressive, cultivating a particular identity and communicating it to one's friends and neighbors, it would similarly be a mistake to reduce eigensinn simply to *dissent* or *counter-hegemony*, two other terms commonly used in the literature. Ordinary Germans did not so much react to existing power relations and status hierarchies as they acted to colonize their own world (Harootunian 2000; Ross 1995). Through their customs of conviviality, they constituted self and society proactively, laying claim to power and status in the shifting historical sands of the twentieth century. They just acted as if they were ordinary.

Method

Hildesheim is an ideal location for a study of conviviality in the first half of the twentieth century. According to the census of 16 June 1925, Hildesheim closely reflected the demographics of the Weimar Republic (*SDR*, vol. 401, pp. 56–57, 333, 364; see also Gebauer 1950: 176–96). As in the rest of Germany, women (52.5 percent) outnumbered men (47.5 percent) due to higher rates of death among men during the war and the in-migration of women. Interwar Hildesheim was also a town of the young: the interwar generation (those under the age of twenty-five in 1925) comprised 43.7 percent of the population. Although considered by many to be a Catholic island in the Protestant North-German ocean, the majority of the residents in the town of Hildesheim were in fact Protestant (64.3 percent), though high percentages of Catholics could be found in some of the villages in the surrounding countryside. The size of the influential urban Catholic minority (33.1 percent) as well as the small urban Jewish community (1 percent) both corresponded to the religious composition of the Reich as a whole.

Hildesheim's socioeconomic structure, summarized in Table 1, also corresponded to the Reich, though less precisely. According to the same census, Hildesheimers belonged to all major occupational groups: the educated and industrial bourgeoisie, the new and old middle classes, the agricultural, the industrial and domestic proletariat, as well as the unemployed (*SDR* 407: 120, and 404/14: 80–86). To be sure, the first wave of industrialization in Hildesheim after 1871, based in agricultural machinery and food

Table 1

Class Structure in Hildesheim in 1925

Class of (typically male) Head of Household	Hildesheim population	%
Middle classes[a]	9,673	16.5
White collar workers[b]	14,639	25.0
Wage laborers[c]	25,642	43.8
in industry		30.5
no profession[d]	8,568	14.7

[a]*Selbständige*, including the owners and directors of industry and agriculture, master artisans, self-employed, entrepreneurs, tenant farmers, administrators, upper bureaucrats.
[b]*Angestellte/Beamte*, including technical personnel, supervisors, salespersons, office personnel.
[c]*Arbeiter*, including domestic, factory, and support workers (*mithelfende Familienangehörige*).
[d]*Ohne Beruf* including families living off of pensions, inmates in prisons, poor houses and asylums, students or orphans living independent of the family, and people lacking a specific occupation. Unemployed persons are listed under the occupation they last maintained.

processing, was relatively late, gradual, and on a smaller scale than in a metropolis like Hamburg or heavily industrialized regions such as the Ruhr; still, it was more significant than in most rural villages. The typical worker in Hildesheim labored in a small handicraft shop rather than in a large factory (Riekenberg 1982: 8–23; Uthoff 1967). According to the 1925 census, 44 percent of the employed breadwinners in Hildesheim worked in businesses that had fewer than ten employees. Another 36 percent worked in mid-sized businesses: i.e., that had between ten and one hundred employees. This circumstance gave Hildesheim the atmosphere of a town of small artisanal shops and corner stores. At the same time, one-fifth of the employed breadwinners (19 percent) worked in businesses with more than one hundred employees, and there were several large factories employing hundreds or even thousands of workers, including Senking for stoves, Wetzell for plastics, Ahlborn for agricultural machinery, and a sugar refinery (*SDR* 416/7b: 62–78, even pages).[4]

This wide range of industrial organization can also be seen in terms of the kinds of work done in Hildesheim. As Table 2 illustrates, the town's economy was relatively diversified, not excessively dependent on any single branch of production. A plurality of Hildesheim's interwar population was involved in the industrial and commercial branches of the economy, but many other areas of production were also significant to the local economy: even more so if one were to include the immediate countryside with its heavy focus on agricultural production (*SDR* 407: 32, 66–67). Hildesheim's

Table 2
Employment by Branch in Hildesheim in 1925

Branch of Industry	% of Hildesheim population
Agriculture & Forestry	1.6
Industry & Handwork	44.0
Machinery & Automobile	10.6
Nourishment & Confections	5.0
Clothing	5.4
Construction	8.0
Trade & Transportation	23.5
Administration, etc.	8.8
Health, etc.	3.0
Domestic Service	4.4
No Occupation	14.7

moderate industrialization perhaps prevented the formation of an especially revolutionary proletariat; still, Hildesheim contained an otherwise complete range of classes and industries, each with sizable minorities in the town.

The second major wave of industrial expansion in Hildesheim during the Third Reich did not significantly alter the diversity of the local economy, though it did increase the scale of production. In 1934, the Vereinigte Deutsche Metallwerke set up shop in Hildesheim, to produce parts for airplanes, and Bosch established the Trillke-Werke in 1937, to make parts for tanks and military trucks. Each employed thousands of workers and helped Hildesheim recover from the Depression. Many other branches of local industry benefited from rearmament as well. After 1933, Wetzell filled only military contracts: for airplane parts, gas masks, and rubber dinghies. After 1939, Senking produced tank parts, Ahlborn torpedoes, and the sugar factory glycerin, an explosive. Even the canning factory Warnecke grew on account of military contracts. Remilitarization shifted the center of the local economy towards metal working in the 1930s, employing a quarter of the workers already by 1939, but Hildesheim still preserved its traditionally diverse economic structure (Notzen-Hillmann 1989: 131–38; Teich 1979; Uthoff 1967: 48–53).

Hildesheim is representative only of a particular kind of communal unit, what Mack Walker called a *home town* (1971). In 1925, the Reich population was divided more or less evenly between city (26.7 percent), town (37.7 percent), and village (35.6 percent). In spite of urbanization, the relative population of Germans living in provincial towns remained approximately the same from 1875 to 1925, while there was a demonstrable shift from rural to metropolitan regions in both absolute and relative terms (*Wirtschaft und Statistik* 6/9 [14 May 1926]: 292–94). In spite of the losses during the war, Hildesheim's population grew from fifty-one thousand to sixty-three thousand between 1910 and 1933, primarily due to in-migration (*SDR,* vol. 401, pp. 56–57; vol. 455/14, p. 53). This growth was facilitated in part by the incorporation of outlying villages (Moritzberg in 1911, Steuerwald in 1912, and Neuhof and Drispenstedt later in 1938). Interwar Hildesheim's population thus stood at the center of the range for provincial towns (2,000–100,000). Neither a metropolis nor a village, Hildesheim is representative of that third Germany composed of mid-sized, provincial urban centers.

Hanoverian since Napoleon, and Prussian since Bismarck, Hildesheim faced multiple and often shifting allegiances in its long and complicated history. These various episodes were still evident in the interwar years, to the informed viewer, in the names of the different historical districts. As illustrated in Figure 1 (see Introduction: "New Manners"), Hildesheim's urban landscape included the medieval Altstadt and Neustadt with their half-timbered houses and Romanesque churches; the nineteenth-century, bourgeois suburbs of the Oststadt, Kalenberger Graben, and Galgenberg with their brick walk-ups and villas; the villages Altes Dorf and Steuerwald whose names were changed in popular usage to the Nordstadt once the area north of the railroad station was transformed so radically by industrialization; along with similar working-class villages of Moritzberg to the west and Marienberger Höhe to the south (Voss 1928: 102; Wolff 1989: 77–81). Framed in an historical hierarchy of value, this narrative of historic districts is part of the way that Hildesheimers represented the town as *Alt-Hildesheim* (following Azaryahu 1988, 1990).

The official narrative of urban geography also included the notion that some of the neighborhoods were *defended communities* (Suttles 1972), districts presumed to be socially homogenous in order for outsiders and insiders to orient themselves in a chaotic and potentially dangerous landscape. For instance, I often heard the prejudice that the Nordstadt was a working-class district and Marienburger Höhe a den of thieves (*Klemmputz*). In reality, Hildesheim was relatively well integrated residentially, with a variety of different kinds of people within close proximity of one another and many Hildesheimers living in multiple locations in town over the course of their lives. In part, I selected this kind of community because it was large enough to give residents the opportunity to know only some of their neighbors, and small enough to offer the fantasy of knowing them all.

I also chose this kind of community because of the centrality of these kinds of communities in shaping the culture of everyday life in Germany more generally (Allen 1965; Applegate 1990; Koshar 1986; Walker 1971; cf. Harootunian 2000). Prior researchers from the United States have often focused on the towns from this region of north-central Germany. Rudy Koshar studied Marburg (1986). Peter Fritzsche studied Braunschweig, Osnabrück, Oldenburg, Celle, Lüneburg, and Goslar (1990). William Sheridan Allen studied Northeim (1965; see also von Saldern 1989). In contrast to these many other locations, however, Hildesheim did not contain a university, though it did contain many schools; and service and administration did not dominate Hildesheim's economy, though it did comprise a significant portion of it. Hildesheim contained a more diversified social structure than any other town in the region.

Uniquely typical of the Reich, Hildesheimers consistently voted in almost the same percentages as Germans did more generally. This fact is particularly worth noting in the case of the Nazi party, since Hildesheimers so often insist that their town was not a center of Nazi activism. During Reichstag elections, the National Socialist German Workers' Party (NSDAP) in Hildesheim was almost always just a few points behind national returns. The one minor exception was the election of 14 September 1930, when the NSDAP received 18.3 percent of the vote nationally but inched over that figure in Hildesheim to 18.9 percent. On 31 July 1932, 34.2 percent of Hildesheimers voted for the Nazi party, and on 5 March 1933, 37.7 percent did. These figures were, once again, just a few points lower than the national results of 37.2 percent and 43.9 percent. The NSDAP thus became the single largest party in Hildesheim in two out of the three final Reichstag elections of the Weimar Republic. These electoral results suggest that Hildesheim was quite typical in its strong support for Hitler. By contrast, the differences between local and national results for the Communist Party were also consistently lower, but usually by a larger amount (4–10 percent). The Communist Party never had anywhere near as significant a following in Hildesheim as the Nazis (cf. Rohe 1992: 296–97; Knott 1980: 13; Thimm 1999: 11–22).

Hildesheim's uniqueness did not go unnoticed among contemporaries. Local chronicler Adolf Vogeler described Hildesheim in 1929 as follows:

> Even before the war, our town was the mirror of our great Fatherland, perhaps more so than any other [town] of the same size; not just in economic terms, because of its fortuitous combination of a world-class industrial sector and significant trade with its proximate, neighboring, blossoming agricultural sector; but also because of the curious nature of the population which found its expression in the mixture of Christian confessions and in the almost equal representation of all major party-political directions. (iii)

Vogeler was writing in the spirit of local boosterism, yet he was also roughly correct. To its inhabitants, Hildesheim represented the definition of normalcy. As a trope of moderation, it can be seen in a variety of contexts: e.g., in their description of their own geology, geography, and weather (Bötel ca. 1911; Dienemann 1964; Evers 1964: 55–62; Hauthal ca. 1911; Seeger 1969; Uthoff 1967; cf. Bötel 1924: 38; and idem in Pfeiffer ca. 1911: 77–78). In political terms, this culture of normalcy was revived after the war to explain why ordinary Hildesheimers were not responsible for Nazi crimes against humanity. As Jürgen Ludewig insisted, "Nothing happened here. Hildesheim was relatively peaceful and quiet, you know, also during the Nazi era. No one got shot here by—by SA men or by communists. That never came about. The people were more or less all *balanced*. No, that did not take place here" (*ausgleichend;* G/107a R/50, my emphasis). Hildesheim is useful for this particular study because its inhabitants believed so strongly that they were ordinary Germans: typical and representative of Germany writ large, politically common and moderate, and ontologically inhabitants of a place that, at least in the modern period, did not make history.

For the purposes of an ethnographic history, Hildesheim is also representative in an experiential sense. On their streets, Hildesheimers encountered a wide variety of different people: members of different classes, confessions, and parties, as well as Slavic seasonal laborers, flashers, and prostitutes. They lived through the same wars, revolutions, inflations, depressions, coups, violence, terror, and bombings along with most Central Europeans. And they faced the full panoply of pressures due to social differences, modernization, and commodification. This book views these events from their perspective to see how ordinary people responded to such extraordinary times.

Like all historical sources, many of mine are problematic when taken in isolation or without critical reflection. By no means have I eliminated all bias on my or their part, nor historical inaccuracies due to failures of memory, translation, or interpretation. I tried to minimize those inaccuracies by evaluating multiple kinds of sources as well as divergent perspectives. I not only compared what these different sources had to say about similar issues but also compared the views of different informants to others of the same kind. Where possible, I even compared what my interview partners said to other interviewers (SAH 902/1). I was particularly sensitive to contradictions between and within sources that, to my mind, disclosed otherwise hidden meanings.

That all said, I relied primarily on narrative interviews to write this book, and these sources do have particular strengths and weaknesses. Most scholars tend to believe that the historical past cannot be understood outside the politics of memory, particularly in the case of the Third Reich; oral histories therefore seem to pose insurmountable challenges to the historian. It is my claim that we can best understand the problem of memory in the context of its original, everyday-life history, best reconstructed from the subjective viewpoint offered by oral history because it locates world history in the context of how ordinary people lived their own lives. I base that claim on the fact that *habit memories* (Connerton 1989) like self-cultivation are relatively consistent in spite of and precisely because of the many revolutionary changes in German politics and society. I address the question of what narrative interviews can reliably tell us about everyday life in my final chapter on epistemologies of the Holocaust, where I make sense of Nazi-era memories in terms of Nazi-era history. Here, I would like to describe the mechanics of the interview process in more detail.

From the middle of 1992 to the end of 1994, I conducted a series of four interviews with each of a cohort of elderly Hildesheimers who were born between 1900 and 1930 and had lived in the town of Hildesheim for a significant number of years between 1900 and 1950. By and large, this cohort was proscribed for me by pragmatic limitations of time, place, generation, human frailty, interest, and feasibility. Where I was able to find interview partners, I took them until my time, money, and enthusiasm ran out. By April of 1994, I had amassed a collection of just under two hundred hour-long audio cassettes recording the memories of thirty-six individuals: twenty-seven of whom I had met in Hildesheim, six in Israel, and three in the United States. Had I used a purely random method for gaining access to interview partners, I would have had far fewer representatives of minority groups, such as Catholics and especially Jews, whose memories were crucial. Instead, this *surviving sample* (Hudson 2000: 174) represented the major social distinctions in interwar Hildesheim.

Half of my interview partners were men, half were women. They were born between 1899 and 1930. Their average age was eighty in January 1993; their roughly even distribution is illustrated in Table 3; most have since passed away. Most (69 percent) were raised in families with two or three children, some (22 percent) in larger families of four to six children. Only one had nine children and only two were the sole offspring of their parents.

Of the Christians, two-thirds were Protestants and one-third were Catholics, as in interwar Hildesheim. One-fifth of the total cohort were Jews. Another two individuals were the children of mixed marriages: one Catholic–Protestant, one Jewish–Christian. This large divergence from the actual size of the Jewish community (1 percent) was necessary since I was investigating the Nazi revolution. When asked if they had been raised religiously, only half of my interview partners answered positively; many also understood this question to refer to whether they regularly attended church

Table 3
Age and Gender Distribution of Interview Partners

Year	Men	Women	Total
1899–04	3	3	6
1905–09	4	5	9
1910–14	2	1	3
1915–19	4	4	8
1920–24	5	2	7
1924–30	0	3	3
Total	18	18	36

Table 4
Class Distribution of Interview Partners

Class	Interview Partners and their Spouses	Interview Partners' Parents
Owning Middle Class	0%	13%
Educated Middle Class	18%	4%
Old Middle Class	4%	10%
New Middle Class	20%	8%
Artisans	11%	6%
Workers	10%	18%
No "Estate"	26%	1%
Housewife only	11%	40%

or synagogue, but subsequently denied that their family had had strong spiritual attachment to God or their faith.

For the sole purpose of assessing the class diversity of my sample, I categorized my interview partners and their parents in terms of their objective relationship to the means of production. As seen in Table 4, most occupational groups were appropriately represented:[5] the owning and the educated bourgeoisie, the old and the new middle classes, artisans and workers, housewives, and even one individual without an "estate" (*Stand*). Politically, my interview partners represented all major Weimar parties with the sole exclusion of communists (though several had personal connections there), just as they represented most postures within the Nazi system: resistance fighters, collaborators, conformists, non-conformists, inner migrants, convinced Nazis, and many who saw themselves as apolitical.

Almost all spoke High German as their primary language in public and in private. Some mentioned dialect- or other language-use at home: Yiddish, Polish, Hebrew, and (mostly) the local rural dialect. Some 72 percent were born in town, and the remaining quarter moved there at an early age. They lived in 129 separate locations: half in the core of town (the Altstadt and the Oststadt), about one-fifth in the social periphery (Nordstadt, Neustadt), and another sixth in the geographic periphery (Moritzberg, Marienburger Höhe, Galgenberg, Grosse Venedig/Kalenberger Graben). One-third of them never moved out of town at all, an additional third moved out of town and subsequently moved back to Hildesheim, and the final third moved away and stayed away, usually due to forced emigration. Insofar as my sampling procedure tended to exclude those Hildesheimers who left Hildesheim on their own to seek greener pastures elsewhere, the permanence of Hildesheimers should not be overstated, and certainly not in any one neighborhood: half of the interview partners moved three or more times to new permanent homes, even if just within the bounds of Hildesheim. Only three interview partners remained in the house where they had been born. Because of the very small scope of most neighborhoods, even moves within Hildesheim required establishing new neighborly relations. The parents of my interview partners were also more mobile than I suspected. Of twenty-one fathers who had a record in the town registry (unfortunately not very reliable: SAH 102/7427), only three had never registered a new address since their birth or arrival in town. The rest had moved on average four to five times in and around Hildesheim before my interview partner was even born, one as many as twelve times.

The most serious problem with the selection process concerned those murdered in the Holocaust.[6] On 30 December 1992, one Jewish Hildesheimer wrote an eloquent letter explaining why he did not want to participate in my research project:

It is not we, the survivors, who are the real witnesses. We survivors are not only a small, but also an abnormal minority: we are those who did not reach the deepest point of the pit due to the betrayal of duty, skill or luck. Those who reached it, those who looked into the face of the Medusa, can never return to report, or they have become mute. (cf. Levi 1988: 83–84)

The history of Jews in Germany is over, this former resident concluded: "repressed, forgotten—forgive me, but I have no desire to begin a search for times since past." I could hardly compel him to speak, but his attitude is misguided as a methodological assertion. The Jews of Hildesheim shared the same local culture of conviviality with their non-Jewish neighbors because it was precisely this mechanism that they all used to negotiate their similarities and differences. Surviving Jews and even their non-Jewish neighbors had relied on these same customs as much as the silent or silenced Jews. Moreover, historians can best gain insight into the ordinary processes of everyday life through memories of behavior under extraordinary circumstances, when "silent normality breaks down" (Niethammer 1995: 279). Precisely because he survived exclusion and murder, this Hildesheimer could have been a very insightful source to help us understand how ordinary people had helped place their neighbors and themselves on the road to Auschwitz.

My interview partners and I used our first interview session to get to know each other more personally. The initial session focused on general biographic data and was recorded on paper. The second and third interviews were recorded on tape and focused on neighbors and friends respectively. In the last interview, we shifted our attention to political events, as traditionally defined, and tried to relate conviviality to them. We also met informally afterwards to look at personal documents or images (reproduced with their permission), to discuss the interviews, and to ask questions.

I opened the interview on neighborliness by asking them detailed, systematic questions about the specific spaces of their residences at different stages in their lives (usually every seven years); the interview on friendships worked in much the same way. Systematically recording the names of neighbors and friends introduced me to these spaces and relationships, helped my interview partner revive memories, and led us both to rich anecdotes about conviviality: *memory traces* (Benjamin 1968) grounded in concrete local-historical circumstance yet mediated through a subjective perspective. The more I focused our attention on narrating their memories of their neighbors, the more they trusted me, the more we were able to break through the "conspiracy of silence" surrounding this particular history, and the more closely our discussions approached their actual, past habits (Connerton 1989: 37; Krondorfer 1995: 118, 163–65). The interviews also corresponded to the very distinction at stake in this book: the first three presumed the myths of normalcy in which friends and neighbors lived their lives insulated from world history, while the last interview undermined the myths of normalcy by relating those convivial relations to larger historical events and processes. Though politics entered into our discussions during the first three interviews, the last interview of the series was nonetheless often the most challenging (Bergerson 2002b).

Whether garnered through a personal encounter, through reading their words in public or private documents, or through looking at their photographs, I refer to this vast array of "informants" collectively as *Hildesheimers*. I refer to the specific group of people with whom I had the pleasure to talk personally, and who hold pride of place in this study, as my *interview partners*.[7] I use a consistent set of pseudonyms for the latter. The fact that I have relied upon so many divergent primary and secondary sources demands that I address theoretical and methodological issues directly in the text. This is an unfamiliar practice in historical scholarship, but it is becoming increasingly common, especially as more scholars work on the interdisciplinary margins of our discipline. I have therefore placed most references in the text itself in the style of the social sciences and humanities, as described in note 2 of the introduction.

Notes

Introduction: New Manners

1. Kaplan 1998: ch. 5; Rosenstrauch 1988: 76.

2. G/157b R/150, G/159a R/200. These abbreviations refer to the tape, side, and cycle number on which the excerpt can be found on the relevant audio cassettes. Here, G/157b R/150 refers to cassette number 157, side b, of this research project on conviviality (*Geselligkeit*; SAH Best. 904–2) at approximately 150 out of 420 cycles into the tape. Although I typed transcripts for these interviews, I refer to cycles on the tapes, rather than pages from the transcripts, because the latter can never be as accurate as the former and the former is the actual source. Copies of tapes and transcriptions are available from the author, though the masters reside at the Hildesheim town archives and are under the administration of its director. Typically references will appear in the text. For archival documents, I provide the institution and collection number where the source can be found (e.g., SAH 102/3019). I describe the document itself directly in the text. The collection title can be found in the bibliography. For newspaper or journal articles, I provide the issue or volume number and the page (e.g., 142: 5). I mention the year and topic in the text. The title of the newspaper or journal could appear in either location. Unless otherwise noted, images refer to my personal collection of reproductions of images belonging to my interview partners: D/345 would refer to slide (*Dia*) 345. To protect their anonymity, I do not credit these individuals.

3. G/94b R/135.

4. Bauman 1989; Kaplan 1998; Reed and Fischer 1989; Rosenstrauch 1988.

5. Schmid 2002; Schneider 1998: III. 2; cf. Addicks 1988; Jan 1968a and 1968b, 1988; Hein 1988; Teich 1979.

6. Fritzsche 1998; Rosenstrauch 1988.

7. Herbert 1983; cf. Goldhagen 1996.

8. Broszat 1981; Kaplan 1998; Petropolous 1998; Schoenbaum 1966.

9. Cf. Arendt 1951; Passerini 1992.

10. I have already described the role of the mass media in the Nazi revolution from the perspective of everyday life: for daily papers and the radio see Bergerson 1997 and 2001 respectively. This book will not address several other arenas for conviviality that are closely related to normalcy and the Third Reich: public festivals, art, architecture, film, local characters, the visits of national statesmen to Hildesheim as well as some of the earlier history of exchange relations and migrant populations. These issues are inextricably imbedded in the broader history of Alt-

Hildesheim, the *imagined community* (B. Anderson 1983) with which almost all of my interview partners strongly identified, and which will be the subject of a forthcoming book.

11. Browning 1998; Gellately 2001.

12. Lüdtke 1995: 5, his emphasis.

1. Civility

1. Even cross-dressing had become one of the options for women in Hildesheim. Thekla Mestmacher claimed that both girls and boys wore school caps: only the girls did not have caps with peaks (*Schirm;* D/908; G/13a R/180). But later, she showed me a photo from her youth in which she wore a boy's cap and man's tie. She judged herself "totally ugly." Clearly, the attitudes of her parents' generation still remained strong in her memory. Moreover, gender was still evident for those who were cross-dressing. When Georg Brzezinski showed me a photo of his sister's first day at school, it was obvious that she was a girl in spite of the school cap. Still, he explained that girls did not actually wear school caps: his sister must have borrowed his (cf. D/1294, G/192a R/300). Though she had broken the rules of headdress, George could dismiss his sister's behavior as so much eigensinn.

2. Niveau

1. All of my interview partners agreed that Catholics and Protestants were uniformly distributed around town: both on its streets and in its buildings. This conclusion is confirmed by the few existing archival records of parishioners: "Strassenverzeichnis der St. Bernwardsgemeinde und Seelenzahl, 1937–8" in the unnumbered file, St. Bernward in Hildesheim: Allgemeine Angelegenheiten insbes. die kirchliche Statistik, 1909–55 at the BAH as well as the more detailed "Kirchenvorstandwählerliste, St. Godehardi-Gemeinde, Hildesheim, 1911 and 1937" at the Pfarrarchiv St. Godehard, also not numbered.

3. The Stroll

1. Though many of my oldest interview partners (those born before 1914) did not remember this custom at all or remembered it unclearly, these events stand at the very brink of the earliest memories of my oldest interview partners. There may also have been more of a class distinction at work in the prewar context. Among these older Hildesheimers, the lower classes were also less able to recall the stroll as an institutionalized custom or were explicit about the fact that they did not participate in it (G/45b R/180, G/68a R/275, G/141a R/355; cf. G/21b R/00, G/71a R/00, G/71b R/20).

2. Disparaging the size of his heimat, Gerhard Mock called them *The Upper 100* (G/111b R/95).

3. I interviewed Sofia by mail using a written questionnaire because we could not arrange a personal meeting. I do not include her as part of my thirty-six interview partners because she alone responded in writing. Her comments here can

be found in Questionnaire 2, Section G, Question 2e, copies of which are available from the author.

5. Coordination

1. The exclamation mark denotes an emphatic insistence on an older tradition—just as political a statement as *heil hitler!*

2. When behavior in the present corresponds to expectations based on prior experiences, one experiences a sense of cultural *conjuncture*. When past experience and present behavior do not correspond, either due to a shift in custom or a change in circumstance, one experiences a sense of cultural *disjuncture* (Connerton 1989; Kren and Rappoport 1980; Plato 1985; Sahlins 1985; Schutz and Luckmann 1973; Scott 1991: 793; Ten Dyke 2001).

3. The term derives from the French Revolution at the end of the eighteenth century: the Civil Constitution of the Clergy had forced church figures to swear an oath of allegiance to the new Republic. Many of those recalcitrant clergy who refused to swear paid with their lives.

6. Polarization

1. A special note of thanks goes to Hans-Dieter Schmid, who generously provided me access to copies of all of the documents he collected, including the trial records, as well as to the Archiv der Sozial Demokratie, Bonn, and the Bundesarchiv in Potsdam, Koblenz, and Zwischenarchiv Dahlwitz-Hoppegarten, who permitted me to view his copies of the files rather than requiring me to go to those archives in person. These sources are all listed in the bibliography with an asterisk.

2. See also the Report of the District Attorney (*Oberstaatsanwalt*) to the People's Court about the miner Heinrich Malessa on 12 March 1938 and the Judgment against him on 14 November 1938 in the same file. Yet another group, centered around the worker Alfons Reinecke, listened to Radio Moscow, but the documentation about this matter is very limited (BA-P NJ 9662, Bd. 2, November 1936).

3. He was probably a Walloon rather than Flemish.

4. He may have been incorrect in terms of the timing of these events. He claims that he was rehired in March 1934, but for him to be able to see Braun get arrested in September in 1933, as he claimed, he had to have been rehired in March 1933.

5. The fact that Braun was not really a communist does not belie Bernhard's pride at participating in what he believed to have been a Popular Front. To be sure, he had also read Schmid's article, and may here be simply reiterating an official narrative rather than his personal memories; but the thesis of the Popular Front certainly corresponded to his experience or else he would have denied it, as he did many other elements of official history during my interviews with him.

6. Bernhard listed them as Franz Engelke, Hans Höberling, and Josef Hesse. The Judgment in Berlin lists them as Eger, Engelke, and Hess. The local Gestapo's use of physical and psychological terror is well documented: see the Reports of Erich

Bruschke, Gustav Hoppe, Minna and Erich Braun, Wilhelm and Getrud Heitmann, Fritz and Anna Henze, Dietrich Disslich, and Hermann Jürgens to the Criminal Police in Hildesheim from 23 May to 14 August 1947 about the vicious interrogation methods of Gestapo Officer Kurt Wenzel, the most notorious officer in the anti-socialist department, in BA-K Z42 VII/1851; "Aussage des Parteisekretärs Gustav Hoppe in der Sache gegen Gestapo-Leiter in Hildesheim, Leitzmann im Jahre 1936–37," 29 January 1948, VVNH NL Teich; the anonymous postwar report, "Vernehmungen durch die Gestapo" in *idem.;* as well as G/124b, R/230, Teich 1979, and Thimm 1999:73–82. In the particular case of these three men, however, Bernhard claimed that the Gestapo did not beat them but did interrogate them for hours at a time "with a dazzling light in their face."

7. Patriarchal presumptions about gender also helped the judges and prosecutors to determine the degree to which individual cases were matters of real politics or mere conviviality. See Judgment D (pp. 17, 19), Judgment B against Hartung (p. 8), and the Judgment against Gustav Voss (pp. 29–30, 33–35).

7. Administration

1. As a system of shared conventions for referring to authentic experience, language can never assure its users that a given symbol (a *signifier*) reflects an actual subjective experience (the *signified*): for instance, whether two people actually see the same color when they each look at a red rose and refer to that rose as red. Yet particular historical circumstances are exacerbating the philosophical limitations of language when two people, both wearing a swastika, wondered whether the other was sincerely committed to Nazi ideals. The more that ordinary people adorned themselves with Nazi symbols out of convenience rather than conviction, the more they effectively disengaged those signifiers (like the swastika) from the signified (sincere Nazi convictions). As Nazi symbols were increasingly used to obfuscate authentic attitudes about the Nazi regime, it became increasingly impossible to measure them absolutely. It is all the more impossible to do so decades later.

2. Some Hildesheimers suggested that the stroll declined in importance by the mid-1930s due to the fact that residents lacked the money to spend on such informal convivial activities, participated instead in formal activities of sociability like the HJ, or because the Nazis did not approve of such "degenerate" activities. More likely, they simply grew out of this adolescent activity or, as Jews, were no longer welcome there personally (G/3b R/370, G/136a R/60, G/117a R/80). Johanna Ernst said that she took the stroll after she stopped the activities associated with the Association of German Girls and even met her husband there in 1937 during a blackout (G/131a R/315, G/132b R/60).

3. A similar example of the administrative management of racial differences can be seen in the case of Catholic services in Slavic languages in the St. Magdalene Church. See BAH GII (neu) 828: Bischöfliche Generalvikariate Rundschreiben, Nr. 7646, 23 July 1942; Aktenvermerk betr. Ukrainergottesdienst in St. Magdalenen in Hildesheim, 17 July 1943; and Michael Moskalik, Berlin, to the Bischöfliche Generalvikariate, 6 July 1944. For statistics on Ukrainians in the region, see the records of the Hildesheim Employment Office found in BAH GII (neu) 828, Bishop of Hildesheim to the Apostolic Visitator, Berlin, 6 March 1942. The Trade Surveillance

Office also distinguished between civilian and military forced laborers for West Europeans, between adults and children for East Europeans, and between Germans, foreigners, and criminals (e.g., SAH 808-1/22 Ahlborn, 1944, Arbeitslager).

Appendix: A Ringing Tour

1. German historians use this term but it is somewhat of a misnomer for scholars in other disciplines, since non-historians often treat structures as more static while the polycratic model of the Nazi state has always placed agency, process, and temporality at its conceptual core. German historians also use the term *functionalism* but that is also a misnomer since this revolutionary process is fundamentally dysfunctional.

2. Otto arguably used the ringing tour to feel like he belonged in his neighborhood in spite of sociological differences, while he used different forms of eigensinn to retaliate against the bourgeois adults who often derided him for his lack of good breeding. I discuss Otto's tactics for dealing with the problem of class in Chapter 8, "Epistemologies." My point here is that Otto used eigensinn to negotiate the problem of class flexibly, moving between identifications with class and neighborhood, sociability and conviviality, as situation and self demanded.

3. Cf. Ginzburg 1985: 48, who traces this quotation to Karl Marx in error; see also Röhr 1995: 330–31. To be sure, social structures can come to feel beyond the control of individual agents even in societies that are relatively traditional and small in scale simply because they are abstract and resistant to any one agent's selfish interests. By contrast, the culture of normalcy involves a rejection of the particularly Western, particularly modern conception of history, developed over the course of the nineteenth century, in which the masses learn to take personal responsibility for the grand historical developments of their imagined communities. See my forthcoming history of normalcy in Alt-Hildesheim as well as Bergerson 2002a, and Harootunian 2000.

4. I generated these figures by averaging the number of workers per business within isolated branches of the economy. These figures were most accurate for those branches with only a few businesses, and the tendency of such an analysis will be to overemphasize mid-sized companies over the extremes of larger and smaller companies, but because each branch was subdivided in great detail, this is still a reasonable approximation of the structure of the local workplace.

5. These charts are valid only as a representation of my interview partners as a cohort. They do not depict actual generational changes: for instance, a disappearance of elites, or a rise in those without a profession. In order to aggregate the data for purposes of selection only, my overly simplistic assessment of class identities ignores the subjective and enacted components of identity, temporary or permanent upward or downward mobility over the course of a lifetime, and the various relationships on which one could base identity. See Katznelson and Zolberg 1986: 13–22.

6. I was also unable to include in this cohort representatives from several types of Hildesheimers who would have been instructive in a study of neighborliness and friendship: gay men and lesbians, Roma and Sinti, Polish migrant workers, tourists, exchange students. These groups entered the purview of this study only indirectly through statistics or narrative accounts of them by those who belonged

to the norm. I will have more to say about them in my broader, forthcoming history of normalcy in Alt-Hildesheim.

7. This history would not exist were it not for our collaborative effort to get at the truth of the past. I do not wish to ignore the power relations inherent in the interview process, but I do wish to emphasize the degree to which I helped shape the narratives of the past through the kinds of questions I posed, my body language, and so on.

Sources

Bundesarchiv-Koblenz,[*] Bestand

Z42 VII/1851

Bundesarchiv-Potsdam,[*] Bestand

NJ 1198. 10 0 Js 78/37. Georg Heitmann u. A.

NJ 1215, 10 0 Js 78/37. Georg Heitmann u. A.

NJ 1268. 10 0 Js 78/37. Richard Hartung u. A. Copy in NJ 5620.

NJ 3365. 10 0 J 72/34. Hans Kirk u. A.

NJ 4973. 10 0 Js 78/37. Gustav Voss u. A.

NJ 6783. 10 0 Js 19/38. Heinrich Malessa u. A.

NJ 9662/1. O. J. 572. 33. Johannes Hesse u. A.

NJ 9662, 15 J. 101 2/362. Johannes Hesse u. A.

NJ 15414/1. 17 J 437/35. Hans Pasch u. A.

NJ 17762. 10 0 Js 17/38. Otto Eger u. A.

St 3/321. Reichssicherheitshauptamt Abt. IV.

Z/C 13209. 10 0 Js 117/35. Heinrich Schaper u. A.

Bistumsarchiv Hildesheim, Bestand GII-neu

[n. n.] Strassenverzeichnis der St. Bernwardsgemeinde und Seelenzahl, 1937–8. St. Bernward in Hildesheim. Allgemeine Angelegenheiten insbes. die kirchliche Statistik, 1909–55.

822. Die Seelsorge für ausländische Wanderarbeiter. 1944–45.

823. Die Seelsorge für ausländische Wanderarbeiter. 1944–64.

824. Die Seelsorge der Wallonen. 1944–45.

---

[*]These sources were provided to the author as photocopies with the permission of the archive.

827. Die Seelsorge für italienische Arbeiter. 1944–45.

828. Die Seelsorge für die unierten Ukrainer des griechisch-katholischen Ritus in Deutschland. 1940–66.

Pfarrarchiv St. Godehard, Hildesheim

[n. n.] Kirchenvorstandwählerlist. St. Godehardi-Gemeinde. 1911 and 1937.

Stadtarchiv Hildesheim, Bestand

102/84. Reichstagswahlen, 1912.

102/87. Reihstagswahl am 6. Juni 1920.

102/91. Reichstagswahl am 14. 9. 1930.

102/6316. Türkische Schüler. Schüler aus Buchara.

102/6670. Schund- und Schmutzliteratur.

102/7396. Protokollbücher der Magistrat der Stadt Hildesheim.

102/7427. Melderegister. 1900–45.

102/8360. Schüler-Hilfsdienst zur Strassenreinigung im 1. Weltkreig.

102/9210. Beerdigungsscheine für Wehrmachtsangehörigen auf kirchlichen Friedhöfe.

102/9211. Beerdigungsscheine russischer und polnischer Kriegsgefangener und Privatpersonen.

102/9212. Kriegsgräberlisten.

103/8941. Exhumierung und Umbettung von Leichen, meist Kriegsgefangenen. 1941–48.

103/8942. Jahres-Berichte des Garten- und Friedhofamtes. 1947–76.

500. Lokale Zeitungen (*Evangelischer Gemeindeblatt, Hildesheimer Abendblatt, Hildesheimer Allgemeine Zeitung, Hildesheimer Volksblatt, Hildesheimische Zeitung*).

801. Kruse-Chronik der Stadt Hildesheim. Vols. 3–8. 1900–50.

808–1/22. Arbeitslager in Hildesheim. 1943–45. Copies of Hann. 140 Hildesheim/43. 44. Hauptstaatsarchiv Hannover.

904–1/20–21, 35–37, 42–43, 46–47, and 55–56. "Leben in Hildesheim." Interviews by Stefan Wolff et al. Tape recordings. Hildesheim, Germany. 1988–89. Tapes and transcripts used for this study also available from the author.

904–2. "Geselligkeit in Hildesheim zwischen den Kriegen." 126 audio, 13 written interviews (mostly) by the author. Tape recordings (198 mostly 60-minute cassettes.) Hildesheim, Germany; Tel Aviv and Haifa, Israel; Chicago, Washington, and New York, U.S.A. 1992–94. Tapes and preliminary, uncorrected transcripts also available from the author.

Verein der Verfolgten des Nationalsozialismus-Hildesheim[*]

Nachlass Hans Teich.

General Bibliography[†]

Allen, William Sheridan. 1965. *The Nazi Seizure of Power: The Experience of a Single German Town, 1922–1945.* New York: Franklin Watts.

———. 1992. "The Collapse of Nationalism in Nazi Germany." In *The State of Germany: The National Idea in the Making, Unmaking, and Remaking of a Modern Nation-State,* ed. John Breuilly, 141–53. New York: Longman.

Althusser, Louis. 1971. "Ideology and Ideological State Apparatuses." In *Lenin and Philosophy and Other Essays,* 127–86. New York: Monthly Review Press.

Amann, Anton. 2000. "Alltagssoziologie: ein Forschungsfeld im Wandel." *Soziologische Revue* 23: 17–35.

Anderson, Benedict R. 1983. *Imagined Communities: Reflections on the Origin and Spread of Nationalism.* London: Verso.

Anderson, Elijah. 1990. *Streetwise: Race, Class, and Change in an Urban Community.* Chicago: University of Chicago Press.

Appadurai, Arjun, ed. 1986. *The Social Life of Things: Commodities in Cultural Perspective.* Cambridge: Cambridge University Press.

Applegate, Celia. 1990. *A Nation of Provincials: The German Idea of Heimat.* Berkeley: University of California Press.

Apter, Andrew. 1992. *Black Critics and Kings: The Hermeneutics of Power in Yoruba Society.* Chicago: University of Chicago Press.

Arendt, Hannah. 1951. *The Origins of Totalitarianism.* New York: Harcourt Brace Jovanovich.

———. 1986. *Eichmann in Jerusalem: A Report on the Banality of Evil.* New York: Penguin Books.

Augstein, Rudolf. 1987. *Historikerstreit: die Dokumentation der Kontroverse um die Einzigartigkeit der nationalsozialistischen Judenvernichtung.* München: R. Piper.

Auslander, Leora. 1996. *Taste and Power: Furnishing Modern France.* Berkeley: University of California Press.

Azaryahu, Moaz. 1988. "What Is Remembered: The Struggle over Street Names in Berlin, 1921–1930." *Telaviver Jahrbuch für deutsche Geschichte* 17.

[†]A Hildesheim-specific bibliography follows.

———. 1990. "Renaming the Past: Changes in 'City Text' in Germany and Austria, 1945–1947." *History and Memory* 2, no. 2: 32–53.

Balfour, Michael. 1988. *Withstanding Hitler in Germany, 1933–45*. London: Routledge & Kegan Paul.

Bankier, David. 1992. *The Germans and the Final Solution: Public Opinion under Nazism*. Cambridge: B. Blackwell.

Bauman, Zygmunt. 1989. *Modernity and the Holocaust*. Ithaca, N.Y.: Cornell University Press.

———. 1997. *Postmodernity and Its Discontents*. New York: New York University Press.

Bendix, Regina. 1997. *In Search of Authenticity: The Formation of Folklore Studies*. Madison: University of Wisconsin Press.

Benjamin, Walter. 1968. *Illuminations*. New York: Schocken Books.

———. 1978. *Reflections*. New York: Schocken Books.

Benz, Wolfgang. 1990. *Herrschaft und Gesellschaft im nationalsozialistischen Staat*. Frankfurt am Main: Fischer.

Bergerson, Andrew Stuart. 1993. "'Aber es war eine schöne Zeit'— Erinnerungen einer Nordstädterin." In *Die Welt hinter der Bahn: Auf Spurensuche in der Hildesheimer Nordstadt*, ed. Günther Hein et al., 228–34. Hildesheim: Gerstenberg.

———. 1997. "Integrating in the Accusative: The Daily Papers of Interwar Hildesheim." *Issues in Integrative Studies* 15: 49–76.

———. 2001. "Listening to the Radio in Hildesheim, 1923–53." *German Studies Review* (February): 83–113.

———. 2002a. "Hildesheim in an Age of Pestilence: On the Birth, Death and Resurrection of Normalcy." In *The Work of Memory: New Directions in the Study of German Society and Culture*, ed. Alon Confino and Peter Fritzsche, 107–35. Urbana: University of Illinois Press.

———. 2002b. "Aufklärung durch Erzählung: mündliche Geschichte und bürgerliche Gesellschaft nach Hitler." In *Inspecting Germany: Internationale Deutschland-Ethnographie der Gegenwart*, ed. Bernd Jürgen Warneken and Thomas Hauschild, 222–49. Münster: Lit Verlag.

———. 2004. "Eigensinn, Ethik und das nationalsozialistische *reformatio vitae*." In *Suche nach Nähe: Interpersonale Kommunikation in Deutschland seit dem 19. Jahrhundert*, ed. Moritz Föllmer, 127–56. Stuttgart: Franz Steiner Verlag.

Berman, Sheri. 1997. "Civil Society and the Collapse of the Weimar Republic." *World Politics* 49, no. 3: 401–29.

Bessel, Richard. 1987. *Life in the Third Reich*. Oxford: Oxford University Press.

————. 2003. "Functionalists vs. Intentionalists: The Debate Twenty Years On; or, Whatever Happened to Functionalism and Intentionalism?" *German Studies Review* 24, no. 1: 15–20.

Best, Heinrich. 1989. *Politik und Milieu: Wahl- und Elitenforschung im historischen und interkulturellen Vergleich.* St. Katharinen: Scripta Mercaturae Verlag.

Binder, Gerhart. 1968. *Irrtum und Widerstand: die deutschen Katholiken in der Auseinandersetzung mit dem Nationalsozialismus.* München: Pfeiffer.

Blackbourn, David, and Geoff Eley. 1984. *The Peculiarities of German History: Bourgeois Society and Politics in Nineteenth-Century Germany.* Oxford: Oxford University Press.

Blickle, Peter. 1998. *Obedient Germans? A Rebuttal: A New View of German History.* Charlottesville: University Press of Virginia.

Bloch, Ernst. 1962. *Erbschaft dieser Zeit.* Vol. 4. Frankfurt am Main: Suhrkamp Verlag.

Botz, Gerhard, und Josef Weidenholzer, eds. 1984. *Mündliche Geschichte und Arbeiterbewegung.* Wien: Böhlaus.

Bourdieu, Pierre. 1984. *Distinction: A Social Critique of the Judgment of Taste.* Cambridge, Mass.: Harvard University Press.

————. 1989. *Outline of a Theory of Practice.* Cambridge: Cambridge University Press.

Bracher, Karl Dietrich et al., eds. 1962. *Die nationalsozialistische Machtergreifung: Studien zur Errichtung des totalitären Herrschaftssystem in Deutschland 1933/34.* Köln: Westdeutscher Verlag.

Broszat, Martin. 1981. *The Hitler State.* London: Longman.

————. 1985. "Plädoyer für eine Historisierung des Nationalsozialismus." *Merkur* 39, no. 5:373–84.

Broszat, Martin et al., eds. 1977–83. *Bayern in der NS-Zeit.* Vols. 1–6. München: Oldenbourg.

Broszat, Martin, and Saul Friedländer. 1988. "A Controversy about the Historicization of National Socialism." *Yad Vashem Studies* 19: 1–47.

Browning, Christopher R. 1998. *Ordinary Men: Reserve Police Battalion 101 and the Final Solution in Poland.* New York: HarperPerennial.

Brüggemeier, Franz-Josef. 1983. *Leben vor Ort: Ruhrbergleute und Ruhrbergbau, 1889–1919.* München: Beck.

Busch, Otto. 1954. *Die Farben der Bundesrepublik Deutschland: Ihre Tradition und Bedeutung.* Frankfurt am Main: Bollwerk.

Calhoun, Craig, ed. 1992. *Habermas and the Public Sphere.* Cambridge, Mass.: MIT Press.

Certeau, Michel de. 1988. *The Practice of Everyday Life*. Berkeley: University of California Press.

Childers, Thomas. 1983. *The Nazi Voter: The Social Foundations of Fascism in Germany, 1919–1933*. Chapel Hill: University of North Carolina Press.

Comaroff, Jean. 1985. *Body of Power, Spirit of Resistance: The Culture and History of a South African People*. Chicago: University of Chicago Press.

Comaroff, John, and Jean Comaroff. 1992. *Ethnography and the Historical Imagination*. Boulder: Westview Press.

Confino, Alon, and Peter Fritzsche, eds. 2002. *The Work of Memory: New Directions in the Study of German Society and Culture*. Urbana: University of Illinois Press.

Connerton, Paul. 1989. *How Societies Remember*. Cambridge: Cambridge University Press.

Crew, David F. 1989. *"Alltagsgeschichte: A New Social History from Below?" Central European History* 22, no. 3–4: 394–407.

———, ed. 1994. *Nazism and German Society, 1933–1945*. London: Routledge.

Dahrendorf, Ralf. 1965. *Society and Democracy in Germany*. New York: W. W. Norton.

Davis, Belinda. *Home Fires Burning: Food, Politics, and Everyday Life in World War I*. Chapel Hill: University of North Carolina Press.

Diehl, James M. 1977. *Paramilitary Politics in Weimar Germany*. Bloomington: Indiana University Press.

Diner, Dan. 1990. "Historical Experience and Cognition: Perspectives on National Socialism." *History & Memory* 2, no. 1: 84–110.

Douglas, Mary. 1966. *Purity and Danger: An Analysis of Concepts of Pollution and Taboo*. New York: Praeger.

Dundes, Alan. 1989. *Life Is Like a Chicken Coop Ladder: A Study of German National Character through Folklore*. Detroit: Wayne State University Press.

Edwards, John Carver. 1991. *Berlin Calling: American Broadcasters in Service to the Third Reich*. New York: Praeger.

Eley, Geoff. 1989. "Labor History, Social History, *Alltagsgeschichte*: Experience, Culture and the Politics of the Everyday—A New Direction for German Social History?" *Journal of Modern History* 61: 297–343.

Elias, Norbert. 1978. "Alltag als Bezugspunkt soziologischer Theorie." In *Materialien zur Soziologie des Alltags*, ed. Kurt Hammerich and Michael Klein, 22–29. Opladen: Westdeutscher.

———. 1982. *Power and Civility: The Civilizing Process*. Vols 1 and 2. New York: Pantheon.

———. 1988. "Violence and Civilization: The State Monopoly of Physical Violence and Its Infringement." In *Civil Society and the State: New European Perspectives,* ed. John Keane, 177–98. New York: Verso.

———. 1996. *The Germans: Studies of Power Struggles and the Development of Habitus in the Nineteenth and Twentieth Centuries.* New York: Columbia University Press.

Evans, Richard J. 2001. *Lying about Hitler: History, Holocaust and the David Irving Trial.* New York: Basic Books.

Falter, Jürgen W. 1992. "The Social Bases of Political Cleavages in the Weimar Republic, 1919–1933." In *Elections, Mass Politics, and Social Change in Modern Germany: New Perspectives,* ed. Larry Eugene Jones and James Retallack, 371–97. Cambridge: Cambridge University Press.

Feldman, Gerald D. 1986. "The Weimar Republik: A Problem of Modernization?" *Archiv für Sozialgeschichte* 26: 1–26.

Fitzpatrick, Sheila, and Robert Gellately, eds. 1996. Volume on Practices of Denunciation in Modern European History, 1789–1989. *Journal of Modern History* 68/4.

Foucault, Michel. 1977. *Discipline and Punish: The Birth of the Prison.* New York: Pantheon.

———. 1978. *The History of Sexuality.* Vol. 1. New York: Pantheon Books.

———. 1980. *Power/Knowledge: Selected Interviews & Other Writings, 1972–77.* New York: Pantheon.

———. 1984. "What Is Enlightenment?" In *The Foucault Reader,* ed. Paul Rabinow, 32–50. New York: Pantheon.

Fraenkel, Ernst. 1969. *The Dual State: A Contribution to the Theory of Dictatorship.* New York: Octagon Books.

Frazer, Nancy. 1990. "Rethinking the Public Sphere." *Social Text* 25, no. 6: 56–80.

Friedlander, Henry. 2003. "Eine Berliner Pflanze: An Unusual Kristallnacht Story." *German Studies Review* 24, no. 1: 1–14.

Friedländer, Saul. 1987. "Some Reflections on the Historicization of National Socialism." *Tel Aviver Jahrbuch für deutsche Geschichte* 16: 310–24.

Fritzsche, Peter. 1988. "Between Fragmentation and Fraternity: Civil Patriotism and the Stahlhelm in Bourgeois Neighborhoods during the Weimar Republic." *Telaviver Jahrbuch für deutsche Geschichte* 17: 123–44.

———. 1990. *Rehearsals for Fascism: Populism and Political Mobilization in Weimar Germany.* Oxford: Oxford University Press.

———. 1994. "Where Did All the Nazis Go? Reflections on Collaboration and Resistance." *Tel Aviver Jahrbuch für deutsche Geschichte* 23: 191–214.

————. 1996. "Nazi Modern." *Modernism/Modernity* 3, no. 1: 1–22. http://muse.jhu.edu/journals/modernism-modernity/v003/3.1fritzsche.html (accessed 30 January 2004).

————. 1998. *Germans into Nazis.* Cambridge, Mass.: Harvard University Press.

Frykman, Jonas, and Orvar Löfgren. 1987. *Culture Builders.* New Brunswick, N.J.: Rutgers University Press.

Gates, Henry Louis, Jr. 1988. *The Signifying Monkey: A Theory of African-American Literary Criticism.* Oxford: Oxford University Press.

Gay, Peter. 1970. *Weimar Culture: The Outsider as Insider.* New York: Harper & Row.

Gebhard, Miriam. 1999. *Das Familiengedächtnis: Erinnerung im deutsch-jüdischen Bürgertum 1890 bis 1932.* Franz Steiner Verlag: Stuttgart.

Gellately, Robert. 1988. "The Gestapo and German Society: Political Denunciation in the Gestapo Case Files." *Journal of Modern History* 60, no. 4: 654–94.

————. 1990. *The Gestapo and German Society: Enforcing Racial Policy, 1933–1945.* Oxford: Clarendon Press.

————. 2001. *Backing Hitler: Consent and Coercion in Nazi Germany.* Oxford: Oxford University Press.

Gerstenberger, Heide. 1987. "Alltagsforschung und Fascismustheorie." In *Normalität oder Normalisierung? Geschichtswerkstätten und Fascismusanalyse,* ed. Heide Gerstenberger and Dorothea Schmidt, 35–49. Münster: Westfälisches Dampfboot.

Geyer, Michael. 1987. "The Nazi State Reconsidered." In *Life in the Third Reich,* ed. Richard Bessel, 57–68. Oxford: Oxford University Press.

Geyer, Michael, and John Boyer, eds. 1992. *Resistance against the Third Reich, 1933–90.* Chicago: University of Chicago Press.

Gilbert, Martin. 1981. *Auschwitz and the Allies.* New York: Holt, Rinehart, and Winston.

Ginzburg, Carlo. 1980. *The Cheese and the Worms: The Cosmos of a Sixteenth-Century Miller.* New York: Dorset.

————. 1985. "Was ist Mikrogeschichte." *Geschichtswerkstätte* 6: 48–52.

Gittig, Heinz. 1972. *Illegale Antifascistische Tarnschriften 1933–1945.* Leipzig: VEB Bibliographisches Institut.

Goldhagen, Daniel Jonah. 1996. *Hitler's Willing Executioners: Ordinary Germans and the Holocaust.* New York: Alfred A. Knopf.

Graml, Hermann. 1992. *Antisemitism in the Third Reich.* Oxford: Blackwell.

Gramsci, Antonio. 1971. *Selections from the Prison Notebooks.* New York: International Publishers.

Gross, Jan T. 2001. *Neighbors: The Destruction of the Jewish Community in Jedwabne, Poland.* Princeton, N.J.: Princeton University Press.

Gruner, W. 1995. "Public Welfare and the German Jews under National Socialism." German Society's Responses to Nazi Anti-Jewish Policy, 1933–1941. Yad Vashem Conference, 10–13 February. http://www.history-of-the-holocaust.org/LIBARC/LIBRARY/Themes/Policy/Gruner.html (accessed 30 January 2004).

Guenther, Irene V. 1997. "Nazi 'Chic'? German Politics and Women's Fashions, 1915–1945." *Fashion Theory* 1, no. 1: 29–58.

Habermas, Jürgen. 1981. *Theorie des kommunikativen Handelns.* Frankfurt am Main: Suhrkamp.

———. 1989. *The Structural Transformation of the Public Sphere: An Inquiry into a Category of Bourgeois Society.* Cambridge, Mass.: MIT Press.

Hall, Stuart, and Tony Jefferson, eds. 1976. *Resistance through Rituals.* London: Hutchinson.

Hall, Stuart et al., eds. 1980. *Culture, Media, Language.* London: Hutchinson.

Hamilton, Richard F. 2003. "The Rise of Nazism: A Case Study and Review of Interpretations—Kiel, 1928–1933." *German Studies Review* 24, no. 1: 43–62.

Hammerich, Kurt, and Michael Klein, eds. 1978. *Materialien zur Soziologie des Alltags.* Opladen: Westdeutscher.

Harootunian, Harry. 2000. *History's Disquiet: Modernity, Cultural Practice, and the Question of Everyday Life.* New York: Columbia University Press.

Henry, Frances. 1984. *Victims and Neighbors: A Small Town in Nazi Germany Remembered.* South Hadley, Mass.: Bergin and Garvey Publishers.

Hebdige, Dick. 1979. *Subculture: The Meaning of Style.* London: Methuen.

Herbert, Ulrich. 1983. "'Die guten und die schlechten Zeiten': Überlegungen zur diachronen Analyze lebensgeschichtlicher Interviews." In *"Die Jahre weiss man nicht, wo man die heute hinsetzen soll": Faschismuserfahrungen im Ruhrgebiet,* ed. Lutz Niethammer et al., 67–96. Berlin: J. H. W. Dietz Nachf.

———. 1985. *Fremdarbeiter: Politik und Praxis des 'Ausländer-Einsatzes' in der Kriegswirtschaft des Dritten Reichs.* Berlin: Dietz.

Herzstein, Robert E. 2002. "Daniel Jonah Goldhagen's 'Ordinary Germans': A Heretic and His Critics." *The Journal of the Historical Society* 2, no. 1: 89–122.

Hilberg, Raul. 1992. *Perpetrators, Victims, Bystanders: The Jewish Catastrophe, 1933–1945.* New York: Aaron Asher Books.

Himmelfarb, Gertrud. 1994. *On Looking into the Abyss: Untimely Thoughts on Culture and Society.* New York: Knopf.

Hobsbawm, Eric, and Terence Ranger, eds. 1983. *The Invention of Tradition.* Cambridge: Cambridge University Press.

Horster, Detlef. 1990. *Habermas zur Einführung.* Hamburg: Junius.

Hudson, Pat. 2000. *History by Numbers: An Introduction to Quantitative Approaches.* London: Arnold.

Hunt, Lynn, ed. 1989. *The New Cultural History.* Berkeley: University of California Press.

Huyssen, Andreas. 1986. *After the Great Divide: Modernism, Mass Culture, Postmodernism.* Bloomington: Indiana University Press.

Jameson, Frederic. 1991. *Postmodernism; or, The Cultural Logic of Late Capitalism.* Durham: Duke University Press.

Johnson, Christopher H. 1993. "Lifeworld, System, and Communicative Action: The Habermasian Alternative in Social History." In *Rethinking Labor History,* ed. Lenard R. Berlanstein, 55–89. Urbana: University of Illinois Press.

Jones, Larry Eugene. 1988. *German Liberalism and the Dissolution of the Weimar Party System.* Chapel Hill: University of North Carolina Press.

Kaeble, Hartmut et al. 1978. *Probleme der Modernizierung in Deutschland: Sozialhistorische Studien zum 19. und 20. Jahrhundert.* Opladen: Westdeutscher.

Kant, Immanuel. 1786. *Grundlegung zur Metaphysik der Sitten.* Riga. [Stuttgart: Reclam, 1978.]

Kaplan, Marion A. 1998. *Between Dignity and Despair: Daily Life in the Third Reich.* Oxford: Oxford University Press.

Katznelson, Ira, and Aristide R. Zolberg, eds. 1986. *Working-Class Formation: Nineteenth-Century Patterns in Western Europe and the United States.* Princeton, N.J.: Princeton University Press.

Kershaw, Ian. 1983a. *Popular Opinion and Political Dissent in the Third Reich: Bavaria 1933–1945.* Oxford: Clarendon Press.

———. 1983b. *The "Hitler Myth": Image and Reality in the Third Reich.* Oxford: Clarendon Press.

———. 1989. *The Nazi Dictatorship.* London: Edward Arnold.

Koshar, Rudy. 1986. *Social Life, Local Politics, and Nazism: Marburg, 1880–1935.* Chapel Hill and London: University of North Carolina Press.

Kren, George, and Leon Rappoport. 1980. *The Holocaust and the Crisis in Human Behavior.* New York: Holmes and Meier.

Krondorfer, Björn. 1995. *Remembrance and Reconciliation: Encounters between Young Jews and Germans.* New Haven, Conn.: Yale University Press.

Lan, David. 1985. *Guns and Rain: Guerrillas and Spirit Mediums in Zimbabwe*. Berkeley: University of California Press.

Lange, Dieter. 1972. "Das Prager Manifest von 1934." *Zeitschrift für Geschichtswissenschaft* 19: 860–72.

Laqueur, Walter. 1981. *The Terrible Secret: Suppression of the Truth about Hitler's "Final Solution."* New York: H. Holt.

Leber, Annedore. 1957. *Conscience in Revolt: Sixty-Four Stories of Resistance in Germany, 1933–45*. Westport, Conn.: Associated Booksellers.

Lefebvre, Henri. 1971. *Everyday Life in the Modern World*. New York: Harper & Row.

———. 1987. "The Everyday and Everydayness." In *Yale French Studies: Everyday Life*, ed. Alice Kaplan and Kristin Ross, 7–11. New Haven, Conn.: Yale University Press.

Lepore, Jill. 2001. "Historians who Love Too Much: Reflections on Microhistory and Biography." *The Journal of American History* 88, no. 1: 129–44.

Lepsius, M. Rainer. 1973. "Parteisystem und Sozialstruktur: zum Problem der Demokratizierung der deutschen Gesellschaft." In *Die Deutschen Parteien vor 1918*, ed. Gerhard A. Ritter, 56–80. Köln: Kiepenheuer & Witsch.

Levi, Primo. 1988. *The Drowned and the Saved*. New York: Vintage Books.

Liebersohn, Harry. 1988. *Fate and Utopia in German Sociology, 1870–1923*. Cambridge: MIT Press.

Lipstadt, Deborah E. 1986. *Beyond Belief: The American Press and the Coming of the Holocaust, 1933–1945*. New York: Free Press.

———. 1993. *Denying the Holocaust: The Growing Assault on Truth and Memory*. New York: Free Press.

Lösener, Bernhard, and Friedrich A. Knost, eds. 1941. *Die Nürnberger Gesetze mit den Durchführungsverordnungen und den sonstigen einschlägigen Vorschriften*. Berlin: Franz Wahlen.

Lüdtke, Alf. 1982. "The Historiography of Everyday Life: The Personal and the Political." In *Culture, Ideology and Politics*, ed. Raphael Samuel and Gareth Stedman Jones, 38–54. London: Routledge & Kegan Paul.

———. 1986. "Cash, Coffee-Breaks, Horse-Play: 'Eigensinn' and Politics among Factory Workers in Germany ca. 1900." In *Confrontation, Class Consciousness, and the Labor Process: Studies in Proletarian Class Formation*, ed. Michael Hanagan and Charles Stephenson, 65–95. New York: Greenwood Press.

———. 1993. *Eigen-Sinn: Fabrikalltag, Arbeitererfahrungen und Politik vom Kaiserreich bis in den Faschismus*. Hamburg: Ergebnisse.

———, ed. 1995. *The History of Everyday Life: Reconstructing Historical Experiences and Ways of Life*. Princeton, N.J.: Princeton University Press.

Lüdtke, Alf, Inge Marssolek, and Adelheid von Saldern, eds. 1996. *Amerikanisierung: Traum und Alptraum im Deutschland des 20. Jahrhunderts.* Stuttgart: Steiner.

Lukács, Georg. 2002. *History and Class Consciousness: Studies in Marxist Dialectics.* Cambridge, Mass.: MIT Press.

Maier, Charles A. 1988. *The Unmasterable Past: History, Holocaust and German National Identity.* Cambridge, Mass.: Harvard University Press.

Mallmann, Klaus-Michael, and Gerhard Paul. 1994. "Omniscient, Omnipotent, Omnipresent? Gestapo, Society, and Resistance." In *Nazism and German Society, 1933–1945,* ed. David F. Crew, 166–96. London: Routledge.

Mann, Reinhard. 1987. *Protest und Kontrolle im Dritten Reich: nationalsozialistische Herrschaft im Alltag einer rheinischen Grossstadt.* Frankfurt am Main: Campus.

Marcuse, Herbert. 1960. *Reason and Revolution: Hegel and the Rise of Social Theory.* Boston: Beacon Press.

Mason, Timothy. 1972. "The Primacy of Politics: Politics and Economics in National Socialist Germany." In *Nazism and the Third Reich,* ed. Henry Ashby Turner, 175–200. New York: New Viewpoints.

———. 1976. "Women in Nazi Germany, 1925–40: Family, Welfare, and Work." *History Workshop* 1: 74–113 and 2: 5–32.

Matzerath, Horst, and Heinrich Volkmann. 1977. "Modernisierungstheorie und Nationalsozialismus." In Theorien in der Praxis des Historikers, *Geschichte und Gesellschaft,* Sonderheft 3, ed. Jürgen Kocka, 86–117. Göttingen: Vandenhoeck & Ruprecht.

Medick, Hans. 1995. "'Missionaries in the Rowboat'? Ethnological Ways of Knowing as a Challenge to Social History." In Alf Lüdtke, *The History of Everyday Life: Reconstructing Historical Experiences and Ways of Life,* 41–71. Princeton, N.J.: Princeton University Press.

Morse, Arthur D. 1968. *While Six Million Died: A Chronicle of American Apathy.* New York: Random House.

Mosse, George L. 1975. *The Nationalization of the Masses: Political Symbolism and Mass Movements in Germany from the Napoleonic Wars through the Third Reich.* New York: H. Fertig.

Müller, Klaus-Jürgen, and Hans Mommsen. 1986. "Der deutsche Widerstand gegen das NS-Regime: Zur Historiographie des Widerstandes." In *Der deutsche Widerstand, 1933–1945,* ed. Klaus-Jürgen Müller, 13–21. Ferdinand Schöningh: Paderborn.

Negt, Oskar, and Alexander Kluge. 1993. *Public Sphere and Experience: Toward an Analysis of the Bourgeois and Proletarian Public Sphere.* Minneapolis: University of Minnesota Press.

Neumann, Franz L. 1942. *Behemoth: The Structure and Practice of National Socialism.* New York: Oxford University Press.

Niethammer, Lutz et al., eds. 1983a. *"Die Jahre weiss man nicht, wo man die heute hinsetzen soll": Faschismuserfahrungen im Ruhrgebiet.* Berlin: J. H. W. Dietz Nachf.

———. 1983b. *"Hinterher merkt man, dass es richtig war, dass es schiefgegangen ist": Nachkriegserfahrungen im Ruhrgebiet.* Berlin: J. H. W. Dietz Nachf.

———. 1985. *"Wir kriegen jetzt andere Zeiten": Auf der Suche nach der Erfahrung des Volkes in nachfaschistischen Ländern.* Berlin: J. H. W. Dietz Nachf.

———. 1988. *"Die Menschen machen ihre Geschichte nicht aus freien Stücken, aber sie machen sie selbst": Einladung zu einer Geschichte des Volkes in NRW.* Berlin: J. H. W. Dietz Nachf.

———. 1992. "Where Were You on 17 June?" In *International Yearbook of Oral History and Life Stories,* 44–69.

———. 1995. "Zeroing In on Change: In Search of Popular Experiences in the Industrial Province in the German Democratic Republic." In Alf Lüdtke, *The History of Everyday Life: Reconstructing Historical Experiences and Ways of Life,* 252–311. Princeton, N.J.: Princeton University Press.

Oliver, Peter. 1975. "Oral History: One Historian's View." *Journal— The Canadian Oral History Association* 1: 13–19.

Ostovich, Steven T. 2002. "Epilogue: Dangerous Memories." In *The Work of Memory: New Directions in the Study of German Society and Culture,* ed. Alon Confino and Peter Fritzsche, 239–56. Urbana: University of Illinois Press.

Parsons, Talcott. 1954. "Democracy and Social Structure in Pre-Nazi Germany." In *Essays in Sociological Theory,* ed. Talcott Parsons. 104–23. Glencoe: The Free Press.

Passerini, Luisa. 1985. "Erzählte Erinnerung an den Faschismus." In *"Wir kriegen jetzt andere Zeiten": Auf der Suche nach der Erfahrung des Volkes in nachfaschistischen Ländern,* ed. Lutz Niethammer, pp. 361–68. Berlin: J. H. W. Dietz Nachf.

———. 1992. "Introduction to Memory and Totalitarianism." In *International Yearbook of Oral History and Life Stories,* 1–19.

Peters, John Durham. 1993. "Distrust of Representation: Habermas on the Public Sphere." *Media, Culture & Society* 15: 541–71.

Peters, Ludwig. 1994. *Volkslexikon Drittes Reich: die Jahre 1933–1945 in Wort und Bild.* Tübingen: Grabert Verlag.

Petropoulos, Jonathan. 1998a. "'People Turned to Ashes, Their Property Did Not': Plundering and the Pursuit of Profit during the Holocaust." At the German Historical Institute symposium "The Genesis of Nazi Policy," University of Florida, Gainesville.

————. 1998b. "Holocaust Denial: A Generational Typology." In *Lessons and Legacies,* ed. Peter Hayes, 239–47. Evanston, Ill.: Northwestern University Press.

Peukert, Detlev. 1982a. "Arbeiteralltag—Mode oder Methode?" In *Arbeiteralltag in Stadt und Land: neue Wege der Geschichtsschreibung,* ed. Heiko Haumann, 8–39. Berlin: Argument.

————. 1982b. *Inside the Third Reich: Conformity, Opposition, and Racism in Everyday Life.* New Haven, Conn.: Yale University Press.

————. 1987. *Die Weimarer Republik: Krisenjahre der klassischen Moderne.* Frankfurt am Main: Suhrkamp.

Plato, Alexander von. 1985. "Wer schoss auf Robert R., oder: Was kann Oral history leisten?" In *Unsere Geschichte,* ed. Hannes Hogi and Volker Ulrich, 266–80. Reinbek: Rowohlt.

Prause, Karl. 1930. *Deutsche Grussformeln in neuhochdeutscher Zeit.* Breslau: M. &. H. Marcus.

Postone, Moishe. 1986. "Anti-Semitism and National Socialism." In *Germans and Jews since the Holocaust: The Changing Situation in West Germany,* ed. Anson Rabinbach and Jack Zipes, 302–15. New York: Homes & Meyer.

Rahden, Till van. 2000. "Words and Actions: Rethinking the Social History of German Antisemitism, Breslau, 1870–1914." *German History* 18, no. 4: 413–38.

Reed, Anthony, and David Fisher. 1989. *Kristallnacht: The Unleashing of the Holocaust.* New York: Peter Bedrick Books.

Roderick, Rick. 1968. *Habermas and the Foundations of Critical Theory.* New York: Macmillan.

Röhr, Werner, and Brigitte Berlekamp, eds. 1995. *Terror, Herrschaft und Alltag im Nationalsozialismus.* Münster: Weltfälisches Dampfboot.

Rohe, Karl. 1992. *Wahlen und Wählertraditionen in Deutschland.* Frankfurt am Main: Suhrkamp.

Rosenstrauch, Hazel, ed. 1988. *Aus Nachbarn wurden Juden: Ausgrenzung und Selbstbehauptung, 1933–1942.* Berlin: Transit.

Ross, Kristin. 1995. *Fast Cars, Clean Bodies: Decolonization and the Reordering of French Culture.* Cambridge: MIT Press.

Sabean, David. 1984. *Power in the Blood: Popular Culture and Village Discourse in Early Modern Germany.* Cambridge: Cambridge University Press.

Sahlins, Marshall. 1985. *Islands of History.* Chicago: University of Chicago Press.

Saldern, Adelheid von. 1989. *Staat und Moderne: Hannover in der Weimarer Republik.* Hamburg: Ergebnisse.

Schäfer, Hans Dieter. 1982. *Das Gespaltene Bewusstsein: Über deutsche Kultur und Lebenswirklichkeit, 1933–1945*. München: Hanser.

Schermer, Michael, and Alex Grobman. 2000. *Denying History: Who Says the Holocaust Never Happened and Why Do They Say It?* Berkeley: University of California Press.

Schmid, Hans-Dieter. 1995. "'Anständige Beamte' und 'üble Schläger': Die Staatspolizeistelle Hannover." In *Die Gestapo: Mythos und Realität*, ed. Klaus-Michael Mallmann and Gerhard Paul, 133–60. Darmstadt: Wissenschaftliche Buchgesellschaft.

Schoenbaum, David. 1966. *Hitler's Social Revolution: Class and Status in Nazi Germany 1933–1939*. New York: W. W. Norton.

Schutz, Alfred, and Thomas Luckmann. 1973. *The Structures of the Life-World*. Evanston, Ill.: Northwestern University Press.

Scott, Joan W. 1988. *Gender and the Politics of History*. New York: Columbia University Press.

———. 1991. "The Evidence of Experience." *Critical Inquiry* 17: 773–97.

Sedgwick, Eve Kosofsky. 1990. *Epistemology of the Closet*. Berkeley: University of California Press.

Sewell, William H., Jr. 1992. "A Theory of Structure: Duality, Agency, and Transformation." *American Journal of Sociology* 98, no. 1: 1–29.

Sheehan, James J. 1981. "What is German History? Reflections on the Role of the Nation in German History and Historiography." *Journal of Modern History* 53, no. 1:1–23.

Siebert, Renate. 1992. "Don't Forget: Fragments of a Negative Tradition." In *International Yearbook of Oral History and Life Stories*, 165–77.

Simmel, Georg. 1989. "Dankbarkeit: ein soziologischer Versuch." In *Aufsätze und Abhandlungen, 1901–1908*, vol. 2, ed. Alessandro Cavalli and Volkhard Krech, 308–16. Frankfurt am Main: Suhrkamp.

Smith, Dorothy E. 1987. *The Everyday World as Problematic: A Feminist Sociology*. Boston: Northeastern.

Snyder, Louis L., ed. 1976. *Encyclopedia of the Third Reich*. New York: McGraw-Hill.

Stegge, Paul. 1994. "Locations of Struggle: The State, The Street and Contested Meanings in the Weimar Republic." Unpublished M.A. thesis, History, University of Chicago.

Stern, Frank. 1992. "Antagonistic Memories: The Post-War Survival and Alienation of Jews and Germans." In *International Yearbook of Oral History and Life Stories*, 21–43.

Stevenson, Jill. 1975. *Women in Nazi Society*. New York: Barnes & Noble.

Stolzfus, Nathan. 1996. *Resistance of the Heart: Intermarriage and the Rosenstrasse Protest in Nazi Germany*. New York: W. W. Norton.

Suttles, Gerald D. 1972. *The Social Construction of Communities*. Chicago: University of Chicago Press.

Ten Dyke, Elizabeth A. 2002. "Memory and Existence: Implications of the *Wende*." In *The Work of Memory: New Directions in the Study of German Society and Culture*, ed. Alon Confino and Peter Fritzsche, 154–72. Urbana: University of Illinois Press.

Theweleit, Klaus. 1987–1989. *Male Fantasies*, vols. 1 & 2. Minneapolis: University of Minnesota Press.

Thompson, Paul. ca. 1972. "Problems of Method in Oral History." *Oral History* 1, no. 4: 1–47.

———. 1978. *The Voices of the Past*. Oxford: Oxford University Press.

Tönnies, Ferdinand. 1988. *Community and Society*. New Brunswick, N.J.: Transaction Books.

Trommler, Frank. 1992. "Between Normality and Resistance: Catastrophic Gradualism in Nazi Germany," *Journal of Modern History* 64 suppl.: 82–101.

Turner, Henry Ashby. 1975. "Fascism and Modernization." In *Reappraisals of Fascism*, ed. Henry Ashby Turner, 117–40. New York: New Viewpoints.

Turner, Stephen. 1994. *The Social Theory of Practices: Tradition, Tacit Knowledge, and Presuppositions*. Chicago: University of Chicago Press.

Turner, Victor W. 1969. *The Ritual Process: Structure and Antistructure*. Ithaca, N.Y.: Cornell University Press.

Veblen, Thorstein. 1967. *The Theory of the Leisure Class.* London: Viking Penguin.

Wagner, Caroline. 1998. *Die NSDAP auf dem Dorf: eine Sozialgeschichte der NS-Machtergreifung in Lippe*. München: Aschendorffsche.

Walker, Mack. 1971. *German Home Towns: Community, State, and General Estate, 1648–1871*. Ithaca, N.Y.: Cornell University Press.

Wehler, Hans-Ulrich. 1985. *The German Empire, 1871–1918*. Lemington Spa: Berg.

Wierling, Dorothee. 1992. "A German Generation of Reconstruction: The Children of the Weimar Republic in the GDR." In *International Yearbook of Oral History and Life Stories*, 71–88.

Wördehoff, Bernhard. 1990. *Flaggenwechsel: ein Land und viele Fahnen*. Berlin: Corso bei Siedler.

Wyman, David S. 1984. *The Abandonment of the Jews: America and the Holocaust, 1941–1945*. New York: Pantheon Books.

Hildesheim Bibliography

Addicks, Dirk et al. 1988. *Verfolgung der jüdische Bürger/Innen Hildesheims: Hintergründe, Berichte, Dokumente.* Hildesheim: Vereinigung der Verfolgten des Naziregimes—Bund der Antifascisten.

Adressbücher der Stadt Hildesheim. 1910, 1914, 1920, 1924/5, 1930, 1935, 1940, 1951. Hildesheim: August Lax.

Arndt, Klaus. 1983. *Ernst Ehrlicher.* Hildesheim: Bernward.

Behrens, Carl. 1990. "Erinnerungen an die Zeit des Nationalsozialismus in der Region Hildesheim." *Alt-Hildesheim* 61: 139–47.

Brinkmann, Jens-Uwe. 1993. *Hildesheim—so wie es war.* Düsseldorf: Droste.

Bötel, Th. ca. 1911. "Das Klima von Hildesheim." In *Niedersachsen: Hildesheim Nummer,* ed. Hans Pfeiffer, 77–78. Bremen: Schünemann.

Fresow, Berthold. 1982. "'Meine Liebe zu Hildesheim ist nie erloschen. . . .'" *Alt-Hildesheim* 53: 89–95.

Gebauer, Johannes Heinrich. 1950. *Die Stadt Hildesheim: ein Abriss ihrer Geschichte.* Hildesheim: August Lax.

Gerlach, Bernhard, and Hermann Seeland. 1950. *Geschichte der Bischöflichen Gymnasium Josephinum in Hildesheim.* Hildesheim: August Lax.

Gerland, Otto. 1908. *Die ortspolizeilichen Bestimmungen der Stadt Hildesheim.* Hildesheim: August Lax.

———. 1921. "Was uns die Galgenberg erzählt." *Alt-Hildesheim* 3: 15.

Hein, Günther, ed. 1993. " . . . *auf freiem Platze als freier Tempel befreiter Bürger": Aspekte jüdischen Lebens in Hildesheim, 1848–1938.* Hildesheim: Museumspädagogischen Dienst.

Jan, Helmut von. 1968a. "Zur Geschichte der Hildesheimer Juden." *Hildesheimer Informationen* 11: 24–29.

———. 1968b. "Aus blinder Hass verwaltete: vor 30 Jahren ging in Hildesheim die Synagoge in Flammen auf." *Hildesheimer Heimat-Kalender* 70–71.

———. 1988. "Die Katastrophe der Hildesheimer Juden 1938–1988: Zum Gedächtnis der 50jährigen Wiederkehr." *Alt-Hildesheim* 59: 97–109.

Kloppenburg, Heinrich. "Neueste Geschichte von Hildesheim: umfassend die Zeit vom 1. 1. 1911 bis 31.12.1920." SAH: manuscript, 1923.

Knott, Anton Josef. 1978. "Die Machtübernahme im Hildesheimer Rathaus: Wie die Demokratie in der Stadt 1933 ihr Ende fand." *Hildesheimer Heimat-Kalender,* 74–77.

———. 1980. *Das Wahlverhalten der Hildesheimer in der Zeit von Bismarck bis Hitler, 1867–1933.* Hildesheim: Bernward.

———. 1984. "So streng waren damals die Bräuche: Einspruch nach erster Bürgervorsteherwahl in Moritzberg." *Hildesheimer Heimat-Kalender*, 55–59.

Krebs, Hans Adolf. 1990. *"Meine Liebe zu Hildesheim hat nie aufgehört."* Hildesheim: Roemer-Pelizaeus Museam Ausstellungskatalog.

Krebs, Hans Adolf, with Anne Martin. 1981. *Reminiscences and Reflections.* Oxford: Clarendon Press.

Lüddecke, Wolf Dieter. 1987. *Polizey-Diener der Stadt Hildesheim.* Hildesheim: Bernward.

Meyer-Hartmann, Hermann. 1993. *Geheime Kommandosache: die Geschichte des Hildesheimer Fliegerhorstes.* Hildesheim: Gerstenberg.

Monte, E. del. 1974. *Une ville du temps jadis: Hildesheim. Ein Reisebericht aus dem Jahre 1883 von E. del Monte veröffentlicht in der Zeitschrift "Le Tour du Monde."* Hildesheim: Gerstenberg.

Notzen-Hillman, Gerhard. 1989. "Wirtschaft und Arbeit in Hildesheim 1933–1945." *Alt-Hildesheim* 60: 131–38.

Politz, Anne-Gret. 1971. "Die NSDAP im Raum Hildesheim: Anfänge und Entwicklung bis 1933." *Alt-Hildesheim* 42: 42–55.

Polizeiverordnung über die Regelung des Verkehrs und die Aufrechterhaltung der Ordnung im Stadtkreis Hildesheim vom 1 Dezember 1932. 1932. Hildesheim: August Lax.

Riekenberg, Michael. 1982. *Die Novemberrevolution in der Stadt Hildesheim: eine lokalhistorische Studie.* Hildesheim: Bernward.

Saeger, Carl. 1934. "Die farbige Behandlung unserer hildesheimer Fachwerkbauten." *Alt-Hildesheim* 13: 22–25.

Schlewecke, Georg [Kurt Adolph]. 1987. *Stirb Er anständig! Kindheits- und Jugenderlebnisse mit dem Dritten Reich, 1932–1945.* Hannover: Lutherisches Verlagshaus.

Schmid, Hans-Dieter, ed. 2002. *Hildesheim im Nationalsozialismus: Aspekte der Stadtgeschichte.* Hildesheim: Gerstenberger.

Schneider, Jörg. 1998. "Die jüdische Gemeinde in Hildesheim von 1871–1942." Ph.D. dissertation, Georg-August-Universität zu Göttingen.

Teich, Hans. 1979. *Hildesheim und seine Antifaschisten: Widerstandskampf gegen den Hitlerfascismus und demokratischer Neubegin 1945 in Hildesheim.* Hildesheim: Vereinigung der Verfolgten des Naziregimes— Bund der Antifascisten.

Thimm, Barbara. 1995. "'In Deutschland regierte ein Mann. . . .': Eine Untersuchung der seit 1945 erschienenen Stadtführer für Hildesheim auf ihren Umgang mit dem Nationalsozialismus." *Hildesheimer Jahrbuch* 67: 337–50.

———. 1999. *Spure des Nationalsozialimus in Hildesheim.* Hildesheim: Gerstenberg.

Uthoff, Dieter. 1967. *Der Pendelverkehr im Raum um Hildesheim: eine genetische Untersuchung zu seiner Raumwirklichkeit.* Göttingen: Geographisches Institut der Universität Göttingen.

Verwaltungsberichte der Stadt Hildesheim. 1909, 1914, 1928, 1936. Hildesheim: Gerstenberg, later Hildesheimer Beobachter.

Vogeler, Adolf. 1929. *Kriegschronik der Stadt Hildesheim.* Hildesheim: August Lax.

Voss, Heinrich. 1928. "Die Entstehung und Entwicklung des Grundrisss der Stadt Hildesheim." Ph.D. dissertation, Techn. Hochschule Hannover.

Wichard, Rudolf. 1975. *Wahlen in Hildesheim, 1867 bis 1972.* Hildesheim: Georg Olms Verlag.

Wolff, Stefan. 1989. "Die Entwicklung des Hildesheimer Stadtgebiets." *Alt-Hildesheim* 60: 77–81.

Index

ANDREW STUART BERGERSON is Assistant Professor of
History at the University of Missouri–Kansas City.